George Jellicoe

By the same author

Jutland. The Unfinished Battle
The Last Days of the High Seas Fleet

George Jellicoe

SAS and SBS Commander

Nicholas Jellicoe

Pen & Sword
MILITARY

First published in Great Britain in 2021 by
Pen & Sword Military
An imprint of
Pen & Sword Books Ltd
Yorkshire – Philadelphia

ISBN 978 1 39900 944 7

Typeset by Mac Style
Printed and bound in the UK by CPI Group (UK),
Croydon, CR0 4YY.

Pen & Sword Books Limited incorporates the imprints of Atlas,
Archaeology, Aviation, Discovery, Family History, Fiction, History,
Maritime, Military, Military Classics, Politics, Select, Transport,
True Crime, Air World, Frontline Publishing, Leo Cooper, Remember
When, Seaforth Publishing, The Praetorian Press, Wharncliffe
Local History, Wharncliffe Transport, Wharncliffe True Crime
and White Owl.

For a complete list of Pen & Sword titles please contact

PEN & SWORD BOOKS LIMITED
47 Church Street, Barnsley, South Yorkshire, S70 2AS, England
E-mail: enquiries@pen-and-sword.co.uk
Website: www.pen-and-sword.co.uk

Or

PEN AND SWORD BOOKS
1950 Lawrence Rd, Havertown, PA 19083, USA
E-mail: Uspen-and-sword@casematepublishers.com
Website: www.penandswordbooks.com

For George, in loving memory, always.

And to the memory of those friendships of his cut short by war:
Peter Pease, Wolfgang and Leberecht von Blücher, Alan Phipps,
Mark Howard, David Jacobsen, Andy Lassen, André Zirnheld.

Contents

Maps and Diagrams

Foreword

The heroic deeds of the Special Air Service, Special Boat Service and Long Range Desert Group made their way early into my schoolroom – mainly, I admit, in comic form via the War Picture Library. I loved reading about the desert raids in jeeps, of machine guns chattering away and German planes going up in flames. I was extremely fortunate in belonging to a family that was well connected to 'derring-doers'. Shimi Lovat of Commando (and Pegasus Bridge) fame was my mother's brother; David Stirling was an uncle by way of my innumerable Catholic cousins; and Fitzroy Maclean was my stepfather. As I grew older I met many of their wartime colleagues like David Sutherland, Georges Bergé, Johnny Cooper, Jason Mavrikis and, of course, George Jellicoe. I was struck by their kindness, their humour, their manner and above all their modesty.

George Jellicoe held a special place in my upbringing because he was the last person to see my father alive. In October 1943 my father, a Royal Navy Signals Officer, was attached to the British Brigade Headquarters on the Greek island of Leros with his Signals detachment. George, who had known my father previously, was also there with his Special Boat Squadron. After a hard-fought battle with German commandos in which both sides sustained heavy casualties, the Brigade was forced to surrender. George, learning that my father was missing, obtained parole from the German commander and went off to look for him. He spent some hours searching the now silent, rugged hillside; all around him were men wounded and dead, both British and German. He never found my father; he had been killed earlier on the steep eastern side of the Brigade location. George, having given his word, reported back to the Germans. He was subsequently marched off, only to escape later, as he was determined not to become a PoW. I have always been so grateful to George for trying to find my father in such difficult conditions, for recounting the events of that miserable day to my mother some time later, and for encouraging me to visit the island, especially Mount Meriviglia and the very well-kept British War Cemetery.

Nicholas Jellicoe has written a most accurate record of his father's eventful life. There is a lot to tell about the man, his extraordinary courage and leadership, his toughness and humility, his vitality and easy capacity for making friends, his sense of fun, and his everlasting friendship for and admiration of the Greek people.

Sadly, George never wrote about his life. He might have been tempted to record his adventures, particularly as a soldier – and goodness, they were real adventures – the Western Desert operations, his raiding force of buccaneers in the Dodecanese, the landing on mainland Greece, chasing the Germans out of Athens and beyond.

I have always been impressed by how servicemen of that time seldom talked about their wartime experiences. It wasn't so much a reluctance to relive some horrid memory but more an honourable reluctance to boast. Many is the time I heard David Stirling reproaching younger fellows with 'No swanking, no swanking'.

In the spring of 1943 George, at the age of twenty-four, was promoted to Major and was selected by David Stirling to command the newly formed Special Boat Squadron. His combination of intelligence, huge energy, courage and sound judgement shown on previous operations in the Western Desert made him an ideal choice. He set up his base on the Palestinian coast at Athlit, romantically situated at the foot of Mount Carmel, next to the ruins of a vast Crusader castle – always a bit of a scene-setter was George. The Squadron was part of Raiding Forces Middle East, consisting of the SBS, LRDG and the Greek Sacred Squadron. They worked in tandem with the Levant Schooner Flotilla, itself made up of men from the Royal Navy, Royal Marines and the Royal Hellenic Navy. It was a truly joint, international Special Force, indeed very much what is now the norm in today's more limited warfare operations. However, glancing at past photographs, they look like a bunch of pirates wearing all sorts of non-military clothing and carrying a great mixture of weapons. Not quite the same nowadays.

Nicholas Jellicoe has caught the atmosphere of these varied operations so well: the raids on Sardinia and Crete, his father's rather fruitless contact with the Italian Governor on German-occupied Rhodes, securing the airfield on Kos, the fierce fighting on the islands of Simi and Leros. He has made many references to some very interesting facts, and his research is really commendable. Particularly impressive is his record of the Aegean operations, notably Leros; indeed, I believe it is probably the most balanced and accurate account that has been written of both the British and German actions. He identifies how George had built up a great respect for the Sacred Squadron and in particular their overall commander, General Christodolous Tsigantes. He was a man of high intelligence, culture and humour, and a fine leader. He was particularly fearless in action and yet he always claimed he had never met a braver man than George Jellicoe.

These seadogs of the Aegean struck fear into the heart of the German forces. They disrupted their planning, destroyed their logistics and their morale, and as a result stiffened the resolve of the Greek people. George's activities in the Aegean and then on mainland Greece were already well known to the Greek authorities, and they saw him, despite his turning up in Athens on his bicycle, as the forerunner of the Allied forces and salvation. To the Greeks George Jellicoe was symbolic of British power and the tangible proof that the British were not far away. The citizens of Athens were ecstatic and showered him with rose petals; he was even offered a wreath of fresh laurel.

George's association with Greece remained important to him for the rest of his life. He had an everlasting friendship with the Greek people for, as David Sutherland wrote in his excellent autobiography, 'They guided us, they fed us and they died for us.' George's affection for General Tsigantes was particularly special. He was 'almost as a folk hero in Crete and mainland Greece'.[1]

Peacetime was less exciting for a man of Jellicoe's nature, but little he did was boring and, as Nicholas rightly describes, 'he lived life at a breathless pace.' He married twice and had eight children. He pursued careers as a diplomat, politician and businessman. He was Secretary of Defence for the Navy, made a Privy Counsellor, was Leader of the House of Lords, Chairman of Tate & Lyle Sugar, President of the Royal Geographical Society and more.

He was a natural successor to take over from David Stirling as President of the SAS Association and was responsible for raising over £2m for their welfare fund following the Regiment's losses in action during the Falklands War. He stood down in 2000 and was unanimously elected the first Patron of the SAS, a position he held till his death.

He visited Greece many times after the war, staying with friends like Paddy Leigh Fermor or joining some SAS Association trip to the Greek islands. On one occasion on Rhodes, George was sitting with a bunch of SAS Old Comrades when a pretty sun-tanned girl in a bikini walked past. Wartime anecdotes stopped for a moment; when they resumed, George had disappeared.

Major General Jeremy Phipps CB
Heathfield House
Hawick
Scottish Borders

Jeremy Phipps sadly passed away on 16 March 2021. RIP.

Introduction

Tucked into a small bay on the western Peloponnese coast is a rugged outcrop of rocks known as Jellicoe's Leap. Paddy Leigh Fermor, the renowned travel writer and ex-SOE officer, named it after his wartime friend George Jellicoe who, much to his chagrin, beat him to the punch by being first to take the perilous leap into the crystal clear waters of the Aegean.

By then, Jellicoe had already made his mark on the world. After a short wartime military career, he had left the Army having commanded the Special Boat Squadron in the Greek islands and on the mainland till its liberation, after riding into Athens on a bicycle as the Germans evacuated. He had followed the military with an equally short but worthy career as a diplomat, serving in the Middle East and in Washington, along the way working closely with two of the three original Cambridge spies, Kim Philby and Donald Maclean. He was then halfway through what would become a distinguished political career, which would see him as the last man to hold the fabled title First Lord of the Admiralty, became the Leader of the House of Lords and, when he died, be recognized as the oldest parliamentarian of his age. Not content with three extraordinary careers, his numerous responsibilities would include posts as Chairman of Tate & Lyle and the Medical Research Council, President of the Royal Geographical Society and close association with numerous worthy causes. He was a man who embraced life, lived every moment and leapt at its opportunities rather than being taken along by the current.

George Jellicoe's arrival into this world was anything but ordinary. He grew up alongside his five sisters, the apple of his father's eye.

After fathering only girls, his father, Admiral Sir John Jellicoe, was delighted to finally have a son. His mother could not have been quite so enthusiastic: she was unconscious for two days after delivering his 13lb heir.

Jellicoe led as full a life as any man, living every day as if it were his last. He had grown up in the shadow of someone whom Winston Churchill had described as 'the only man on either side who could have lost the war in an afternoon'. In 1916, his father had been Commander-in-Chief of the Grand Fleet at Jutland, where British naval supremacy had been severely challenged but upheld at a high cost. After the war, he joined his title to Scapa Flow in homage to the Orkney Islands and the folk who had protected his fleet for the first two years of the war.

Sir John Jellicoe's prominent public career shone a spotlight on his son that would influence everything he would do. Yet, unlike the case of many others of his class, these advantages did not prevent him from approaching life with modesty, vigour and enthusiasm.

George Jellicoe was a man of extraordinary depth, knowledge and ability. Sir Peter de la Billière talked of the 'innate' sense that Jellicoe had to excel 'in so many fields from politics to business to diplomacy', leading a life characterized by 'courage … leadership and wit'.[2] A former ambassador and long-time friend and colleague, Nico Henderson, had a stab at summing up Jellicoe: 'He is not a complicated, but in fact a many-sided character. There are in fact four Georges: George the First, the unabstemious, boisterous Lothario … hero George … the aesthete … and finally we have pensive George, scholar and public servant.'[3] Wherever he went, he 'raised the wattage'.[4]

The Second World War catapulted Jellicoe forward. Aged twenty-seven, he ended the war a Lieutenant Colonel, acting Brigadier, a highly-decorated veteran of Britain's Special Forces, the SAS and SBS. The Admiral, his father, did not reach the rank of Commander till he was thirty-one. And 'like most real heroes, [Jellicoe] spoke little and spoke less about his war.'[5] But in Greece, a country where history is never forgotten and for whose freedom he fought, his name is still 'revered'.[6]

A dazzling diplomatic career in Washington, Brussels and Baghdad followed, but then came to a crashing end with his decision to resign and stay with the woman he loved. Later, in government, Jellicoe's political ambitions were to be scuppered by a second scandal with an ironic twist. His name was found in the diary of a call girl. The name had been connected to a location not the person – a place named after one of his forebears, Father Basil Jellicoe, a young and courageous social reformer in the thirties.

In his political career, he rose to become the Leader of the House of Lords and ended it as the 'Father of the House', a title given to its longest serving member. George Jellicoe, in fact, became the longest serving parliamentarian in the world. In his obituary, the *Guardian* said that his departure from Government had 'deprived the Conservative party of one of its most intelligent, hard-working and forward-looking leaders, at the peak of his powers.'[7] Jellicoe was by nature a modest man but had a unique spark of life and an engaging, self-deprecating humour. He may have come from a highly privileged background, but anyone who knew him, whatever their station, never held it against him, even Trades Union negotiators during the thorny years of the Heath Government.

After his second career ended abruptly, he went on – never one to stay down for long – to become the first non-family Chairman of the sugar refining company, Tate & Lyle, and then of the Davy Corporation, at the time, the 'largest engineering contractor in the world'.[8] He ended his very active public life serving as President of the Royal Geographical Society.

He was a man who had travelled the world, touched many lives and supported many causes. He left behind many feeling all the more enriched, if saddened by his passing.

Jongny, Switzerland
April 2021

Acknowledgements

E ven if this is a book about a man with whom I could not have been closer, it's inevitably the case that others bring different perspectives and a wider understanding to a son's recounting of his own father's life. A life lived to its fullest.

I have particularly appreciated help from those within the Special Forces community. At the very top of that list is Major General Jeremy Phipps, Alan Phipps' son and a former Director of UK Special Forces. He and Lord Carrington both spoke at the Guards Chapel in London at my father's Memorial Service in 2007 and he generously wrote the Foreword for this book. I received help from the SAS Regimental Association of which my father had been a past President, meeting Lt. Cols. Keith Edlin and Chris Dodkin on the harbour front in Sfakia, southern Crete, after they had just walked the Samaria Gorge. For years both generously provided me with whatever help they could. I would like to include my thanks to Damien Lewis, whose knowledge as an ex-marine was very welcome. He introduced me to Jack 'Zucky' Mann who worked with both my father and Andy Lassen as a radio operator. It has become more special, now that I have a better idea about my father's war years, to meet the people with whom he fought. I now have a far better appreciation of just how tough their lives were. Another who fought side by side with George was Jack Sibard, a member of the Free French SAS. He was on the '42 Heraklion raid. Sadly, Jack died in 2019 but he and I spent a day together reminiscing at his home in Bordeaux in 2018. In Copenhagen, I met with Andy Lassen's elegant younger sister, Bente Bernstorff-Gyldensteen. We talked about Andy, a man my father adored and admired, over a delicious lunch of schnapps and pickled herring. All the relatives of those who fought together share a special bond so I'm grateful for the conversations I've had with so many of them.

Greece has brought me together with others who had either known George directly or were, somehow, connected. Sadly Jason Mavrikis is no longer with us; Mavrikis had fought with Lassen and been with him when he liberated Thessaloniki. You would never know it, so modest and quiet these courageous men were. We spent many hours together in Athens and on Crete. I met with Eleni Tsigante, the General's granddaughter and Nikos

Nickoloudis on another trip to Athens. Both Kostas Mamaloukis and Peter Schenck spent days with me retracing my father's footsteps, the first on Crete, Peter on Leros. On Leros I was privileged to meet one of the few Leros survivors, Albert Poulter, who'd been on HMS *Intrepid* when she, and the RHN Queen Olga (*Vasilass Olga*) were sunk by Ju.88 bombers. My thanks also to Theofanis-Marios Kotzampopoulos, Themis Codjambopoulos and Savvas Vlassis who all helped me with their knowledge of the Greek Sacred Squadron.

I owe a very large debt to Thomas Harder for his invaluable advice, materials, introductions and criticism. As the author of *Lassen's War*, Thomas patiently helped me thread together much of George Jellicoe's war on the Greek islands and the Peloponnese. James Holland wrote a wonderful profile of my father in his book, *Heroes*. He kindly lent me all his interview notes. Gavin Mortimer's many books on the SAS, SBS and the LRDG have been an inspiration. Tony Rogers (*Churchill's Folly*) helped me with on-the-ground details from Leros as did Julie Peakman (*Hitler's Island War*). Others whose paths I have crossed offered their help without knowing me. One was Paul McCue who corrected some of the errors about Athlit, the SBS base. It was through a correspondence with Bruce McComish that Martin Solomon came to life.

Many people talked to me about George's later life; when I decided not to include an account of his life after he left the Foreign Office, much of their recollections were dropped from this book. Nevertheless, they allowed me to leave a personal account for the family. I am indebted to HRH, the Duke of Kent, Lord Howe, Dr. Rita Gardiner (The Royal Geographical Society), Lady Damaris Stewart, Lord William Waldegrave and Lord Carrington with whom I talked before he sadly passed in 2019. Collette Jackson recounted some wonderful stories about her time with George. The family will always be deeply grateful for all the care and attention she brought, not only to my father's last days, but to other members of the same family.

I am always grateful for the patient help from my cousins, James Loudon, Philip Wingfield, Richard Latham and Christopher Balfour for sharing their own stories and for patiently proof-reading mine. Thanks to both our daughters, Zoë and Francesca, the former for her welcome editorial suggestions (along with those of George Chamier), the latter for help with the book's maps and diagrams. Phillipa, George's real companion in life, generously read and re-read the manuscript, spending many hours with me talking of George's life and the connections that I had failed to mention or misunderstood.

Those who, like myself, come to writing late in life often share a common regret: we failed to value the time we had with those around us when we could have saved so many priceless memories for posterity. There are those with whom I now wished I had talked more: David Sutherland, Steve Hastings, Carol Mather, Jason Mavrikis, Paddy Leigh Fermor and Walter Milner-Barry. I would have loved to have met Bill Cumper, Porter 'Joe' Jarrell, Georges Bergé or Augustin Jordan. Or John House, George's driver. He must have seen so much of the other side of my father.

Many of the photographs are from the author's collection; whilst every effort has been made to trace the copyright holders of others, the publishers and I apologize for any inadvertent omissions. Similarly, there are bound to be errors in my telling of the story of George Jellicoe's life. Over time, I hope these will be corrected and happily invite comments and suggestions. I am always grateful to anyone who helps make this a better and more accurate accounting of an extraordinary life. One of those is my old friend John McCartney, who helped find many of those errors that managed to survive to the very end and gave me another Leros connection with my father.

Abbreviations

AHSF	Anglo-Hellenic Schooner Force (incorporated the Levant Schooner Flotilla)
Ar.196	Arado single-engine seaplane (German)
BCA	*Bataillions de Chasseurs Alpins* (France)
BLO	British Liaison Officer
Buffs	4th Battalion, Royal East Kent Regiment
BYMS	Brooklyn Yard Minesweeper
CA.309	Caproni, CA.309 bomber, the Ghibli (Italian)
CIGS	Chief of Imperial General Staff (UK)
CGS	Chief of General Staff
COPP	Combined Operations Assault Pilotage Party
Coy.	Company
CR.42	Fiat Falco single-engine biplane fighter-bomber (Italian)
CSDIC	Combined Services Detailed Interrogation Centre
DCM	Distinguished Conduct Medal (UK)
DCO	Director Combined Operations
DSO	Distinguished Service Order
EAM	National Liberation Front (Greece, *Ethnikón Apeleftherotikón Métopon*)
EDES	National Republican Greek League (*Ethnikós Dimikratikós Ellinikós Syndesmos)*
ELAS	Greek People's Liberation Army, military arm of EAM (*Ellinikós Laïkós Apeleftherotikós Stratós)*
EXFIL	Extraction
Faughs	2nd Battalion, Royal Irish Fusiliers (also RIF)
FFL	*Forces Françaises Libres* (France)
Fi.56	Fiesler Storch. German light reconnaissance aircraft
FO	Foreign Office (United Kingdom)
FOB	Forward Operating Base
FUP	Forming-up Point
Gestapo	*Geheime Staatspolizei* – Secret State Police (Germany)
GRU	*Glavnoye razvedyvatel'noye upravleniye* – The Main Intelligence Directorate of Russian Military Intelligence, Formed 1992 (Russia)

GSS	Greek Sacred Squadron, *Ieros Lochos*
HDML	Harbour Defence Motor Launch
He.111	Heinkel He.111 twin-engine bomber (German), first used in the Spanish Civil War in 1936.
I-Boot	*Infanterie-boot* (LCI)
INFIL	infiltration
Ju.52	Junkers Ju.52 (German)
Ju.87	The Junkers 87B2 (German) had two crew, 230mph cruising speed, three 7.9mm machine guns, bomb payload 1,540 lbs
Ju.88	Junkers Ju.88 (German)
KGB	*Komitet Gosudarstvennoy Bezopasnosti* – Committee for State security, 1954-1991 (Russia)
KORR	King's Own Royal Regiment
LAF	Libyan Arab Force
LC	Landing craft
LG	Landing Ground (LG12, for example, was Sidi Haneish, LG21, Fuka)
LFA	Land Forces Adriatic
LRDG	Long Range Desert Group
LSF	Levant Schooner Flotilla
LST	Landing Ship Tanks
MAS	*Motoscafo armato silurante* (Italian). Equivalent to British MTB
MC	Military Cross (UK)
Me.109	Messerschmitt. Sometimes referred to as the Bf109 because of its manufacturer (Bayerische Flugzeugwerke)
Me.110	Messerschmitt
MEHQ	Middle East Headquarters
MERF	Middle East Raiding Forces
MG34	*Machinengewehr.* Heavy infantry machine gun (German)
MI.9	British Military Intelligence Dept. handling escape and evasion and support to European resistance movements
MID	Mentioned in Dispatches
MM	Military Medal (UK)
MO.4	Special Operations Executive (SOE) in the Middle East
MTB	Motor Torpedo Boat (UK. British equivalent of a German *E-Boot*)
NKVD	*Naródnyy Komissariát Vnútrennikh Del* – The People's Commissariat for Internal Affairs, 1934-1947 (Russian)
NSA	The National Security Agency (American)
Pltn.	Platoon
OCTU	Officer Cadet Training Unit

OFLAG	*Offiziere Lager* (officers' camp)
OR	Other Ranks
PIAT	Portable infantry Anti-Tank (British equivalent to American bazooka)
RAC	The Royal Automobile Club, Pall Mall, London
RFHQ	Raiding Forces Headquarters
R boat	Light naval landing craft, known as a Eureka
RIF	2nd Battalion, Royal Irish Fusiliers (also 'Faughs')
RMBPD	Royal Marine Boom Patrol Detachment
RTU	Returned to unit
RWK	Queen's Own Royal West Kent Regiment
ULTRA	The American description of British-decrypted German radio traffic using the Enigma encoding machines (because of its ultra-exclusivity of distribution)
UNRRA	United Nations Relief and Rehabilitation Agency
SAAF	South African Air Force
SAS	Special Air Service
SB	Security Battalion (Greek Police Battalions)
SBR	Special Boat Regiment
SBS	Special Boat Section/Service/Squadron. Each has a very different connotation
SDF	Sudan Defence Force
SIS	Secret Intelligence Service most usually known as MI.6
SM.179	Savoia-Marchetti 179 3-engine bomber (Italian)
SP	Self-propelled
SOE	Special Operations Executive
SRS	Special Raiding Squadron
STALAG	Shortening of *Stammlager*, itself a shortening of *Kriegsgefangenen-Mannschaftsstammlager* (literally, prisoner of war camp)
TJFF	Trans-Jordan Frontier Force
WP	Wireless Post
Z.506	Cant twin engine seaplane (Italian)

A Note on Spelling

Chosen	Alternatives
Appetici (Leros)	Apetiki
Bagoush	Bagush, Baggoush
Berka	Berca
Calchi	Halki (English), Chalki (German)
Kastelorizzo (Greek)	Kastellórizo (English), Megisti (German). Castellorizo or Castelrosso (Italian)
El Dhaba	El Daba, Al-Dhaba
Fuka	Fukka, Fouka
Grifo Bay (Leros)	Kryfos
Kalymnos (English & German)	Calino (Italian)
Karpathos (English and German)	Scarpanto (Italian)
Kos (English and German)	Coo (Italian). Cos
Leros (English and German)	Lero (Italian)
Lipsi (English and German)	Liso (Italian)
Martuba	Matuba, Maturba, Martuba
Nisiros	Nisyros (English and German), Nisiro (Italian)
Palma Bay (Leros)	Vaghia Bay
Parteni Bay (Leros)	Partheni
Pasta di Sopra (Leros)	Pano Zymi
Patmos (English and German)	Patmo (Italian)
Piscopi (Italian)	Tilos (English and German)
Portolago (Italian)	Lakki (contemporary Greek)

Quirico (Leros)	Querico, Mt. Ag. Kyrikos
Rhodes (English)	Rodi (Italian), Rhodos (German)
Simi (Italian)	Symi (English and German)
Stampalia	Astypalaia (English), Astypalea (German)
Timimi	Tmimi, today called 'Al Tamimi'
Vathy (Samos)	Vathis, Vathi

Part I

The War Years

Chapter 1

1939: War and the Loss of Innocence

W hen war came, George Jellicoe had few illusions as to what lay ahead. With uncanny foresight, an entry in his 1939 diary noted, 'I anticipate a five-year plus war.' The war would profoundly change him. As for others of his generation, it would be a rite of passage. If, that is, you were lucky enough to have survived.

When he had left Cambridge in June 1939, Jellicoe's mind was set on getting into the Foreign Office. The outbreak of war would change all that. The summer of 1939 had been particularly beautiful and Jellicoe spent it down on the Isle of Wight. He would be there for about five weeks before the Officer Cadet Training Unit (OCTU) course started at Sandhurst. He enjoyed the last days of peace, spending quite a bit of time in the company of 'a particularly attractive lady who'd rented the cottage on the beach'. Jellicoe's dalliances with the fairer sex started at an early age.

Jellicoe referred to himself in these years as being 'quite apolitical'. He was more interested in being with his friends, playing golf and, as he misleadingly put it, 'occasionally, very occasionally doing a bit of work' (Jellicoe always underplayed his application). Nevertheless, he followed the Abyssinian crisis and the Spanish Civil War closely.

'The first major event which profoundly touched [him]' had been the Munich agreement, a year earlier. He felt 'impotent pain and rage' at the way in which Britain had signed away the rights of many Czechs to Hitler.[1] It was Jellicoe's great turning point – his 'great awakening'. It was now that his awareness developed into the intensity that came to characterize his intellect. He was deeply 'ashamed' of the agreement his country had signed.[2] At the time he was staying with the Wavells. Archie John Wavell, the son of the great Field Marshal, was a close friend, and in later life Jellicoe would often pick up a copy of his father's anthology of poems, *Other Men's Flowers*. Maybe it was a way to keep his son's memory alive.

While others went to Spain or joined up, Jellicoe had instead gone to St Moritz to face the challenge of the Cresta Run and spent 'the best part of six months' in France, visiting St Jean de Luz, Tours and Paris. By now, both his French and German were near-fluent.

Jellicoe was already well-travelled. After Winchester, he had spent time in Germany for what he called his 'post-exam spree'. He had wanted to get both his French and German 'up to par' in preparation for his intended Foreign Office career and so, while in Germany, he mixed in diplomatic circles as much as he could. At a dinner at the Italian Embassy, he started to dance with Mussolini's daughter, Countess Eda Ciano, married to the Foreign Minister – rather too intimately and by error during the Italian National Anthem. She whispered provocatively in his ear, 'You certainly like to fly close to the flame, George.' He drove around with an artist friend, somewhat older than he, who put his growing concerns to rest, reassuring him that there would be no war:

> I'm absolutely certain that if the Führer does decide to do something foolish, the Army chiefs will not allow him to go too far.[3]

This German friend would be killed in December 1941 in the ice and snow just outside of Moscow, as Hitler's armies ground to a halt.

Four years after his father died, George Jellicoe took his seat in the House of Lords for the first time. It was 25 July, just two months before Europe once again descended into the chaos of war. He was in the Lords on the first or second day of September and remembered thinking that Britain was going to 'rat on the Poles'. War was declared on 3 September 1939.[4]

Jellicoe had been to Claridge's the same afternoon and had allowed a bellboy to go back to his room to fetch his gas mask, instead of going himself. He felt so 'deeply ashamed' that he decided to spend the rest of the day helping the hotel staff fill sandbags. He was amply rewarded for his guilty conscience: thereafter, he could always get a room at Claridge's, and always at preferential rates.

In October 1939, the 21-year-old Jellicoe joined up and, armed with his new serial number – 124546 – entered the Royal Military College (RMC), Sandhurst, just another face among the first batches of innocently enthusiastic wartime cadets. He was a little late as he had enjoyed the last few weeks of a glorious summer on the Isle of Wight. While he wasn't there long before coming down with pneumonia, he received his commission in the Coldstream Guards on 23 March 1940, days after the Finnish war had ended. He spent much of the time recuperating in Sunningdale, at a house his mother purchased at Whinshill near Ascot, rather than at St Lawrence on the Isle of Wight. This day, 23 March, was a date that would curiously play a prominent role throughout his life. On that particular day in 1944, he would marry Patsy O'Kane, my mother, and nine years later, in 1953, I would be born.

One of his roommates at Sandhurst was Alan Hare. He later became chairman of the *Financial Times* and, a position that was of much more interest to Jellicoe, of Château Latour. Another Sandhurst friendship which came with more tangible benefits was with Bobby Henderson. His aunt, Laura Henderson (neé Forster) owned the Windmill Theatre near Piccadilly, and Jellicoe would go up to London to see the 'young ladies' of the theatre with his friends. Years later, he would recall with amusement that 'they were allowed to uncover one bosom as long as they stood quite still and this was the enormous erotic thrill we got.'[5]

In late January 1940, Lieutenant Lord Jellicoe joined the 5th Scots Guards Ski Battalion, where he trained for a number of weeks under the command of Major Jimmy Coats MC, first at the Quebec Barracks at Bordon Camp near Aldershot, and then in France. 'In twenty-three days' Coats had 'to assemble, organize, equip, inoculate and train a body of men not only from all the ranks of the Army, but from civilian life as well, who had never served together before.'[6] It was an enormous task. Coats was not only a very good skier, he had also been involved in the Cresta Run and, no doubt, already knew Jellicoe. A bigger problem, in many ways, was that out of the 1,000 men who volunteered in January and February 1940, a full 60 per cent were officers: 'Too many chiefs; too few Indians'. The obvious option was demotion, but many didn't want to do this: 167 officers left. From the Coldstreams came Jellicoe, along with Lieutenant Colonel Coats, Lieutenants Bridge, Thorny and Waken. On 5 February, the ragtag group, now known as 'The Snowballers', assembled, in preparation for embarking for Finland, where the whole operation was to be under the command of Colonel Kermit Roosevelt, President Roosevelt's second son. He committed suicide in 1943.

It would have been a tricky operation. The British wanted to block Swedish iron ore imports to Germany, but Churchill made it clear that British troops should not be the cause of any provocation towards the Russians, at this point allied to Germany. In August 1939, the two states had entered an 'unholy alliance', a two-fronted assault on Poland the immediate objective. Alluding to the story of the Russian Imperial Navy's circumnavigating the world en route to Tsushima in 1905, Jellicoe said that 'you could have followed the route of the 5th Scots Guards to Chamonix by the number of champagne bottles which came out of the train', there were so many old school friends assembled together. On 2 March, they left 'in the greatest secrecy' for Chamonix and arrived in the local station at St Gervais-les-Bains-le-Fayet, where they took a mountain train up to the mountain base, to be met by the *111ème Bataillon des Chasseurs de Haute Montaigne*, under whose aegis they would be training. It was a fiasco. Their ski equipment didn't arrive until three days later, leaving them precious little time before their departure on the morning of 11 March when, despite all the security, Lord Haw-Haw was able to announce the precise hour the troops would ship out. The American-born Anglo-Irish fascist William Joyce's voice was instantly recognizable: very nasal and affectedly upper-class tones sounding 'Germany calling, Germany calling' opened each broadcast. Regularly broadcasting from Berlin, he was later imprisoned in the Tower of London and in 1946 became the second-to-last person to be executed there as a traitor.

Jellicoe was (and remained for the rest of his life) an accomplished and fearless skier. He loved being in Chamonix for 'two or three weeks, skiing every day' especially, I imagine, because he would have been surrounded by good skiers.[7] Matters quickly turned more serious. On 14 March, they boarded a Polish ship, which Jellicoe characterized as 'a rather fine Polish liner', the MS *Batory*, only to find out, once at sea, that the Finns had stopped fighting.[8] With this news, the ship turned around on 16 March. Uncharacteristically, Jellicoe felt relieved. They were not well enough trained, and he was sure that the expedition would have ended in disaster: 'Our bones would be bleaching on some sort of tundra very quickly.'[9] Carol Mather of the Welsh Guards was scathing about the lack of professionalism:

> About one fifth had only three days on skis, and therefore could not ski. About one sixth had no military experience or were specialists, and therefore could not shoot. Only about one in five knew how to use a Primus stove or how to fit skins on skis. Only one man in 50 had used snowshoes.[10]

They were both RTU'd, returned to unit, in Jellicoe's case back to the Coldstreams to train at Pirbright in Surrey. For Mather, back to the Welsh Guards.

Jellicoe quickly became bored and spent much of his time in London nightspots like the Bag o' Nails. He was itching for action and would get up to all sorts of no good. Not surprisingly, he frequently found himself confined to barracks – at Pirbright and later at the Holding Battalion in Chelsea at the Duke of York barracks and then at Regent's Park.[11] The first chance he got, he applied for the Commandos. At White's Club, he was interviewed by Robert Laycock, recently made a Colonel, and asked why he wanted to join.'Lucky' Laycock didn't wait for the reply. Laughing, Jellicoe recalled the prompt Laycock gave him: 'I suppose, Jellicoe, you want to have a crack at the Boche'.[12] My father was too timid to tell him the real truth. Like others, he was, bored 'sitting on [his] arse'. Laycock took him on.

Origins of the Commandos

The first Commando units were the Independent Companies, 'the name of which had been borrowed from Boer raiding-parties'.[13] Colonel Colin Gubbins (1896–1976) had already helped the Czechs and Poles at the start of the war, and his experience was needed to help prepare Britain for a possible invasion. In March 1940, he was called back to raise a 3,000-strong force. Apparently, the idea had been proposed to Sir John Dill by Colonel Dudley Clarke as they were inspecting Dunkirk survivors. Dill proposed an idea to Churchill who backed it fully. The new Commandos were sent to fight in Norway but were disbanded on their return and integrated with the Royal Marines to form the new units. The 'Leopards', as they were originally named by Churchill, formally became part of the British Army on 12 June 1940. On 24 June, they carried out their first cross-Channel raid on Boulogne aimed at destroying the harbour installations.

Private enterprise and established regiments such as the Guards figured prominently. A large area of land on Scotland's north-west coast, between Arisaig and Glenfinnan, was closed off and declared a military training area. This was essentially the land either side of the Fort William–Mallaig road and railway. Old barbed wire military fencing still restricts easy access. Inverailort House was commandeered as a billet for the Independent Companies after Norway and would remain an endurance training centre for the rest of the war. Arisaig would become a 'killing school' used by Eric Sykes and William Ewart Fairbairn. They had both been in the Shanghai Municipal Police (Sykes an expert pistol shot, Fairbairn an ex-Royal Marine) and later used their experience to train the new Commando and SOE recruits in fieldcraft, reconnaissance, killing and sabotage. The F-S commando throwing knife is named after them: they had commissioned it from the Wilkinson Sword Company. The knife cost 13/6 and 250,000 of them were produced.

It was an area which had been set up to train a guerrilla army that could carry on resistance – behind enemy lines – if the planned 1940 German invasion, Operation Sealion (*Fall Seelöwe*), had succeeded. Major Bill Stirling, David's brother, was chief instructor, and Major Lord 'Shimi' Lovat, his cousin, was a 'fieldcraft' instructor with David's other brother, Peter. Lovat became one of the legends of D-Day, advancing to relieve Major John Howard's airborne troops at Pegasus Bridge to the sound of bagpipes, dressed in a characteristic white Aran sweater. Fitzroy Maclean, later to command

Jellicoe's SBS M detachment, trained there and was friends with Peter. The men were taught how to live off the land, in fact, how to poach. Some of Jellicoe's friends did the training. One was a rather older man who had fought in the First World War, Edward Beddington-Behrens, later a great patron of the arts, married to a princess, Irina Obolensky. Another was David Niven, the actor. Jellicoe thought him an 'amusing chap'. His high-profile Hollywood connections left most around him speechless.

On 6 June 1940, as Allied troops were being encircled on the beaches of Dunkirk, the British Cabinet discussed and approved the order to set up ten Commando groups, each with around 500 men, to be under the command of MO.9. The search was on for 40 officers and 1,000 men. Six days later, a Royal Marine, Sir Alan Bourne, became the first head of what would become Combined Operations, then called Offensive Operations. The following month, Special Operations Executive (SOE) was set up by Churchill's War Minister, Sir Hugh Dalton, the Labour party politician, economist and outspoken critic of appeasement in the 1930s.

When LAYFORCE, by this time, had been rechristened 'Belayforce' in 1941, it seemed as though little had been achieved. In fact, its valuable experience inspired Roger Courtney to form the Special Boat Section and David Stirling, the Special Air Service.[14] No.11 Scottish Commando left for Syria, No.8 became the basis for the SAS, and Courtney transferred the Folboats to HMS *Medway*, from which they would operate as part of the 1st Submarine Flotilla.

Following the near-crippling defeat of Dunkirk, the British licked their wounds. They had managed to get more than 140,000 troops out, but had left behind copious supplies and weaponry – around 700 tanks, more than 10,000 machine guns and 500 or so Anti-Aircraft (AA) guns. The very same month, June, Churchill's cry, 'Set Europe Ablaze', rang out. If the British could not fight a superior military power by conventional means, Churchill would use what he had learned as a junior officer in South Africa, forty years earlier. 'I felt as though I were walking with destiny and that all my past life had been a preparation for this hour and for this trial.' The Commandos epitomized his indomitable spirit.

The training was very effective, even if the organization was sometimes haphazard, a mix of private enterprise, military organization and the old school network. Almost all the early recruits were from the Scots Guards and had served together in the disastrous Norway campaign against Generalleutnant Dietl's seasoned German Special Forces. During the 1940 Narvik campaign, Dietl had successfully held off an Allied force of

25,000 soldiers with 2,500 mountain troops and 2,000 sailors. Though the training was tough, there were, to the best of Jellicoe's recollection, hardly any dropouts.

No.8 Commando, the unit to which Jellicoe was seconded, came under the command of another Coldstreamer, Mervyn Griffith-Jones. After the war, he served as a prosecutor at the Nürnberg trials. As usual, it was heavily made up of recruits from various Guards battalions. Jellicoe became one of two subalterns, the other being the much older Davis Cup tennis player and later publisher, Ian Collins. In the same Troop were Jim Almonds, Pat Riley, Jim Blankney and Bob Lilley who would later be known as 'The Tobruk Four'. Almonds, a former policeman, had been caught poaching and only narrowly missed a court martial; Riley was an American whose family immigrated to Cumbria when he was seven; Malcolm Pleydell, later to become the SAS regimental doctor, remembered Lilley: 'black tussled hair, his serious voice, and his small dark eyes which wrinkled up when he laughed'. There was 'no acting, no showing off, but just very straightforward and honest'.[15]

The unit trained at Burnham-on-Crouch in Essex where a pub, The Welcome Sailor, served as J troop's temporary headquarters. The Commando wasn't housed in barracks but was billeted amongst the local population. This was the time of the Battle of Britain. As Jellicoe's unit trained day in day out on the ground, 'the Few' were up above in the skies, heavily outnumbered, fighting for their lives. Even Burnham could not escape the German air assault, and six townsfolk were killed. A 22-year-old pilot with 603 Squadron, Peter Pease, died in the skies above Maidstone on 15 September 1940. A lime tree, planted in 1990, now marks the spot where his Spitfire plunged into the ground at Kingswood in Kent. A very touching headstone reads, 'Some of the Many honour one of the Few'. Peter had become one of Jellicoe's closest university friends when Jellicoe dated his sister, 'Pixie'. Pease's brother went on to become head of Barclays Bank. Who knows what would have been Peter's own future? Many said that he could have become Foreign Secretary. Languages and an interest in foreign policy was something he shared with Jellicoe, and like Jellicoe, he had travelled extensively in Germany.

Jellicoe now started to understand that he had much to live up to. His father might have helped open opportunities, but the young Earl now had to prove that he was worthy of the trust placed in him. His frivolous side gave way to an increasingly sober appreciation of the fickle nature of life. It would not be too long before, under fire, he would also learn what it really meant to be responsible for another man's life and how to master his own inevitable fear.

In the six or so weeks that he was there, Jellicoe concocted some interesting training exercises. One involved sending the men out tasked to bring back an odd assortment of very specific items – a cockerel, a hen, a bowler hat, a lady's bicycle and even a car.[16] Although the items were returned, what their poor unsuspecting owners felt was not recorded.

Jellicoe's training continued in Scotland at Inveraray and on the Isle of Arran. The unit was housed on Lord Brocket's estate. This noble earl was known to have had Nazi sympathies, was a member of the Anglo-German Fellowship and had even gone to Hitler's fiftieth birthday celebrations. Jellicoe 'felt fully entitled to poach his deer.'[17] He later added that he was actually encouraged to do so by 'a man called Lovat'.

Three commando groups – Nos.7, 8 and 11, plus a single troop from No.3 Commando – were grouped together into a larger force, officially named Force Z, but later known as LAYFORCE (after 50 and 52 Commando joined), taking its name from the newly promoted Colonel Robert Laycock. They didn't know it, but the target for which they were training was Rhodes, and this operation was only cancelled when the emergency evacuation of Greece took precedence.[18]

On the Firth of Clyde, at Gourock, Jellicoe and his men boarded a transport to take them out to their ship, the *Glen Roy*, 'a 10,000 ton, 17-knot converted merchantman'. That would be their floating home for the next few months.[19] She was old and noisy: her engines could be heard for miles. As she lay at anchor in the roads off Arran, Jellicoe and Ian Collins, gathered No.3 Troop on deck. Before boarding they'd been given a farewell lecture by Admiral Sir Roger Keyes, the 'hero' of Zeebrugge and a strong critic of Jellicoe's father. When Britain resorted to irregular military action, he became one of its senior proponents.

At 2230 hours on 1 February the *Glen Roy*, *Glen Gyle* and *Glen Earn* all weighed anchor and set sail for Egypt, escorted by a cruiser, HMS *Glasgow*, and four destroyers.[20] On board were two of the Commando units, No.8 Guards and No.11 Scottish Commando. Jellicoe made no comment about the comforts. For him they might have been fine, but they were certainly not for others. 'Our living conditions were abysmal as we were billeted in the holds, vast caverns with no portholes and no source of fresh air from the decks above.' What was worse was that the heads 'frequently overflowed onto the deck with extremely unpleasant consequences.' Johnny Cooper, later acclaimed as an SAS 'Original', unsurprisingly found that the only way he could escape 'the odour of excrement and vomit below' was to volunteer to work the AA guns above deck.[21]

No.8 Commando boasted an impressive roster. There were, in Jellicoe's own words, 'lots of sprigs or spriglets of aristocracy', names like Gavin Astor,

Randolph Churchill, Lord Fitzwilliam, Julian Berry, Carol Mather, Lord Sudeley, Evelyn Waugh and Philip Dunne. And, of course, from the Scots Guards, David Stirling. So many were members of White's that it became the troop's nickname. And then, of course, there were the men who really made up the fighting strength of No.8 and would join Stirling's SAS. Men like Jock Lewes, Jim Almonds, Bob Bennett, Jim Blakeney and Johnny Cooper. Also there were those who would form the core of the SBS: Roger Courtney, Tommy Langton, Bob Lilley, Carol Mather, Johnny Rose and Jim Sherwood. Many knew each other from pre-war days.

Randolph Churchill, the Prime Minister's son, was clearly ill-at-ease once at sea. Almonds had a very sharp eye for detail as well as a wonderful way with words. He was watching Churchill one day as he came up on deck:

> He would stand, facing towards the bows, clinging to the railings with his left hand, while holding the other slightly out to the side like a circus tight-rope walker. Sliding his hand along the rail, he would make his way forward by jerky little jumps.[22]

Dick Holmes, who would later serve with the SBS, remembered how Bill Cumper described Randolph. It didn't lack sting: 'Christ! He's so stupid even the other officers notice it!'[23]

Jellicoe said that he didn't think Randolph ever 'really fitted into things', but it was clear that he was 'extremely brave. There's no doubt about that at all.' Fitzroy Maclean was more forgiving than many: 'I began to realize what marvellous company Randolph could be. Maddening, of course, in a dozen different ways, but endlessly stimulating and entertaining.'[24] At No.8's Essex training ground at Burnham-on-Crouch with Jock Lewes, Randolph had cooked up an impromptu breakfast – an hour before an exercise – of steak and onions at the local blacksmith. When he'd been training at Lochailort he'd been sent home by Shimi Lovat for arguing with his instructor. He'd actually been in the right, but his attitude had been extremely arrogant. Mather trained with him and concluded, 'Truth to tell, he was no good with the men', although 'there was something lovable about this rumbustious, outrageous, over-grown school-boy who, while excelling at nothing, added lustre to our lives.'[25] He was not popular, being 'much too outspoken and militant in his convictions'.[26] He would very often pull rank and could be extraordinarily rude to people who weren't in a position to answer back. Later, in Cairo, 'he would sit in Shepheard's Hotel openly with a bevy of girls 'obviously ... not chosen for their conversational power'.[27] One club, the Muhammed Ali, had to change its rules to stop Churchill bringing in these sorts of women. No wonder Alan Moorehead, the war correspondent, summed him up as 'aggressive, headstrong, opinionated'.[28]

Evelyn Waugh 'became much more of a misfit later on.' He wrote about his experiences in No.8, describing it as 'boisterous, xenophobic, extravagant, imaginative, witty, with a disproportion of noblemen, which the navy found disconcerting.'[29] He and Jellicoe would regularly end up in some Soho nightclub. One time, they were thrown out of a particularly louche establishment called the Jamboree Club. When Jellicoe's mother saw an article describing the event, her immediate thought was that it must have been something to do with the Boy Scouts, so instead of a ticking off, her son was rather surprised to get a pat on the back.

Jellicoe also became a close friend of 'Phil' Dunne and would later marry his daughter, Philippa, after his first marriage to my mother, Patsy, had failed.

Many others would be lifelong friends. Julian Berry would become my godfather, and his wife, Pamela, remained friends with Patsy for many years. I hardly knew or remember Julian. Along with Tom Hall, he would become one of the three initial investors in the Haute Savoie ski resort, Méribel.

Jellicoe, Carol Mather and David Sutherland from the Black Watch became very close, lifelong friends. Sutherland would take over command of the SBS from Jellicoe, while Mather would work as one of Montgomery's Intelligence officers during the Ardennes offensive. With No.8 was also a young officer, Roger Courtney, commanding a special amphibious unit, the Folboat Section. He might have been described by Sutherland as 'a hard-drinking white hunter with a big line of bullshit and a persuasive tongue', but he is regarded by many as the father of the SBS.[30]

On the outward journey, they played a lot of cards, mostly gin rummy. There wasn't much else to do. According to Jock Lewes, whom Jellicoe first met on that voyage, conditions were 'very crowded ... there is practically no exercise space.'[31] Only rarely was David Stirling, whom he also first met then, ever seen. He usually remained in his cabin, earning himself the nickname, 'The Giant Sloth'.

Stirling's pedigree, like that of many in No.8, was impeccable:

> The son of General Archibald and the Hon. Margaret Stirling, of the Stirlings of Keir, a Scottish family of ineffable distinction, Roman-catholics, landowners, rich and solidly interconnected to the great mafia of Anglo-Scots aristocracy which permeates British military and political history.[32]

He was the weakling of the four siblings and suffered a speech impediment until the age of six. It was so difficult to understand him that his sister would 'translate his needs to the family'. It was his way of being the centre of attention.[33] Stirling did not survive Cambridge: he was 'sent down' for drinking and gambling. What his companions also didn't know was that he was a depressive and a man who had tasted many sides of life: he had studied art in Paris, trained as a climber and had wanted to be the first man to climb Everest.

On the *Glen Roy*, he went back to what he knew best: gambling. Stirling's fortunes could rise and, just as fast, fall. Randolph Churchill lost £400 to him one night, but by the time they arrived in Egypt he was down £800. His gambling, his son maintained, caused the collapse of his first marriage.[34] 'In the closed world of the ship, the men greeted this news with sardonic amusement: a private's pay came to 14/- a week.'[35] Jellicoe also spent most of the time losing money to him.[36] Evelyn Waugh said that he nearly lost even more than Churchill. He had 'lost almost three years' wages, only to win it all back on a single lucky card.'[37]

Stirling had not, by that point, impressed many people. His superior in the Scots Guards concluded that he was 'an irresponsible and unremarkable soldier'.[38] Even in his early days in Cairo, he continued to behave in the same way. He was even described as a 'malingerer' and came close to a court martial as he spent most of the time at the Scottish Military Hospital. He would visit the wards when he needed to recover from a hangover: 'a couple of deep snifters from the pure oxygen bottle ... the hangover vanished in seconds.'[39]

He had a strongly irreverent sense of humour. Hastings noticed the 'hint of impish humour' that could accompany his 'penetrating directness'.[40] In many ways, his early impediment pushed him to want to make a name for himself and was probably why he soon developed into the 'merciless practical joker' that he became. When confronted by his sergeant about the state of his rifle, his response was perfect:

'Stirling, it's bloody filthy. There must be a clown on the end of this rifle.'
'Yes, sergeant, but not at my end.'[41]

On 10 February, the *Glen Roy* arrived in Freetown, Sierra Leone. Nine days later, they finally made Cape Town, the men by then roasted chestnut brown after almost two weeks at sea. Stirling and Jellicoe got off together, Churchill by himself, a rather lonely figure wandering off into the harbour streets. As the long sea journey continued, Jellicoe got to know some of the naval officers, like the 71-year-old Admiral Cowan and the young Peter Beatty, Sir David Beatty's son. Cowan had been persuaded to join 8 Commando by Sir Roger Keyes.

On 7 March 1941, they finally reached Port Suez and dropped anchor. It had been a terrible trip, and most of the men were deeply demoralized. Here the core three Commando groups (7, 8 and 11) were joined by two other groups, Nos.50 and 52, which had been in East Africa.

No.8 mustered on deck and gave the ship's captain, John Padgett, three cheers. They had sailed across 14,000 miles of ocean without harm. Three days later, 'issued with Wolseley helmets', they temporarily disembarked and made their way to an 'arid plot named Geneifa Camp'.[42] It was not their final destination. On 9 April, they re-boarded and sailed, accompanied by the destroyer HMS *Decoy*, going on to Tobruk and entering the harbour while an air raid was in progress. Then onwards to Alexandria to re-board the *Glen Roy*. Morale in No.8 'reached rock bottom'.[43] It was nothing close to the picture that Keyes had painted. Back then, the Admiral had talked passionately about 'an enterprise that will stir the world'. It wasn't surprising that the men were thoroughly disillusioned. Jock Lewes talked sarcastically of the inflated promises:

> Very soon we will be performing a feat of arms which will astonish the world. When this does come, easily the most astonished will be ourselves.[44]

Jellicoe joined one of the raids which turned out to be abortive. They had to use an old 'Yangtze gunboat', an old Insect-class destroyer, the *Aphis*, built in 1915. She was an old boat and 'in heavy seas was hell to sail in', but she was also courageous: the 625-tonner had steamed into Bardia harbour on one occasion and, single-handedly, shelled shore installations for twenty minutes.[45] On the way to attack a German airfield about 60 miles west of the front lines, she was heavily bombed by Italian and German aircraft for two days. She was lucky not to have been sunk; at one point, Jellicoe remembered seeing a bomb, falling short, bouncing right over the ship. All the while, there was Cowan, 'who'd insisted on coming, with a Tommy gun, well into his 70s, shooting at these Italian bombers coming over'.[46] The old Admiral was a legend. He went on to fight on land, totally ignoring his own safety. The 'little admiral', who had fought on the Nile in 1898, fought at Jutland with Jellicoe's father and had even been a Naval ADC to Lord Roberts, now became the Commandos' 'mascot'. Eventually, in Tobruk, he was taken prisoner but not before he'd emptied his revolver at a tank. Because of his age, he was repatriated back to Britain, something which utterly disappointed the old man, who then went back out on service again. Cowan 'ended his days hunting with the Warwickshire Hunt. He was a very energetic man, a great martinet: he'd been a very stern disciplinarian when he was C-in-C in the Mediterranean Fleet in the Inter-war Period.'[47]

Trying to raid the large German airfield at Ain el Gazala and approaching the destination in such a 'huge, clumsy and slow gunboat' was totally ill-conceived, in Jellicoe's opinion. He enjoyed the company of the young Aussies from the 4th Australian Infantry Division, although he admitted that, as a well-known titled Guards officer, he was an exceedingly easy target for 'good Australian ribaldry which was plentifully bestowed and was extremely good for these two young officers', he and Ian Collins.[48]

All in all, the month in Tobruk was one that Jellicoe enjoyed. There were two twin Vickers K machine guns mounted at the bottom of the garden.

> The Stukas used to come over morning and evening, and it was really rather like a pheasant drive. I used to thoroughly to enjoy that … it had rather been like shooting at high pheasants (although) never hitting them, we never hit anything.[49]

He and Carol Mather decided that a two-man attack on Ain el Gazala stood a better chance of doing some useful damage than 'the ponderous presence of a gunboat with a cargo of 100 troops to disembark'.[50] It was the failure of the *Aphis* venture that set them both off on a 'hare-brained scheme'.[51] When the two went to see General Morshead, the Australian commander enthusiastically agreed to their plan. Jellicoe's name certainly helped, but it was just as much the Australian way of waging war. One day, six German tanks broke through the wire and were headed their way. Morshead's Chief of Staff, Colonel 'Gaffer' Lloyd, was told the news. Hardly looking up, (he) said to the agitated messenger, 'Tell the bastards not to come in here. We're too bloody crowded already!'[52]

Mather and Jellicoe planned to go in with an 'R' boat, a light naval landing craft called a 'Eureka'. It was made by the Higgens Boat Company, the US firm that later built the famous, mass-produced landing craft. After three attempts, they gave up. The skipper turned out to be 'a rotten navigator' and, besides, the boat didn't even have the right navigational equipment.[53] When he was talking with James Holland, Jellicoe admitted that it was just as well. The two had thought that after the raid they could get back through the German lines and, more importantly, be allowed through the Allied lines by soldiers of the 18th Indian Cavalry (King Edward's Own). 'It was an absurd idea', he concluded.[54]

After a month, thoroughly disgruntled, Jellicoe left the Commandos and went back to his old regiment, the Coldstream Guards, to the 3rd Battalion, where he had a 'marvellous person as his Company commander, John Lloyd'. Captain John Lloyd would win an MC after beating back an attack by SS troops at Monte Sole Massif. 'In terms of casualties (estimates ranged from about 770 to more than twice that number)', this operation was 'the worst carried out by the SS in Western Europe in the Second World War'.[55] Jellicoe became 'really bored at standing by' for what he termed 'not particularly well-planned operations' in the Commandos.[56] In his own platoon were many miners, mainly from County Durham and Northumberland. It was a fond memory for Jellicoe. When, in later life, Jellicoe wanted to join the ranks of the Labour Party, he told me that he'd been rebuffed with a polite but firm recommendation: 'First, go work down a mine, lad.' He wouldn't have taken that piece of advice the wrong way. He had great respect for people, no matter what their station. The miners were no exception: 'They were a very good lot … and they looked after this young Subaltern pretty well.'[57] Later, I think he probably would have fought alongside many of the same soldiers when the Durham Light Infantry was sent to the Dodecanese islands in late 1943.

The daily routine became pretty much set: going out into the desert to establish contact with the Germans and then bringing back intelligence or prisoners. They would go out with the 4th South African Armoured Car Regiment in their Marmon-Herrington armoured cars. Once, when Jellicoe was out trying to lift a German prisoner for interrogation, his unit ran into some front-line troops. He was armed with a Beretta that had belonged to his father and tried to put it to use, but the old automatic jammed. It's now in the National Maritime Museum in Greenwich, although I don't believe they have, unfortunately, any idea of that event.

The battalion advanced further west to Marsa al Brega. About a mile and a half south of the coastal road was marshy land. Jellicoe took half a dozen men out on a patrol but soon found that they could no longer see what was going on to their south. Dunes blocked the view. They could hear quite a lot of noise, however, so needed to get to high ground to observe. Once there, they found that Rommel was on the counter-offensive and that their route had been cut off. They had to leg it back, a trip of roughly 120 miles.

They walked through the night and lay up in the day. Before long, they started to run out of water, and when they saw what appeared to be a well, Jellicoe went forward with one of his men to take a closer look. The two of them were spotted. Shots rang out. Jellicoe said rather dryly that 'at thirty yards or so, I didn't feel like spending too much time investigating their precise identity.'[58] Even at that short a range, the enemy missed, but at 200 yards, just when he thought he was safe, Jellicoe was spun around as a bullet impacted his right shoulder. He was very lucky, because the bullet only missed his spine 'by a fraction'. Nevertheless, he was knocked over, and he would suffer painful muscle cramps for the rest of his life.

There was little choice but to walk through the night. Luckily, they spotted some armoured cars from the Indian Division. Their doctor was Malcolm Pleydell, and after being given a field dressing, Jellicoe later introduced him to David Stirling and he became the SAS medical officer. He would write about his days in the SAS under the pseudonym Malcolm James. Jellicoe got back to his Battalion three days later, although his wound inevitably turned septic. When Jellicoe talked about the incident (he often used to recount it as an example of his own stupidity), he modestly joked about the predicament he'd found himself in and the distance he'd covered with an open wound: 'Nothing really ... eighty miles, that sort of thing. No, it wasn't epic.'[59]

Just before they left the besieged Fortress Tobruk, there seemed to be some light at the end of the tunnel. On 22 June the cry went up, 'The Russians are in!' Bren guns were fired off madly although 'there was not an enemy aircraft' in sight. Hitler had launched his attack in the east. The vast Russian steppes would bleed Germany to death: after the autumn mud slowed progress, winter snows brought her armies to a stop, 15km from Moscow's Red Square.

My father used to tell me the story of his wounding with a rather different slant in a typical *Boy's Own* manner. He would say that he had been on a raid and an Italian sentry had spotted him. When he thought he was out of range, he had flicked the man a V-sign – and had been shot for his troubles. It sounded better but, in fact, he thought that the men he'd run into were Senussi tribal troops under British command and that they'd mistaken him for the enemy. It had been his fault 'for not running away faster'.[60] The Senussi had no love for the Italians. When Mussolini invaded Libya in 1922, they led the armed resistance. Many of their leaders were killed and their lands confiscated.

A story that Jellicoe recounted from his Tobruk days was the occasion on which he was nearly responsible for the death of the Corps Commander, General Lumsden. His platoon had been covering one of the gaps through a minefield on the southern perimeter of Tobruk. Lumsden had come back from a night-time recce and asked Jellicoe to show him the way back to Brigade headquarters. Jellicoe obligingly walked in front of the staff cars, but suddenly realized that his compass bearings had been thrown off by the cars' engines. He had to 'explain to a slightly peeved Lieutenant General that he'd made a slight error of navigation' and had walked back into the minefield.[61] Given the circumstances, the General was surprisingly forgiving.

The war in the desert now turned against the British. Despite the 'heroic' defence by the French at Bir Hakeim, Tobruk fell and the Eighth Army beat a 'pretty disorderly retreat'. Jellicoe had already left. His wound had been looked at by the staff at the Tobruk Casualty Clearing Station who'd ordered him shipped back to the 64th General Hospital in Alexandria. Jellicoe, who admitted that he was 'rather sort of stuck-up and snobbish' about literature, spent ten days reading Proust.[62] His memory had started to fail when he was being interviewed, and he couldn't remember Proust's most famous book, *À la recherche du temps perdu*. George the aesthete. Later in life, his love would be Russian literature, Lermontov in particular.

As he recuperated, however, Jellicoe's mind wasn't totally on reading. His roving eye settled on a beautiful, 24-year-old nurse with 'snow-white hair'. Her name was Miss Donna Bugle so they called her 'Penny Whistle', rhyming 'Dollar' with 'Donna'. Apparently, or so he said, she nearly became the Duchess of Wellington. Jellicoe remembered her fondly as someone who was a genuinely good Samaritan. She 'couldn't have looked after us more kindly.'

*   *   *

At the end of June, LAYFORCE was officially disbanded. Jock Lewes had always liked 'Colonel Bob' and described him as 'very positive' and 'empathetic', but he also criticized him for lacking an 'essential' quality of leadership – 'judgement of character', nor was he able to get a real and challenging role assigned to his men.[63]

Ironically, it was that failure that became the catalyst for the formation of the Special Air Service. All the pent-up expectations of the men who had joined No.8 Commando had to find some outlet. Initially, it was in the defence of Tobruk. Stirling had also arrived in the besieged town, probably the second week in July, as part of a sixty-strong force led by six officers – Laycock, Lewes, Captain Mike Kealy, Captain Philip Dunne, Gordon Alston and Tommy Langton.

Tobruk was a hell-hole. The port, protected by its surrounding high ground, was 70 miles from the Libyan border. Around it, Auchinleck had thrown up a 30-mile-wide perimeter defence. Every day, the Germans and Italians would shell and bomb them Lewes complained to Mirren, the girl whom he would have married had he lived: 'I don't like being shelled much, it is just like waiting for the dentist to hurt.'[64] The experience made men weary. Lewes was no exception:

> But in the salient we were nobody's baby – attached for rations … and then onto the next fair in the covered wagon. It was like being a tramp, going from home to home, given a meal and a hole in the ground at each.[65]

Origins of the Special Air Service

The Special Air Service was brought together by David Stirling and Jock Lewes, initially with heavy enrolment from the Guards (primarily the Scots Guards) and the various Commando units that had been involved in LAYFORCE, particularly No.8 Commando.

On 15 July 1941, Stirling managed to get into the five-storey Art Deco building on Tonbalet Street that served as MEHQ Cairo. Once inside, he presented his plan to the newly-promoted Chief of Staff, who later further passed Stirling's ideas to Auchinleck. Stirling was allowed to recruit sixty-eight men and officers plus seven support staff and form a unit, initially called The Special Air Service Brigade, L Detachment.

It was Lieutenant Colonel Dudley Clarke who designated Stirling's new unit's name (J and K Detachments already existed in his make-believe organization). He had been running his own deception plan with phoney parachutists under the same name. L Detachment was later renamed the 1st SAS Regiment. Up to late 1942 its total strength never exceeded one hundred.

The number of recruits would allow for teams of the requisite eleven men. Each team fit into a slow-moving Bristol Bombay transport aircraft used for parachutists, i.e. two teams of five men and one officer. With a maximum speed of 100 mph, it was so slow that if the wind speed exceeded 50mph, pilots usually turned the plane back.

Lewes was the first to join Stirling in his new venture. He brought with him Roy Davies, his batman, Jim Almonds, Pat Riley, Jim Blakeney, a Grimsby trawlerman, Bob Lilley and Johnny Cooper, 'blessed with a blade of cutting wit'.[66] Recruits were drawn heavily from the old LAYFORCE, from which Ritchie had said he could select officers and men, and through the connections each man coming to the regiment could bring with them. Slowly other units were incorporated: a Free French group of parachutists (very often called the 'Free French Squadron') under the command of Georges Bergé, and then more seaborne Special Force elements as Stirling expanded.

Stirling was the thinker, the dreamer. Lewes more the enabler, the man who made the dreams come true by dealing with the detail. At the start, he organized training. Stirling sold the idea of a unit based on long range insertion by parachute, but following the first disastrous drop was persuaded, probably by Guy Prendergast, to change the approach to insertion with the help of the Long Range Desert Group (LRDG). When needed, Stirling could also call on the Royal Navy for amphibious support.

Another change occurred in 1942 when the unit 'changed from parties operating on foot to very heavily and specially modified long-range jeeps', a forerunner of the Sidi Haneish massed jeep raid. Normally, the unit would be equipped with what it needed, but 'on one occasion the RAF landed transport aircraft far behind in enemy territory bringing in much needed ammo, petrol, water & food', returning with wounded and in some instances freed PoWs found by the unit.[67]

The impact of the SAS had been significant. Apart from the intelligence brought back or the distraction it caused the enemy, its sheer destructive force was hard to exaggerate: Throughout the whole North African campaign, no fewer than 350 confirmed enemy aircraft were totally destroyed, together with petrol dumps, ammo and bomb dumps, torpedo dumps, stores wrecked and countless vehicles of all types including A.F.Ws etc.

Stirling started to get an idea of what lay ahead. While he did not appear to be the prototypical leader, he was driven. It was in his blood: his mother was Margaret Fraser, daughter of the 16th Lord Lovat, the man who ran Lovat's Scouts in the Boer War.

Stirling had been recovering in hospital from a bad jump. Being bedridden gave him time to think about the failings of Laycock's Commando and the idea of using the long, exposed flanks that German supply routes offered to a small group coming out of the desert. David announced his intentions when Hermione Ranfurly went to see him at Heliopolis with his brother, Bill:

When I have got my legs to function again, I have a scheme to put to headquarters … it may be difficult to get them to accept it, but it is vital they do.[68]

Jellicoe's later comment, concerning Stirling's 'extraordinary imagination … persuasiveness and an ability to get through to the top and get his own way', in part explains how Stirling got past the guards at Middle East Headquarters to present his case. It became the stuff of legend. Despite being on crutches, recovering from his June parachute drop, he dashed inside to get in front of Auchinleck's Chief of Staff, General Ritchie.

After a desultory apology, Stirling handed the general a hand-written paper outlining his ideas for a special unit. He held his breath. Ritchie 'got very engrossed and had forgotten the rather irregular manner in which it had been presented.'[69] Neil Ritchie and Stirling's father were friends and used to shoot grouse together. Connections like these gave Stirling all the access he needed. After leafing through the report, Ritchie looked up and said, 'This may be the sort of plan we're looking for. I'll discuss it with the

Commander-in-Chief and let you know our decision.'[70] A few days later, Richie received the 'Auk's' blessing, and Stirling was on a roll.

His ideas for the SAS have survived in the pencil-written document he showed to Ritchie. It was dated 16 July 1941 and entitled 'The Case for the Retention of a limited number of special service troops, for employment as parachutists'. It may have sounded bland; it was anything but. It was written as a reaction to the news of LAYFORCE being disbanded in the last week of June. He'd heard the news from Evelyn Waugh, while bedbound. What Stirling saw was,

> the unique opportunity for a small, well-trained and well-led force to carry out surprise attacks on the rear of the formidable but fully extended Afrika Korps while using the empty desert to the south as Lawrence used the Arabian desert, to emerge out of and then to fade back into.[71]

Jellicoe summed up Stirling's appreciation of the vulnerability of the enemy:

> He had very quickly understood that an open desert flank was a heaven-sent opportunity for the right sort of Special Forces activity, that the rather clumsy commando tactics were not the right way to go about it, and that it was better to do it by small groups of highly trained people.[72]

The view that he would make a success of his new venture wasn't shared by all. Carol Mather's assessment was probably typical:

> We really could not give [his scheme] credence and we thought we knew David too well for it to work. Another fiasco [i.e. after the disbanding of LAYFORCE] was the last thing anyone could take.[73]

Mather wasn't alone. Sutherland, too, had to admit that he had seriously misjudged Stirling: 'In effect, I had to eat humble pie in asking to re-join him.'[74]

Stirling's core idea was to drop Special Forces by parachute rather than further stretch naval resources or rely on ground infiltration. That is why he had been learning – very unsuccessfully – to parachute. He may have focused on infiltration by parachute as a way of preventing the plan being thrown out because of the perception that it duplicated what the LRDG were already doing. Stirling later admitted that parachute insertion was an important element for selling the idea of his force: 'Psychologically the parachute was the ideal propaganda means of putting over the proposition of the role of the unit.'[75]

Stirling knew Jock Lewes was thinking along these lines and so he went to see him: to help hone his thinking in to a stronger and more convincing case that Stirling could – through his connections – get in front of the right person. Stirling took a number of trips back to Tobruk on the *Aphis* in July and August to meet with Jock. The final ideas are Lewes', not really Stirling's. Stirling was merely the mouthpiece. Nevertheless, he seized on the opportunity: to tie in with the planned launch of Auchinleck's offensive that November.

Stirling had heard Lewes talking about the German's recent use of paratroopers in Crete and the idea stuck. When Laycock gave Lewes the go-ahead, Lewes found the supplies he needed: fifty parachutes that were intended for India. With the help of the Parachute School at Ringway, he started to learn what he could. Ringway (officially known as the No.1 Parachute Training School, RAF) was where the British undertook most parachute research and development.

When Stirling started to push Lewes to combine forces and to fold his operation into what would become the SAS, Lewes quite understandably hesitated. He needed considerable persuasion that Stirling wasn't a 'fly by night' or, as he himself put it, a 'good time Charlie'. Stirling recognized the reasons for this hesitation: 'I think Jock wanted to be sure that if we got the thing working, I was going to stay with it and tackle the enormous problems at MEHQ.'[76]

Stirling also wanted independence of command, reporting directly to Auchinleck. Instead he and Lewes shared a disdain for a certain type of officer, the type that would only go 'by the book'. The men would scathingly refer to MEHQ officers as the SRDG, the Short-Range Desert Group, since they only seemed to frequent the bars near their offices. Stirling saw them as 'unfailingly obstructive and uncooperative … astonishingly tiresome'.[77] He would also refer to them as 'fossilized shits'.

Instead, Stirling was told that he would report to Brigadier Dudley Clarke. It turned out to be a better choice. Later, Stirling told Gordon Stevens that these early frustrations turned out to be fundamental to the success of the SAS:

> One of the reasons that the SAS concept has survived longer perhaps than might be expected is because of the fact that it was forged in hell, forged behind the lines, and with the running battle with Middle East Headquarters. That forced me all the time to be a step ahead.[78]

With Ritchie's interim blessing, Stirling went searching for men and a home.

Jock Lewes was an accomplished athlete and a professional soldier. The 28-year old Australian from Paramatta had gone to Christ Church, Oxford, where he'd won a Blue as an oarsman and had become President of the University Boat Club. He had rowed against Tommy Langton, who would be part of the 1937 Oxford and Cambridge boat race eight and later join the SBS. In late 1938, Lewes joined the Tower Hamlet Rifles and, in February 1940, became an instructor at the Small Arms School in Hythe, Kent. At Bisley he met David Stirling's brother, Bill. When war was declared, he transferred to the Welsh Guards from which he went on to No.8 Commando and to LAYFORCE.

According to Lewes, 'Stirling was away for most of 1941.'[79] It wasn't a complaint; it was a recognition that it took each of them to bring their very special and unique strengths to build the SAS. While Lewes would bring the men to the peak of physical fitness and hone their new skills in navigation, explosives and infiltration, Stirling spent most of his time in Cairo fighting the unenviable but necessary war with MEHQ, a conflict that became Stirling's signature style.

Lewes wrote that he was 'proud to play second string' because the quality of training would count for more than 'premature command': 'Together we have fashioned this unit. David has established it without, and I think I may say I have established it within.'[80]

It was probably Bob Laycock who suggested Mayne to Stirling. The 6' 3" Northern Irishman, ex-rugby player and Irish Guardsman, had come through the Litani raid in Syria with accolades. Lieutenant Colonel Dick Pedder's No.11 Commando had landed on the Litani river in the first opposed and near-disastrous commando landing of the war. Of the 185 men who went into action, 30 were wounded and 104 killed. Mayne had not only succeeded in getting ashore, but his No.7 Troop had captured ninety prisoners, eight machine guns and three mortars. He also captured 'a sort of HQ place' full of military supplies and, as he put it later, 'more to the point, beer and food'.[81]

As a boy, Blair (Paddy) Mayne was anything but the man he became:

> An intelligent boy, kind, good natured and shy, he devours books and avoids social gatherings wherever possible. His mother dotes on her three boys ... when the eldest boy commits suicide, she draws closer ... particularly to the quieter Blair. This bond is exceptional, reaching an almost spiritual closeness later in life ... there were two different people in Paddy Mayne.[82]

Jellicoe, also, could be witheringly cold when angered; not as volcanically destructive as Mayne, but frightening nevertheless. His fury could be ignited in a flash. It wasn't always the 'controlled aggression' that men in the Regiment sometimes refer to; very occasionally, the eruption got the better of him. Maybe that was why Mayne (and Jellicoe, reputedly), could deal with Stirling's 'diverse and volcanic character'. Mayne was not only a rugby player of international reputation, he was also almost equally skilled as a boxer. Aged eleven, so the story goes, he had even knocked his coach clean out.

Mayne had been a practising lawyer in Belfast and was tough, superb in a corner but difficult to command. Stirling likened him to one of Shakespeare's characters: 'He had, I suppose, something akin to Hotspur, the young Harry Percy, quick-tempered, audacious, vigorous in action but not one who took kindly to being thwarted, frustrated or crossed in any way.'[83] When he was part of No.11 Commando 'he was known in Arran to sit on his bed and shoot the glass panels of the windows with his revolver.'[84] It took a certain amount of ingenuity to conceal things like this from the local police. Stirling's first meeting with him wasn't easy. Mayne did not like the public-schoolboy type and when addressed as 'Paddy' by Stirling, 'he replied curtly that his name was "Blair".'[85]

He was very strong: 'As a teenager, he was able to physically rip a telephone directory in two, and I have personally seen him uproot a street lamp in a Cairo street', Jellicoe recalled.[86]

Underneath Jellicoe and Mayne shared the same intense dislike of convention. Mayne's early evaluations confidently predicted that he would never amount to much: 'unpromising material for a combat regiment, undisciplined, unruly and generally unreliable'.[87] But by the time he was in No.11 Scottish Commando he was starting to become the kind of officer for which he would later be known: 'deadly calm' under pressure but just as menacing when off-duty. When a fellow officer, Gerald Bryan, didn't fill his water jug, Mayne lashed out: he 'picked [him] and hit [him] one hell of a blow on the face that knocked [him] against the wall … [he] was hardly out the door, when he loosed off in [his] direction a full magazine of the .45 revolver that he always kept by him.' Typically, these episodes were of little significance to and soon forgotten by Mayne. The next day, he comfortingly asked Bryan who had hit him, protectively adding, 'Just tell me and I'll sort the bugger out.'[88] One man dared to openly challenge him: Pat Riley. Later in the war, on his way to Sicily, Mayne was about to 'clock' another officer and Riley stepped in to 'defuse' the situation:

> There was no time to lose. I pulled Paddy round and hit him hard on the jaw. He went down … but he just got up without a word. Then after a minute he said, 'Come on Pat, let's have a drink.'[89]

Mayne moved to Cyprus with his unit following the Litani raid. He had 'run amok with a rifle and bayonet' and had 'chased everybody out of the mess'[90] including his commanding officer, Colonel Geoffrey Keyes, the son of the famous Admiral of the Fleet, Roger Keyes. The next day, Keyes had come back to complain and Mayne knocked him out clean. Paddy was placed under arrest. Small surprise then, that when he and Stirling talked, Stirling's only condition was that this behaviour would not be acceptable in his unit, that 'this commanding officer wasn't for hitting'.[91] For Mayne, who had been sitting in gaol thinking about going to China to train the Chinese Nationalist Army, Stirling's offer was welcome.

Mayne was a Jekyll and Hyde character. Drunk, he morphed into a belligerent and, frankly, extremely dangerous person. He would disappear into Cairo for lengthy binges with his close friend, Eoin McGonigal. He could also 'sulk phenomenally' and did not take kindly to being slighted, even by Stirling.[92] Malcom Pleydell compared his style to Jellicoe's. It was much harder, none of the relaxed sophistication that was Jellicoe's, as he put it, 'nothing of the rather clever and witty nature that made Jellicoe's conversation so characteristic'.[93] Nevertheless, Jellicoe always looked to the three of them – Stirling, Lewes and Mayne – as the Regiment's founding fathers; and, like Stirling, to Bergé, in almost equal proportion. Each played an equally important part. Mayne was 'a natural gang-leader, a born bandit-chief. While Stirling always seemed to have his head in the clouds, looking for lessons and patterns, Mayne concentrated on the job in hand.'[94]

Peter Davis, at one point in charge of D Squadron's training, recounts his meeting with Jellicoe in Kabrit where most of the SAS training was carried out:

> Although a shrewd and capable leader, (Jellicoe) was the complete antithesis in character to Paddy Mayne. Possessing a strong personal charm and magnetism, he did not seem to conceive the seriousness and danger of the job that he was training his men to do. He seemed too light-hearted to take the job seriously but people who knew him soon realized that this was a pose.

Jellicoe once had to bail Mayne out of jail. A call was put through by the Provost Marshal asking Jellicoe if he knew a certain officer called Mayne, who had had a disagreement with a group of Australians in a bar:

'Six stout Aussies had been laid out cold and the list of broken chairs, tables and other missiles read like a sales catalogue.'[95] Jellicoe managed to persuade the Director of Military Operations, who 'took a view based on strict wartime priorities', that Mayne was too valuable to be lost. As a result, he was 'spirited away in a jeep'.

The first people to come on board were the NCOs that Lewes had recently commanded: men like Pat Riley, Bob Lilley, Jim Blakeney and 'Gentleman Jim' Almonds (because he never cursed) – the so-called 'Tobruk Four'. Malcolm Pleydell, the future SAS chief medic, thought highly of Almonds, saying that he was 'more sensible and intelligent than the average officer'.[96] He and Pleydell 'had in common an insatiable curiosity about their environment'.[97] Soon others came: Reg Seekings, 'what you would call dour … a very good soldier but not too intelligent', and Johnny Cooper, 'bright and outgoing'.[98] As far as Seekings was concerned, it was an overly tough judgement. He was dyslexic and would stay up well after his mates had gone to bed, doing double-duty to pass the tests; nevertheless, when he was interviewed by Stirling he hit the button right on the head. Asked why he wanted to join, he replied, 'I'd seen a film of these German paratroopers and always wondered why we didn't have this in the British Army.'[99] Cooper had lied about his age to get in. His father was furious, but in the end acquiesced. His parting words were conciliatory: 'Be it on your own head, but look after yourself.'[100]

The unit's new home would be a godforsaken stretch of sand south of the Great Bitter Lake: Kabrit, 90 miles east of Cairo. It was a desolate, miserable place, where 'a wind like Emery paper scoured the Great Bitter Lake, but the amenities were still a shock … to new officers.'[101] Jellicoe recalled that he never found the flies difficult; it was the south wind which could be 'very unpleasant'.[102] Fitzroy Maclean remembered seeing the place for the first time, passing camps, huts and dumps, 'clouds of flies, an uninviting smell of food rising from every cookhouse; the sickly smell of disinfectant rising from the latrines'; this was how his memories of the place came back to him when he was writing *Eastern Approaches*.[103] Nearby was a 'very trim' naval base, HMS *Saunders*, and a railway station.[104] Pleydell remembered an oddity on the roads of the naval base: the 10 *knot* speed restriction. But because Kabrit was where both a naval base (HMS *Saunders*) and a Blenheim bomber base, RAF Kabrit, were located, it was targeted for bombing, and acoustic anti-shipping mines were regularly dropped into the canal.

From the first day at Kabrit, Stirling instilled a unique style, a sense of purpose and independence in the men. Lacking any equipment, he decided to 'liberate' what he needed from a nearby New Zealand base. Bob Bennett said that Stirling made this the focus of 'their first operation' although the idea might have come from Gerry Ward, the Company Quartermaster Sergeant.[105] Anything was fair game: tents, tables, chairs, even a piano (years later, the New Zealanders asked for it to be returned). The Kiwis were amply kitted out, so he felt no qualms about his first raid, even though some of his men apparently did. A Londoner called Kaufmann did much of the scrounging. He 'flogged the army stores to these kiosk blokes in return for cigs and stuff the boys couldn't get easily', Seekings explained. From the RAF base, he even 'pinched a load of bricks, rounded up some prisoners

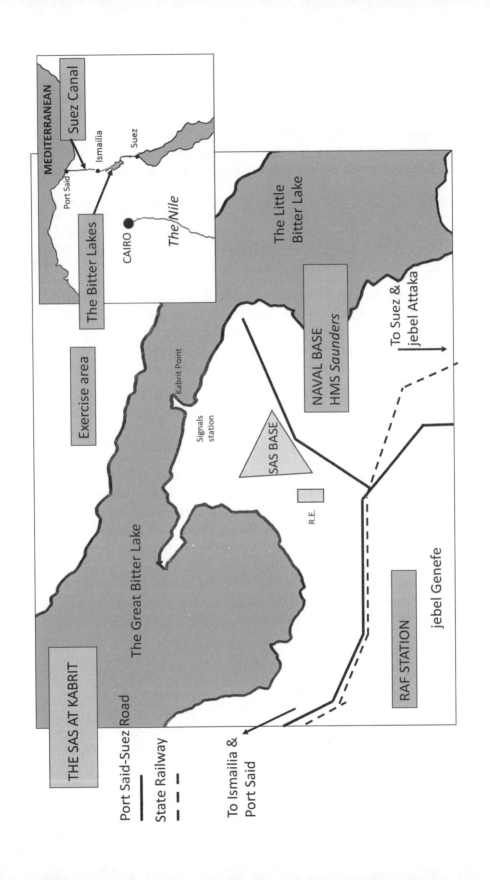

THE SAS AT KABRIT

Port Said–Suez Road _____
State Railway -------

To Ismailia &
Port Said

RAF STATION

jebel Genefe

The Great Bitter Lake

Signals
station

Kabrit Point

Exercise area

SAS BASE

R.E.

NAVAL BASE
HMS *Saunders*

To Suez &
jebel Attaka

The Little
Bitter Lake

MEDITERRANEAN

Suez Canal

The Bitter Lakes

CAIRO

The Nile

Port Said

Ismailia

Suez

and made them build a brick canteen.'[106] Kaufmann himself, however, didn't make the cut; he was RTU'd.

Around his unit's new camp, Stirling became a familiar sight. Being exceptionally tall (he was 6' 5"), he could only fit into a jeep with his knees visible on either side of the steering wheel. It made for fond memories:

> *Parfaitement reconnaissable dans sa petite Jeep – trop petite pour sa grande taille – d'où ses genoux émergeaient de chaque côté du volant ... un vrai Arabe sur son petit bourricot!* (He was completely recognizable in his little Jeep – much too small for his height – his legs splayed out each side of the driving wheel. Like an Arab on his tiny donkey). [107]

Other things didn't go so well. For one, the food was 'terrible', said Seekings. And Sergeant Major Yates soon found himself the object of a tirade of abuse from the men whom he had ordered to dig holes for tents which were yet to arrive. The men's grumbling grew into open insurrection, and it was only Jock Lewes' forceful – and provocative – intervention that saved the day:

> Jock stood on the lecture room table and told the men that they had to prove they were not cowards. 'Prove it!' he told them, 'Prove it! The trouble with you people is that you've all got a bloody yellow streak a yard wide down your backs. That's your problem unless you prove it otherwise.'[108]

There was a deadly silence; you could have cut the atmosphere with a knife. These were, after all, seasoned soldiers. All of them had more than proved their worth under fire. Eventually, the stand-off came to an end when Jock agreed to the men's challenge: he would do anything they would ... and, most importantly, vice versa. 'That's a bet.'

Coming out of the ill-fated experiences of the commando, Stirling focussed on the need for, and the efficiency of, a small – very small – force structure:

> The basic unit would be a four or five man sub-unit. The commando technique was such that an entire commando, six hundred or so men, couldn't succeed in tackling more than perhaps two landings on the same night, and more than three-quarters of the force would be taken up defending those who were actually operating. We preferred for every sub-unit of four or five men to tackle a full target on their own, and if they failed it would be more than compensated for by the very fact that with sixty men we could attack, theoretically, up to fifteen or twenty targets on the same night.[109]

Stirling won the argument with Lewes on the basic unit size; Lewes had wanted ten- or twelve-man teams. In Stirling's scheme, each four-man unit

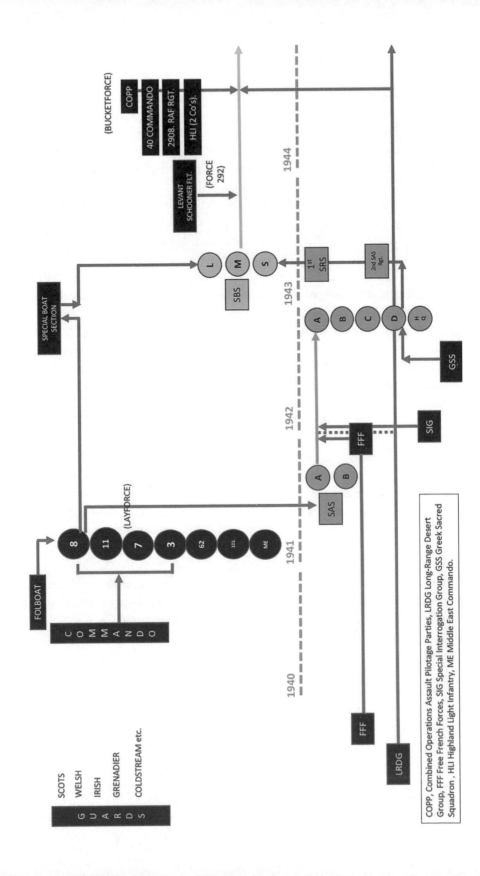

COPP, Combined Operations Assault Pilotage Parties, LRDG Long-Range Desert Group, FFF Free French Forces, SIG Special Interrogation Group, GSS Greek Sacred Squadron , HLI Highland Light Infantry, ME Middle East Commando.

would be known as a 'patrol'. Each team member would be a specialist – a mechanic, medic, navigator or demolitions expert. Each man would work with a 'mucker'. Inter-dependence was fundamental.

L detachment was split into two Troops, A under Lewes and B under Paddy Mayne. Within them, the men were further divided into 'sticks' of eleven men – an officer and two five-man units.

In addition to Mayne (who led the PT sessions and would handle punishment) and Lewes (who doubled up as the training officer and taught fieldcraft), three other officers came on board: Lieutenant Bill Fraser from the Gordon Highlanders who taught map reading, Lieutenant Charles Bonington and Lieutenant Eoin McGonigal, weapons officer. Both McGonigal and Fraser were recruited by Stirling from the Commando depot at Ganeifa; Fraser's family had strong military ties – both his father and grandfather had served as sergeants in the Gordon Highlanders. Bonington's son would later become a household name: Chris Bonington, the climber (originally, as Charles' father was German, the family name was Bonig). Bonington had left Scotland for Australia, where he found work as a journalist. Initially, he joined the Australian Army as a sergeant and then became an intelligence officer in the 1st Cheshire Regiment. To help get the unit licked into shape there was a Company Sergeant Major, George 'Bill' Yates, and a Company Quartermaster Sergeant, Gerry 'Daddy' Ward.

'There was a distinct whiff of the Foreign Legion about the infant SAS.'[110] The camaraderie was solid, the discipline tough and the loyalty absolute. It was, in Steve Hastings' words, 'an idiosyncratic collection of people, officers and men with the minimum distinction between them, whose only bond seemed to be a reflection of their extraordinary commander's personality'.[111] The absence of parade ground discipline was immensely appealing'. Seekings put it this way: 'You were treated as one of a team, and this made a big difference. That's what everybody was after.'[112] Stirling looked for men who would question an order. An officer wasn't sacrosanct. Of course, the approach presented its own set of challenges: 'In a sense they weren't really controllable. They were harnessable.'

By design, there was a larger ratio of officers to ORs in the SAS than in most units, because the patrols were based on small numbers. So it was not uncommon for those coming on board to go down a rank, losing either a 'pip' or a 'stripe'.

Stirling always resisted growing the unit too much. More challenges would come with size: much of the bonding that came from the intimacy of the small sub-units could be eroded. He had absolute confidence in his sergeants in principle, more than in the younger officers. 'The real engine room of any effective military organization', he said, 'is the sergeants' mess.'[113] Invariably,

Stirling would wait for a report from his sergeants on any new officer. They – and they alone – would decide if he was good enough for the unit. And they would be briefed first. The officers were there to instil purpose, the men would 'police themselves'.[114]

First names were used between officers and men, and everyone joined the same chow-line. An officer wasn't given priority. The French were amazed. Even Seekings and Cooper admitted that they got a little 'big-headed' in how they treated their officers.[115] 'There was no bawling', as would be the style in regular Army units, remembered Jeff du Vivier. No saluting. None of the usual parade ground stuff. There were even enemy prisoners milling about. Captured Italians would often be kept on and asked to help with camp cooking and cleaning. They would drop these prisoners' post off whenever they made a raid. Cooper remembered how Stirling was in the early days at Largs: 'He did not bark orders; he asked people to do things.'[116]

Stirling understood the importance of pride associated with visibly wearing a unit 'badge'. The unit needed an identity. It's not completely clear where its origins lay. Maybe it was Bob Tait, from 11 Commando, who designed the famous winged dagger (and who'd also won an MM on the Litani River) or Jock Lewes. Some people say that the wings were those of the Egyptian god Isis, that the flaming dagger is not a dagger as such but Excalibur, King Arthur's sword. But Stirling didn't like the suggested mottos, 'Strike and Destroy', 'Descend to Ascend' or 'Descend to Defend'. He eventually came up with 'Who Dares Wins'. One of the Sergeants later came up with his own version. Musing over a drink, Bill Cumper looked at his cap badge and said, "'Oo cares 'oo wins?' The chosen colours – Cambridge and Oxford blue – reflected Stirling's and Lewes' university days.

Originally, the unit had 'snow-white' berets, a surplus of which Stirling had found in a Cairo warehouse. They were soon replaced after the men were habitually 'wolf-whistled', especially by Aussies, Kiwis and South African troops.[117]

Lewes understood the fundamental importance of training and happily took the role. He thought that 'complete freedom to experiment in training with his men might well create a totally new and powerful tradition of his within the Army.'[118]

Jock was utterly scientific about his methods. His approach was unique. He would go on increasingly long marches, timing himself, measuring and reducing his water intake to see where the limits of survival lay, but doing so without the reassurance of a friendly pick-up. That way, he could experience genuine uncertainty about life or death. Later, after experience in the desert, the 'wise ones buried their bottles at night.'[119] That way, the first drink would be refreshingly cool.

Lewes' training set the bar so high that men would easily manage the seemingly impossible: 'On one 60-mile march, the boots of Private Doug Keith disintegrated after 20 miles so he completed the remaining distance in stockinged feet with a 75lb pack on his back.'[120]

Lewes would also learn from what he read. He used games based on Kipling's *Kim*, treasure hunts for navigation and Blind Man's Bluff to sharpen the key senses most used at night – hearing, smell and touch. He would teach men little tricks that could save their lives, for example recording distance accurately by transferring pebbles (or bullets) from one pocket to another to keep track of each stretch of 100 yards travelled.

While Commando training would involve full packs for 35-mile daytime marches, the SAS marches would be at night over distances from 12 to 30 miles with what were initially sand-filled packs; the load was later changed to numbered bricks, when it was discovered that the men were emptying their packs at the start of a march and refilling them at the end. Water discipline was such that each man was expected to come back with water in his can. If you started to get thirsty, you'd 'chew' a stone. If you did drink from your canteen, you washed your mouth out with the water; you never swallowed. To the south of Kabrit, just over the two separate rail lines that ran up to Suez, lay the Djebel Attaka – an ideal and arduous training ground, where night exercises under the moonlight on its slippery rocky slopes toughened up even these seasoned troops.

Training the French – or any other unit – in SAS tactics and weapons could, of course, be challenging. More often than not, it was humour that broke the barriers, one man's in particular, Bill Cumper: 'After initial bewilderment, the French who only understood one word in three, took to him wholeheartedly and he to them.' He was universally liked, almost loved. He would turn up to a meeting 'wearing a detonator behind his ear like a cigarette'.[121] Dick Holmes said he kept the lads 'in fits' with his humour.[122] When Cumper, through some ill-founded bureaucratic logic, was taken from the SAS, Stirling immediately got him back:

Apparently, with the eternal wisdom of that mediocre MEHQ freemasonry, they'd sent him to supervise the engineering works at a bloody hospital. Imagine that, the best and most ingenious explosives man we had was now fitting toilet seats in Alexandria. I soon sorted that out ...[123]

The unit's parachute training was arduous. Peter Warr and Bernard Schott were the assigned instructors. Initially, no RAF parachute instructors were available for Stirling's outfit, such was the opposition to it within MEHQ.

The first training routines were inappropriate and dangerous. The men would jump off the sides of a rolling wagon running along a rail track; then they progressed to rolling off the back of a moving truck. Near the camp there was a quarry where they found a narrow-gauge section of railway. An 80-yard section of track and its sleepers were lifted and taken back to the camp. A platform was built on the hopper, and the men would roll off as the contraption gathered speed hurtling down a dune. After a considerable number of injuries, Stirling asked Jim Almonds to construct a jump tower. Several men – including Jeff du Vivier, Bill Fraser and Jimmy Brough – had broken limbs jumping from the back of the truck at 30mph. The tower might have been pretty rudimentary but it worked. It took a while to get it right, but Almonds had help both from the nearby Royal Engineers and Italian PoWs.

In June, they made the first jumps, using an 'obsolete Vickers Valencia [sic] biplane'.[124] A hole was cut in the bottom of the fuselage, but it was a struggle to wriggle through with a bulky chute and invariably men would hit their heads as they dropped into the slipstream:

> If you so much as glanced towards the ground you were certain to bash your head on the rim as you went out. This took a lot of self-control and those who failed were apt to land very sore, if not half conscious.[125]

At the very start, the jumping technique was pretty rudimentary: 'The men secured their "static lines", which pull the canopy from the pack, by simply lashing the lines to seats near the aircraft door.'[126]

Lewes and Roy Davies, his batman from the Welsh Guards, went first. Stirling followed. His parachute snagged on the aircraft's tail, which ripped great chunks out of the silk. As Stirling fell, the chute spilled out air and he landed hard. Very hard. For an hour he was blind and had to be hospitalized in Alexandria, at the Scottish Military Hospital. As he described it, he 'really put a crater in the desert'.[127]

Then they used a Bristol Bombay. First, they experimented. 'We threw out a dummy made from sandbags and tentpoles. The parachute opened okay, but the tent poles smashed on landing.'[128] It didn't bode well. When they tried themselves, the results were disastrous: Joe Duffy and Ken Warburton both died when a clip buckled and disengaged the static line after they jumped. Their chutes didn't open. 'People on the ground heard them screaming as they fell.'[129] Luckily, the dispatcher, F/Sgt Ted Pacey, had reacted immediately to stop the third man, Bill Morris, and Johnny Orton behind him, from jumping. When Duffy's body was found, the chute was half out. He'd tried to pull it out by hand but couldn't twist around enough. The sight of Duffy's horrifying struggle as he plummeted to his death must have left each man weighing the odds of his own mortality.

It later transpired that a similar accident had occurred at Ringway but no warning had been sent to Stirling.

On the next jump, a choice was put to the men by Jock Lewes: to jump or not. Despite the terrible accident, Lewes found no takers for the second option. Not one single man backed out. And Lewes honoured the commitment he had made the men on the first day: he was first out of the aircraft.[130] Eventually, all would have to do six jumps 'starting at 1,000 feet down to 350 feet, with one night jump at 500 feet'.[131] The men didn't deserve the nickname that the LRDG supposedly gave them: 'Stirling's parashites'.

Stirling and Lewes both strongly believed in the importance not only of leading from the front but also of always demanding more from themselves than they would from the men. In that sense, he and Jock Lewes were 'birds of a feather'.

Some of Stirling's training missions were carried out with what appeared to be an almost dangerous lack of planning. In May 1942, along with Seekings, Maclean and Cooper, the men practised planting limpet mines on a tanker in the Great Bitter Salt Lake. Stirling had said nothing about the exercises to the port authorities and only later found out that they would 'often drop man-sized depth charges into the water to deter saboteurs and were inclined to spray the surface with machine gun fire if they saw anything suspicious.'[132] It's one thing to have controlled live fire exercises, another to court death. All the men trained on Folboats in two-man teams. They had to 'canoe the four miles across the Bitter Lakes and back again without stopping'. It was obvious that the men had to be good swimmers. Here they were expected to swim 'at least a mile in full uniform (including their boots)'.[133]

New recruits were needed as the war took its toll and numbers were whittled down. After the Sidi Haneish raid in mid-1942, only sixteen men of the original fifty-five who had done the famous first jump were left. It fell to Geoff du Vivier to lick the new boys into shape. The new intake would include names that would become well-known: Dick Holmes, Sid Downland and Doug Wright. All three came in from the 6th Battalion, Grenadier Guards. Fresh equipment also arrived: the new Willy Bantam Jeeps. Jellicoe was given the responsibility for getting them adapted and having the Vickers K mounted. But Jellicoe was really itching to get back on ops. Neither he nor Stirling was that interested in hanging out in Kabrit (who would have been?) or running back and forth to Cairo to see the people at GHQ.

Tools of the Trade

Special Forces warfare often demanded weaponry and resources entirely different from regular military activity. Equipment had to be hardened for the long desert crossings, and bombs and arms as light as possible.

The **Lewes bomb,** invented by Jock Lewes, was one such SF solution. It weighed slightly over 1lb and could blow up a bomber, but be carried in quantity by one man. It was specifically designed 'to rupture petrol tanks and ignite the fuel which leaked out' rather than blow a plane apart (Holmes, p.158). The bomb consisted of a heavy charge made up of Nobel 808 plastic explosive (Nobel 808, Lewis, *Secret Warriors*, p.6), thermite and aluminium shavings moulded together in engine oil. It was set off using a dry gun-cotton booster and a No.27 primer or could be detonated by a small 'time pencil' fuse, where a specific quantity of acid would eat through a seal to set off a detonator. The pencils were colour-coded to show their time delay (the thicker the copper wire, the longer the delay) and could be as short as 10 minutes. It would give the men a headache when they worked with it because of the strong ammonia fumes. The timers weren't always that reliable. Bob Tait was quoted as saying that 'on a warm night the bombs ignite after 18 minutes' (Wynter, *Special Forces*, p.312). David Sutherland wrote that the SAS continued to use a version of the famous bomb right up to the 1990s, when they were employed against Argentine aircraft on Pebble Island.

In mid-1942, the SAS equipped themselves with the **Willy Bantams,** the M38 Utility General Purpose (GP) vehicle that came to be known as the 'Jeep'. Stirling borrowed his first fifteen of the four-wheel drive jeeps, promising to return them after use! 'Tommo' Thomson helped improve the jeep's performance and durability. Following the LRDG practice, extra condensers were fitted to the radiators (to recycle water) and the suspension strengthened. All windscreens were removed, extra fittings were mounted to hold two spare tyres, three extra jerry cans on the bonnet and sand mats on the sides.[134] Even then, 'Few jeeps survived more than two operations in the desert.'[135] 'The springs were breaking because of the heavy gun mountings; the recoil put tremendous strain on them.' As time went on, extra armour was added to the radiator and even armoured glass from Hurricanes.[136] Extra tanks were built on to the front and back of the jeeps, since the jeeps 'drank petrol'. Additional 'three tonners would take the petrol.'[137] At top speed, the jeeps could run at 60mph and had an operating range of about 300 miles (McCrery p.19).

Vickers K guns, found in an Alexandria warehouse from old Gloucester Gladiator biplanes, were mounted on fifteen jeeps in four days, according to Jellicoe.[138] Mayne had suggested this in June to Stirling, to save men walking the last distance to an objective.[139] With 1,200 rounds a minute, their firepower was awesome, although they had a habit of overheating. The drums were considered better to use than belt ammunition. Johnny Cooper, however, made the point that this was not usually a problem as 'our actions were very short and sharp' (Stevens, p.100). On the ground, the men would use an assortment of weapons – both Allied and Axis. The favourites were the .303 Bren, capable of 500 rounds per minute (RPM) with a maximum range of 2,000 yards, the Thompson sub-machine gun, capable of 750 .45 RPM with a range of 300 yards, the 9mm Sten which only had a 175-yard range, the German Schmeisser (MP420 *Maschinenpistole*) and the Italian Breda. The 4-second Mills 36 grenade was commonly used for close-in action. Various mortars were used – 2" with a 500-yard range, the 3" for 2,800 yards or the 4.2" for a 4,100 yard range.

Training was one thing, equipment another, and here they were often let down. In the story of the early SAS, the poor quality of equipment comes up repeatedly. The rubber dinghies were notorious. Twice they caused failure at the last minute: once during a training exercise on the Great Salt Bitter Lake, the second time during the first Benghazi raid, on which Stirling had gone with Maclean, Rose, Cooper and Churchill, 'there to see the fun'.[140]After successfully passing numerous sentry posts with the aid of Maclean's fluent Italian, and having also gone back and recovered their explosives from Stirling's 'Blitz Buggy' five minutes before they were timed to go off, both of the dinghies turned out to be punctured and unusable. The only thing they could do was blow up a petrol dump. The buggy was, in fact, an old souped-up Ford station wagon which had been cut down, painted in desert brown and even had Afrika Korps TAC signs on it. Stirling would drive it at dangerously high speeds. In the March 1942 Benghazi raid, the Folboat they brought proved equally useless.

Explosives training was conducted by Bill Cumper, a 20-year old officer who had been promoted from the ranks. After Jock Lewes came up with the practical and light Lewes bomb – and following his death – it was Cumper who put all the new recruits through their paces. The level of professionalism was admirable. Explosives training was always related to the target. An Egyptian Railways' employee of the Egyptian Railways came to Kabrit to teach the men where to optimally place their bombs: always on a curve so that the explosion would also lead to a derailment, and because curves were more difficult to replace. On aircraft: if a bomber, consistently on one wing, port or starboard, to make spare-parts scavenging more difficult, and on fighters 'on the nose' to destroy both engine and cockpit. Bob Bennett, for example, said that with a 9F, 'you just pulled the window back, put it [a Lewes bomb] in the cockpit, or stuck it on the wings. It was best in the cockpit', while 'on the big planes, they used to bomb Malta, you had to throw them up. The wings were about twelve to fourteen feet high.'[141]

It was clear from the start that the unit had needed a new bomb more suitable for airfield raiding. The existing one was heavy. It weighed 5lbs and took a lot of time to prepare. Neither excessive weight nor time were things the raiders wanted to deal with when they had to get in to blow up planes in small numbers, at night and at speed. MEHQ sent an explosives expert 'whose name has not been recorded', and he told Lewes that what he was asking for was out of the question.[142] It was all Lewes needed to hear. He set to work. He'd always loved chemistry, and the task appealed to him. With childhood memories of doing chemistry together, he wrote to his brother, David, then an RAF officer, 'You would love it here – all manner of explosive toys to play with.'[143]

For hours on end Lewes would work in a small shed. From time to time, he would test his new concoctions on an old wing with an oil drum, representing the aircraft's wing fuel tank, sitting on it. 'Small explosions punctuated the day, ringing out like a loose cannon.'[144]

The timers were also unreliable. And they were just as critical. Coming back from the 14 June 1942 raid near Benina, Bob Lilley saw that one of the time pencils had somehow ignited. Along with Stirling, he and the others were lucky to get out of the car before it blew up. The next month, on the 7 July raid, twenty of the forty primers failed to work after they had been placed. It must have been heartbreaking for the raiders. They could have doubled their 'kill'.

Cumper and Jellicoe had an easy-going relationship. When Pleydell first arrived, Cumper joked at the doctor's arrival. 'Blimey!' he said to Jellicoe in an aside as he shook Pleydell's hand. 'A sawbones! What's going on around 'ere, George? 'Cos if things are going to start getting rough, I'm 'opping it.'[145] Cumper was a very effective soldier and received a field commission. Captain Cumper was also considered the 'best Royal Engineer officer in the Middle East'. His way with words was quick-witted, sharp and memorable: Lodwick famously described him having 'a tongue like the bite of a centipede'.[146] He once overheard a newly-arrived officer, still wet behind the ears, mutter at Cumper's looks and demeanour, 'What an uncouth fellow!'

Cumper heard the stage whisper and immediately faced off with him: 'Me? Uncouth? D'yer hear that? What's biting yer, cheddar? Me, wot's bin in the Army man and boy for twenty years? Ain't I good enough for yer?'

For the next few days it was 'Uncouth speaking', 'Uncouth to yer'. 'Cumper of Kufra' was the stuff of legend.[147] Men would earn the most apt of nicknames. There were two mates, one tall, the other short, whose more obvious nicknames, 'Lofty' and 'Shorty', logically evolved after they had driven off the road into the Nile. The couple were to be known henceforth as 'the Mermaids'.

From early on, the SAS proved themselves up to the task. An RAF officer had been sent by Ritchie to have a look at their methods. He scoffed at the idea that they could possibly raid one of his airfields and get away with it. As he said it, Stirling threw down the gauntlet. Right there, he wagered the officer £10 that his group could successfully raid the base at Heliopolis, adding, 'Tell them we'll be paying a visit around the end of October.'[148]

Stirling divided his men into four groups, each of ten men, and brought them through the desert unobserved. Each man carried 'four water bottles, a pound of dates, half a pound of boiled sweets, and some army biscuits'.[149] They got into the field and placed little stickers on each of the planes to represent the real bombs they might have placed. On each note, the word 'Bomb' was facetiously written. The RAF officer had to eat his words. The 100-mile trek across the desert was a real test of endurance for the unit. In their Italian haversacks each carried some hessian cloth as desert camouflage and enough stones to simulate the weight of eight Lewes bombs. When the ragged group got back from their successful raid, they looked more like escaping PoWs.

Joining Stirling's group was probably *the* defining moment of George Jellicoe's life. It was the turning point around which his life and, maybe, his fondest – and saddest – memories revolved. It came about when he bumped into David Stirling at the bar of Shepheard's hotel in Cairo, probably in late May 1942. It was a place 'where everybody met everybody'.[150] It was 'sheer chance'. He didn't think 'he had an appointment or anything.'[151] Jellicoe recalled the conversation:

'Very nice seeing you, George. I'm looking for a second in command. Would you consider it?'

'I'd be delighted and honoured, if my battalion would release me.'

What he said next was typical of Jellicoe, always playing down his importance, as he added, smiling, 'And not to my surprise, my battalion had no difficulty about releasing me.' However, he qualified what he said by saying that Stirling 'was used to pulling strings'.[152]

Jellicoe had been getting bored in Tobruk and had heard about Stirling's group and that it had 'already achieved some really spectacular successes.' This David Stirling was a very different man from the *Glen Roy* days.[153] Jellicoe knew both David and Jock Lewes from his No.8 Commando time. Stirling's youngest sister, Irene, was also keen on Jellicoe; Veronica Fraser, who was married to Alan Phipps and later to Fitzroy Maclean, suggested that it was probably more serious than that, as 'she was hoping soon to become engaged.'[154] The fact that Jellicoe knew and admired both Jock Lewes and David Stirling was good enough reason for him to come on board when Stirling eventually approached him.

Stirling very likely wanted Jellicoe to 'improve the administration of the unit and to liaise with the Free French under his command'.[155] According to Jellicoe, organization was something the group 'rather lacked, to say the least'.[156] He was probably looking for someone who could bring what he himself lacked and had always delegated. Without Lewes, the SAS probably could not have even got off the ground. He was a 'marvellous training officer' but also a practical innovator, the inventor of the famous bomb whose well-designed destructiveness was instrumental in achieving such success in SAS raids. His early death was 'a very great loss to the SAS.'[157]

Jellicoe would become 'one of Stirling's finest officers'.[158] Technically, he was Stirling's Second-in-Command (2i/c), although Jellicoe may have been uncertain of this. Some have suggested that Jellicoe was never given the 2i/c spot. According to Asher, Stirling had also promised the job to another officer, Captain the Hon. Robin Gurdon of the Scots Guards. Gurdon would be killed in July 1942. That may have been true: Gurdon was a much admired officer, usually 'immaculate … in his clean shirt and corduroy trousers', someone who 'always managed to preserve that air of being very much the nobleman.'[159] Stirling was more than likely keeping his options open till Jellicoe proved himself. He was up against fierce competition. Nevertheless, that George Jellicoe was also now part of Stirling's crowd must have been 'seen as a huge vote of confidence' in the group.[160]

Jellicoe still needed to get his leaving of the Coldstreams sorted. Such was Stirling's pull that approval came through almost at once – so fast, indeed, that Jellicoe was not able to take up his new position as he had come down with malaria in Beirut and was still on sick leave There he had initially stayed with Bill Astor who, it seems, soon tired of having a sick officer under his roof, so sent Jellicoe packing within two days off to another Casualty Clearing station. Astor would later be implicated in the Profumo affair when he had an affair with Mandy Rice-Davies. It was she who befriended Christine Keeler and introduced her to Stephen Ward, the osteopath who treated John Profumo, the young Secretary of State for War.

From Beirut, Jellicoe went to an Australian Hospital. No 'white-haired' beauties this time. Even though he liked the Aussies, he 'didn't fancy being looked after by Australian male nurses.' Discharging himself, he went back to Cairo, where Stirling shared a flat with his brothers, Peter and Bill. Peter was a Third Secretary at the British Embassy, while Bill worked as an Assistant to General Arthur Smith, Chief of the General Staff (CIGS).

The flat was notorious. It was located in the Garden City quarter, where it overlooked the British embassy and backed on to the Belgian. Above lived an embassy employee, Adam Watson, and the game the flatmates played – 'livening up Watson' – was to shoot live rounds through the ceiling. Whenever the landlord visited, the numerous bullet holes pitting the flat walls would be covered up with pictures of the British Royal Family. Apart from Peter Stirling's room – the only one with a large bed – the rest were 'like left luggage offices', camp beds, suitcases and German ammunition strewn all around. 'One day, Peter Stirling woke up to find a donkey and a rose bush tethered to the bed.'[161] The flat was a visual cacophony, the very definition of casual chaos.

The war let loose the public schoolboy in these men. Their butler, Mohammed Aboudi, affectionately known as 'Mo', took care of everything. It was Mo who looked after the guest lists, the cooking, the laundry, even 'chasing up military equipment and vehicles ordered from recalcitrant Army HQ'. He later wrote a 'light-hearted' account of these days, *All about Mo*. Hermione Ranfurly wrote of a typical dinner in 1942:

> I dined with Peter Stirling at his flat. David was there and told me of his raids on Jalo and Gailo beyond Misurata … His score of enemy planes destroyed … is now fantastic. David hates talking about his nocturnal raids so I felt very honoured to hear a detailed account. Mo, with the dignity of an English butler, served dinner and handed round captured Italian wine, murmuring, 'Mussolini, Sir?'[162]

On another occasion, Jellicoe was at the flat talking through a raid and briefing the group on the route to be taken. 'The briefing was late … because Mo had hidden the secret maps in the bathroom, in a praiseworthy if vain attempt to tidy the place up.'

Stirling also probably thought Jellicoe would be useful in promoting increased ('more effective' were Jellicoe's words) liaison with MEHQ. Certainly, his language skills were a particularly valuable asset, because of the Free French. Stirling had studied in Paris, so his French was good but not as good as Jellicoe's. It was also delivered with a strong stammer. He knew that there were Free French troops who were just itching to get into the action but weren't being employed. He wanted to see if they could become part of his outfit, to fill his immediate manpower needs.

Stirling went to see General Catroux, de Gaulle's military commander of the Free French forces based in Cairo (later, he would recall the meeting and mistakenly say that he met with de Gaulle himself). Initially, the meeting did not go well. Castroux, like de Gaulle, did not like the English and saw Stirling as just another Englishman. No French forces would take orders from an English officer. As he was leaving, Stirling muttered under his breath. It was theatrical, and probably well-rehearsed. He pointed out that he was a Scot, not English, and that he had grown up 'dans l'ancienne alliance entre la France et l'Écosse contre les Anglais'.[163] The story is colourful but I suspect it might also have been told for Bergé's benefit when the two met up again at 1985. The plucky Gascon had 'immense admiration' for Stirling.[164] It was mutual. Jellicoe, too, liked Bergé as well as his 2i/c, Augustin Jordan. Jellicoe described Bergé as 'a marvellous commander in his own right'.[165] The three developed a close working relationship and a friendship that lasted the rest of their lives.

The two French SAS commanders were very different characters. Asher described Bergé, a southerner, as 'excitable and mercurial', 'irascible but keen-as-mustard',[166] the other, a northerner, as 'saturnine and phlegmatic'.[167] The tough but small Bergé (he was only 5' 6") was 'very powerfully built, stocky, dark haired, square jawed, with very deep-set brilliant green eyes and a ready laugh. Famously quick-witted and with a sharp tongue, he is a true Gascon, tough, radiating energy, enthusiasm and humour. An early Bob Hoskins.'[168] Bergé had been convalescing from a wound when he heard the news of the Armistice. Six days later, on 23 June, aboard the Jean Sobieski, he arrived in Portsmouth and met with de Gaulle, who gave him the go-ahead to form a parachute group within the Free French Forces. On 15 September 1940, the 1ère Compagnie de l'Infanterie de l'Air was activated and trained at Ringway with the British. When he and his men arrived at Kabrit, he had already been decorated with the British Military Cross. In short, Bergé was a fighter and he had already a lot of experience under his belt. He'd been one of the first men parachuted back into occupied France on a mission to blow up a power station feeding a German submarine base in Brittany.

Jordan was also thirty but was almost totally different to Bergé: 'Taller (5' 11"), slender, with an angular chiselled face, delicate features, sharp watchful eyes and great polish. Thoughtful, careful, quiet-spoken. Patrician and a touch frosty, but with quiet sardonic humour … very much the northerner, to Bergé's southerner.'[169] He could seem very aristocratic (he played polo) but was a natural diplomat (and later entered the Quai d'Orsay, the French Foreign Office).

Jordan had met Bergé in Damascus. Both of them were unhappy. Bergé had arrived too late for the Syrian campaign, Jordan too late to join General

Le Gentilhomme in Ethiopia. At the outbreak of war, Le Gentilhomme had been Commander-in-Chief of French forces in Somaliland, but after denouncing the new Vichy government he ended up in London, where he was promoted and sent back to work under Wavell, as the commander of the newly-created *1ère Division légère française libre*, DLFL.

Jellicoe would always joke that the Free French were 'very, very free; and very, very French'.[170] Joke he might, but Bergé actually instilled a strong sense of competition in his men, right at the outset. He hardly needed to. Like the Greeks, the French had a burning hatred for the Germans. It was born from occupation and a history of wars. In their own country, these soldiers faced the death sentence for joining de Gaulle. 'They have quite literally everything to fight for.'[171] Talking of Stirling's men, Bergé was under no illusions that the French would have to work twice as hard:

> *Nous avons un handicap terrible à remonter. Ils ont déjà plus de cent avions détruits à leur actif! Voyez comme il faut que nous mettions les bouches doubles pour les rattraper!* (We have a terrible challenge to live up to. They already have a hundred planes to their name. We will have to work double time to catch up!)

Whether you stayed in the unit or not wasn't decided by how well you trained; it was under fire that the real mettle of a man could be seen. Lewes' training was developed to build confidence and it was so tough that, invariably, the real thing was easier.

When Bergé's men joined the SAS, he brought with him six officers, twelve NCOs and forty-two men.[172] They set up camp a little apart from the rest of the SAS, their tents dug in around a small parade ground. The tents that the French used were relatively spacious: five or six men would share each one and, in order to keep them cooler and to protect against air raids, they were dug deep into the sand. At the centre of each was a flagpole on which flew the flag of the Cross of Lorraine, the symbol of continued French resistance. That the French tents were separated from the rest of the SAS powerfully symbolized their unit's pride and the challenge they set themselves: to be as good as, if not better than the British.

Georges Bergé led his men on a similar raid to the British against Heliopolis. It was to test them after the three gruelling months of training. Bergé demanded a very high standard: 'We must not only catch up with, but overtake Stirling's men.'[173] Bergé divided two dozen men into two groups, one under himself, the other under Lieutenant Jordan, and walked the 130km across the desert to get to the target. It was gruelling.

Les hommes n'en peuvent plus, Roger Boutinot est epuisé comme ses camerades et certains ont les pieds en sang mais tous le monde s'accroche. (The men couldn't give any more. Like his comrades, Roger Boutinot was exhausted. Some of the men's feet were bleeding but they still pushed on).[174]

Despite Heliopolis airfield being *'sévèrement gardée'*, the group claimed seventy aircraft 'destroyed' after they'd successfully placed the same adhesive stickers. The raid strongly validated Stirling's decision to bring the French on board. Jellicoe would become the co-ordinating point with the SAS.

Chapter 2

The SAS: Early Failures and New Tactics

In early November 1941, the SAS received its first challenge: to support Auchinleck's Operation CRUSADER by raiding the Libyan airfields, both to create a diversion and, more obviously, to make a dent in enemy air power. The Allied offensive was supposed to finally start on 18 November, after having already been delayed from the 11th and then the 15th.

It was decided that the SAS would make a parachute drop to attack five major Axis airfields, RV about 50 miles inland and exfil with the LRDG. The airfields were spread out, three around Tmimi and two at Gazala, and they were where the new Me.109-Fs were being deployed.

At 1930 on the evening of 16 November, five 216 Squadron Bristol Bombays took off from their base at Bagoush after what Bob Bennett referred to as 'The Last Supper'. Bennett remembered it well: 'What went through my mind was: what a beautiful meal this is, and what's it in aid of? I think the RAF thought they'd never see us again.'[1] The RAF's hospitality seemed suspicious, even if welcome. 'Treated like men going to the gallows' was one description of the event.[2] They outstayed their welcome with the 'Crabs' (RAF). Kershaw, Blakeney and Storie 'liberated' some alcohol from its very insecure storage and were caught red-handed by the camp commander. The next morning, Lewes was preparing to give them a dressing down; instead, he couldn't help it but laugh.

When they finally embarked, aboard the five aircraft were the fifty-five men of L Detachment, each plane under the command of an officer: Stirling, Mayne, Lewes, McGonigal and Bonington. It was not going to be a smooth ride, the wind already blowing hard at around 35mph, at that time twice the recommended strength for a jump. One man didn't go; Jim Almonds' son had died and he was planning to go back for the funeral. It probably saved his life.

The Bombay was not a plane that many liked:

They used to flip on their backs, their centre of gravity moved feet instead of inches. They had a rear gun turret they couldn't use, so they used that area as a lavatory. But you had to warn the pilot before you moved, so that he could take an extra grip on the things, to stop her flipping.[3]

Flying in through thick flak was terrifying: one plane was shot down (later they learned that another plane had been 'talked-down' by an English-speaking German controller into landing on an enemy airfield). Although the wind remained almost as strong, Stirling decided to ignore the warnings. He had been told of the probable conditions by Brigadier Sandy Galloway, the General Staff Co-ordinator, who said the decision on whether to go ahead with the drop would 'rest' with him. It was a lonely moment for Stirling. He desperately needed to establish the unit's value. It must have felt as though 'it's now or never'.

Some people said it 'was the worst storm to hit the region in thirty years'. Bob Bennett said that 'by the time they reached the area we seemed to be flying completely blind, and the objectives below were completely obscured.'[4] Stirling added, 'It was a night without any moon, pitch black, so there was no way you could see the ground, particularly with all the desert blowing up, all the flying sand.'[5]

When du Vivier landed he was immediately dragged over the rocks, badly hurting his leg, but thankful to be alive. The same happened to Reg Seekings. A new foldable entrenching tool had been given to the jumpers. It had not been tested and would have deadly results. With the harnesses on, the parachute shrouds quickly became entangled. Try as the men might to snap the buckle open, it was almost impossible to do so when being dragged over the desert at speed. It was probably then that Jock Cheyne broke his back, even if Bob Tait said that he got lost and simply was not seen again.[6]

Lewes gave his men what turned out to be very sensible advice just before the jump: each man should note the wind direction, then 'set the back bearing of this on your compass and you will have the best chance of locating the man who has jumped before you.'[7] Cooper and Pat Riley (who was the senior NCO) jumped with Lewes. He remembered hitting the ground hard and then hurtling over rocks and sand at 30mph, carried relentlessly by the wind as he struggled to get the 'chute buckle unclipped. It took around an hour to get the entire team assembled, but Lewes' advice saved his men. The supply cannisters were, of course, nowhere to be found: of ten, 'only two could be located.'[8] They had no food, machine guns, water (although that would soon be solved) and, most importantly, no bombs. You didn't jump with rucksacks. Everything they needed had been in the containers. The mission was useless.

Mayne's plane took off late – at 2020 rather than 1940 – and because of that delay missed some of the flak. As his stick floated down he saw 'flashes on the ground'. It turned out 'to have been caused by detonators exploding in packs whose parachutes had failed to open.'[9]

As if the wind wasn't enough, the heavens seemed to open and torrential rain bucketed down. The men were caught in a hailstorm, soaked and trying to stay upright in the torrent of fast-moving water in a *wadi*. They were 'waist deep in a swirling tide of water', du Vivier said.[10] Bennet recalled that 'six of us were sitting there with blankets over our heads'.[11] It was so bad on the march back to the RV that he even decided to hand over command to Pat Riley, who was able to get them back in one piece using a mixture of cajolery, encouragement and nursing to keep the exhausted men going. They would march for forty minutes, rest – or rather sleep – for twenty, and repeat the process. They finally met up with the LRDG at 2200 on 19 November, cold, exhausted, and hungry. Du Vivier didn't forget what Riley had done that night: 'I shall always be indebted to him for what he did. I'm sure he was for the most part responsible for our return.'[12]

A few hours later, Paddy Mayne also got back. Two men had been left behind because of the seriousness of their injuries: Bill Kendall and Dougie Arnold. They would survive. After dragging themselves across the desert, they surrendered to a group of Italians. Later, they said that they had been treated 'kindly and with great amusement', the Italians apparently believing their story that they were engineers who had got lost.[13]

Of the men who jumped, only eighteen men and four officers came back. Thirty-four didn't make it: three officers, McGonigal, Bonington and Thomas, CSM Yates, Sergeants Lazenby, Stone, Bond and Cheyne. Also Blakeney, Jim Davies and Dougie Arnold. Eoin McGonigal was Mayne's only real friend, and his death hit his fellow Irishman badly. Anyone or anything around Mayne became a target, and he caused havoc in nightclubs and with the MPs. The only group that dropped well was Jock Lewes'.

Was Stirling right to have gone ahead with the drop? Considering what was at stake at the time, undoubtedly yes. Reg Seekings said that some people clearly thought that 'they should never have dropped under those conditions, but if we hadn't there would never have been an SAS.'[14] Stirling's dilemma had been that he might not get another chance. The lessons of Operation SQUATTER were hard. Apart from having to go to such lengths to prove their value, dropping important weapons and gear separately had been a mistake, especially under such conditions. Also, fuses and time pencils needed to be properly waterproofed. But the essential point had been made: they could get to the coast road undetected.

As he was waiting at the RV for his people to come back, Stirling got talking with David Lloyd Owen. 'I think I'll wait here for a bit,' he said, 'and see who else comes in. Let's talk if you've nothing else to do.'[15] As they talked, Lloyd Owen 'sensed throughout that (Stirling) was not really certain that parachuting was the best way to reach his target.'[16] Their informal conversation, sitting and waiting in a lonely desert outcrop, led to the birth of the new partnership between the LRDG and the SAS. It would become the hallmark of future desert operations. The LRDG knew the desert terrain backwards and were very skilled in navigation. They didn't use maps, rather they constantly reckoned their position from the sun, and at night, from the stars. The LRDG would ferry the SAS to the target, drop them off and then pick them up after they had completed their missions. Once back at Siwa, Stirling got approval from the LRDG commanding officer, Colonel Guy Prendergast.

The Long Range Desert Group (LRDG)

Desert navigation using a sun compass, and driving techniques using ladders and mats to carry trucks over slippery sand, were developed in the interwar years by Major Ralph Bagnold, Royal Signals. His written recommendations – based on years exploring the Libyan desert prior to 1939 – for the formation of a desert reconnaissance force were the foundation of the LRDG. Bagnold was the inventor of many of the tools used by the LRDG and the SAS: for example, the sun compass, desert radiator condensers, 5-foot sand ladders and bush mats.

Desert conditions were extremely varied: the Sahara consisted of 'flat sand plains (*serir*), rocky plateaus (*hammada*), deep dry watercourses (*wadis*), treacherous salt marshes (*schott*) and massive deathly dune seas (*erg*).'[17]

When formed in July 1940, the force was already sizeable (eleven officers and seventy-six men) but it grew rapidly and by March 1942 numbered 25 officers and 324 men (McCrery p.18). Bagnold credits Wavell with the foresight to establish the force, saying that 'especially when others had ridiculed any such idea as utterly impossible ... he alone grasped the possibilities and implications' of what Wavell came to call his 'mosquito army'.[18] Ranfurly (p.99) talked of the disappointment at Wavell's replacement in the desert, saying, 'he is one the few senior officers who back young methods of war.'

The LRDG was originally built by Bagnold around three Rhodesian and New Zealand-manned patrols, R, T and W. R and T were combat units; W support. The trucks in the New Zealand patrol (T) were all named after places (T.4., for example, was *Taupo*, *Te Aroha* was another). Later other patrols were added – S, G (made up of recruits from the Guards Regiment) and Y (from the Nottingahmshire Yeomanry). By the end of the war, 325 New Zealanders had served in the LRDG.

The vehicles they used were 1.5 ton American, open-topped Chevrolet trucks camouflaged in 'a bold design of rose-pink and olive-green, which, oddly enough, made them practically invisible against the desert' (Maclean, *Eastern Approaches*, p.166). The 'two-wheel drive only' Chevy was 'relatively light and fast and not too greedy on the juice'. [19] Normally armed with .303 Lewis guns or, on the back, Vickers .50 water-cooled machine gun, occasionally the vehicles would carry captured weapons like the Italian 20mm Breda, captured in February 1941 at Beda Fromm on Libya's east coast. The unit's first fourteen trucks were bought from Ford dealers, nineteen more 'had to be begged, second-hand, off the Egyptian army.' (Bagnold, p.33)

Benefits from the SAS-LRDG partnership were many: the raiders could be dropped closer to their targets with greater safety, they could carry in more supplies and explosives, and the two groups had many other interchangeable skill sets that would be enhanced by working together.

Back at MEHQ, Stirling met both Cunningham and, in the afternoon, his replacement, Ritchie. It was bizarre timing. Cunningham had just been informed of his replacement by the CGS, Arthur Smith. At first, Stirling was despondent, but a chance encounter with another Scots Guards officer, Brigadier John Marriott, opened up new opportunities. As Stirling put it, 'He and I entered into a conspiracy.'[20] Marriott introduced Stirling to Brigadier Denys Reid, whose group would help provide his men with the military infrastructure they needed to keep functioning out in the desert, away from Kabrit: 'If you're looking for a supply base to leech onto, Denys is your man ... He's well placed to help.'[21]

Stirling assembled his men. Despite the staggering losses, he reassured them that the SAS was not done, and that they would now raid with the LRDG's help. It was a perfect combination: the LRDG was 'reconnaissance', the SAS were 'raiders'.[22] To all the LRDG's strengths, Stirling offered an equal amount from the SAS:

The irrational tenth ... like the kingfisher flashing across the pool: a never-failing audacity, a gift for daring improvisation, which invariably took the enemy by surprise.[23]

Stirling had to keep the news of what had happened quiet. If word of the disaster got out, it could destroy the unit before it had even had a chance to prove its worth: 'It was absolutely essential to keep quiet and not report to MEHQ.'[24] The men went back to Kabrit, collected all the supplies that they could and left as quietly and quickly as possible for Jalo once Stirling had quietly updated Jock Lewes. This was clandestine communication. He got in contact with Lewes 'not by open signalling, because I couldn't afford that in case Middle East HQ rumbled where I was.'[25]

On 5 December, at 0245, Stirling flew with his men to the desert oasis and arrived that night. Jalo, a small stretch of green abundance seven miles long by two wide, had only just been captured from the Italians by an armoured brigade. When he could see the oasis in the morning light, Cooper commented that it was 'a typical Foreign Legion outpost, out of *Beau Geste*'.[26] From equipment left behind, the SAS took two Lancia Trentequattro trucks, each armed with Breda 20mm guns, which would serve them well as disguised transport.

Chapter 3

Operations in 1941

With Captain Gus Holliman in command and Mike Sadler navigating, an eighteen-man Rhodesian Squadron was assigned to take the SAS 350 miles to the airfields at Sirte, Nofilia and Tamet.[1] On 8 December they set off in seven trucks. It was going to be a long journey.[2] They managed to cover almost the whole distance without being seen, until an Italian spotter plane, a Ghibli, saw them and tried, unsuccessfully, to bomb them.

At Sirte, Stirling and Brough had little luck. It was frustrating. On the field, thirty Caproni CA309 bombers presented an inviting target. Not wanting to lay his bombs before Mayne, Stirling waited, only to see them all take off in pairs. All he could do was destroy twelve supply trucks that he found outside.

Thirty miles away, Mayne's luck held. Holliman took 'three of his trucks down the coastal road for the rendezvous with David Stirling. The other three would approach the field from the north', dropping Mayne off three miles from the field.[3] Years after the war, in 1955, Mayne wrote about the attack: 'It was just after ten o'clock as we left the truck. An ideal night for the job. No moon, and pleasantly cool for walking.'[4]

Before tackling the parked planes, he was distracted by sounds coming from a guard hut, where 'about thirty off-duty German and Italian pilots … were relaxing, drinking and playing cards.'[5] Mayne surprised them and, as he had been trained to do, shot the first man who moved with his Thompson and then sprayed the whole room with fire. As he left, he even shot the lights out. With Mayne that evening was a Londoner called Hawkins. He would not last in the unit but would be RTU'd for the simple reason that Mayne did not like 'his continual use of a certain epithet'. It was an odd thing to do to a fellow soldier whom he admitted was a 'good man', given his own behaviour – either when drunk or killing.[6]

At Tamet, Mayne destroyed twenty-four of the Fiat C42 Falco biplanes, fourteen with Lewes bombs and, when he'd run out of explosives, simply by ripping out the aircraft instrument panels. He dealt with as many as ten in this manner.[7] He'd seen the glow inside a cockpit and realized that a mechanic had forgotten to turn off the switches. Mayne wanted

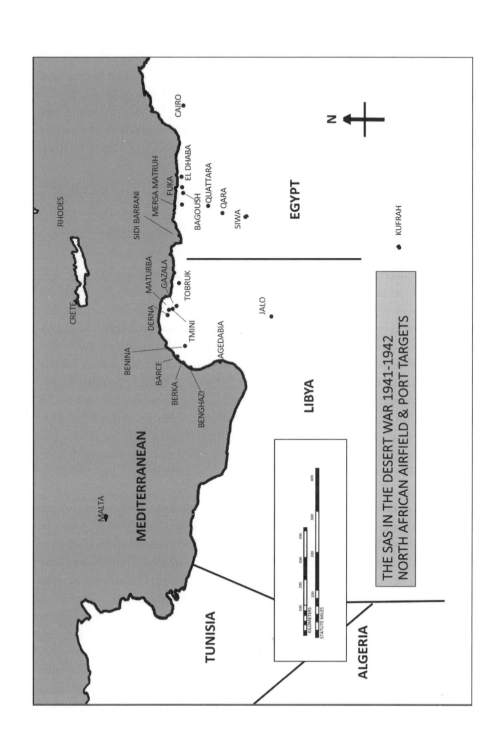

THE SAS IN THE DESERT WAR 1941-1942
NORTH AFRICAN AIRFIELD & PORT TARGETS

the dashboard as a souvenir. They'd run out of bombs as they'd been 'too generous at the petrol hut and around the dumps.'[8] At this stage of mobile warfare, with the constant changing of forward airfields, the enemy had not the means of establishing proper perimeter defence, and the planes were seldom guarded; neither were the cockpits locked.[9] Mayne later described the attack rather dryly. This was in stark contrast to the report which came out in the press and talked of the aggression of Mayne's attack on the airfield's officers' mess:

> Drinking songs turned to shouts of fear and those who were not killed or wounded desperately trying to make for the doors and windows were mown down. They were 50 miles behind the front line but a British patrol was in their midst. Not one left the room alive.

As he left, Mayne 'threw a time bomb on the roof of the mess.'[10]

Some of the planes that Mayne blew up at Tamet were probably the same ones that took off from Sirte and had left Stirling and Brough fewer targets.

Jock Lewes took an eleven-man group plus Lieutenant Morris's LRDG party to raid the field at Agheila while Almonds and Lilley stayed at the camp. The next day, they drove back east to Mersa Matruh and, at Mersa Brega, stopped at a roadside fort. In the car park Almonds counted forty-seven enemy vehicles. Riding their captured Lancia, they blended in without being spotted. They were so convincing that, at one point, an Italian sentry came over and asked for a light. After the man had been pushed into the truck, astonished at being treated like this by 'Germans', Lewes quietly told him that they were British. At first, the Italian took it as a joke but soon saw that his life was hanging by a thread. He was taken prisoner. They planted as many bombs as they could in the truck park. The seven-minute fuses didn't give them much time before going off. Under attack, enemy soldiers retreated back to the fort, where they locked themselves in. The plan to use the Breda heavy machine gun to shoot things up didn't work. The early morning air was so cold that the oil had congealed. Instead, the raiders contented themselves with planting Lewes bombs on more rather unexciting telephone poles, on trucks and on cars. As they drove out, they passed a 'brightly painted truck and trailer ... a travelling brothel'.[11] On 18 December they were back at Jalo.

Reid now asked for their help. He was planning an operation that would link up with Marriot but was worried about crossing miles of featureless desert and being spotted by roving Axis aircraft. He needed Stirling's men to blow up some more planes.

On 19 December, Bill Fraser took a group out to raid Agedabia, north-east of Mersa Brega. With him were Bob Tait, Philips, Byrne and

Jeff du Vivier. They knew each other well. Byrne and Fraser had both served at Dunkirk. As well as Tait, who was now navigating, Philips had been in No.11 Commando with Fraser, an interesting man who always had 'an irresistibly jolly expression'. But it was misleading.[12] He was an experienced officer who had also fought at Litani. Mayne, however, disliked Fraser because he was homosexual. He was wrong about Fraser, who didn't lack guts, could display as much bravado as the others and 'did all of his parachute jumps in one morning so that he could sport his wings in Cairo the next day.' (The SAS were only allowed to wear their wings on their sleeve once they'd completed eight training jumps. Only when three successful operational jumps had been made could the patch be transferred to the left breast.[13]) Consequently, when Mayne was around, and particularly when he was 'drink taken', Fraser would prefer to spend time alone with his dog, a dachshund called Withers, a little creature with 'deep and very soulful eyes'.[14]

The LRDG dropped them off on 20 December within 16 miles of the target. As they were lying up, Philips was spotted by a young Arab shepherd boy. Fifty years later, another SAS man, part of team Bravo Two Zero, also called Philips, would also be seen by a shepherd. In North Africa the team was lucky. In Iraq, they weren't. The latter team had to exfil rapidly, heading towards Syria, and lost men to the cold and others to capture and torture.

Each man carried 'a water bottle, a compass, eight Lewes bombs, a tin of chocolate, plus other rations consisting of raisins, cheese and broken biscuits'.[15] At 2115 they got to the airfield perimeter, passing through without problems: 'the tripwires were tripped over without results!' Fraser later said.[16] The next three hours were spent moving slowly but deliberately, silently planting bombs, after the first plane was located at 0005. The attack proceeded at a glacially slow pace; it was necessary to be able to blend in with the night. It must have been agonizingly tense. The bombs were planted on the aircraft, conveniently parked together in pairs, near the hangar, 'one batch of CR.42s standing wing to wing'.[17]

> On the way back, we counted well over forty explosions and heard the bomb dump go off with a blood-curdling, deafening roar. Though we must have been at least a half mile away by this time we felt the concussion press on our lungs.[18]

The enemy opened up with machine guns, pouring heavy fire down both sides of the airfield, hoping to catch the escaping attackers. Byrne described the 'tremendous din' of 'ammunition crackling and exploding in the burning aircraft'. As they were getting away, a group of Blenheim bombers flew over and used the opportunity of a completely illuminated field to drop more bombs.[19]

They had destroyed thirty-seven aircraft. Most were Italian, Fiat CR42 fighter-bombers, but there were at least seven Me.109Fs amongst them, 'parked snout to tail ... covered in blanket-like cowlings'.[20] Along with the aircraft, an ammunition dump was also destroyed. 'It was as perfect a raid as any the SAS ever carried out.'[21] Jeff du Vivier apologized for the two aircraft that were left on the ground, explaining that they had run out of explosives. The apology was – obviously – quite unnecessary.

At 0555, eight hours after getting past the perimeter defences, they met up again with the LRDG troop and exfiled back to the camp at Jalo, getting there on 23 December. It was an awful irony that the only casualties on the operation were two LRDG men killed by a couple of RAF Blenheim bombers. One of the Rhodesians, Bob Riggs, had been frantically waving at the recognition signs, only 'to be blasted off his feet'.[22] The two casualties must have been the more painful to bear given the futility of the deaths.

Back at Jalo, the unit celebrated their biggest bag of aircraft so far. The celebrations wouldn't last long. Stirling and Mayne were going back to target Sirte and Tamet again, while Lewes and Fraser headed to Arco dei Fileni.

Two teams were to be used: with Stirling went Cooper, Seekings, Rose, Cattell and Brough; with Mayne, Ed McDonald, White, Hawkins, Chesworth and Bob Bennett. Reg Seekings and Johnny Cooper had, till that point, not got on well. Seekings said that Cooper was 'a big mouth'. From that evening, however, they became inseparable, in the same way that Bob Bennett and Sergeant Lilley struck up a great friendship. They all had a strong dislike for civilian life.

Mayne's Tamet group spent Christmas Day in the desert:

> The LRDG shot a gazelle and we made base that evening, and the New Zealanders cut this gazelle up. We made a little fire in the sand, and we had the gazelle, and rum and lime – we had a very, very nice Christmas.[23]

Bennett and Mayne were dropped off six miles from Tamet and just walked on to the airfield.[24] They were amazed at how badly protected it was on the first raid. 'It always fascinates me the number of times these airfields were done, you'd have thought they'd be like a fortress. But no, a bit of wire and a couple of machine gun posts – we never had much trouble getting into them', said Bennett.[25] This time it seemed that 'there were signs of greater vigilance than a fortnight earlier ... guards were sited in groups of seven or eight around the field.'[26]

Once on the tarmac, they lobbed bombs up on to the wings, 12ft above the ground, of the Savoia bombers parked 50 yards apart amongst the trees. The time pencils were set for 30 minutes but started to go off prematurely, and the party was fired upon as they were getting back out. Mayne didn't take too well to that and finished off the Italian sentries with grenades. 'That was rather a mistake as I don't like being fired at', he dryly explained.[27] He called out '*Freund!*' but in 'a very un-German-like brogue' as he tossed a Mills grenade.[28] With fifty-one aircraft disabled between the two raids, Tamet airfield now 'became known in the unit as "Paddy's own".'[29]

After one unsuccessful attempt to break on to Sirte in which Stirling also nearly got shot by one of the LRDG taxi service, they had raced in Gus Holliman's trucks along the Via Balbia: 'The party regained their trucks and drove along the road shooting at the vehicles parked alongside it with small arms and a Bofors gun, and also put thermite bombs in two large lorries.'[30]

Fraser then set off to raid Arco dei Fileni, 60 miles to the east of Nofilia, which Lewes was going to hit. On Christmas Day 1941, the two groups (fifteen LRDG and a further ten SAS) dutifully left their camp with the New Zealander T.2. patrol led by Second Lieutenant Morris. 'Arco dei Fileni' was so called because Mussolini had ordered a large triumphal arch built there on the edge of the desert. The Nofilia group – Fraser, Bob Tait, Philips, Byrne and Sergeant du Vivier – was dropped off around ten miles from the target and walked in after having spent two days lying low, waiting.[31] So that they could watch the aircraft traffic pattern, they lay low in a '*ber*', an underground well, set in a depression, at the end of the airfield.

The raid, however, would be abortive: 'Large formations of aircraft came and went, which gave the impression that it was used by day to land reinforcements or as a refuelling point, but it appeared to be empty at night.'

Fraser led the team back to the RV point, but after three frustrating days waiting for the LRDG to appear, decided that they needed to get back on foot. T.2.'s CO, Morris, had decided against doing so after the events following Lewes' Nofilia raid.

By 7 January their water and food had run out: they had only found a small amount on an abandoned German truck. That night, they surprised the occupants of another truck, this time Italian:

> The occupants were sleeping inside, and became hysterical when captured. They were for some time under the impression that we were German soldiers. Some food was obtained and the radiator drained for water.[32]

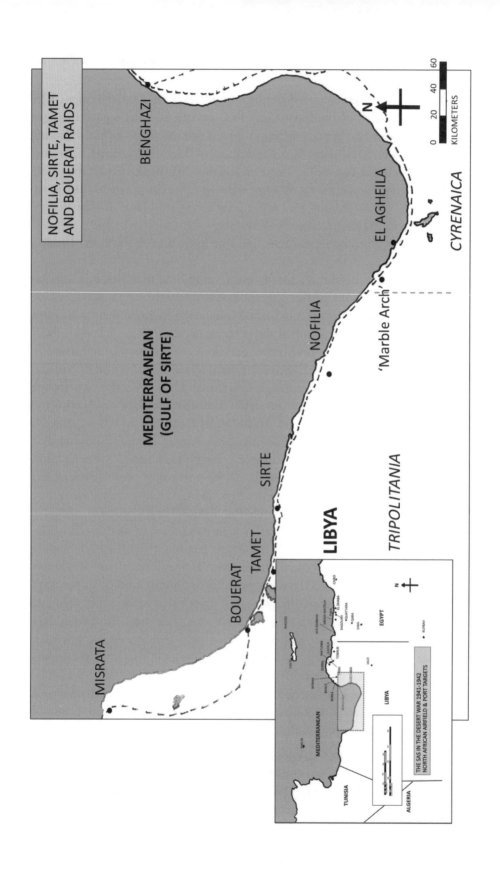

NOFILIA, SIRTE, TAMET AND BOUERAT RAIDS

BENGHAZI

MEDITERRANEAN
(GULF OF SIRTE)

MISRATA

BOUERAT

TAMET

SIRTE

NOFILIA

'Marble Arch'

EL AGHEILA

CYRENAICA

LIBYA

TRIPOLITANIA

N

0 20 40 60
KILOMETERS

THE SAS IN THE DESERT WAR 1941-1942
NORTH AFRICAN AIRFIELD & PORT TARGETS

MEDITERRANEAN

TUNISIA

ALGERIA

LIBYA

EGYPT

N

The next night, they managed to get a German truck driver to take them part of the distance north of Mersa Brega. Philips disguised himself by wrapping up in a blanket to look like an Arab. He stepped out in front of the truck as it was leaving a truck park. As it slowed, the others jumped on. The driver had little choice if he wanted to live. In moonlight, they were able to walk through the lines, although spotted and fired upon. A few days later, Senussi tribesmen gave them food, and the next night, 10/11 January, they were found by a friendly Allied patrol.

After dropping Fraser's party, T.2. continued on along the coast another 60 miles with Lewes and dropped the second party off within 18 miles of Nofilia the next day, 28 December, at 1500. Fraser, along with four others. Almonds, Storie, Lilley and Bob White, spent most of the day of 28 December watching as planes landed and took off. It looked like the same thing was happening.

At one point they counted forty-three aircraft on the tarmac: brand new Stukas in factory-fresh paint. Once they got in, however, their luck ran out. They had penetrated the airfield easily and started to place bombs, Lewes on one, Almonds on another. And that was it. There were no more aircraft. They only found the two. And their fuel tanks were empty at that, so they wouldn't catch fire. They were thoroughly discouraged, even if, during the afternoon, several planes had landed, bombed up and taken off again. Picked up again by Morris' patrol at 1800 on 28 December, they continued on the next day, 31 December, with the intention of collecting Fraser's team. They never got there.

At around 1000, an Me.110 swooped in low, guns firing.[33] As the plane flew off, the rear gunner kept on firing the 20mm cannons. Bullets zipped by at a withering 650 rounds per minute. Jim Almonds and Lilley were riding behind Lewes' LRDG Ford. Almonds saw the others jump out but thought that Lewes had stayed on longer 'fiddling about with some papers'.[34] Almonds and Lilley kept going and then, seven miles further on, were attacked again by a pair of Stukas.

It was after that attack that Almonds learned that both Storie and Lewes had been hit critically. Lewes' back was 'shattered'. A 20mm shell had hit him in the thigh and half his leg was blown off by the exit wound. 'He'd bled to death in about four minutes.'[35] They spent the rest of the day getting one of the trucks, Lewes' old one, working to go back to Jalo that evening.[36]

Jim Almonds described the last moments before Jock's death:

Sighted a lone Messerschmitt 110 Fighter heading our way. Kept still in hope he would not see us. He passed right overhead and was going away, everyone breathing a sigh of relief, when one wing dropped and round he came. Circled us very low and then attacked, armed with four machine guns forward and two cannon … His second burst got our truck but did not hurt anyone or set us on fire. It soon became obvious that it was only a question of time before we should all be killed if we stayed with the trucks so we left and got behind a rock. Mr Lewes had been wounded in the leg … [37]

Jock had sent a telegram to his girlfriend, Mirren Barford, a few days earlier on 23 December. He sounded as though he was on top of the world:

Back today with Pullable Beard and possible Medal. Off again tomorrow. Merry Christmas and all love John Lewesx [38]

Mirren's letter of acceptance of his offer of marriage proposal was on its way to Jalo. He would never see it or know that she would have chosen to spend her life with him. Separated by thousands of miles, Mirren felt something had happened and she left the party which she'd been attending.

Lewes was buried in the desert about 'twenty miles south-east of Nofilia'. They dug a shallow grave, scratching his name on his helmet. Almonds later wrote of his sadness at the time: 'No one will stop by his grave or pay homage to a brave heart that has ceased to beat – not even a stone marks the spot.'[39] In 2018, John Lewes, Jock's nephew, a schoolteacher and the author of a biography of Jock, mounted an expedition to see if the gravesite could be found using what information he could from Jim Storie, who had buried his uncle.

Fitzroy Maclean, soon to be an important member of the unit and later to make his name fighting with Tito's partisans in Yugoslavia, felt that Stirling's strength was his 'remarkable vision, resourcefulness and imagination'. Stirling was the first to recognise the debt that he owed Jock Lewes. He said as much when he wrote to Jock's parents a year later:

There is no doubt that any success the unit had achieved up to the time of Jock's death and after it, was, and is, almost wholly due to Jock's work.[40]

In 1992, Jellicoe had a chance meeting in a hotel in Tirana, Albania. The man he met was Mirren's brother. In his letters, he also wrote of Jock as 'a very highly principled person, a very clever person indeed and I could understand even more why David had had such a high opinion of him.'[41]

Stirling was despondent. He'd lost the man with whom he'd really built the SAS. Pleydell always thought that Lewes was 'the man who was responsible for its construction and organisation'. Stirling felt the same and wrote as much to Jock's father.[42] Lewes' loss was a 'very great loss to the SAS'. He was everything that Stirling wasn't – 'serious, single-minded, systematic and analytic'.[43] Gavin Mortimer summed up the relationship between the two men succinctly: 'Stirling was the backbone but Lewes was the brains.'[44]

It's interesting to pause for a moment and consider how very different the three key players in the early SAS were. David Stirling, Paddy Mayne and Jock Lewes were a study in contrasts. It was extraordinary, in fact, that Mayne and Stirling hit it off so well: Mayne was a Protestant Ulsterman from a poor background, had been educated at a grammar school and was socially awkward. Stirling was a Scottish Catholic aristocrat, Ampleforth- and Cambridge-educated and totally at ease in the highest of social circles. Lewes was 'academically brilliant ... exceptionally beautiful ... [but] quite humourless and very practical.'[45] If ever there was a way to illustrate the real strengths of diversity, this was it. Although so very different, each respected the others' strengths and made allowances for their shortcomings.

John Verney talked about this balance in *A Dinner with Herbs*:

> Your capacity was daily tested and exposed, and when the vital point arrived – there was no advantage to be gained by that or any other similar pretence. We pretty soon came to know one another's physical and mental capacities, and with them our own. Strength and skill were respected, and a fair degree of both were essential, but everyone recognised that there were other qualities, such as a cool head, or a good temper, that might well prove more valuable.[46]

What was disturbing about the raid was that the Germans had clearly strengthened airfield defences, 'by at least a division'.[47] And when they got back to the RV, they waited and waited. The LRDG was nowhere to be seen.

There was nothing to be done but 'hoof it out'. After waiting for four days, Fraser and his four companions set off on an epic eight-day journey to walk back to a British outpost at Hasselet, almost 200 miles. On 2 January they started walking, along the way stealing water and what food they could find. When their paths crossed, Bedou tribesmen helped them, giving them dates and water. It was down to the wire. Just as they started to run out of food again, they found some old tins of meat in a burnt-out German truck. Then they found some cans of pasta and were looking forward to a nourishing, hot meal when, not by enemy fire, but by their own Primus stove exploding, they nearly met an untimely end.

By mistake, they stumbled into some Italian positions and would not have made it back out had not a single Blenheim begun strafing the Italians. The bomber provided the diversion they needed to get through. On 10 January they finally made it back to their lines, looking so bedraggled that even their own men were not inclined to recognize them. The raiders were brought back in under guard, at the point of bayonets, by some very suspicious guards.

> We must have looked a grim sight. With our long matted hair and beards. Faces and hands caked in dirt and torn, ragged clothes. They must have thought we were a band of savages.[48]

Chapter 4

The 1942 Raids: North Africa and Crete

For the Allies, morale in the early months of 1942 was at its lowest, on just about every front: in Russia, in the Middle East where Rommel's Afrika Korps was steamrollering across the desert, and in the Far East where, following the destruction of the US Pacific Fleet at Pearl Harbor, Singapore, Hong Kong and the Philippines had fallen to the Japanese.

On 17 January, Stirling got underway for Bouerat, a little further west along the coast from Tamet, after he'd first gone through Jalo to pick up some of the men en route. 'Progress was slow owing to breakdowns and difficult country.'[1] On 25 January, an attack was planned on a large fuel dump. The four-team attack was meant to include a Folboat assault on shipping, but there was little shipping to be had as the intelligence had been old and, in any case, their Folboat – typically – was damaged. It might have been, as Asher points out, that they had made a mistake in assembling the boat beforehand and it was damaged in the back of the 15cwt Ford when going over some potholes. Mayne had not been convinced about the attack and in many ways he'd been right. Nevertheless, they did manage to destroy eighteen tankers, each one of which was loaded with 4,000 gallons of fuel. It was a well-timed raid. Two days before, on 21 January, Rommel had launched his attack to regain Benghazi, and the destruction of fuel and warehoused foodstuffs meant a significant loss to him of much-needed supplies.

The attackers were surprised at what sheer audacity could achieve: at one point, Riley and Sergeant Badger 'passed within a few yards of two Italians, who did not even speak to them.'[2] But they had had a close call as they were trying to get away; their Thompson machine guns, filled with desert dust, jammed. They only got out after heavy enemy mortar and machine gun fire was successfully suppressed by unleashing an answering hail of fire from one of the Vickers K.

On 31 January they were back in Jalo which, because of Rommel's latest advance, was in the process of being abandoned. Rommel's forces had retaken much of Cyrenaica and, because Stirling had been out of touch since losing his radio truck a week earlier, he had not known that the base at Jalo could no longer be used. Stores were being set on fire by men of G.2 patrol who, along with Stirling's raiders, went on to Siwa the next day.

Mayne did not go on the raid. After losing Lewes, Stirling had asked him to take over Jock's training role. Raw recruits were pouring into the unit and they needed to be brought up to standard quickly. In mid-January, Stirling had met Auchinleck and had been given the go-ahead to double his force, adding another six officers and forty men. Mayne was upset and took Stirling's request as a personal affront. Deep inside, there was rivalry between the two: Mayne felt that Stirling was trying to catch up with his own score of aircraft destroyed. There was little doubt that Mayne had had the lion's share, and there might even have been some truth to his suspicion. However, Stirling was his C.O. Mayne went off and 'sulked' in his tent, spending his time reading Penguin paperbacks. When Stirling got back, they had a blazing row. The Scotsman luckily realized that it was he who had made a gaffe. Mayne was his best operations officer, a natural combat leader, not a trainer. The row cleared the air.[3] Pat Riley, then a sergeant major, took over the training.

Mayne and Stirling buried the hachet. They spent some time talking, and Stirling discovered that Mayne had wanted to be a writer (he was keen on James Joyce). They had found their common ground: Stirling had wanted to be an artist.

But in the back of his mind, Stirling must have had some concerns. No training had taken place at all while he had been gone. 'It was fairly common knowledge', wrote Lorna Almonds, 'that Stirling did not think of Mayne as a 2i/c for the SAS.'[4] Mayne had his strengths *and* his weaknesses.

Some of the new manpower would come from the French. Jeff du Vivier, who spoke fluent French, and Johnny Cooper, who couldn't, took the French on board and helped them integrate. Cooper had just been awarded his DCM but was still seen as the 'kid'. Most of all, the French loved Bill Cumper, now a full Captain. He'd even taught them to swear in rhyming Cockney. 'Trezz beans' was his way of complimenting good performance.[5] There was not much love lost, however, between the French and Mayne. Augustin Jordan, Bergé's 2i/c, referred to the Irishman's love of killing by calling him '*le grand tueur*' (the great killer). Either that or, because of his size, '*l'armoire*' (the cupboard).

On 2 March, Stirling held a briefing in Alexandria, saying that he wanted to 'change the direction of SAS attacks'.[6] The next week, from 8 to 13 March, Mayne, newly awarded his third pip, led a series of attacks on airfields and installations in and around the port town of Benghazi. He was very nonchalant about the promotion when he wrote to his sister, Frances: 'I am becoming a Captain. I am rather sorry as I was fond of my two pips. I have had them a long time but it is back-dated to 1st September so it means a few extra shekels.'[7]

On 15 March, at 1000, the combined LRDG–SAS patrol left Siwa. It was a large raiding force – Stirling, Mayne, six SAS ORs, three SBS officers and three SBS ORs together with a Belgian, Captain Bob Melot and two ORs from the Senussi Regiment. Melot was 'a wonderful man', a 'fluent Arabic speaker … speaking the lingo is the key to that sort of work', Bob Bennett commented.[8] They set off from Siwa, guided by LRDG Second Lieutenant Olivey's S.2. patrol.

John Olivey would, at the end of 1943, end up on Leros fighting with Jellicoe in the Dodecanese islands. He greeted one of the newcomers, David Sutherland, in a typically jaunty manner: 'Good to have you with us. You're joining the best patrol in the business. To and from Benghazi will be like a Cook's tour.'[9] For Sutherland, it would turn out to be anything but. Inevitably, they talked about the loss of Jock.

As they crossed the miles of desert heading to Benghazi, they used an old camel route, the *Trigh-el-Abd*, known to have once been used as a slaving route. It cut days from the desert crossing.

In the scrub, Sutherland's car, an old Ford disguised to look like a German staff car, with an Afrika Korps palm tree emblem stencilled on, ran over an Italian Thermos bomb. Although he was only slightly wounded (as was Sergeant Moss), the injuries were bad enough for him to be sent back to Siwa while the rest of the group continued on to Benghazi. In the evenings, around an open fire, Mayne would sometimes instruct on small arms handling. One of those evenings was described in the SAS Diary:

> The party went into action with rum and lime, rum and tea, rum omelette and just plain rum … Captain Mayne went through the weird rites of how one should NOT fire and NOT take to pieces at night, MGs, LMGs, Tommy-guns, pistols and God knows what other intricate pieces of mechanisms. Casualties: Incredible as it may seem, nil.[10]

Three days of hard driving brought the raiders to Gasr el Gehese, six miles south-east of the port town. It was a convenient lookout point in the Djebel Akhdar, the 'Green Mountain' overlooking the airfield, from which one could scope out the operation's key entry and exit points. The Senussis and Bob Melot went forward to do a recce. By 20 March, they were ready.

As part of a four-man team with Bob Bennett, Rose and Byrne, Mayne hit Berka satellite (he'd actually planned to hit the main Berka field but was not able to). It was a well-planned operation. Bombs were placed on more than a dozen aircraft, some fuel dumps and twelve large aerial bombs. But they arrived late for the RV and had to hoof it for 30 miles. It wasn't that bad: Mayne loved the landscape. For him it wasn't as people imagined the desert: 'Some of the people who know the South Downs say that it is very like it – low hills and valleys, lots of wild flowers and grass.'[11]

Mayne and Bennett had waited for Rose and Byrne (who'd split up after disagreeing about which way to head) at the RV, but when they didn't show, made off on foot, intent on reaching Tobruk. Byrne ended up as a prisoner. En route, Senussi tribesmen – although suspicious at first – took care of Mayne and Bennett. By an extraordinary coincidence, Rose headed to the same Senussis, also intent on asking for their help, and was reunited with his fellow SAS.

On the evening of 21 March, Stirling headed to another airfield, Benina. When he found no aircraft, he went on to the port, arriving there in the early morning, at 0510. It was too late to plant any bombs, and the group headed back to Gasr el Gehese, where they lay up till the night of 24/25 March. When darkness fell, they went back to Benghazi. Once there, after the monumental effort of crossing hundreds of miles of desert, the equipment failed again. The Folboat was missing a piece and wouldn't unfold. Again, they headed back, and again passed the Benina depot, where thirty or so aircraft were reported. Looking forward to a good bag, they went back the next night, 26 March, only to find it empty apart from two Messerschmitt fighters and three other aircraft which were successfully dealt with.

Discounting Stirling's aborted raid on Benghazi, the other airfield raids mostly went well. At Barce, Fraser claimed one aircraft and four repair wagons. After leaving Siwa on the 16th with Gus Holliman's S.1 patrol, it had taken four days to reach Barce, only to find it empty again.

At Benina, five hangared aircraft were claimed, and at Berka, Mayne's efforts accounted for another fifteen. Separately (he was with Morris's T.1. patrol), Lieutenant Dodd's attack on Slonta was unsuccessful, while Fraser's other attack (he was taken in by Gus Holliman's S.1. patrol) on Barce could only claim one aircraft and a number of 'workshop' trucks No general attack was made as it was deemed to be too heavily defended. On 27 March, the group (minus Mayne's party) headed back to Siwa.

When they got back to camp, Stirling could do little else but think about what had gone wrong, in order to work on how to successfully raid Benghazi the next time. He had a new officer on board, now a Member of Parliament, Fitzroy Maclean. Stirling 'entrusted [him] with the task of experimenting with small collapsible rubber boats' to try and avoid another fiasco.[12]

In April, a small group of SBS were detailed to make an extensive beach reconnaissance along the Palestine/Lebanon border and along the border between Turkey and Syria. The success of von Kleist's armour in the Caucasus was starting to cause concern that a German push through Persia might be 'on the cards'. It's an interesting note on the interconnectedness of the different theatres of war.

The next month, May, Stirling returned to Benghazi with Fitzroy Maclean, Randolph Churchill and four others. With Robin Gurdon's G.2. LRDG patrol, they left Siwa on 15 May. They'd been briefed at the Naval Intelligence Office at Raz-el-Tin with all the latest details of intelligence and aerial photo recon. There was even a full-scale wooden model of what they would be attacking. They approached Benghazi again using the *Trigh-el-Abd*, headed north and then skirted east of the town to Msus. Very much as Mayne had, Maclean described the last part of the journey as feeling as though he were back home, it was so lush: 'We might have been in the Highlands of Scotland. We were driving across brownish-green hills and moorland thickly covered with scrub with, here and there, stunted trees.'[13] The whole area was populated by friendly Senussi tribes, who had no love for the Italians.

Stirling had not wanted Churchill to be included, but Randolph was relentless. Finally, Stirling weakened, and he was allowed to come along as an observer. It was only when one of the detonators went off in Seekings's hand that he came on fully as Reg's replacement. He was heavily overweight and even though he would lose over ten kilos, to Stirling's mind he was still 'damn fat'.[14]

Stirling had put up with Randolph because of his connections, most obviously with the Prime Minister, but also because he was a source of amusement; but he was quite prepared to slap him down when needed. Churchill drank a lot: one time, he handed Cooper what the latter thought was water. The 'kid' took a deep gulp of neat rum and spluttered. 'Captain Churchill, we never drink on ops', Stirling is supposed to have snapped 'icily'.[15] Roger Boutinot, one of the French Squadron, recalled that 'He used to bring a case of whisky every night and we put it in a big dustbin with some pineapple and mixed it all up. He was drunk all the time I met him outside my tent. He was fast asleep, completely nude.'[16]

On 21 May, after lying up all day 45 miles east of the port, the raiders left, all tightly packed into Stirling's Blitz Buggy, the two LRDG trucks following behind. It was a good night for the raid: 'there was no moon, but brilliant starlight.'[17] After parting with their escort, they drove into the town to find sirens wailing, an air raid in progress. At one point, it looked like they were being followed and Stirling stepped on the gas. Rose recalled, 'We were simply scorching along, whipping around corners on two wheels, and all the time making enough noise to raise the dead.'[18] They soon dumped the Blitz Buggy, with its 'distinctive screech' and filled it with charges planned to go off on a short time delay. Laden down with equipment, a sentry approached them. Maclean was a master of Italian and was completely unfazed by these obviously precarious moments. As though it were quite a normal occurrence, he asked the sentry's help: 'We have just met with a motor accident. All this is our luggage. Can you direct us to a hotel where we can spend the night?'[19] He might have been talking to a bell-boy at the Ritz. The audacity of it was extraordinary.

Mary Soames, Churchill's daughter, remembered Maclean as a man who combined the characteristics of ruthlessness and integrity with a sense of fun: 'He looked rather *douce* and benign – but benignity with a twinkle – an appearance which belied the steel and thirst for adventure.'[20]

When they were trying to inflate the infuriatingly useless rubber dinghies, another Italian challenged them. Without hesitation, Maclean 'tore a strip' off the poor man, deriding his slovenliness. It was frustrating to have planned so intricately, to have acted so audaciously and then be tripped up yet again because of poor equipment. And then, with only five minutes left before the charges were supposed to go off, Stirling decided to reclaim his car.[21] Johnny Rose said they only had seconds to spare: 'I didn't waste any time in chucking away the detonator, I can tell you! It landed on the other side of a wall and went off with a bang.'[22]

After the failure to inflate the rubber boats, time was running out again and the decision was taken to hole up for the day in a deserted house and wait for the next night. That proved impossible. There was too much security, and they had to pack it in.

Driving back from Benghazi in the 'buggy with nine lives', Stirling's group hit the Benina depot a third time. They left a couple of token bombs on two parked planes and machinery – 'no more than a pin prick', Cooper said, but Stirling and the boys were chuffed.[23] At 0600 on 23 May, the raiders rejoined their LRDG minders and were back in Siwa three days later.

Back in Alexandria, on 28 May the group went off together for a drive along the coast road to Cairo. With them was a journalist, Arthur Merton of the *Daily Telegraph*. Going far too fast in his beloved Blitz Buggy, Stirling lost control and rolled it over. Rose, Maclean and Churchill were all injured, Churchill's spine so badly that he had to be evacuated to Britain. Mayne's commentary was as forgiving as he could be: 'He was not a bad lad, plucky enough but very bad manners. He had done a couple of parachute jumps with us but is no athlete.'[24] When Maclean woke up, having been unconscious for three days, he found himself in a hospital bed in Alexandria with a broken arm and fractured collar bone. Stirling was hardly scratched, suffering just a sprained wrist. Merton, the only 'outsider', wasn't so lucky. He was killed.

Rommel's 26 May offensive soon overran Tobruk. It had withstood eight months of siege in 1941; now it fell in as many hours. Five generals and over

30,000 troops surrendered. With Axis victories in Libya, the decision was now taken to infiltrate Special Forces groups on to selected Axis airfields to find some way of relieving the pressure on Malta. The Malta commander made it clear to Churchill that the island couldn't hold out much longer – they were running out of all supplies – and Stirling was tasked with a series of airfield raids across the Mediterranean; most were in the Benghazi sector, around Derna, but there were others on Crete. It was the first real strategic use of the SAS.

Raids were organized by SAS and Special Boat Service elements throughout the western Mediterranean, timed to coincide with two important convoys. The two units, SAS and SBS, had frequently operated together,

> partly because of an identity of aim and partly through sharing of personnel and supplies. It was therefore logical that the efforts of the two units should be coordinated and that if the SBS was raiding a harbour, the SAS should be attending to a nearby airfield.[25]

But they had also started to change the role of the SBS, from beach reconnaissance and 'shore-side sabotage' to small-scale assault raiding. A struggle was on as to who would bring the various units under one wing. Stirling wanted to broaden his reach, while the units prized their continued independence – as did the SAS.

It was vital that the convoys got through, in whole or in part. One was coming from Gibraltar, the other from the east, on 11 June, from Alexandria. All convoys had to run the gauntlet of attacks from the air.

While the SAS were tasked with Benghazi, Barce, Martuba and Derna in Libya, the SBS raids would hit three Cretan airfields at Maleme, Kastelli and Tymbaki. A fourth raiding group, run by the French SAS, would target Prassos airfield at Heraklion. Stirling wanted to see what he could learn from SBS tactics.

The North African fields were divided up. The French would lead the raids on Heraklion, the two fields at Derna (Derna-West and Derna-East), Martuba (two fields, Martuba-5 and Martuba-3, inland and to the southeast of Derna), Barce and Berka-3, the main airfield; the British would take care of Berka-1 and Benina.

As always, the raiding parties would start out from Siwa. On 8 June, the three groups (led by Stirling, Mayne and Lieutenant André Zirnheld of the Free French) set out in seven 30cwt Chevrolet trucks and Stirling's Ford (which was destroyed two days later when it hit another Thermos bomb). Different LRDG groups supported the desert traverse – G.2. (Lieutenant Gurdon) supported Stirling, S.1. (Captain Holliman) the FFF Barce raid and R.1. (Captain Guild) the Martuba /El Dhaba raids, and the fourteen

Free French and thirteen SIG operatives commanded by Lieutenant Jordan and Captain Buck.

Malcolm Pleydell, the doctor, had only just arrived at Kabrit. He knew Jellicoe from the Coldstreams and found him full of 'nervous energy, the quick movements and restlessness that were so characteristic of him'.[26] As he was about to leave for another mission, Stirling's parting words to Pleydell were an apology for leaving him behind: 'I know it must seem awfully rude of us to push off like this just as you arrive.'[27]

The raid on Derna Airfield

The Derna/Martuba assault teams were made up of fifteen Free French as well as thirteen operatives from Herbert Buck's Special Interrogation Group (SIG).[28] A group of German-speaking Jews from Palestine had been put together initially to gather intelligence by mingling with enemy PoWs. Now they were given a chance to participate in an action that would take them behind enemy lines. It was a completely new role. Despite knowing what might lie in store for them should they be captured, they were enthusiastic. One of their number, 26-year-old Maurice 'Tiffin' Tiefenbrunner, who would survive the war and later took part in a film about the exploits of SIG, talked of his feelings as he was briefed:

> He said we would be trained by experienced people to behave like German soldiers, put on German uniforms and go into enemy territory and do intelligence as well as sabotage work ... This was one step further to my aim to hurt the Nazis as much as possible ... I and the other volunteers said we were willing to take the risk and go.

Like the others, Jordan's Free French team left Siwa on 8 June, Buck was in the leading car, a Kübelwagen, the classic militarized version of the Volkswagen, the Free French followed in a truck, and out ahead was the R.1. LRDG patrol. Three days later, on 11 June, they were dropped off ten miles north of Baltet es Zelagh (roughly 100 miles into the desert, SSW of Derna). The LRDG 'taxi drivers' promised to be back at the RV on 18 June.

SIG had been founded by Captain Herbert Buck, a 'highly intelligent man' under the aegis of MO.4, the name by which Special Operations Executive, SOE, was known in the Middle East.[29] He'd studied at Oxford and was a man of 'average physique and a thinker rather than a doer'.[30] He'd managed to escape by pretending to be more seriously injured than he actually was and then managing to evade capture by donning an Afrika Korps hat and simply sauntering through German and Italian troops as though he belonged. He thought that since he had done it, others could. No doubt, it helped that he could speak rudimentary Arabic.

The cover story was that Buck, travelling under the name of Hauptmann Heinz, was escorting a convoy of trucks from Agedabia to Derna and that he was to be given all assistance he demanded. These airfields were heavily guarded, and a new ruse was to be used. The SAS men would pose as prisoners being transported under guard. They would be travelling in captured Afrika Korps trucks and jeeps driven by SIG men. Inside each truck a mounted machine gun was hidden.

En route, the SIG changed into German uniforms to assume their new 'role' of escorts. One of their number, Brückner, drove one truck with nine Frenchmen in the rear; the other was driven by Buck, dressed as Hauptmann Heinz, along with Essner and more Free French and some other SIG. On top of each truck rode one SIG man behaving like a guard but acting as a lookout.

The SIG Germans, Walter Essner and Herbert Brückner, both of whom were non-Jews, had served in the French Foreign Legion and had been recruited by the British Combined Services Detailed Interrogation Centre (CSDIC) as double agents in November 1941. They'd been captured when fighting with the Afrika Korps' 361st Regiment.

Approaching their destination later the next day, 12 June, the group was stopped by an over-curious guard at an Italian roadblock who wanted to search one of the disguised trucks. Buck, pistol drawn, made it clear to the poor man that he could only proceed with such a search at his own peril. They continued, but knew now that they somehow had to get the password. Around midday, with Jordan driving, one of the trucks took off to have a closer look at the Derna and Martuba airfields, specifically Derna-West and -East, Siret el-Cheibra (Derna-South) and Martbuba-5 and Martuba-3. Inside Jordan's truck were his other team leaders, de Bourmont and Tourneret, along with Vidal and one of the Royer brothers.

Closer to the target, they were stopped at another Italian roadblock, where Buck casually asked for the challenge and password, using the excuse that they were tired and were coming back from combat at the front. Security seemed lax, even though the sentries had actually been warned about British commandos being on the loose.[31] As they were waved through they were helpfully informed that the required passwords were 'Siesta' and 'Eldorado'.

They drove by a number of invitingly full airfields – Me.110s parked at Derna-West (a signpost stated that they were Me.110 fighters of the 7th and 8th Squadrons) and a dozen Ju.87 Stuka fighter-bombers at Derna-East. However, they weren't able to get to Martuba-5. It was already getting late, around 1730, and they decided to return to the group RV.

Because of the incomplete recce, Jordan decided to re-allocate de Bourmont from Martuba-5 to Derna-West. Jordan's own group would attack Derna-East, while Corporal Tourneret would head for Martuba-3 with two of the Palestine Jews as drivers. The other trucks would take de Bourmont to Derna-West and then carry on with Jordan's team to Derna-East. At 2200 Jordan ran through the final planning with the groups.

At 2230 (12 June), they set off. Brückner was driving the truck heading to the two Derna airfields. On board with Jordan's team was de Bourmont's, the idea being to drop them off at Derna-West and carry on to Derna-East with his own men.

It seemed as though the engine was giving problems, and Brückner got out, opened the hood and started tinkering with it. As they arrived at the first stop, Derna-West, Brückner got out again, this time casually saying he was going to ask for a spanner. One of the Jews, Peter Haas, calmed the anxious French: '*Il est allé chercher un clé*' (He's gone to look for a spanner).[32] The next thing Jordan heard were shouts of '*Franzosen, raus!*', and a Frenchman was pulled out of the truck. Other Free French and SIG operatives were similarly dragged out.

After the French officer was forcibly pulled out, his men and the SIG operatives followed but, in the confusion, Jordan managed to slip away. From where he was hiding, he watched as Gillet, Prados, le Goff, James and Jouanny emerged with their hands above their heads. Peter Haas didn't. As a Jew, he knew what to expect if he were to be captured. He must have pulled the pin on a grenade, blowing up the truck in a massive explosion and killing himself with his last act. The Germans scattered as 'half a ton of explosive' went up.[33] As it did, le Goff was hit in the head and soon lost consciousness. 'Loulou', as le Goff was affectionately known, was very nearly bayoneted by one of the Germans who was stopped by an officer. Although Gillet, James and Jouanny were immediately taken prisoner, the Germans did not succeed in capturing everyone.

Tourneret's group, dropped off a couple of kilometres short of Martuba-3, heard the explosion from Derna-West and within minutes saw columns of troops racing towards the scene by truck. Tourneret made the decision to try and get back to the Buck RV. He arrived around 0500 and met up with de Bourmont and Marcel Drezen, who'd also both managed to get away, but they had walked into a trap: Brückner had clearly told the Germans everything he knew about the attack and the RV points to be used afterwards. Drezen was badly injured in the firefight.

At the Derna-West ambush, a few miraculously managed to evade immediate capture. Vidal got clear of the airfield but was taken prisoner on 13 June. Prados, in desperate need of water, gave himself up. The last,

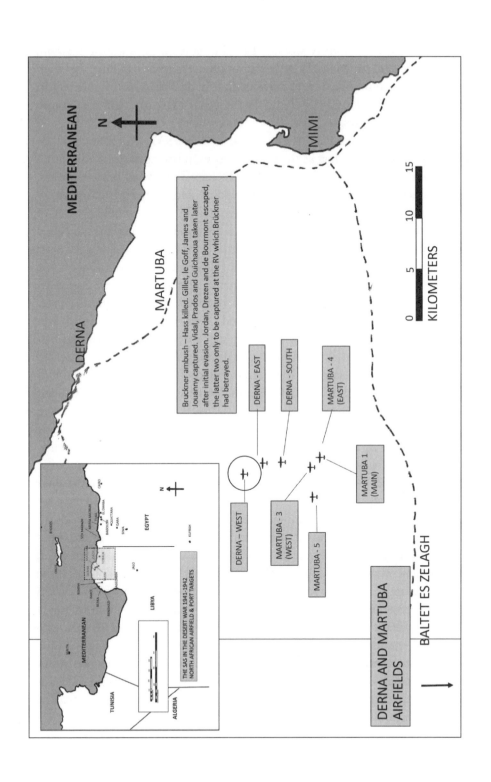

MEDITERRANEAN

N

DERNA   MARTUBA

Bruckner ambush – Hass killed. Gillet, le Goff, James and
Jouanny captured. Vidal, Prados and Guichaoua taken later
after initial evasion. Jordan, Drezen and de Bourmont escaped,
the latter two only to be captured at the RV which Bruckner
had betrayed.

TMIMI

DERNA - EAST

DERNA - SOUTH

MARTUBA - 4
(EAST)

DERNA – WEST

MARTUBA - 3
(WEST)

MARTUBA 1
(MAIN)

MARTUBA - 5

MEDITERRANEAN

RHODES

CRETE

SIDI BARRANI

BARDIA
EL ADAM
QUAITARA
SIWA

CAIRO

EGYPT

TUNISIA

LIBYA

ALGERIA

JALO

KUFRAH

N

THE SAS IN THE DESERT WAR 1941-1942
NORTH AFRICAN AIRFIELD & PORT TARGETS

DERNA AND MARTUBA
AIRFIELDS

BALTET ES ZELAGH

0   5   10   15

KILOMETERS

Robert Guichaoua, slightly wounded in the hand, continued the mission. Climbing aboard an Me.110, he left an unpinned grenade behind and then made for the mountains. He was picked up four days later, on 17 June, by an Italian patrol who found him lying on the road. He hadn't eaten or drunk any water in four days.

After Haas had blown up the truck at Derna-West, Jordan and de Bourmont ran away as fast as they could and soon became separated. Jordan waited at the north end of the airfield for his men, but it was clearly hopeless, and he decided to head back to the RV point. He waited till dawn on 19 June. Tieffenbrunner recalled Jordan's return: 'He was completely out of breath' and needed some time 'until he could speak' of what had happened with Brückner.[34]

When Buck and Jordan arrived back at Siwa on 21 June, the Frenchman appeared 'shrunken and disconsolate'. It was obvious that they had been betrayed. Brückner had managed to get away by using the spanner ruse, but Essner wasn't so lucky. After the raid, Essner would be handed over to the Military Police and shot while trying to escape. Tiefenbrunner had been suspicious of Brückner from the beginning and had kept a watchful eye on him. He felt that having the two of them along on the raid was 'too dangerous'.[35] Another SIG veteran from 51 Commando, Sergeant Major Israel Carmi, shared the concern.[36] Even Paddy Mayne had disliked Brückner, but for different reasons: the German sergeant 'revelled in obscene talk and gestures, especially after some drinking.' Mayne had apparently asked Brückner to stop using such language, and the German had muttered something under his breath which Mayne caught. Tommy Corps, a one-time boxer from Newcastle, intervened before Paddy could deliver an 'anaesthetic'.[37] Brückner had known just about everything there was to know.

The warnings were ignored. Tieffenbrunner's misgivings were conveyed directly to Buck by Isaac Levy, the British Army Jewish chaplain. However, it is possible that knowledge of the airfield raids might also have come from a far more unlikely source: American diplomatic channels. The US Military Attaché in Cairo, Colonel Bonner F. Fellows, had unwittingly signalled 'details of the coming airfield raids'. Unbeknownst to him, the Black diplomatic code was being read by the Germans.[38]

There was a real danger of more of the French being captured as a result of this betrayal. Jordan wasn't able to dwell on the fate of his comrades for long. Bergé's own betrayal and capture on Crete would now mean that he now took command of the French.

The Special Interrogation Group

The **Special Interrogation Group (SIG),** informally known as 'The Lions of Judah', was the brainchild of Captain Herbert Cecil A. Buck. Buck had been an officer in the Indian Army (1st Punjab Regiment) and had later joined the Scots Guards. From the Scots Guards came the unit's other source of inspiration, Lieutenant David Russell, who was, like Buck, a fluent German speaker. Buck had been captured in January 1942 and had escaped using the stolen uniform of the German uniform of a driver he'd killed. At Oxford he'd studied German, which he already spoke well (his father was British, his mother was German). In March 1942, his idea of more actively exploiting this deception was approved and he was put in charge of a group of fluent German speakers, largely recruited from émigré German Jews. On 17 March he selected the SIG team, mainly from 51 Commando.

51 Commando had been formed in Palestine and used as the core unit in the abortive October 1941 'Raid on Rommel', when 'no fewer than forty-three of the fifty-six commandos had been killed, wounded or captured' (*Scotsman*, 11 January 1999). Originally it was formed under the command of Lieutenant Colonel Henry J. Cator, who would later take over as the first overall Commander, Special Forces in March 1943. Others were recruited by Buck from the Jewish units, Palmach, Hagenah and the Irgun (like Dov Cohen), or even from the Free Czech Forces and the French Foreign Legion. The commandos were taught German weapons handling, intelligence gathering, sabotage and marching songs, and each was given a background story, a German Army pay-book (*Soldbuch*) and even fictitious girlfriends. It is said that many of their photos were of British ATS girls in Cairo. Striving for perfection, Buck took what he called 'a necessary risk for training purposes' and recruited two actual Afrika Korps privates as instructors, Walter Essner and Herbert Brückner. CSDIC had vouched for them. It would turn out to be a fatal mistake.

The unit consisted of around thirty-eight men and included Karl Kahane, 26-year-old Maurice 'Tiffin' Tiefenbrunner, Corporal Charlie 'Chunky' Hillman and Private Opprower. Kahane had served in the German Army and fought in the First World War; Tiefenbrunner had left Marseilles on a ship for Palestine with 950 other Jews in June 1939; Opprower's father had been taken from his home in Berlin to a concentration camp when Opprower was just sixteen years old. Tiefenbrunner's escape ran foul of the British, and when they refused to allow his ship to dock, he beached it on Tel Aviv beach and was temporarily (for two weeks) taken prisoner by the British before the declaration of war.

The immediate use for the group was intelligence: to mix with PoWs and pick up unguarded conversations. The group's arrival at the Siwa oasis on 7 June 1942 caused a small sensation. Their transport included an Afrika Korps Volkswagen and Opel truck and a British 3-tonner made to look as if it had been a captured trophy: it had the Afrika Korps palm tree logo stencilled on.

Most of their initial work focussed on gathering intelligence. In one of their first operations, they posed as Military Police on the Bardia road, stopped German military traffic and collected significant amounts of unit information.

Their first assault mission was with the SAS on 13/14 June 1942 on the Derna and Martuba airfields. It was a disaster. One of their number betrayed the party. In 2013, one of the last surviving members of the SIG died: Maurice Tiefenbrunner. He had originally objected to SIG taking in the two men who would later betray them. SIG was disbanded in September 1942 and absorbed into the ranks of the SAS. Tiefenbrunner had liked Buck's recruiting speech: 'He said we would be trained by experienced people to behave like German soldiers, put on German uniforms and go into enemy territory and do intelligence as well as sabotage work.' Fourteen Free French and two SIG operatives were killed or captured and, despite claiming twenty-seven planes destroyed at Martuba, 'after a sterling start the SIG had crashed and burned spectacularly.'[39]

Martuba Airfield

With the Derna groups heading off in one direction, the Martuba group headed south at 2230. They were dropped off two kilometres from their target. As they were sitting waiting, a series of explosions was clearly audible. Probably the RAF, they all thought. Shortly after, however, a large convoy was heard passing by, on the way to 'their' field.

When they arrived at the perimeter, something seemed wrong. It was clear that the airfield was '*bien sévèrement gardé*' (pretty strongly guarded).[40] The convoy they'd seen earlier had brought in additional troops.

At the moment they were to launch their attack, a wall of machine gun fire was unleashed which '*les "arrosèrent" copieusement de tires d'armes automatiques*' (sprayed them copiously with automatic weapon fire).[41]

The attack was called off and the decision taken to regroup at the RV point. Geiger suggested that they go on further to where the LRDG would

RV, around four hours march, but Tourneret, '*discipliné et respectueux à l'extrême des consignes et des ordres donnés refusa cette proposition*' (disciplined and extremely respectful of procedure and orders, refused the very idea).[42] He would go by the book and head for the local RV. His decision was fatal. Geiger and Jean Royer weren't at all convinced, but decided they could not disobey Tourneret.

Around 0500, just as they thought they were near the RV, two shadowy figures were seen. They dived for cover but soon recognized de Bourmont and Drezen. Now they understood the explosions: they were told about the ambush at Derna-West. Grabbing some rations off their trucks, the LRDG RV was now agreed upon by all as the better option. No sooner was the decision taken than light machine gun fire broke the silence.

They were surrounded. They tried to fight it out but had little weaponry apart from their pistols and Geiger's Beretta, for which he only had a couple of 10-round magazines. Drezen was wounded early on by a rifle bullet from a Mauser. The shot shattered his femur. With Drezen down and ammunition running out, Tourneret decided to surrender.

The prisoners were herded into a small shelter – two metres by three – ready for interrogation. They were surprised at the Germans' knowledge of the operation: '*les Allemands ayant appris des details qu'eux-mêmes ignoraient*' (the Germans already knowing details about which they themselves were ignorant).[43] They were stunned. An Italian officer now started abusing them, shouting at them and kicking them.

The rules of war did not seem to apply to the Free French. De Gaulle's government-in-exile was seen as renegade. The Axis only recognized Pétain's Vichy government. Their captors threatened a death sentence by firing squad:

> *Vous serez fusillés! Dès demain à l'aube. Vous êtes Gaullistes, des traitres à votre patrie.* (You'll be shot, starting tomorrow at dawn. You are Gaullists and as such, traitors).[44]

The French were taken from one camp to another. It would be a long journey into captivity. On 16 August, from the d'El Coffia camp near Benghazi, the remaining dozen Free French boarded a transport, the *Nini-Bixio*, one of two ships that had survived a severely attacked convoy. What had been purgatory now became hell: the very next day, 17 August, just after 1530, the ship's alarm was sounded and, on the hour, the first of two torpedoes hit her. The chaos was overwhelming, men desperately trying to climb out of the holds, scrambling over each other to climb on to the bridge, jumping into the sea. Almost 3,000 of the 7,000 prisoners who had embarked failed to answer the roll call when dry land was reached on 18 August at the Greek port of Pilos. Seven French SAS had disappeared. Prados had managed to dissuade Pierre de Bourmont and Lucien Geiger from jumping. He probably saved their lives.

De Bourmont, Vidal and Prados escaped to Switzerland and rejoined 2nd RCP. Two who'd been badly wounded – Le Goff and Drezen, who'd had his leg amputated – were both repatriated the following April to Alexandria and immediately sent to hospital in Beirut. For Drezen, a young dancer, it was a particularly cruel outcome. A few were lost at sea: Gillet, Jouanny, Tourneret, James and the brothers Georges and Jean Royer, who hadn't listened. Geiger, despite several attempts at escape, remained a prisoner of war till 1945. Robert Guichaoua, the only man who claimed an aircraft, died of dysentery. He was barely twenty. It was a terrible outcome to a meticulously planned raid, scuttled by deceit and betrayal.

Barce

Sixty miles to the north-east of Benghazi, another French patrol headed by Sous-lieutenant Jacquier, made its way to Barce airfield with the help of the LRDG's S.1. patrol. In the group were René Martin, Caporal-Chef Pierre Lagèze, Roger Boutinot and an Englishman, Sergeant Badger.[45] He'd been with Stirling since the beginning and had already participated in the mid-January Bouerat and March Barce raids, so knew the area. The Free French were dropped off far from their destination and walked through the night. At daybreak, they found themselves still on the Djebel, still a fair way from the target, and decided to rest up during the day.

That night, they started again, '*un parcours pénible et épuisant*' (a painful and exhausting journey), only arriving at Barce around 0200.[46] As Jacquier's party was approaching the airfield, all the aerodrome lights were on. Roger Boutinot, who accompanied the young officer, concluded early that it 'was clear that they were waiting for us'.[47] Brückner must have tipped them off about the other raids as well.

As they reached the field, an Italian sentry challenged them. Lagèze boldly replied, '*E Benito che ritorna della cantina!*'(It's Benito coming back from the canteen) and then continued singing in Italian. It was full of bravado and had more than a whiff of Fitzroy about it. Initially, the approach seemed to work. The Argentinian-born Lagèze, a fluent Italian and Spanish speaker, had been with Bergé from the beginning and had been at the Inchmery House camp at Exbury, Hampshire. Soon, however, it was clear that the Italians hadn't been taken in at all, and Jacquier took the decision to rapidly fall back.

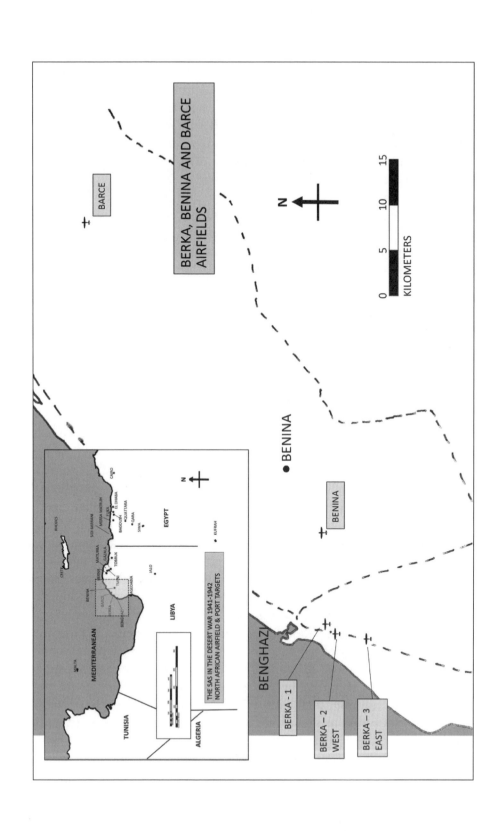

BERKA, BENINA AND BARCE AIRFIELDS

BARCE

N

KILOMETERS
0   5   10   15

BENINA

BENINA

BENGHAZI

BERKA – 1

BERKA – 2 WEST

BERKA – 3 EAST

MEDITERRANEAN

CRETE

RHODES

MALTA

TUNISIA

ALGERIA

LIBYA

EGYPT

CAIRO

SIDI BARRANI

MERSA MATRUH

FUKA

EL DHABA

QATTARA

QARA

BAGOUSH

SIWA

TOBRUK

DERNA

MATURBA

BARCE

TMIMI

BENINA

BENGHAZI

AGEDABIA

JALO

KUFRAH

N

THE SAS IN THE DESERT WAR 1941-1942
NORTH AFRICAN AIRFIELD & PORT TARGETS

They decided to use their bombs on some ammunition dumps they found as they were making their way off the field. When it came, the explosion was huge; so large, in fact, that the RAF concluded in a later recce the raid had actually been effective: '*constaté que l'explosion avait détruit 7 avions situés à proximité, et probablement endommagé quelques autres*' (surmised that the explosion destroyed seven planes parked nearby and probably damaged a few more).[48]

Berka-1 and Berka-3

Gurdon's LRDG, sometimes curiously known to the SAS as 'Carter Patterson' (the name of a British haulage firm at the time), dropped the Berka airfield raiders off around 30km from their target on the night of 11 June. For the rest of the night they marched and finally lay up within a few kilometres of the field. Berka would be hit by both British and French SAS raiders – Berka-1, the satellite, by Mayne, while Berka-3 would be André Zirnheld's target.

On Berka-1, the second time back, Mayne's group were caught on the tarmac as bombs started to go off. In the first raid in March, he'd claimed fifteen planes. This time, the Italians 'had learned to space their aircraft out on the airfields to make them less vulnerable to air attack and to assign individual sentries to each machine.'[49]

Explosions from the French attack on the nearby main airfield (Berka-3) alerted the field's security. Initially, the enemy guards were confused, and when explosions were heard from the adjacent airfield, Italians and Germans opened fire on each other by mistake. The team – Bob Lilley, Arthur Warburton and Private Storie – could do little but take cover and pray. When Italian sentries spotted them right out on the open tarmac, a fierce firefight developed, and soon grenades were being used at close quarters.

Before leaving, they managed to destroy a few more aircraft on top of what the RAF had already hit, although one French account records, '*Ils n'ont pu détruire qu'un seul avion*' (They were only able to destroy a single plane).[50]

André Zirnheld's group might have caused some of the confusion since, according to Storie, they 'went in an hour before their time.' They arrived at the edge of the base around 2300 while the RAF was pummelling Benghazi, and at 2330 they went in after Victor Iturria had taken care of two Italian sentries.

As Fauquet was placing the Lewes bombs, Bouard and Zirnheld were being covered by Jean le Gall, the small Frenchman they all called '*le p'tit Jean*', 'considered a crack shot *(un tireur d'élite)*, perhaps the best of the *1ere*

Compagnie.[51] They were able to destroy six aircraft that night, while the RAF's attack might have taken another ten. Only Bouard was slightly wounded.

After the attack, Zirnheld's group joined back up with Mayne to their north, and the following evening, 14 June, the two rejoined the LRDG. All were back except for Corporal Warburton. After the raid, he and Lilley had separated and Warburton was later captured. Mayne and Storie met up later with Lilley at a Senussi campsite.

Benina

This time, Stirling was lucky. The three raiders – Stirling, Johnny Cooper and Reg Seekings – slipped quietly into the Benina Repair depot. It was his third raid on it. Stealth was essential, but as Cooper and Seekings pushed the huge hangar doors back, 'the rollers creaked' loudly.[52] They all froze, certain that the awful noise had alerted the guards. But there was no challenge.

As they entered, Stirling went to the left and Cooper to the right. All of a sudden Cooper heard, 'All right, Cooper, this one's mine. You go into that far corner and use it on that Ju.52.'[53]

Cooper had little choice but obey his C.O. They looked inside the other hangars, and in the third Seekings found thirty promising-looking crates. When opened, they were found to contain what looked like new aircraft engines carefully packed. While Seekings stood guard, Cooper and Stirling planted their bombs.

Leaving the field, Stirling did something he later regretted – 'a silly show of bravado', an act even he described as being 'close to murder'.[54] He opened the guardhouse door, rolled in a Mills 36, shouting 'Share this amongst you!' The grenade rolled under the sleeping guards' beds, killing most while they slept. It was quite likely that he'd been high on Benzedrine, speed, taken to keep alert and awake on long operations. He'd been complaining of a massive headache, a tell-tale sign, although he'd suffered from headaches frequently since his first bad parachute drop.

This act was very unusual for Stirling. His men understood that, although Reg Seekings tried hard to persuade Stirling that this kind of terror was appropriate and had a purpose: 'Your average soldier's not bothered about equipment. A tank blown up means nothing to him. There's more where that came from. But finding his mate dead in the morning – that hits him hard.'

After the Bouerat raid, the Germans bombed Kabrit, and Seekings saw his opportunity as Stirling dismissed the loss of aircraft, thinking of the dead. The penny dropped: 'Damn it, you're right, Reggie ... yes, I see what you mean, damn it.'[55]

Learning from the SBS: the Heraklion raid

After agreeing to join Stirling, Jellicoe immediately relocated to Kabrit. When Malcolm Pleydell arrived at Kabrit on 6 June, Jellicoe was already there. He was soon quickly immersed in training his men, 'making ... horrible bangs on the beach'.[56]

When David Sutherland was initially briefed by Mike Kealy, the latter thought the omission of Heraklion from the targets 'odd'. He was to target Malame along with Ken 'Tramp' Allott and Cyril Feebery, 'a bull of a man'.[57] Kastelli would be George Duncan's responsibility, while Sutherland and Riley were assigned Tymbaki.[58] The Kastelli raid would claim German lives and secondary targets (like ammo and fuel dumps); Tymbaki turned out to be an intelligence failure – there were no aircraft on the field; and Maleme was so heavily guarded that Kealy decided against an attack, despite having brought with him eight New Zealanders who knew Crete well from the previous year. There were so many guard dogs patrolling that 'the place sounded like Crufts on show day.'[59]

No mention of Heraklion. Crete was mainly an SBS operation, but Stirling wanted to learn from their 'experience'.[60] He worked behind the scenes to get one of the targets re-assigned to his unit. Heraklion was going to be the 'first SAS seaborne operation' and Jellicoe's first major operation.[61] Duncan's raid on Kastelli with SBS men from M section succeeded in blowing up a bomb dump. The Kastelli raid bagged another eight aircraft, six trucks, four bomb, seven petrol and two oil dumps. The explosions were so massive that 'at least 70 Germans were killed.'[62] There were no aircraft at Tymbaki; it had been abandoned. Maleme was 'so heavily defended they just could not get onto it'.[63] When the Germans assaulted Crete in May 1941, they had lost so many *Fallschirmjäger* (paratroopers) in the battle for Maleme that 'they had no intention of allowing infiltration.'[64] That left Heraklion.

It's been said that Jellicoe was selected to accompany the 'quick-witted' Georges Bergé for two reasons: 'first he spoke fluent French', but that he also 'knew Crete well', is wrong, I think. As far as I know, he had never been there.[65] It seems as likely that it was because the French would need help with the Navy, and Jellicoe clearly had, as he said, 'rather easy access'.[66] Just before the raid, Fitzroy Maclean met Jellicoe, by now a Captain, and Bergé in Alexandria at the start of June: 'Jellicoe at this stage of his career was about 23 years old, brown as a nut, with a nose like the Iron Duke's, [and] an extensive capacity for irony.'[67]

At dusk on 4 June, the group started to prepare. They were then taken to Cairo by truck and out to the Greek submarine HMS/M *Triton* by the M/S *Corinthia*, which they had boarded the previous evening, 6 June. She was one of six submarines built by the French between 1927 and 1930. The next day, Sunday, as dusk was falling, the group embarked on the *Triton*.[68] They made the RV outside of Alexandria harbour, away from prying eyes.[69] The submarine was apparently 'pretty ancient' and 'getting a bit long in the tooth'.[70] Her commander, Kontoyannis, a 30-year-old Lieutenant, was 'absolutely first rate', Jellicoe later remembered.[71]

The plan was to surface just east of a small island, Dia, north of Heraklion. From the sub the group would paddle ashore on to a beach at Karteros, just 3km or 4km to the east of their target, the airfield.

The three-day trip went without major incident. Capitaine Bergé used the time to study and re-study their maps and the little photo recon material they had, and to make sure their equipment was sorted. Jellicoe wasn't, however, particularly pleased or impressed by his companions. He once complained that the Free French ate melons on board and threw the rinds on the deck, causing some strong words to be uttered when the Greek crew members slipped on them.[72]

In the group were four Free French and a Greek guide and interpreter, a young Cretan Lieutenant, Kostas Petrakis, known as 'Costi'. The unit's overall commander was Bergé, and with him were three other Free French: Corporals Pierre Léostic, Jack Sibard and Jacques Mouhot. All had been on the gruelling Heliopolis raid in March.

(I met Jack Sibard [he hated being called 'Jacques'] in March 2018. Aged ninety-seven, he was living just outside Bordeaux with his wife. We talked non-stop, for more than six hours. I was astonished at his lucidity and recall of facts. It was far better than that of most younger people. Jack was proud of being Corporal Sibard but he corrected me, abruptly: '*Caporal – chef*'.)

None of them thought that he was going to be chosen when Stirling announced the targets and teams. Sibard, who later wrote about the events, was '*inquiet et déçu*' (worried and disappointed) and went to see Bergé to voice his feelings.[73] He was one of the early French squadron members. In fact, as No.34, he was only one place behind Bergé's 2i/c, Jordan, and was at Kabrit before Zirnheld.

Bergé immediately reassured him, saying that he would be going on another mission, '*la plus dangereuse*', elaborating, '*elle sera pénible*' (it will be tough). Given that this was Sibard's first combat mission, it must have been somewhat unnerving, although he had already proved his courage at sea when he'd been torpedoed at the end of May 1940.[74] Bergé gave them all ample warning.

Bergé had just been promoted. He was superstitious and, on the second night, when he told them, he also said that he would only feel that he'd earned his new rank after they'd successfully pulled off the mission.

Je dois vous signaler que j'étais promu commandant avant l'organisation des missions. Mais je ne voulais faire état de cette promotion qu'au de retour de notre mission. Quand nous aurons réussi à faire sauter les avions, vous pourriez m'appeler 'commandant' (I should tell you that I have been promoted to major and will be in charge of organizing operations. But I didn't want this promotion to take effect until we have returned from the mission. When we have succeeded in blowing up the planes, then you can call me 'major').[75]

Léostic had lied about his age when he had joined the Free French in England aged sixteen. When 'Pierrot', as he was known to his friends, arrived at Kabrit, barely eighteen, he 'usurped Jonny Cooper's place as the "kid"', and Bergé had clearly taken him under his wing.[76]

On the afternoon of 10 June, they arrived at the drop-off point and surfaced. They couldn't stay long above water, however: around 1600 the boat had to dive deep, to around 60 feet (according to one of the French accounts, 42 metres),[77] as they were nervous of aerial detection; a German convoy was seen approaching and passed overhead. After two hours they surfaced again. For Mouhot, a heavy smoker and used to the outdoors (he'd been a ski instructor), being trapped inside the sub was very tough, *'irrespirable'* (unbreathable) as one account puts it.[78]

From the drop-off point they made as close an inspection of their target as they could through the periscope. Luck was with them: *'J'ai constaté qu'il y a beaucoup des avions au sol'* (I saw that there were many aircraft on the ground).[79] Bergé and Jellicoe would land the group from the submarine in darkness, just after midnight.

Drifting quietly, the sub was around 10km north-east of Heraklion. In the darkness, the dinghies were taken up on deck and, with the help of the sailors, inflated. Suddenly, as Lieutenant Kontonyannis stood on the bridge of the submarine waving the group off, there was a sharp burst of gunfire. Everyone held their breath, but it was only AA directed at an RAF raid. Jellicoe, Petrakis and Mouhot went in the first of three dinghies, all of them 'captured German rubber boats';[80] Bergé, Sibard and Léostic in the third. The second was loaded with the group's ammunition, explosives and stores.

Not only were they going to be far from shore – they should have been a mile off, rather than three – but a very strong easterly current was running. It would be a long haul. When they touched land, they'd been pushed roughly 30km eastwards down the coast to the Gulf of Malia. The beach at Karteros would have been, at most, a couple of kilometres south-east of the airfield.[81] Milatos beach was almost 40km away. It was an inauspicious beginning.

As they landed, one of the three rubber boats started to leak badly, and Jellicoe, 'always very nattily dressed, sacrificed his best service dress cap as a bailer.'[82] After all the boats had been weighed down with stones, Jellicoe and Mouhot stripped, swam out and sank them.

Back on his native soil, Petrakis was overcome with emotion, tears in his eyes as he touched the ground, murmuring *'Patrida, Patrida'. 'L'émotion de notre ami nous a touché profondement'* (The emotion of our friend touched us deeply).[83] It was around midnight.

Each man was laden with Lewes bombs (Sibard was carrying sixteen of the eighty they had brought), often an Italian Beretta sub-machine gun and a Colt .45, ammunition, two grenades and rations; some also carried radio batteries, and each had a survival kit. The rations were basic: dates, raisins, bully beef, hard tack and chocolate. Sibard didn't like the 40-round Beretta 38 and also carried a Special Forces 'knuckle-duster' knife. Bergé had insisted on the stock of his Beretta being cut off, which made the gun less accurate and less easy to control. Before leaving, Pleydell had been asked by Jellicoe to put together some emergency kits 'in a waterproof covering' which would include salt, morphia tablets, vaseline and dressings.[84] In the desert, an 'essential rubber tube for condensing salt water drop by drop' was normally included but it was probably left out as Jellicoe wanted the kit to be 'as small as possible'.[85] The kit also included a small saw and a map printed on a silk scarf. (I still have my father's map outlining the Adriatic and Aegean.) In both Jellicoe's and Sibard's opinion, they each 'had far too much heavyweight equipment.'[86]

The Free French SAS

Who Dares Wins / Qui Ose Gagne

As France disintegrated in May and June 1940, two rival camps emerged. Marshal Pétain signed the Armistice with Germany on 17 June declaring that France should collaborate; General de Gaulle, the very next day, broadcast the new resistance message from London. When he was officially recognized as the leader of France's Government in exile, he had fewer than 2,000 men under his command in England.

On 29 June de Gaulle visited Trentham Park Camp. From the 14,000 men of the French Norwegian expeditionary force, only 200 stayed behind in England; the majority went back to Morocco or were repatriated to France on 1 July, two days before the terrible events of 3 July 1940, when the British fleet sank the French fleet at Mers el-Kébir.

Captain Bergé went to see de Gaulle the day after he'd arrived from Saint Jean de Luz. With the latter's blessing, he formed the first French parachute unit on 15 September, the *1ère Compagnie de l'Infanterie de l'Air* (*1e CIA*), which moved to Manchester's Ringway training centre in November. In February 1941, the men were trained and started their first missions. Working with SOE, one of the first tasks was to destroy a bus carrying pilots from a *Kampfgeschwader* (bomber unit) (100) in Meucon. In June a group was sent to blow up the electrical power station at Pessac which powered a German submarine base.

By May the unit comprised one hundred men (nine officers, ten NCOs, seventy other ranks) and now included new recruits like Roger Boutinot, Jean le Gall, Louis le Goff and Émile Logeais. The same month, the unit was moved to Exbury in Hampshire, where they were based at Inchmery House, opposite the Isle of Wight. In July they were embarked for Africa and arrived in Beirut 23 September, finally reaching the SAS camp at Kabrit on 1 January 1942. It had been a long journey. They now became L Detachment's 3rd Squadron, the Free French Squadron.

Under the command of Commandant Bergé and his 2i/c, the 31-year old Lieutenant Augustin Jordan, the Free French formed a group in the desert. Jordan had managed to get to Britain from North Africa, where he'd served in the Colonial Service, in 1940. Jellicoe was particularly close to Jordan, whom Jack Sibard regarded as being the real 'brains' in the Free French. Jordan was multilingual – he spoke English, German and Spanish – and was also a very good night sky navigator. Bergé, who had served in one of the original French parachute units, the *601ème Compagnie d'Infanterie de l'Air*, had escaped France after Dunkirk. Later. Stirling would acknowledge Bergé as one of the founders of the SAS, but in my conversations with Jack Sibard, the latter was less than complimentary about the French SAS founder. He was hopeless at navigation and not a strong tactical leader. Jordan was.

The lack of equipment and access to aircraft made an approach to Stirling the rational solution. While his men had been parachute-trained, Bergé demonstrated the validity of what David Stirling would put together already in January 1941 when, together with the LRDG, with twenty-five men in five trucks, they successfully raided the Italian air base at Murzuck in western Libya. When the Free French arrived at the Kabrit 'Combined Training Centre' on 2 January 1942 to form 'The French Squadron', they were met with great enthusiasm by the British – they were not only fellow parachutists, most of them were seasoned troops, some of whom had already fought in the battle of France and in Norway. They were special. All of them had decided to fight on and not surrender.

Those that left England in July 1941, a heavy toll was exacted: five of the nine corporals and seventeen of the thirty-nine other ranks would die in combat over the next years.

Petrakis, dressed as a civilian, took the lead position as guide. It was 'extraordinary rough-going', Jellicoe said.[87] The six-hour march through the night was gruelling: *'le cheminement est extrêmement pénible'* (the going was extremely tough).[88] The French (Jellicoe decided against it) dumped some of the heavy loads, but the rough journey was made psychologically worse by the fact that their nationality was correctly – and almost immediately – detected by the Cretans whom they encountered, despite their speaking German as a ruse.[89] They stood out that much. At one point they stopped to listen to the RAF bombing Heraklion. It was to be the final air raid before the SAS attacked on the ground. By the next morning, they were still a good ten miles from the target and decided to hole up for the day in a cave. Sibard was the first assigned to take guard.

At dawn on 11 June they awoke to see that their hideout was very close to a group of peasants in the vineyards, *'à quelque centaines de metres de notre refuge'* (a few hundred metres from our hideout) in Sibard's account. Petrakis went over to them to see what information he could glean and was, seemingly, convincing enough: *'Il se fait passer pour un maquisard cretois'* (He passed for a Cretan partisan).[90]

Jellicoe and Bergé sat outside shivering in the cold early light of the Cretan morning. They were both of them buoyed up by Jellicoe's Benzedrine, while the rest of the group slept.

That night, they set off again. Bergé had thought that they could reach their target by dawn and they finally got to the southern perimeter of the airport just before 0300, 12 June. It was too late to attack, and they decided to hole up in a large cave throughout the day and work through the details and organization once again.

That night, they left their new hideout, leaving some of the weapons behind so as to be light and agile as possible. They were each armed with a Colt or Beretta and a knuckle-duster dagger. The Frenchmen left their telltale berets behind, fearing that their outline could give them away. Jellicoe, however, was not to be persuaded to give up his officer's hat:

Lord Jellicoe a tenu a conserver sa coiffe dont aucun officier de sa Majesté ne saurait – n'est il pas vrai – se séparer (Lord Jellicoe was determined to keep the hat from which an officer of His Majesty could not be separated)[91]

Once in position, overlooking the airfield, they stopped to assess the target. Attentively, they watched the sentries pacing through their designated zones, '*le cent pas*' (a hundred paces).[92] When they thought they'd got the timing down, they moved forward towards the outer road. Their clothing was making a terrific racket brushing against the dry bushes, and their clambering, despite the utmost care, set off landslides of pebbles. The noise ('*des pierres qui dégringolent bruyamment*' – stones which rattled loudly[93]) had a chilling effect on the men: they all froze. The other raids on the island had really stirred up the sentries, who appeared to have been alerted. They could not believe that they hadn't been heard. They tried again. But the route was impossible.

With only an hour to go before the sun came up, Bergé decided to postpone the attack, observe the field during the day and try again that night. Sibard said it was 'wise'.[94] With day breaking and all suffering from thirst, Mouhot and Sibard went off to find water – not from a stream, but at a peasant's house, pretending to be Germans: '*Wasser bitte!…Nero, Nero*'.[95] Despite their efforts, it was unlikely that anybody was taken in. They went back to their hide, where Petrakis was waiting for them. He looked in horror as they arrived without Bergé or Jellicoe, but they explained that they were fine and that had decided to hold off the attack.

Sibard and Mouhot continued their search for food and water and were successful at finding both. A young girl helped them get water out of a deep well, and they were able to enjoy a meal of fresh lamb at a mill near the hide.

They planned to attack after midnight, at around 0100 on the morning of 14 June. While the men slept, Bergé and Jellicoe noted the visible enemy dispositions, where planes were most concentrated and where they were most vulnerable. They planned to go in at the south-west corner, target the easternmost aircraft concentrations and leave by the same general route.

From their vantage point overlooking the field, they counted sixty-six German bombers.[96] (When I went back there with my father I walked to where he thought they had been, on a large rounded hillock with a complete view over the target.) Most of the aircraft were twin-engine Ju.88's. The aircraft had true multi-purpose characteristics. The Germans knew it as a '*Mädchen für alles*' (maid of all work); it could function as 'a bomber, a night fighter, a heavy fighter, a reconnaissance aircraft and even as a torpedo bomber'.[97] There were also triple-engine Ju.52s and fighters, Me.109s.[98] To keep going, Bergé and Jellicoe took more Benzedrine, while the men ate plums and grapes. This was a very bad mistake; before long they were writhing on the ground, suffering severe colic.

Despite the obvious difficulty, they grabbed some sleep, and when they awoke again ran through the briefing materials one last time, along with the intelligence photos.

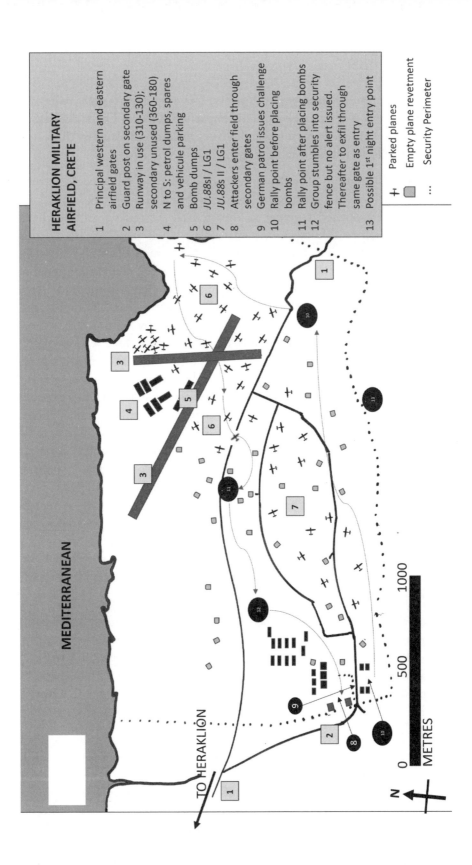

HERAKLION MILITARY AIRFIELD, CRETE

1 Principal western and eastern airfield gates
2 Guard post on secondary gate
3 Runway in use (310–130); secondary unused (360–180)
4 N to S: petrol dumps, spares and vehicule parking
5 Bomb dumps
6 JU.88I / LG1
7 JU.88s II / LG1
8 Attackers enter field through secondary gates
9 German patrol issues challenge
10 Rally point before placing bombs
11 Rally point after placing bombs
12 Group stumbles into security fence but no alert issued. Thereafter to exfil through same gate as entry
13 Possible 1st night entry point

✝ Parked planes
◻ Empty plane revetment
··· Security Perimeter

MEDITERRANEAN

TO HERAKLION

N

0   500   1000
METRES

L'attaque est prévue pour ce soir. Étudiant une dernière fois les photos de la base aérienne, il est entendu que nous attaquerons côté sud (The attack was to be this evening. Studying the photos of the airfield for a last time, it was decided to attack from the south).[99]

Around 2200, a group of Ju.88s came back down. The pilots could be seen quite clearly, obviously recounting a successful raid to the ground crews.

They were crouched together as they moved forward in an arrowhead formation, each man hugging the next as closely as possible: *'tête dans les jambes du précedent'* (head against the legs of the man in front).[100] Finally the group, minus Petrakis, were able to penetrate the airfield's perimeter, advancing very slowly and with maximum stealth, Bergé in the lead. They had 'almost cut their way through, with Bergé at the head of our file and Jellicoe at its tail', when a passing patrol, alerted by sounds, came over. Jellicoe said, 'I thought that the patrol had not seen us. But I was wrong.'[101]

A torch shone out, catching them in its beam.[102] One of the enemy patrol, Jellicoe continued, 'stopped within a foot of [my] head.'[103] They were saved by Corporal Mouhot's quick thinking. The Breton started to snore loudly – 'ghastly, lingering, drunken'.[104] What he did was 'inspired', said Jellicoe. It was clear that he and 'the Lord' hit it off. Mouhot described Jellicoe as having a face that was *'ouvert et franc'* (open and frank) and said that he *'me félicite de mon à propos'*, congratulated him for his quick-thinking.[105] (Jellicoe was also known as 'Curly', 'His Reverence' or 'The belted Earl'.)[106]

He openly admitted that he had no idea of what to do – throwing a grenade would have neutralized the patrol but ended the operation. Surrender, the same. The German, however, took Mouhot's theatrics as a reassuring sign merely of the presence of a drunken Cretan. Mouhot later said that the guard had even treated him with a degree of brotherly understanding for his drunken state:

L'allemand me pousse d'un pied amical, fraternal, éteint sa torche électrique et rejoint ses camerades en me gratifiant d'une phrase à laquelle bien sûr je ne comprends rien, sinon, que, dans le ton, elle n'est pas hostile, mais plutôt complice, comprehensive. (The German gave a friendly tap with his boot, turned off the torch and rejoined his comrades, talking of me in a way I don't understand but know, from the tone, not to be hostile, more friendly.)[107]

Once they were about twenty yards in, the small group hid in a building that turned out to be a bomb store. An RAF Blenheim then came in to drop its load of bombs on eight landing Ju.88s. Sibard had a nice turn of phrase to describe it: *'Le RAF va encore pilonner la base'* (The RAF was going to hammer the base again). They used the confusion to plant their 90-minute stick charges on a group of sixteen Ju.88s. Mouhot and Sibard placed the charges, with Bergé, Jellicoe and Léostic covering them. Mouhot jumped on to Sibard's back to reach high enough (the wings could be twelve feet from the ground). By the second plane a sentry was sleeping. Mouhot was unfazed and stuck the Lewes bomb near the fuel tanks.

They were about to cross the runway to a larger group of planes, but backed away when armed guards were seen. Instead, they found another six targets by one of the hangars. There was also one small plane, a reconnaissance Fieseler Storch, that they included in the 23-plane 'bag'. The Blenheim's arrival was not by chance. It had already been agreed that had the airfield not been dealt with on the first night – which it had not because of the problems of the landing – but that the RAF would have a go.

Sighting some hangars, Jellicoe, 'avec son flegme britannique' (with British phlegm), went off alone.[108] Once there, he found crates full of engine parts in which he left some Lewes bombs. He did the same with some trucks.

Mouhot was not through with his job when his first bomber exploded. The Lewes bombs had gone off faster than they thought. They had set them on 90-minute delay, but the Blenheim attack had delayed them on the ground. However, the Germans did not react as though a ground attack was in progress. They must have thought the explosions were caused by delayed action aerial bombs ('bombes à retardement') from the Blenheim.

The SAS group then breezily walked out by the main gate, following around a dozen German garrison troops and pretending to be part of the armed guard. As they left, they laid even more charges on any truck they came across. It was now around 0230.

Finding the other aircraft as they were leaving, a total of nineteen twin-engine Ju.88 bombers, a single Dornier 17 (the so-called 'Flying Pencil'), an Me.109, a single-engine Fiesler Storch, four trucks and a petrol dump were destroyed using Lewes bombs.[109] As they withdrew to their cave, more explosions were heard.

Outwardly, Jellicoe was overjoyed with the results. He clapped Mouhot on the shoulder; the former swimming instructor at the Molitor baths in Paris had saved the day: 'Bravo Mouhot! Grace à vous la mission a réussi' (Bravo Mouhot! Thanks to you the mission has been a success).[110] Privately, he thought that they could have done better. He wrote in his report that 'The target was a fat and sitting bird. I feel that the results achieved were not commensurate with the opportunity presented.'[111] If the RAF had not bombed, they felt he could have bagged more.[112]

As they headed out into the night, Jellicoe noticed that the Pole Star was not where it should have been. Bergé had become confused and had led them north in error. The rendezvous point was already a minimum of 60km to the

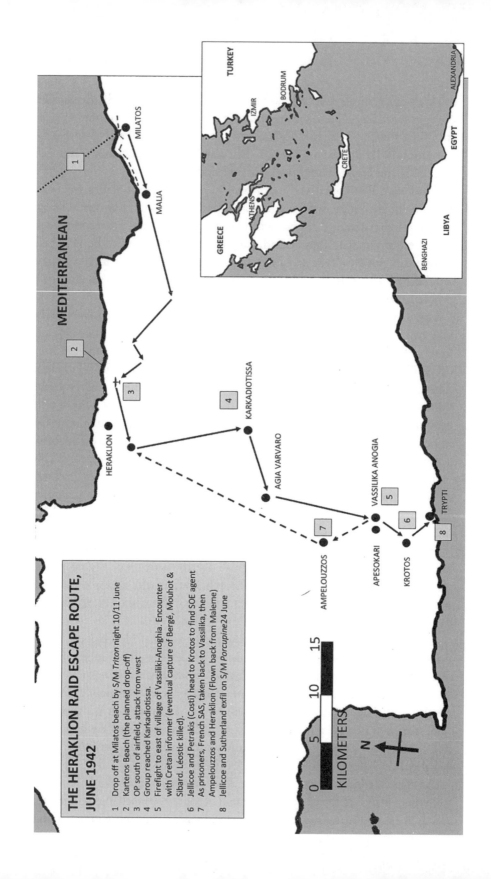

THE HERAKLION RAID ESCAPE ROUTE,
JUNE 1942

1   Drop off at Milatos beach by S/M *Triton* night 10/11 June
2   Karteros Beach (the planned drop-off)
3   OP south of airfield, attack from west
4   Group reached Karkadiotissa.
5   Firefight to east of village of Vassiliki-Anoghia. Encounter
    with Cretan informer (eventual capture of Bergé, Mouhot &
    Sibard. Léostic killed).
6   Jellicoe and Petrakis (Costi) head to Krotos to find SOE agent
7   As prisoners, French SAS, taken back to Vassilika, then
    Ampelouzzos and Heraklion (Flown back from Maleme)
8   Jellicoe and Sutherland exfil on S/M *Porcupine* 24 June

south over very rough terrain. On the 17th they reached the small village of Karkadiotissa. Petrakis went to find some food and was rewarded by a shepherd who gave him a small sheep. Two other Cretans acted as guides to take them further south. Marching through the night of the 18/19th, they made it to nearly 20 kilometres north-east of where they wanted to be. That evening, Petrakis and Bergé came back '*les bras chargés de victuailles*' (arms full of food).[113] They did not stay long as they didn't feel comfortable with the location. Instead, they carried on and crossed the Mesara plain, east of Tymbaki, which had been assigned to Sutherland. It was 'the only really difficult bit because it was very open there' and offered little cover for the roughly seven or eight kilometres they had to navigate.

The group chose a spot a little to the east of a small hamlet, Vassilika-Anoghia. In the valley, two Cretans found them lying up. They offered to go and bring back wine and food, an offer gladly accepted. When they did come back, another man was with them. My father thought him 'very nice', and Petrakis had told them not to worry as he knew the man and that he came from the same village. Bergé, however, was 'suspicious of him'. He turned to Petrakis and said, 'There's something about that man I didn't like.'[114] The man had, Cowles recalled, 'dancing eyes, and nervous, artistic hands'.[115] As they were eating, the new Cretan left rather than sit and share their food.

It was now midday and the men took advantage of the shade of the olive trees to grab some sleep. It was then, as they slept, that Bergé asked Jellicoe to push on ahead with Petrakis to make contact at the RV point in Krotos. Bergé had originally tasked Sibard but had changed his mind while the latter slept.

Around 1500, Jellicoe and Costi left the group and headed to Krotos, around 6km (as the crow flies) further south. There they were to meet a shepherd who could put them in touch with an SOE agent, 'a certain Miroyannis', who could signal their submarine, which should have been on the coast 3km further south.[116] Over the hills, the distance was considerably longer and tougher.

Sibard woke up at about 1800 and started to get the others up. The disappointment he felt in not having been chosen by Bergé to go with Costi was quickly replaced by more urgent considerations. Around 1830 Bergé spotted some Germans. It was clear that they had been betrayed by the lone Cretan who had suddenly appeared and just as quickly disappeared.

Petrakis may have vouched for him, but one never knew the leverage that the occupying Germans had on an individual or what that individual's motives might have been.[117] Some Cretans who had seen them had not lingered; maybe because they thought that they were Germans. Even though the group had been keeping themselves to themselves, the locals 'always discovered' them. During one encounter, local Cretans told them about hostages who had been shot as a reprisal. The list of the executed, chosen from the northern Cretan town of Chania, was long. It must have been shattering. 'That was really depressing' was Jellicoe's way of avoiding just how deeply the event would haunt him through his life. 'The Germans must have known that this had not been done by Cretans.'[118]

Bergé decided to fight it out, hoping that they could make it till darkness. That was hours away, around 2100. It was unwise. Sibard gave his former commander the benefit of the doubt when he wrote *Mission en Crète*, but when he and I spoke, it was clear that he thought Bergé's decision had been wrong. Furthermore, he said, most SAS officers would never have fought it out under those conditions. Given that they had a couple of minutes on the Germans, Sibard would have chosen to get out and evade them.

The four must have been facing two or three platoons from a German battalion, around fifty men, and their defensive position was not good. While there was a wall and a tree for cover, the fact was that they were caught in a bowl; the Germans could shoot down at them from higher ground. Armed with weapons that could only be effective at short range (largely because of the adaptations that Bergé had ordered to their Beretta machine guns), his men had to allow the Germans to close in on them. When one of them was killed, the enemy held off for a quarter of an hour.

Each man was assigned a 90-degree arc of fire to cover: Bergé to the north-west, Sibard looking to the north-east, young Léostic to the south-east and Mouhot to the south-west. Desperately outnumbered and outgunned, the four Free French parachutists, nevertheless, put up a stiff resistance.

Léostic was first to go down. They had already been fighting for over an hour when the young Pierrot disobeyed Bergé's orders to hold his ground. Bravely he shouted, 'My commandant, I cannot obey you any more!' and was shot almost as soon as he broke cover in an attempt to break out to the south. Sibard managed to get about 50 metres away from the group and then ran straight into a German who nudged him in the chest with his Schmeisser. He didn't have a choice. He'd been wounded and was now taken prisoner. Bergé ran out of ammunition and surrendered. Mouhot, also out of ammunition, would not give up: '*Fidèle à sa reputation, Jacques Mouhot reste introuvable*' (True to his reputation, Jacques Mouhot remained hidden and kept fighting).[119] But Mouhot's efforts were for nought and he too was brought in, hands above his head. With the Germans was the '*gros bonhomme*' (fat fellow), the same nervous Cretan who had betrayed them.

The prisoners were immediately driven back to Vassilika-Anoghia and then on to the command post at Ampelouzos, before being taken to the Luftwaffe barracks in Heraklion. Luckily, they were not in the hands of the

Gestapo. Hitler's *Kommandobefehl* (the order that captured irregulars should be shot without trial) came into force in October 1942, and their lives were at grave risk. Initially, they were threatened with death by firing squad. Bergé stood his ground. It was only by firmly and confidently stating that the same action would be taken against captive Germans in British hands that the three survivors managed to negotiate their own own reprieve. According to Sibard, they maintained that eighteen Germans were in Allied hands and would be shot if anything happened to them. Three for eighteen did not sound like a good exchange to the officer, so eventually the Frenchmen were transferred to Brindisi on 2 July and thence to a camp near Frankfurt. Mouhot was able to escape and managed to rejoin his unit in August 1943. Jack Sibard also escaped from his work camp and managed to get back to Britain in May 1943, but his escape was seen as so incredible that his British interrogators thought he was a German plant. Consequently, he was incarcerated until 1945. Till his death, the experience remained a bitter memory.

It had all been pretty harrowing. The day after their capture, two officers, one a medical orderly, had come to inspect them. He'd asked about Sibard's wound (which Sibard dismissed as slight) but then asked him to strip. Sibard had been circumcised, causing the officer to furrow his brow and ask, '*Jude?*'

Bergé's loss was dramatic. He'd been one of the first French officers to go back into occupied France – twice – before coming out to the Middle East. After his release from Colditz, Oflag IV C, the camp for inveterate escapers near Leipzig (where he would be reunited with his old commanding officer David Stirling, who would be captured in February 1943, as well as Augustin Jordan), Bergé would head up the new French SAS and eventually become a general.

Jellicoe was lucky to get out alive. He had gone back to the group alone after he and Petrakis linked up with the SOE contact. Petrakis's feet were giving him trouble. Jellicoe searched but couldn't find the group. He thought he must have gone wrong in one of the 'many parallel valleys'. He tried numerous alternatives but at first light came back to where he'd started. He knew it was the right one. He saw that they had left bits and pieces behind but was very suspicious, as 'they were all tidy'. 'He knew immediately that something was wrong.'[120] He was warned off by a group of small Cretan boys who, though he could not understand what they said, made it clear that things had gone badly. He finally understood that they had had the misfortune to chance on one of the very few Cretan Quislings, who had sent a messenger back to warn the Germans at Tymbaki. In his report, he noted that 'contact with the local population was hard to avoid and, in the end, led to betrayal and disaster.'[121]

Sibard had a very different take on why they were betrayed. He confided to me that he'd had to be rather circumspect about Bergé when he wrote *Mission en Crète*. Now, he laid the blame fully at Bergé's door, saying that when the latter had asked for water he had absent-mindedly let down his guard and sent back their British Army canteens. They were bound to raise questions. Furthermore, Bergé had apparently talked rather boastfully about how the Allies would soon be landing on the island, and had said that they were only an advance party. These were the kind of actions that would fan rumours. That was the last thing the group, trying to move around discreetly, should have been doing.

My father once told me that Sibard never really forgave him. Even if Sibard went through the motions of occasional ceremonial reunions in Crete, he didn't really care for Jellicoe. Maybe it was because Sibard was self-made and begrudged what he saw as Jellicoe's coddled upbringing; but it was probably more that he felt that Jellicoe had done little to help him when he had been so unjustly imprisoned by the British later in the war. Sibard said that Jellicoe maintained that he never knew.

The consequences for the local population were terrible. On 14 June, the Germans had rounded up more than fifty prominent citizens, mainly from the small port town of Chania, and shot them. Tito Giorgiadis, a former Governor General, a 70-year old priest and a number of Jewish prisoners were amongst them. Today there is a street called 'The Route of the Sixty-Two Martyrs', dedicated to these and twelve others who had been shot the year before on 3 June.

My father never talked about these reprisals. It was only years later, when I went back to Crete with him, that we attended a commemorative ceremony in the graveyard of a small village church; and even then, the whole story did not sink in. He did not talk about it, either on the way there or on the way back. It was meeting the Director of the Heraklion Museum, Constantinos Mamaloukis, that finally brought home to me the full horror of what had been perpetrated. Kostas invited my wife, Trish, and me to the museum and slowly walked us through one corner where the Martyrs are remembered. It was extremely moving to see the scores of old black and white photographs and personal possessions like rings, combs and watches. Even though only by distant association, I felt an element of guilt, the guilt – or rather, remorse – that my father must have borne.

Petrakis named his son after Pierrot, calling him Pierre-Léostic Petrakis; a heartfelt gesture to a fallen comrade. And in Heraklion his memory remained: a street is named after him.

It was only afterwards, the moment he saw Jellicoe, that Sutherland finally twigged why Kealy had appeared 'so furious' at the briefing he'd attended.

He spied him, in the distance, a figure 'in khaki shorts and shirt'. Even though in three nights Jellicoe's group had 'climbed two ranges of mountains and walked 120 miles',[122] he still displayed a 'jaunty way of walking'.[123] The mountain ranges must have been gruelling – rocky, sparse and lacking any shelter.

Sutherland and Jellicoe sought the welcoming cool of a dark cave. David remembered, much to his distaste, how he 'had begun scratching his back like an ape'.[124] The cave was infested with fleas. A couple of 'very unpleasant' nights in the cave was how Jellicoe put it, though I doubt he would have spent more than one. The idea of Sutherland, 'a serious, freckled-faced officer' who'd gone through commando training on the Isle of Arran, hunkering down in a cave under such conditions makes one chuckle: the men referred to him as 'Dinky' Sutherland because of his knack for constantly appearing well turned-out, even if he'd just come off an op.

In the dark, probably around midnight, on the way out to the MTB, Jellicoe passed another shadowy figure in the dark. It was SOE agent Paddy Leigh Fermor being rowed ashore to work with the partisan resistance.

'I'm Paddy Leigh Fermor. Who are you?'

'I'm George Jellicoe. Good luck.'

Though they only 'exchanged shadowy greetings' across the dark waters, the two would later become lifelong friends. Kardamyli, Paddy's beautiful stone-built house on the Peloponnese, became our 'home away from home' whenever we went as a family to Greece. He died at ninety-four, but I can still clearly picture him, a year before his death, sitting back in a comfortable chintz chair at the British embassy in Athens reciting poetry non-stop. It was an unforgettable evening. He had been impressed by Jellicoe:

> When George and I met by daylight a year and a half later in Cairo, I was struck immediately by the tonic effect of his presence, his initiative and his inflexible determination, and his knack of command. Also, his humour and buoyant spirits. We became great friends. He had a gift for getting on with his own soldiers and sailors and, most importantly, with our Greek allies. [125]

After midnight, in the very early hours of 24 June, they left from the beach south of Krotos at Trypiti, where a British MTB, *Porcupine*, had been waiting, and made for Mersa Matruh. Lieutenant John Campbell would get to her home port the day before the Germans arrived. At this last minute 'a gross muddle was made on shore', according to Jellicoe:

> Many of the population of S. Crete … 'rolled up' to fight their way aboard HMS *Porcupine*. Only thirty could be taken.[126]

Campbell, an old Etonian, was also an 'experienced deep-sea fisherman'. He got into trouble when he refused to obey orders from a colonel to machine-gun crews in the water from schooners that he had been ordered to sink on suspicion of carrying supplies for the Germans.[127] Campbell and Lt. Cmdr. Adrian Seligman, the famous around-the-world yachtsman, both came from SOE to form what would become the Levant Schooner Flotilla, the LSF.

One of the new passengers was the guerrilla leader, Satanas, who died soon after of cancer in Alexandria.[128] When he got back, Jellicoe went directly to Bill Cumper's wedding in Cairo, 'seemingly little the worse for his savage experience in Crete'.[129] In fact, he was in pretty bad shape and very shortly thereafter ended up in the 8th General Hospital in Alexandria. Jellicoe always seemed to land on his feet, so to speak. One of his nurses was Ivy Vassilopoulos, a beautiful Greek girl with whom he had often swum and who had watched them train before he went off. He was well looked after. He was to meet her again in Greece with Philippa. She, along with Jenny Dimopoulos and Teresa 'Tessy' Whitefield, was one of a group of beautiful girls christened 'The Three Graces' who hung out with many of the SBS and SAS.[130]

When I was in Heraklion I also had the chance to meet the son of the German Luftwaffe commander, Commandant Karl Meidert. It was an odd experience, as former adversaries gathered around a small memorial stone outside of the arrivals terminal at Heraklion Airport.

I am sure that my father never held a grudge against the Germans. He had, like his father, many warm memories of Germany. I read in one letter written to his mother (only marked 'Friday', but it would have been 1936, the year when he went to the Olympics in Berlin) of 'meeting Reinhardt Henschell in the Rhineland – and then driving with him and the Crown Princess to Frankfurt'. He had been invited to stay with Fritzi, the Crown Prince, and Cecilia, his sister, in Berchtesgaden. The place did not then, clearly, have its later connotations. His letter was written on the embossed paper of the Cecilienhof, Potsdam. It felt like something from another age.

In the desert, Jellicoe had nothing but praise for how the Afrika Korps behaved:

> We respected them. They behaved extremely well, or so I gather from people who were captured or wounded. There was a certain camaraderie there, I think. Having no civilian population, I think, probably helped it a lot. We had a considerable admiration for Rommel and of course we used to sing German (songs) … We were always tuning in to the German radio to hear *Lili Marlene*.[131]

For his part in the Heraklion raid Jellicoe was awarded the DSO in December. He was just twenty-four. The citation read:

> His cool and resolute leadership, skill and courage throughout this very hazardous operation were mainly responsible for the high measure of success achieved. He ... placed charges on the enemy aircraft and brought off the survivors after the four Free French members of the party had been betrayed and killed or captured.[132]

After the raids

Slowly the raiders started regrouping at Siwa. On the night of 15/16 June Stirling made it back. Zirnheld and Mayne had arrived the night before, on 14/15 June, and Jacquier's group came a couple of days later, on 17 June.

By the 20th everyone who was going to come back had done so. Of the fifteen Free French who'd been on the Derna-Martuba raids, only one, however, reappeared: Augustin Jordan. Some later claimed that it was because he 'spoke fluent German (and) managed to bluff his captors and escaped.'[133] The French discovered that they had lost their leader, Bergé, as well as the rest of the Heraklion team. Léostic was dead, Bergé, Mouhot and Sibard, prisoners. The raids, on paper extremely successful, had literally gutted the French, whose command was now handed over to Capitaine Jean Lambert, with Jordan as his 2i/c.

After the war, Jordan and Jellicoe remained close friends. Jordan eventually became the French ambassador to Austria, and then Poland. Both Bergé and Sibard continued to meet reasonably regularly with Jellicoe till his later years. I once met Jack at Heraklion airport, at the memorial commemorating the raid. He was heavy-set and attractive and struck me as a warm-hearted man. When I met him again, for the last time, in 2017, I was astonished at how physically diminished he'd become but I remained equally impressed by his intellect. I was worried he might not be very talkative or that his memory might have failed. I could not have been more wrong, even if for the first two hours he would not stop talking, understandably I must underline, about the wrongs he had suffered.

Jellicoe never felt comfortable with Sibard. He was never able to put his finger on why. Neither he nor the Cretan Runner, George Psychoundakis, was able to persuade the authorities (British or Greek) of their innocence and of what they had been doing in the war. Both were treated as renegades and liars. The cloud of suspicion over Sibard was not removed until 1956. He'd been a prisoner of the British almost as long as he had been held in German PoW camps. For an astonishing 660 days he'd been locked up under the cruellest of circumstances, sleeping on the floor without a mattress or a pillow. It is no wonder that Jellicoe picked up on a certain coldness.

In 1986 Jellicoe received a letter from an ex-Luftwaffe officer, Gerd Stamp, who'd served in Ju.88s as the A2/A3 officer based out of Heraklion. A month before the attack, on 12 May, a British destroyer, HMS *Jackal*, was sunk south of Crete, around 90 miles north of Mersa Matruh, by a Ju.88 piloted by Hauptmann Helbig from I/LG 1 (*Lehrgeschwader*). It was an extraordinary coincidence that *Jackal*'s captain was a certain Commander Christopher Jellicoe, a distant cousin.

When everyone was back, Stirling had a good overall picture of what had been achieved but it was almost entirely bad news. He learned the details of the fate of the SIG and the Free French, of Jacquier's raid, of Bergé's capture and of the fall of Tobruk. Two South African divisions – more than 20,000 men – had surrendered the fortress town after what many criticized as only a token resistance. While Churchill was furious – 'Defeat is one thing, disgrace another' – he'd played a role in that defeat. He had moved much-needed troops to Greece, giving Rommel the opening he needed. A week or so later, the German advance may have halted at El Alamein, but outside MEHQ 'the acrid fumes of burning paper permeated' the air on 1 July as secret documents were burnt.[134] The day became known as Ash Wednesday. The Germans were within 100 miles of their objective: the Suez Canal.

When Stirling heard Jacquier's report he was furious, and the officer was RTU'd. Only later, when the Eighth Army was advancing back on Tripoli, did they find out that the explosion that Jacquier's men had caused had been so devastating that the airfield was put out of action *'pendant des mois'* (for some months). Stirling had got it wrong. By contrast, he was so pleased with Zirnheld that he offered him a place on the Benghazi-Derna railroad raid.

It's quite difficult to put a reliable number on the aircraft destroyed in the eight raids, because Stirling's reports always underplayed what had been counted on the ground. Routinely, only two-thirds of the actual count was ever reported back.[135] But what they'd achieved was impressive: between Heraklion and Kastelli, probably thirty-one or thirty-two aircraft and ten trucks.

In the North African raids, they got another fifty-two planes or so (five by Stirling at Benina, twenty at Martuba, fourteen at Derna, seven at Barce and six at Berka Main). As well as that combined total of around eighty-four planes, Stirling's attack destroyed an additional thirty aircraft engines, and Zirnheld's count was probably higher than six. Maybe ten. On top of that there were additional explosions that included a number of bomb dumps.

The other benefit of the raids – the distraction they caused – has often been overlooked. Not only did the raids physically account for Axis aircraft, they also played a part in the Allied misinformation campaign, adding to the doubt and speculation that existed in German Intelligence circles about Allied plans. The Germans were jumpy. They were always wondering if any Allied activity might point to an invasion or commando operations somewhere, but did not know where.

Of the seventeen ships in the Allied convoys to Malta, only two got through to Valetta, but these enabled the island to continue its resistance. It makes one pause to consider the huge loss of life that must have taken place at sea.

David Sutherland and Duggan finally got back from their raid on Rhodes aboard the submarine *Traveller*. As she entered harbour, she sported a 'Jolly Roger' with a white dagger over her conning tower, the sign of a successful Special Forces pick-up but no sooner was he ashore, than Sutherland came down with malaria. He had lost around 15lbs on the operation, and both he and Duggan had gone through a terrifying experience getting back to their submarine. They had signalled that they were going to swim out ('Swimming. Come in.'). After an hour, during which the boat twice dived out of sight to avoid Italian MAS, they finally managed to clamber on board.

* * *

The very next month, July 1942, Stirling's group was brought back to help in another strategic role. The group was tasked by Auchinleck with harrying Rommel's supply lines. Every day, Rommel needed '1,500 tons of supplies, including rations and water', and the supplies were sent all the way from Tripoli.[136] Rommel's supply line was his 'Achilles heel'. This time, the mission was designed to tie in with the Eighth Army's Mersah Matruh offensive targeted for 7 July.

On 3 July the LRDG-SAS group left Kabrit and, after an initial escort by military police, disappeared along a track that ran across the northern edge of the Qattara Depression. The depression was actually a salt-bog, 'the lowest point on the continent of Africa, being 134 metres below sea level'.[137] It was considered 'a treacherous area of *mish–mish* sand and saltmarsh'.[138]

From Qara, where they were taken by Robin Gurdon's LRDG, the SAS would raid a number of airfields: Sidi Barrani to the north-west, the al-Dhaba fields to the north-east, Bagoush and the four fields at Fuka between the two. Stirling and Mayne would target Bagoush.

The territory had formerly been in British hands and so was reasonably well known to many of the men.

By 1700 on 7 July the raiders arrived at a laying up point around 15 miles to the south-west of Fuka (at Bir Khalda) for their first series of raids. The

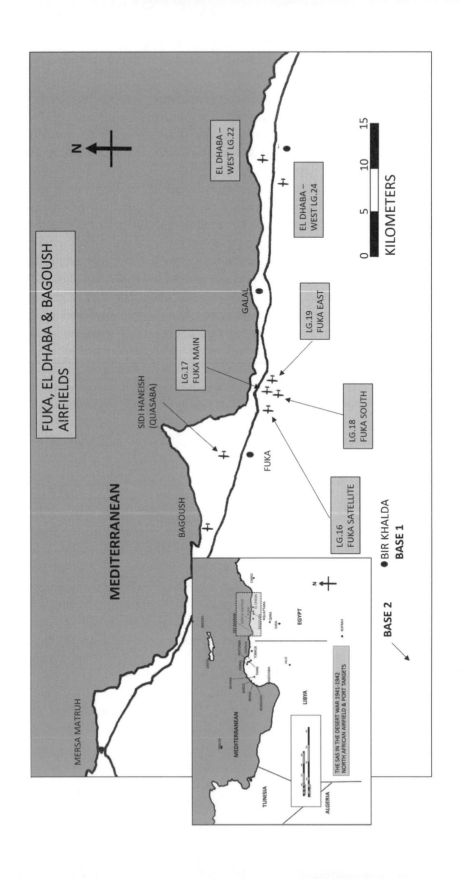

FUKA, EL DHABA & BAGOUSH AIRFIELDS

MEDITERRANEAN

N

MERSA MATRUH

BAGOUSH

SIDI HANEISH (QUASABA)

GALAL

EL DHABA – WEST LG.22

EL DHABA – WEST LG.24

LG.17 FUKA MAIN

LG.19 FUKA EAST

FUKA

LG.18 FUKA SOUTH

LG.16 FUKA SATELLITE

BIR KHALDA
BASE 1

BASE 2

KILOMETERS
0   5   10   15

THE SAS IN THE DESERT WAR 1941-1942
NORTH AFRICAN AIRFIELD & PORT TARGETS

TUNISIA

ALGERIA

LIBYA

EGYPT

MEDITERRANEAN

N

subsequent reconnaissance to establish the correct approach roads was never carried out.

At around 2200 Mayne, driving a jeep, and Stirling, a 3-tonner, pulled up just short of their targets. The journey had been incredibly slow: they were lucky to cover more than five or six kilometres every hour. The going had been, '*Trés ravine, tout en montées et en déscente périlleuse, les pierres tranchantes lascèrent et crèvent les pneus*' (Very undulating, a lot of dangerous up and downs, with slippery stones ripping and puncturing the tyres).[139]

After the sun had gone down, they arrived at 'a minefield blocking the entrance to the track leading down to Fuka' and split into two groups.[140] Mayne would go on to Bagoush, 30-odd kilometres further to the west of Fuka itself, the other two made for the fields at Fuka-16 (the satellite field) and Fuka-19 (Fuka-East). Much further to the west, Captain Alistair Timpson's G.1 patrol would recce Sidi Barani. With him went Stirling's new parachute instructor, Captain Peter Warr of the East Surrey Regiment, and Bernard Schott (who had also been an instructor at Kabrit). Jellicoe, along with Aspirant François Martin, was originally assigned the fields at El-Dhaba, but this was called off when Intelligence reported that it was deserted. Instead, to the east of Fuka, at a midway point with Galal, they would set up another roadblock on the coastal highway.

Bagoush

Stirling and Mayne set off together to head west to Bagoush. It was the first time they'd gone on a raid together. Ten miles or so from their target, they split up: Stirling took three men, including the inseparable Cooper and Seekings, to set up a roadblock on the Bagoush–Fuka road, while Mayne's group of nine continued on to Bagoush in three vehicles, stopping just short of the field a little after 2300.[141] Mayne was in front in one of the new jeeps. The new Willys Bantam jeeps had just arrived from the States, and after Mayne had suggested that they ask for some of the new trucks, they got lucky.

With three others, Storie, Adamson and Mullen, Mayne crept on to the strip. They were spotted, and Italian sentries issued a challenge which was immediately answered by Mayne lobbing a couple of grenades in their direction. This swift response dealt with the immediate danger, and they continued laying bombs, forty of them (each man carried ten Lewes bombs). At 0135 the sky lit up, but only twenty-two explosions were counted. Half the detonators had failed because they were damp. After the raid, when they examined some of the remaining Lewes bombs, they discovered the problem: the fifty or so bombs had become sodden and wouldn't light. Their primers had been inserted twenty-four hours before the raid, thinking that this would give the raiders more time on target. In the cold, damp morning light, crossing the Qattara depression, the damage had been done. One can only imagine the sense of frustration: 'Some of the fuses didn't go off. I had to leave about twenty aircraft sitting there … It's tragic.'[142]

The damp primers, only part of the problem, had been an entirely avoidable problem. However, the Italians had dispersed the planes so well that it was time-consuming for Mayne's group to distribute their little oil-covered 'gifts'. To cap it all, the base was very well patrolled. After another stressful hour, Mayne's party managed to get out and met up with Stirling. His group had seen nothing of any value in the ambush they'd set up. Seekings saw that Paddy was itching for a fight: *'Le capitaine Mayne semble être en bonne forme ce soir, Sir* (Captain Mayne seems to be in good form this evening, Sir').[143]

Failure necessitates innovation. Stirling suggested they machine-gun the other planes, arranged in groups of six. A single jeep and the Blitz Buggy were driven slowly across the tarmac, methodically targeting the remaining planes with machine-gun fire. 'Shoot low. Go for the petrol tanks', instructed Stirling.[144] The Vickers were devastatingly effective although 'after three magazines [they] had a seizure from overheating.'[145] They managed to destroy another fifteen aircraft – mostly CR.42s and ME.109s – which meant they matched Fraser's thirty-seven destroyed the previous December at Agedabia.[146] One of the aircraft destroyed even turned out to be a captured, unused Hurricane.[147]

On the way out, sentries were machine-gunned sleeping beside their tents. Not everyone felt good about this, but Stirling angrily retorted: 'The odds are so heavily against us in this war. We have to put the fear of Allah up them.' Seekings' little talk seemed to have made the difference. Certainly, Mayne had no problem. According to Lloyd Owen, he had probably, 'knifed about seventeen [sentries]'.[148]

On the way back, the group was attacked by two Italian bombers and a single recon plane.

Fuka-19 and roadblocks

A number of groups drove on to target the Fuka airfields: on this raid, 7 July, the French, led by Jordan, were tasked with attacking Fuka-19 on the east.[149]

Around 2300, Jordan's group was dropped off a few kilometres from their targeted field. After roughly an hour, the four-man group under Jordan's lead, Aspirant Michel Legrand, Sergeant René Martin and Chasseur Roger Boutinot, went in.

The field was *'trés sévèrement gardée'* (very heavily guarded): Italian sentries had been posted, two to a plane.[150] As they went in, it seemed that they were undetected: Jordan had airily replied to the Italian sentry's challenge in German, thinking he'd got away with it. They did not find their targets immediately and the fact that they spent around ten minutes looking suggested that they had not done a very thorough recce in the early hours of 6 July.

Once in position, Boutinot prepared the charges and Jordan placed them, while Martin and Legrand gave cover. One Italian sentry, however, hadn't been convinced and now raised the alarm by firing a round. A Breda and two machine guns then opened up, spitting out a mass of fire in their direction, but to little avail: *'les tirs sont très imprecises non ciblés'* (the shooting was bad and off-target).[151] After another *'bonne dizaines des minutes'* (good dozen minutes), the group left towards the west to meet up with their LRDG minders.[152]

Jordan's group bagged eight aircraft with only one casualty: Martin was shot in the hand.[153] While Pleydell was bandaging him up – 'a trivial affair with the bullet slicing across his little finger' – Martin claimed that they'd destroyed more: 'blown up nine planes for certain'. They'd added another six aircraft to the list and 'thought they must have got more'.[154]

The discovery of the Free French at Fuka-19 came at the very moment that Bill Fraser's patrol, at Fuka-16, was crawling in between two sentry posts'.[155] This made his own raid too dangerous, and it was called off.

As he was making his exit around 0300, a Wellington bomber flew overhead. It soon reached Bagoush and dropped its load, just as Stirling was raiding. He was furious, as he'd been assured that no RAF raids would be carried out that night.

Jellicoe's and Zirnheld's targets, the two fields at al-Dhaba, were to be left alone. Updated intelligence stated that they were not being used. Instead, Jellicoe was tasked with setting up a roadblock and taking prisoners.

It was François Martin's first SAS operation and it would turn out to be when the Free French captured their first prisoners. They'd been waiting unsuccessfully for at least an hour for enemy vehicles to pass by. When nothing came, and Zirneld decided to look further down the road when Sergent Brouard announced that he could make out two large shapes. Along with Brouard and Jean le Gall, they found a small tent parked beside a large tanker and pulled out the unsuspecting occupants, two Germans, who mistook them for Italians.

The two Germans, one an 18-year-old *Gefreiter* (private), the other an older *Obergefreiter* (corporal), had been sleeping beside their huge trucks, one a captured British tank carrier. Sitting there stranded, they'd been waiting on the side of the road for a refuelling truck. Jean le Gall took them prisoner:

> *Grand est leur stupéfication d'être capture, à plus de cent kilometres du front par des Français* (Great was their surprise at being taken prisoner by two Frenchmen more than 100 kilometres behind the front line).[156]

Le Gall and Bouard placed explosives, destroying both vehicles. What they then learned must have come as frustrating news: the intelligence on Al-Dhaba was completely wrong. The younger German, who'd just arrived in Africa, said that Al-Dhaba was 'the busiest' Axis landing ground (LG) in the area.

Fuka-16 and Al-Dhaba Airfields

Five days later, the night of 12/13 July, Jordan was back at Fuka, this time assigned to Fuka-16, the satellite field to the west. With François Martin's injury, his group had been changed slightly: he was replaced by Caporal-chef Guégan. Getting on to the field posed no problems but, just as they were placing their bombs on the first two planes, an Italian sentry challenged them and fired off two rounds, raising the alarm. Searchlights started to dance around in the darkness.

Legrand was hit badly in his right arm but continued to place bombs and decided to stay behind – with Boutinot – to give Jordan and Martin cover as they legged it out. Although he could still walk, he was in great pain. Guégan had also been wounded.

Around 2345, Jordan heard the first small explosions go off. Apparently, he couldn't understand why the planes weren't catching fire. Maybe they weren't fuelled. As soon as the flares faded, the group headed off to the RV with the LRDG. Shortly before midnight, they found the LRDG trucks waiting for them.

Just as Paddy Mayne and Stirling had done a few days earlier, the Frenchmen decided to take some of the LRDG trucks back on to the field to hose down some of the remaining aircraft and pick up Boutinot and Legrand. Lieutenant Hunter led the three LRDG trucks, lights out, on to the airfield, and immediately another three aircraft were '*irrémédiablement touchés par cette grêle de balles et detruits*' (completely ripped apart by the hail of bullets).[157] The LRDG hit one of the planes and Guégan, behind on one of the twin-mounted Vickers K, got another.

Just as their fire was starting to hit their targets, their truck came to a lurching stop. They had driven into a ditch. Jordan was thrown free but Guégan was trapped under one of the wheels. The second vehicle narrowly avoided rear-ending them, but the last one hammered straight into the back. The truck was, however, in a good enough state to be able to drive back out.

At 0830 on 12 July, they got back to the main base. Though he did not put it in his report at the time, Jordan later concluded that it was he who had shot Legrand, not one of the enemy sentries. Despite all the mishaps, Jordan's group claimed eight Me.109s.

Knowing now the importance of the Al-Dhaba fields, Jellicoe, along with one of Gurdon's LRDG patrols, François Martin and André Zirnheld, was tasked with raiding them. Or, as the French would say, 'chasser le Stuka'. They started out early: Martin's group would take on el-Dhaba 2, Zirnheld, el-Dhaba 1.

Around 1700, the French group reached a plateau and discovered another airfield no one knew about. However, they were spotted, caught by two roving Italian fighters and badly strafed.[158] They tried waving to the pilots as though they were Axis troops, but the ruse didn't work. It was clear to Martin that they had arrived way too early and should have waited for darkness.

Jellicoe, Mather and Hastings set off in three jeeps to attack 'the most easterly of the German airfields, closest to the Alamein line'.[159] They had set off earlier because of the greater distance and were, therefore, not able to use the darkness for cover. They had been warned that, because of their previous raids, Italian Macchi fighters 'regularly patrolled the escarpment in the evening' and they had, it seems, gone 'against the advice of the SAS veterans with them.'[160] As the sun started to set, no sooner had Jellicoe halted the patrol than they were spotted by three fighters. After these ran out of ammunition, they were replaced by another three and a bomber.

Jellicoe hid in a *wadi* and managed to escape unharmed. The other two jeeps, however, had been badly hit, and his own now had to do double-duty carrying others. Nine, including Jellicoe, Mather and Hastings, clambered on to the one jeep to head west. The problem was the radiator: it was leaking badly, and the engine was over-heating, so they 'stuffed [it] with plastic explosive and peed into it.' Eventually, they got back to within a few miles of the RV after a 70-mile journey.[161] Mather remembered how well the tactic had worked but also that 'it smelt like a chicken coop!'[162] Hastings later concluded that Jellicoe had 'saved us a very long walk, if not indeed our lives.'[163]

On another raid, with two jeeps destroyed and one burning like a beacon, Robin Gurdon was mortally wounded. He had been assigned the next airfield to Jellicoe's target and had also set off earlier. He had stayed with the burning vehicle and continued firing, bleeding profusely from neck and chest wounds.

The mission scrubbed, Zirnheld took over the care of the wounded while Martin, now the most senior officer, took charge of getting the group back. Of the four jeeps, two were destroyed and another abandoned. The nine men had to pile into one jeep, and now that Gurdon was mortally wounded, the only other navigator was Stocker, who'd also been injured.

As night fell, a group of armoured cars could be seen coming their way. It was clear they had to get going. For 150km the jeeps raced ahead of their pursuers, each bump an agony for the wounded lying in the back. Gurdon was still just alive but losing a lot of blood. Stocker, despite his injuries, was helping navigate, but it was clear, in the fog, that he was not sure of their position, and their sun compass had been shot up. It turned out that he almost got them back; he'd ended up only five miles from the RV.

When it was clear that the wounded could not be moved any further, some accounts tell of Stocker going off for help. It probably wasn't him, because of his injuries. At midday, whoever it was re-appeared with medical help.[164] 'He looked as if he was exhausted, and his eyes were reddened with fatigue.'[165] Gurdon had been planning to join the SAS 'probably to take over second in command from me', Jellicoe thought.[166] It turned out to be too late. Robin Gurdon died half an hour later at 1230.

Gurdon's grave was humble, two planks tied together to form a cross. It was terrible that after surviving the agony of the 150km trip across rough desert he had succumbed only hours before Base-2 was located. His batman, Vaughan, 'broke down'. Pleydell 'patted him on the shoulder to comfort him until, all of a sudden, [he found that he too] was crying.'[167] Many had very much admired Gurdon :

> *Son sang froid et sa calme determination, la précision et la rapidité de ses décisions eurent un effet salutaire sur les conducteurs des véhicules qui étaient égaillés, abandonnant leur voiture* (His composure and his calm determination, the precision and speed of his decision-making, had a salutary effect on the drivers who had been dispersed, having abandoned their vehicles). [168]

While not achieving as high a count as the June raids – the raids on Sidi Barrani and al-Dhaba fields were called off – the July raids still proved devastatingly effective, destroying at least fifty-two planes: thirty-seven at Bagoush, seven on Fuka-16, eight or nine on Fuka-19. But everything was overshadowed by Robin Gurdon's death. Any victory they celebrated felt hollow. It must have felt much like the day that Jock had been killed.

While Stirling was reflecting on the success of using jeep-mounted machine-guns, Mayne continued the old raiding style, successfully hitting Fuka again with Jordan on 11 July. Another twenty-two aircraft were accounted for – fifteen by Mayne, seven by Jordan. Fraser's attack was abortive.

With him on the Fuka-16 raid were some of the Free French: Officer Cadet Legrand, the 20-year old Roger Boutinot and Louis Guégan Guess. He'd just arrived at Kabrit on 3 June. A few days before him, another group of officer cadets ('*Aspirants*', as they're called in French) had arrived, including François Martin and his friend Mairet. They'd been in the *6ème Bataillon de Chasseurs Alpins* and all had been at Narvik.

Back at base, the men gathered around a fire. Routinely, a 'Wyndham' radio aerial would be erected for nightly updates and a time check from Cairo.[169] In the anonymity of the darkness, some of them started to sing. Malcolm Pleydell was moved by this 'expression of feeling that defied the vastness of the surroundings'.[170] At first, the French were reticent and just watched. Eventually, they were persuaded to join in, singing '*Madeleine*'. Even the German prisoners did too, singing '*In Hoffmann Stadt da gibts ein Haus*' and '*Lili Marlene*'. Momentarily, friend and foe were brought together in the great void of the desert under a blanket of stars.

A week or so later, on 23 July, Stirling also arrived back at Base No.2.

A change of tactics – Sidi Haneish

Stirling, Mayne and Jellicoe drove the 400 miles back to Kabrit, in order to collect more jeeps and recruits. Around thirty men were left behind to look after the base. The idea of using jeeps in a massed attack had been starting to form ever since the incident with the damp fuses.

At MEHQ, Stirling presented this new suggestion. It was a novel way to destroy enemy aircraft, rather than the traditional, small-group SAS approach. Stirling concluded that fundamentally changing tactics would leave the enemy guessing 'between two methods of defence'.[171]

With the help of Major Peter Oldfield at the new Photo Reconnaissance Wing, an airfield in the Fuka area, Sidi Haneish (also known as Haggag el Qasaba), was selected. It was one of Rommel's important staging airfields for the front, known simply as Landing Ground (LG) 12.

Bringing twenty new jeeps, each fitted with Vickers K aircraft machine guns, the three arrived back after only eight days. A few 'were even fitted with a high-power searchlight.'[172] They then set about planning the raid. Before the final attack, the group laid up forty miles from Sidi Haneish working out logistics, cleaning weapons, loading up ammunition and making up explosive charges. All the Vickers' magazines had to be loaded with rounds 'in proper sequence, tracer, ball, incendiary, armour-piercing'.[173] Jim Almonds explained that this way, you were able to see and correct your fire: 'you could see tracers of incendiaries, coming across like strings of sausages.'[174] Working away busily on the jeeps in a cave, Mather thought the scene reminiscent of Snow White and her dwarves.

Jellicoe 'was in charge of the commissariat' and was responsible for working out what needed for the mission. He sat alone in one corner 'with a large tin of acid drops in front of him, trying to work out the impossible problems of supply'. Paddy Mayne was sleeping, 'his head under one jeep and his feet under another'. He would spend down-time reading 'the inevitable Penguin'. On this particular occasion, it must have been challenging, since both his hands were 'heavily bandaged … he was susceptible to desert sores.'[175]

Around them lay randomly scattered paraphernalia – 'tins of tobacco, sweets, pipes, jars of Eau de Cologne (there was no water for washing) and last year's glossy magazines. George had thoughtfully spent £20 in Cairo on these luxuries.'[176] Jellicoe and Stirling both had a style of which Almonds spoke. When they could, they would both go off 'like boys back from raiding the school tuck shop', bringing 'as many small luxuries as they could carry, including sweets, lavender water and cigars'.[177]

Seventeen jeeps were to be used in the attack itself.[178] On each would be mounted four Vickers K guns. A double-mount up front fired from the passenger seat, two more were mounted on the back. The jeeps would form two double lines of eight jeeps apiece, Jellicoe leading one column, Paddy Mayne the other. All were following Stirling's lead jeep at the apex of the triangle. Once he got Stirling to his target, Mike Sadler's jeep would stay back from the attack itself.

With a rate of fire of 1,200 rounds per minute, the broadside would be devastating.[179] And deadly. Jellicoe and Sandy Scratchley enjoyed the idea that they were practising for an attack on an enemy while behind his lines. Under the light of a quarter moon, Stirling 'decreed live ammunition' be used for the practice run.[180] This was deadly serious. It was going to be absolutely essential that the formation was tight. Precision meant the difference between life and death. There was no room for mistakes. Carol Mather elaborated:

> Every gun fired outwards, and as I was driving and at the end of the left-hand column, my front gun fired across my face and my rear gun behind my head, so it was important to sit very still and not to lean forwards or backwards.[181]

They would start off line-abreast, then close up into the two-column formation to take the moving mass of firepower down the central strip of the airfield between the parked rows of planes. A green Verey light, the signal to 'Open Fire', would be shot by Stirling. Then he would shoot a red one to 'Check Fire' and re-form line-abreast to deliver the final onslaught.

Stirling chose a night with a full moon period deliberately, because an attack then would be completely unexpected – the first one, at least. The date was set for 16 July. After sundown, the formation set off.

Sidi Haneish lay around 75 kilometres north-east of the second SAS camp, a few kilometres west of Bagoush. The attack was planned for 01:00 the following morning, 27 July.

Stirling was riding with Johnny Cooper and Reg Seekings, rolling across the desert at around 20mph. Each jeep followed the dust of the one in front. As darkness was falling, Mike Sadler would get out to take accurate bearings with his theodolite. This responsibility bore heavily on the shoulders of the 22-year old. He had to guide the group across almost 50 miles of desert at night. As they continued, the ground became harder and stonier and punctures increasingly frequent: fifteen of them, each requiring at least five minutes in which to change tyres, slowed their onward progress.

At night the desert sky could be astonishingly beautiful, and because these were the times when there were no flies, the 'best moments were at dawn and dusk.'[182] Mather described how, when driving back with Jellicoe one time, his companion asleep in the jeep beside him, he was tempted to continue driving rather than wake his slumbering partner, 'the desert so soft and silvery, under the clear light of the moon, the stars so big and brilliant and the sky so deep blue'.[183] From December to March, it could also be extremely cold, however. On this particular night the visibility was, apparently, not good, but by Sadler's confident reckoning, they were less than a mile from the field, even though they could see nothing. In an apt turn of phrase, Forgeat calls Sadler 'le Simbad du sable' (Sinbad of the sand).[184] His navigating skills were legendary. When Stirling promoted him in Cairo, he gave him a field commission, telling him that he should 'go and buy some pips'. Sadler also had a curiously strong influence on Stirling's decision-making:

> He had a unique way of being able to deliver unwelcome news which Stirling rather preferred to ignore with an ease that nobody else would have been able to get away with.[185]

Stirling ordered a line-abreast formation, the jeeps driving closer in towards the target with five yards' separation. When 200 yards from the airfield, they came to a stop.

Suddenly, the scene in front of them lit up. All the field's lights had been switched on like 'Brighton beach'.[186] Stirling's immediate reaction was that they must have been seen, betrayed or both. He must have breathed a sigh of relief when he realized that it was because a plane was about to come in. It was the moment to go.[187]

After two minutes, his eyes adjusted, Stirling fired his Verey pistol. He led the roaring jeeps straight in, changing from line-abreast to the two-column attack formation. The seventeen jeeps became a moving wall of fire as all the Vickers simultaneously opened up, shredding the landing He.111

in seconds. 'It was blown to pieces before it came to a halt.'[188] Too late, the runway lights were cut.

The 'sudden savagery of the onslaught' took the defenders by complete surprise. The combination of surprise and the equally sudden unleashing of overwhelming violence has become a hallmark of SAS operations. Jellicoe casually reminisced, 'We just cruised around shooting up their planes.'[189] It was, obviously, a bit more than that.

The jeeps headed down the smooth tarmac, flanked on both sides by a mix of Stukas, Messerschmitts, Heinkels and Junkers, just 50 yards or so from their guns. Planes either ignited when their petrol tanks caught fire or disintegrated in the chainsaw hail of lead. 'It was like a duck shoot', quipped Johnny Cooper, the tracer helping the gunners adjust their aim.[190] Those who were there recalled the intensity of heat from the burning planes and the overwhelming, nauseating fumes from gallons of aviation fuel flooding across the runway.

The first German reaction was mortar fire dropping between the racing columns. Early on, Jim Almond's jeep was knocked out. It wasn't hit; it had probably run right into a slit trench. After they'd run down the column, some of the planes only 15 yards away from the jeeps, another flare went up, the signal to swing the jeep columns around. After two more mortar rounds had fallen, a Breda AA gun opened up from around 300 yards. Steve Hastings' jeep was hit, oil leaking all over his face, but he was uninjured and caught up with the others. Then the jeep in front came to a screeching halt. Two men ran over to Hastings' jeep while the third set the fuse on a bomb to destroy it. Sandy Scratchley's gunner, 21-year old Lance Corporal John Robson, wasn't so lucky. He was hit in the head, his skull sliced in two by a 20mm round from the Breda.

When Stirling's jeep was hit, he dismounted, and the entire formation came to a halt. The fire from the Breda was the cause, and Stirling ordered it destroyed. He took the opportunity of telling them all to switch off their engines and held a quick tactical briefing. After getting a sitrep on the remaining ammunition, he told them that he wanted to double back to complete the circle and then hit another group of aircraft he'd spotted on the perimeter.

The perimeter turned out to be where the all-important Ju.52s were lined up. They, too, were soon turned into piles of torn and flaming wreckage. One more was spotted and then the silhouetted shadow of a running man, jumping up on to the wing. It was Paddy Mayne, determined not to let a single enemy plane go undamaged and placing an explosive charge; his gunners had probably run out of ammunition.[191]

Before leaving the hellish landscape of destruction, Sadler, who had stayed out of the attack to take care of stragglers, stopped to take some photographs.[192] He was amazed by the impressive speed of the German recovery – 'within an hour of the attack there were planes coming in to land.'[193] On his way out, he nearly ran into a halted column of German infantry: 'Collars turned up against the cold … they peered at Mike's jeep as it bumped past them. Mike and his men peered back. No greeting was exchanged. No challenge was offered. No sign of recognition … Mike drove on into the mist.'[194]

Stirling's orders were for everyone to get out and as far away as they could over the two and a half hours remaining before daylight. The raiders now split into three groups to make their separate ways back to Bir-al-Quseir. Each group had been instructed to use the line of telegraph poles that ran from Bagoush to Qara at the north-western tip of the Qattara depression as a marker.

Daylight on the 27th would bring inevitable retribution. 'It wasn't the raid that worried you, it was how the hell you were going to get away afterwards from the Germans', Sadler mused.[195] Paddy Mayne had a nice way of putting it: 'A raid was like a booze-up – you always paid for it the next day.'[196] And payment wasn't just from Axis planes; Allied aircraft were just as likely to strafe you.

Trying to avoid being discovered from the air led to a whole series of counter-measures. Seekings explained that fighters represented the biggest danger:

> We didn't worry so much about bombers. You could hide from a bomber; they were slower, you could fight them off. But you couldn't with fighters. That was what worried us. Once they pointed their nose at you, it was rough.[197]

On the ground, the desert presented some unique challenges: 'The big problem in the desert is casting shadows. You had to break up the shadow.'[198]

This often meant lowering a jeep's profile by digging it in or driving it *into* the rambling branches of a lone bush rather than holding up *beside* it. If an aircraft was heard, the drivers would turn their vehicles around, as it was likely that the direction in which they were spotted travelling would be reported. If spotted, the LRDG's practice was to have all the trucks split off into completely different directions and RV 'at the last place we had spent any time, e.g. last night stop, or a lunch stop'.[199]

Stirling's group got lost and headed for a *wadi* just before the sun came up. The men drove the jeeps into the 'centre of a water course among the tallest bush'.[200] None of them needed to be told what to do: they immediately went to work camouflaging their vehicles. After some brackish tea, Stirling called them together to bury Robson. It was a simple gathering, no words from a book, just a moment or two of quiet, individual reflection, each man lost in thoughts of his own.

> It was a curious burial, just a two-minute silence with a handful of tired, dirty comrades. Yet for a short fraction of time, lost in the middle of nowhere, there was dignity.[201]

Steve Hastings caught himself wondering if anyone would ever again come anywhere near the grave, so desolate was the spot.

The French – Jordan, Zirnheld and Martin – had participated in three jeeps: riding with Jordan on Stirling's left were Caporal Le Gall and Caporal Boven; Caporal-Chef Philippe Fauquet and Caporal-Chef Victor Iturria rode with André Zirnheld; while Caporal-Chef Pierre Henri Lageze and Parachutiste Jacques Leroy joined Francois Martin. After the attack, as they raced for safety, joined by Paddy Mayne, Zirnheld's and Martin's jeeps both started to fall behind – by at least an hour. Two tyres on Zirnheld's jeep blew, one after the other, causing considerable delay. Lagèze helped him out with a spare from his jeep.[202]

They managed to find the telegraph poles on the Siwa road but only just as the fog was dissipating. They hurriedly camouflaged the jeeps to wait out the daylight hours. A large German convoy of around thirty vehicles stopped '*à peine à deux kilomètres de leur cachet, sur un terrain plat*' (scarcely 2km from their hideout, on flat ground). Two Fiesler-Storch spotter planes flew by slowly, lazily passing over but not seeing them.

As they continued to hide in a *wadi*, around 0730, four marauding Stukas attacked.[203] A further two attackers, Me.109s, were weaving back and forth around them. The Stukas made nine separate attacks, during which the men were subjected to intense strafing ('*au cours desquels ils sont soumis à une mitraillage intensif*').[204] The machine gun fire sounded like a summer hailstorm.

Early on, Zirnheld was badly hit. Probably after the second attack. First in the shoulder, a wound which he lightly dismissed to his friend, François Martin: '*Je suis touché au bras. Ce n'est rien.*' (I've been hit in my arm but it's nothing). Then he was hit again, on the penultimate attack, this time in the stomach. Martin could hear the difference in his voice. After Martin had dragged him clear of the jeep, he managed to hold on for a couple of hours, but obviously knew he was dying, '*Mon pauvre vieux, je suis foutu, laisse-moi là et pars avec les hommes*' (My poor old chap, I'm done for. Leave me here and get away with the men).[205] Martin's men got the jeeps going and carefully laid Zirnheld on one. It was hopeless. After a few kilometres, a '*véritable calvaire*' (real Calvary) for the wounded officer, Zirnheld pleaded with them to stop. They did so, and Martin put him in the shade of a small tent. He was slipping away, imploring his friend to stay with him and give him comfort by holding his hand. After 1130 Martin decided he had to get back to Bir-al-Quseir and find Pleydell. To avoid the possibility of aerial detection, Corporal Webster volunteered to go on foot, but Martin decided to go himself with Fauquet and Iturria, leaving Lagèze and Jacques Leroy behind.(Webster had earlier been picked up by the French as they left the fields, after his own jeep had been destroyed by a mortar round).

Martin got back to the *wadi* where the rest of the SAS was lying up. But by the time he returned, around 1230, Zirnheld had already died. He was buried under rocks to protect his body from scavengers, and his comrades made a small cross out of used ammunition boxes. On the rough wood, they had scratched out: '*Mort au champ d'honneur*' (Died on the field of honour). Martin later found the poem, 'A Para's Prayer', written by Zirnheld in 1938 in his notebook. Zirnheld had been a deeply religious man and expressed his faith through poetry. Shortly before, he'd asked Martin to take care of his things for him. '*Je vais vous quitter. Tout est en ordre en moi*' (I'm going to die but I'm at rest). It was 27 July 1943. Eventually, the five Frenchmen and Webster piled on to the one serviceable jeep and drove back to safety. The two Free French Forces jeeps had been the only two returning vehicles that had been attacked. Six jeeps had been damaged in the actual attack. Three were destroyed. One man was killed: John Robson.

In the poem he had written, Zirnheld had asked not for wealth or success, but for 'turmoil and brawl'. He would be happy with whatever his God had left over to give him. Like the other deaths, Zirnheld's was deeply felt, and not just by the French. Later, Jellicoe described him as a 'very fine young officer', a philosopher and a 'beautiful' poet. Stirling was also deeply affected.

A day after Zirnheld's death, Jordan took another patrol out to hit enemy convoys. He very nearly didn't make it back. His own jeep was badly shot up and he could barely drive it back to the base, 150km distant.

Stirling wasn't pleased about the raid that would become one of the revered stories of the SAS. In fact, he was downright angry about how it had been carried out. He complained that many men had wasted massive amounts of ammunition because of 'firing wildly' and not aiming low enough. Although he had asked to change the tactics, it was not done in the SAS spirit of 'maximum achievement for minimum cost'. They had lost equipment and good people. Stirling, however, did not include the Free French in these criticisms.

Ça n'est pas le cas de vos hommes. Vous revenez avec des tambours pleins, et Dieu sait pourtant si vous avez été efficaces! Mais vous n'avez pas tiré sur n'importe quoi ! Vous avez su économier les munitions, je vous en félicite ! (This wasn't the case with your men [talking to Jordan]. You came back with full magazines and only God knows if you were effective. But you didn't shoot at no matter what. You managed your ammunition well and I congratulate you).[206]

Some interesting visitors now arrived. One of the LRDG groups, led by Lieutenant Wilder, had captured two Germans who came down in the middle of the desert in a Fiesler Storch. Jellicoe was close by, 'lying up … six hundred yards' away from where the pilot landed.[207] The ungainly-looking Storch was the German Army's main reconnaissance plane; it had a remarkably short take-off and landing capability.

The Germans landed and walked over to Wilder's group, clearly thinking that they could only be German or Italian troops, only to be shocked when their scout plane exploded behind them. It was riddled by machine gun fire. With the pilot (who had, in fact, once flown Rommel) was a Hamburg medical doctor, the Baron von Lutterotti. The startled Lutterotti, who had clearly thought that the bearded soldiers wearing Arab headdress could only be a German patrol, 'albeit an odd one', whipped out his Red Cross armband, protesting in good English, 'You can't shoot me, I'm a doctor.' He had gone up for a joyride 'and it ended unhappily … *"c'est la guerre"* was his only comment.'[208] What more could he have said?

That evening, there was a strange encounter when the Baron offered his medical services to the SAS and LRDG wounded in the cave. Jellicoe came in complaining of a twisted knee (his knee used to lock, usually at the most inconvenient of moments). Pleydell thought it was one thing, Lutterotti another, but 'they were both right.' When Jellicoe's name was mentioned, the Baron inquired, 'Not the Lord Jellicoe?'

When Jellicoe nodded, the Baron quipped, 'I think you know my wife'.

Apparently, Jellicoe had dined with her in Hamburg before the war in 1936. He knew the Baron's parents well and had stayed with them in Bremen the same year. He had gone to the Berlin Olympics with the doctor when he'd been a student. Jellicoe had been staying at the Cecilienhof in Potsdam with the son of the German ex-Crown Prince, Friedrich 'Fritzi' von Preussen, and with his parents they had gone to lunch in Bremen. Old habits start young. Jellicoe was an 'energetic ladies' man', and the word swiftly spread around camp that 'the earl had done rather more than just dine with the baron's wife.'[209]

That night, a love of the night sky formed an unusual bond between three foes: Almonds, Pleydell and Lutterotti. The German doctor might have sounded as though he was waxing lyrical about the stars; in fact, he was cleverly pumping the doctor for information about their location and the direction to the coast. Pleydell and Almonds, without realizing it, helped the Germans find their escape route. Lutterotti talked romantically about walking at night in Austria under Vega and Antares. 'And there', he noted, 'the little Pole star – very small but very important, I think you understand?' Maybe this was a nod and a wink, suggesting he be allowed to escape. In the night, the Germans quietly slipped away.

The SAS were only 40 miles from German lines, and their escape caused a good degree of nervousness. Details of the force composition and their position would soon be in enemy hands. The group needed to relocate to a new hideout quickly. They went back to the old RV.

The next day, a Stuka came in low over the SAS camp. But nothing happened. No strafing, just a low fly-over. Bob Bennett, who believed the whole thing to be 'a put-up job', thought the Stuka's fly-over was a 'Thank You' gesture.[210] It would not surprise me.

Stirling was now being re-supplied at the oasis by air. It meant that the SAS could remain in the desert raiding, rather than having to make the long journey back to Kabrit.

A Bombay from 216 Squadron landed much-needed materiel on a strip around ten miles from their FOB, but the most urgent need was for more jeeps. He'd asked for another thirty. When Zirnheld was killed, Stirling had even sent Hastings back to look for spares from the wrecked jeep. When he didn't return, Stirling sent another party out, eight jeeps in four groups. With them went Mather, Jordan, Lieutenants Russell and Chris Bailey, who'd worked before with Buck.

David Russell came up with an interesting way to blow up trucks. The sheer audacity of it was astonishing. He'd flag down a passing truck and, as he spoke fluent German, ask for a pump, then slap a quick-fused Lewes bomb under the unsuspecting Good Samaritan's truck and disappear. He did this successfully eight times.

Jellicoe had come in late with two jeeps, each grossly overloaded. He had been sent off to see if he could track down the missing Germans. His driver at that time, Andrew Rodigan, a volunteer vehicle mechanic, wrote about the episode in 1990. They were driving towards an outcrop when, suddenly, 'a figure scurried round the rocks.' Jellicoe 'immediately let loose a burst of fire and demanded surrender, whereupon a figure emerged out into the open, hands up, followed unbelievably by another few.'[211] He had come across a group of South Africans hiding behind an old wrecked Italian lorry. When he spotted movement, the Vickers was swung around and Jellicoe started shooting, only for ten South Africans to emerge under a white flag. Along with 'a voluble South African Sergeant', he had brought in the additional eight stragglers who, it turned out, had escaped from a PoW camp outside of Tobruk. They had been very lucky. They had been making for Siwa, thinking it under Allied control, when they became lost. For 48 hours the oasis had been back in German hands.

The Benghazi fiasco

After the raid, a large number of the men were sent back to Kabrit on one of the three Bombay transports, using a desert landing strip just to the east of the Quara-Matruh track at Bir Chaldee. Ginger Shaw and another officer cleared away the strip of rocks and boulders at night, and then the lumbering planes were guided in by a lighted flare path. Jellicoe, sitting next to Pleydell, 'his heavily bandaged knee showing whitely in the darkness' was on one. During the flight, the plane hit bad turbulence, and some of the men – all battle-hardened veterans by now – started to panic. 'The Lord' spoke, or rather barked, 'Sit down and give the pilot a chance!'[212]

A fortnight after getting back, Jellicoe was off again. He was asked by Stirling to prepare for more raiding. He took a column of jeeps and three-tonners up to Eighth Army Headquarters, where Stirling was meeting with Auchinleck; but Jellicoe's problems with his knee meant that his war in the desert was now over. Luckily, he missed the abortive Benghazi and Tobruk raids, since he had to be operated on for a torn ligament and a damaged cartilage and was out of action for a couple of months. He went back to London in late November to report on his experiences.

In August 1942, the rest of the unit was called back from the desert. Auchinleck was replaced by Alexander, and Montgomery was promoted to take over the Eighth Army. Stirling met with Auchinleck's Chief of Staff, Major General E. 'Chink' Dorman-Smith, who told him that Rommel was heavily relying on three ports for his fuel supplies – Benghazi, Tobruk and Mersa Matruh. He told Stirling to prepare his men for the next planned push in September.

The combined LRDG-SAS group headed out again just north of the Qattara Depression, south of the Alamein lines. The long drives weren't to everyone's taste, but the desert was anything but boring. Conditions would constantly change, from a sea of soft sand to hard-packed salt fields, rocks and mountainous terrain. The jeeps would normally follow the larger trucks, giving them more room for manoeuvre if there was an attack. Sometimes their drivers would just play with the jeeps, zig-zagging around, in and out of the heavier trucks. But you couldn't get bored: focussed concentration was highly recommended. You could very easily lose your sense of depth in the blinding light, like a white-out on a snow-covered mountain. It was only 'when you felt the jeep rise beneath you that you knew you were climbing a dune.' Going up a 'razor-back' dune could be dangerous. You'd accelerate to get up, not see the top, then be flung out as the jeep hurtled down the other side. Hastings talked of an LRDG friend he'd met on the Benghazi raid: Alistair Timpson had damaged his arm, while his driver, Guardsman Wann, broke his back.[213]

Both the Jalo and Siwa oases were now in enemy hands, so a new base at Kufra, much further south, was set up. It was actually 'six separate groups of palms, each with its own wells ... all of these within a radius of five miles'. It was a 'lost oasis with crystal clear salt lakes fringed with palm trees'.[214] Maclean remembered 'two lakes of brilliant turquoise-blue, so salty that you could float sitting upright'.[215] From there the raiders would travel north through the Great Sand Sea and purposely pass the narrow gap at Jalo at midday, when 'the heat haze would make visibility poor' for the enemy. [216]

At the start of September, as part of Operation AGREEMENT, the Allies planned a surprise attack on Tobruk. The attack would be kicked off by a very large air raid, a seaborne attack to the north-west, followed by commando raids on the harbour installations landed by MTBs from the north-east. The brass wanted Stirling's group to go back to Benghazi, but this time with a large force – 214 men – 'half of whom came from other units'.[217] Stirling was dead against the idea: the convoy alone would be tough to hide men crossing the desert. Operation BIGAMY would be huge: thirty Jeeps and forty three-tonner trucks. As part of Force X, the Benghazi operation, Stirling was told to use the whole of L Detachment, the SBS, troops from ME Commando, even two Honey RN personnel and two Honey tanks to clear roadblocks. The latter were hopeless: 'They did indeed start but got bogged down in the sand and never made the operation.'[218] It was an assault group, reminiscent of some of the earlier ill-fated commando raids not an SAS action. Haselden's Force B targeted Tobruk and the SDF, Force A would retake the base at Jalo Oasis. Haselden had been a cotton broker in Egypt and, as a result, his Arabic 'was so perfect that he could be taken for an Arab, even by the Arabs.'[219]

Twenty-two of the Free French participated. They left Kabrit on 20 August and arrived at Kufra on 7 September. They'd only had one day's rest before having to set off for the final stretch to Benghazi. It was a long drive: 800 miles down to Kufra and then another 600 north to the Djebel. Hastings described the potential difficulties:

> The 800-mile journey from Kufra to the Jebel Akhdar, the hills around
> Benghazi, involved crossing a neck of the great sand sea, which stretches

from the edge of the Tibesti mountains in the southern Sahara 500 miles north of Jalo and Jarabub, a passage seldom attempted, except by the LRDG and certainly never by 80 heavily-laden vehicles. [220]

Around the same time, 22 August, a large SAS force left Cairo headed for the same location in seven 3-tonners, accompanied by units from coastal defence, Royal Engineers Signals and AA units. David Lloyd Owen's LRDG units joined up later. Their departure would be difficult to hide from German spies. Using some of the earlier SIG tactics, the idea was for three of the trucks to enter Tobruk as though they were bringing in British PoWs. Halting on the southern side of the harbour, the group was to divide into two units – Lieutenant Colonel Haselden would attack to the west, Major Campbell to the east. Tommy Langton would be responsible for signalling the MTBs, holding offshore.

By the time Haselden fired off his Verey pistol, the attack had already been rumbled: the group had managed to get in without a problem, then a single rifle shot raised the alarm. Langton's men had been seen. Led by one of his junior officers, Lieutenant Roberts, an immediate attack was launched on the German machine gun post that opened up on them. Subsequently, they were able to put a German W/T station out of commission. Langton got through to the seashore, from where he tried to signal the MTBs. En route, he had to deal with a couple of Germans who crossed his path: 'I hit them with my revolver.'[221]

He wasn't able to signal the MTBs, so he, along with Lieutenant Russell, Sillito and Privates Hillman and Watler, boarded one that had made it in and put the boat's guns to work. Furious fire was opened on the Germans on the overlooking hill who were shooting up other incoming MTBs. When they couldn't get the MTB's engines going, they transferred to a landing craft, using that to go out into the harbour.

The Germans now launched their own attack against Haselden in battalion strength. Before he was killed, one of his officers, Lieutenant Barlow, managed to lead some of the survivors out. Left behind to make their own way back were Langton, Ronald Watler and Hillman. The latter was actually an Austrian, Corporal Steiner, from Bruck's SIG. He was a fluent Arabic-speaker.[222] One of the first of the survivors to falter was Sergeant Evans, brought down by dysentery. A day later, the Leslie twins followed. For 78 days they marched, 'with 10 water-bottles, some bully-beef and some goat-meat'.[223] Tommy Langton had also learned some Arabic in Syria and was able to get some food and shelter from Arabs as well as intelligence on which villages would be friendly. Finally, the three were picked up 400 miles west of Tobruk. Langton had lost an astonishing five stone (32kg). When he made it back to Kabrit, a party was held in his honour. It got slightly out of hand, and Paddy Mayne drove a jeep – thankfully without injuring anyone – right through the mess. When he got back from the Middle East, Langton wrote a touching letter to Watler's father in London telling him not to 'worry', saying that Ronald would be 'home soon' and that he was 'very well and fit and enjoying life'.[224]

Before going into Benghazi, Stirling's Intelligence officer, Fitzroy Maclean, sent 'a shifty looking Arab deserter from the Italian army' ahead to gather intelligence.[225] He came back and gave Fitzroy and Bob Melot unwelcome news: the town was being reinforced. It seems as though Stirling's raiders were expected. Melot had been with the LAF and knew his way around. If he was nervous, there was good reason. What they learned was that around 5,000 Italian troops were in the process of being moved from al-Abyar to reinforce the Afrika Korps battalion. Damaged aircraft were now being placed as decoys on the edges of the airfields, where they would be tempting – and time-wasting – targets for the raiders. In the harbour itself, the final straw: shipping targets had mostly been moved out.

Stirling warned MEHQ that the plan had leaked and was told, in no uncertain terms, to go ahead. 'Ignore bazaar gossip' came the reply, and 'no great importance is attributed to this information.'[226]

On 10 September, Paddy Mayne set up an advance group at Wadi Gamra on the Djebel Akhdar. It was a good location from which to survey the Benghazi plain.

On 14 September, they went in. Chris Bailey and Bob Melot took one group to silence an Italian W/T post before the attack at 1600. Stirling's main group would head into Benghazi immediately after a planned midnight RAF raid. The W/T attacks succeeded, but Melot and Bailey were both badly injured. Bailey had been shot through the lung and Melot's torso was peppered with grenade fragments. Without Melot as their guide, Stirling's column got led into the wrong *wadi* and had to backtrack. When the RAF raid came, they were still 15 miles from the target. They only reached the base of the mountain at 0300, a good three hours late.

They pushed on. At 0430, Jim Almonds led the first group of jeeps to drive down to the port facilities. To the side holding up a gate stood Bill Cumper , who 'with typical bravado, proclaimed in a loud voice, "Let Battle commence".'[227] Just as he did so, enemy machine gun fire, mixed with well-placed mortar rounds, opened up. At least 'a dozen machine guns opened up … at point-blank range; then a couple of 20mm Bredas joined in.'[228] It was ear-splitting. The whole area was bathed in brilliant light, tracer zipping between the opposing forces.

After the raid, when he was back in England, Jellicoe wrote to Jim Almond's wife. The raiders, he explained,

> managed to pass through one road-block and your husband who was in the leading truck immediately charged the next obstruction. This they were unable to negotiate and your husband's truck was hit by machine-gun fire and caught fire. So heavy was the fire ... it soon became obvious that it would be impossible to proceed further and the order was given to retire. The co-driver of your husband's vehicle had managed to get back and rejoin the main party but there was no sign of your husband.[229]

Almonds remembered that he got to 'within about forty to fifty paces' of 'two concrete pillboxes and a big heavy chain stretched across between them' when enemy fire was opened.[230] He'd only just managed to get out of his jeep before it went up in a massive explosion. The Lewes bombs had been on board.

The SAS reacted, their training and experience kicking in immediately. Le Gall, *'calme à son ordinaire'*, got behind his machine gun and poured fire back at the well-dug-in Italian positions.[231] Eventually, his jeep was hit, but he stayed at his position as long as possible: *'Il etait resté à bord, à sa mittraileurse, jusqu'au moment ou sa pauvre voiture à été incendée'* (He stayed with his vehicle, manning the machine gun, till it went up in flames).[232]

Just as he was talking with Tony Drongin, his gunner, Seekings saw that he had been hit: 'a bullet had drilled through his thigh and slashed off his penis.'[233] Drongin was barely alive but conscious enough to rebuff attempts to dump him from the jeep. Despite his agony, he managed to hiss at the green officer who'd mistakenly assumed he was dead, 'Corporal Drongin to you, sir!'[234]

Eventually, Pleydell started to operate on the ex-Commando RSM. Drongin apologized to him for the bother. He had been taken back to the *wadi*, which was now also under attack. Maclean saw truck after truck hit and knew that getting the wounded back was going to be tough. In all, twenty trucks went up, including Pleydell's. It was just as bad for Mayne and the SDF, and in all around sixty trucks were lost. Stirling asked Pleydell to organize getting the seriously wounded handed over to either the Italians or Germans under a flag of truce. Among the dead, the French had lost one of their young officers, Guerpillion. The MOs drew lots for who was going to go with them under a white flag.

After the war, Churchill admitted that the ambush was known through ULTRA intercepts, but they had wanted the Germans to pull back their air cover.[235] I'm dubious about that claim. Asher maintains that GHQ knew about the reinforcements but did not think they were associated with Force X; For him 'the main cause of failure was the time lost in descending the escarpment.'[236] Asher places the blame firmly at Stirling's doorstep. More than 5,000km had been driven with precious little to show for it although, indirectly, the Germans' anticipation of the attack pulled some troops off the El Alamein front line. It must be said, however, that protecting the secrecy of ULTRA's existence exacted a heavy toll.

The group nearly didn't make it back, so many trucks had been lost: 'in one day, twenty-five trucks and nineteen jeeps'.[237] In total, fifty men and the same number of vehicles.[238] There was little space for the survivors, and water and petrol were scarce.

Almonds ended up a prisoner and was 'paraded round the town' the next day. He was 'chained up, two hands chained down to one foot'.[239] Mayne himself had nearly been killed. One of his team fell off the jeep he was driving, shot by a strafing plane. Without hesitation, Mayne jumped out and brought the soldier back on his shoulders. Hastings later recounted that they had nearly got away without the severe thrashing they received from the air:

> The trouble came the next evening. All day we had lain hidden in a *wadi* in the jebel while German and Italian aircraft flew around looking for us. There was a particularly persistent Italian bomber which seemed to circle our *wadi* repeatedly. One of our French comrades ... lost his Gallic patience and shot at it. That did it. Called in by the bomber, the planes roared in and we were bombed and strafed until dark.[240]

Once back at the oasis, their troubles weren't over. They were unsure of what lay ahead: the only way to tell if the oasis was back in Allied hands was to see if any German or Italian aircraft were around strafing and bombing.

Despite the obvious error of trying to make a large raiding force out of the SAS, on 28 September, in a meeting with Colonel John 'Shan' Hackett, Stirling was informed of the decision to expand the Detachment into a full regiment with a complement of 29 officers and 572 other ranks. 'Shan' Hackett had fought in North Africa with the 8th Hussars and briefly headed Special Forces reporting to Montgomery, before commanding the 4th Parachute Battalion during MARKET GARDEN in 1944. He and Jim Gavin (as a young Major General, commander of the U.S. 82nd Airborne at Arnhem) remained friends with the Jellicoes after the war. The SBS (the original Special Boat *Section*, not Squadron) would be absorbed into D Squadron, while the Free French would remain with C Squadron. Stirling had harboured a slight feeling of dread at the thought of the meeting but in the end admitted that they had seen 'eye to eye' and could develop a 'very close alliance'.[241] Hackett, however, hadn't been keen on taking the assignment and wrote to Freddy de Guingand about his dislike of organizing 'a lot of prima donnas'.[242]

The SAS was now organized into five squadrons: A, B, C, D, under the command, respectively, of Mayne, Peter Oldfield (with Vivian Street deputizing), Richard Lea and Tommy Langton, a man of extraordinary courage and tenacity. The remaining squadron functioned as HQ staff. After an unsuccessful raid on Tobruk harbour, Langton made the 400-mile trek across the desert to reach British lines. That he and his party survived was a testament to SAS and SBS training.

Anyone with seaborne experience gravitated to D squadron, so it was quite symbolic, if nothing else, that Jellicoe, given his naval connections, was attached to the detachment which would become the basis for the SBS when he took over command in 1943. Courtney's SBS had been 'swallowed temporarily by the Stirling octopus' following losses in personnel and 'without any really valid case for a separate existence'.[243] D detachment also included the nascent Greek Sacred Squadron under the inimitable Colonel Christodoulos Tsigantes, untested as yet in its new Special Forces role. Sutherland thought Tsigantes looked like 'a prosperous restaurateur' although he was 'highly sophisticated and charming, spoke five languages and was fearless in action'.[244]

The Greek contingent had originally been put together in 1942 under the command of Major Antonios Stefanakis. When it made its début in early September 1942 it was known as the 'Squadron of Select Immortals'. After Greece's defeat in 1941, the recruits to the Immortals came from individuals or Greek units fighting in the Middle East. It didn't matter whether they were cadets, enlisted men or officers, although they were heavily drawn from the officer class, as the sheer number could not be easily absorbed into the structure of the 1st and 2nd Greek Brigades.

Gradually, the unit changed its complexion as the new commanding officer, Tsigantes, gave it a more Special Forces flavour, but it wasn't until a meeting with Stirling took place (on Christmas Day 1942) that the future role of the GSS within the SAS was first tabled. The men wore a distinctive beige beret and the Spartan Sword emblem. The motto of the *Ieros Lochos* was memorable, harking back to the days of Spartan courage: 'Bring back your shield or be brought back on it' ('With it or on it'). Tsigantes was the '"General Gigantes" of Lawrence Durrell's *Alexandria Quartet* – the dashing, original and very effective commander of the Greek Sacred Brigade.'[245]

But it was also said that Tsigantes, a rightist, had purged all officers who had any communist leanings. As a result, the Squadron was known as 'the private army of the Greek right', and the unit had been increased to regimental size of around 1,000 men in April to help balance the political forces.[246] Tsigantes himself had been condemned to death in 1935 for his part in an attempted coup but had been reprieved.

The Greek Sacred Squadron (*Ieros Lochos*)

'We used to say that the Greeks fight like heroes,
now we say that heroes fight like Greeks' (Churchill)

The *Ieros Lochos*, known in English as the **Greek Sacred Squadron** or **Sacred Band (GSS)** was formed to bring together many Greeks who had fled their country following its fall to the Axis in May 1941. All were volunteers. During the war the new unit would fight alongside the SAS, the SBS, the Free French, the New Zealand Division and the Eighth Army.

The original unit, formed in 1941 and sent to Egypt for training, was called the 'Dodecanesian Phalanx'. It provided the core organization into which those fleeing from Greece's triple occupation (by Germany, Italy and Bulgaria) could muster. The suggestion of forming a specific unit to bring these men and women together was made by an older and senior Air Force officer, Wing Commander, now Lieutenant Colonel G. Alexandris, and was approved by the commander of the 2nd Greek Brigade, Colonel Alkiviadis Bourdaras. Like the SAS, there were too many officers and not enough ORs, so many officers served in the ranks. The 1st Greek Brigade took part in the battle of El Alamein. The 2nd Brigade was created thereafter.

When Colonel Christodoulos Tsigantes became the unit's new commander on 15 September 1942, it was renamed 'The Greek Sacred Squadron'. There were 'just 150 of us', Korkas, a GSS veteran, said. The GSS became part of Raiding Forces Middle East based at Azzib (modern day Achziv) on the coast road north of Nahariyya, alongside the SAS, LRDG, SBS, the Free French and PPA (Popski's Private Army, named after their commander, Vladimir Peniakoff).

The GSS was sent by Stirling to Tripoli with Jellicoe. When Stirling was captured, command was turned over to the French and Tsigantes reported to Leclerc. In May 1943, Tsigantes persuaded Montgomery to release the squadron from North Africa, allowing it to participate in the war on the Greek islands alongside of the SBS, even if under very tight allied control.

The role of the Squadron in the liberation of Greece was a mixed one. Churchill had wanted to use the Dodecanese islands as a bargaining chip with Turkey: the islands' return to Turkish sovereignty in return for Turkish entry into the war. Consequently, the deeply nationalistic GSS was not trusted by the Allies for mainland operations, and in the Aegean was limited to certain islands only. Furthermore, Tisigantes' strongly right-wing leanings made him a difficult partner when dealing with communist ELAS (the leftists) in the early stages of occupation, as the British still hoped to use their strength to help oust the Germans.

On 7 August 1945, the squadron was disbanded in Athens. Its total wartime losses amounted to twenty-five dead, fifty-six wounded, three missing and twenty-nine captured.

Tsigantes' granddaughter, Eleni, an architect in Athens, played down the General's political leanings when I met her, saying, 'The *Ieros Lochos* consisted of every kind of political ideology ... that was all put aside ... they worked as a team' and that 'he didn't really have a left or right politics. That was the secret of him.'[247] Many might find it hard to agree with her conclusion.

Men whose homeland was under enemy occupation – the Greeks, the French, a Dane like Andy Lassen – harboured an intense desire to fight in a different way, maybe, from the British. As in the SAS, they were prepared to take a demotion. There were too many officers and not enough ORs, so the obvious solution was a series of reductions in rank, much as had happened in the Snowballers. Tsigantes, originally a Colonel, became a Captain; Wing Commander/Lieutenant Colonel G. Alexandris became Corporal Alexandris; Captain Kazakopoulos became a Sergeant Major; RHN Captain Matheos became a Sergeant.[248] There had been considerable opposition to his taking the role, and there was a 'heated discussion' with officers and men of the squadron on 12 September which eventually cleared the way to Tsigantes assuming command three days later.[249]

The next month, October, Montgomery took over command. The expansion of Stirling's unit would not have happened had it been left any longer. Along with Hackett, Stirling went to see 'Monty' early in the month to ask if he could recruit out of the Eighth Army. Montgomery immediately took umbrage, bristling at Stirling's reasonably straightforward request. He didn't like the SAS and thought Stirling 'quite, quite mad':

I find your request arrogant in the extreme ... You failed at Benghazi and you come here asking, no, demanding the best of my men. In all honesty, Colonel Stirling, I am not inclined to associate myself with failure.[250]

Monty's description of Stirling, despite his obvious distaste for the SAS leader, should, however, be seen in context, for he did end by saying, 'However, in a war there is often a place for mad people.' But, it must be said, Montgomery was wholly against their style of warfare.

It is to Stirling's eternal credit that he could deal with such men diplomatically. He was 'always conscious that the fight was not solely against the enemy, but also against the so-called top brass.'[251] I doubt that Mayne would have been able to control himself, facing the sort of cold, insulting tirade that was so often associated with Montgomery. What saved Stirling in this instance was bumping into Brigadier Freddy de Guingand. He hinted at the coming North African landing, Operation TORCH, and a possible role in it for Stirling's men.

During the November 1942 El Alamein push, however, Montgomery wouldn't assign Stirling any role. So, on his own initiative, Stirling organized a schedule of raids against a range of targets along the Libyan coastline west of El Aghelia. Mayne's patrols harried the Germans by blowing up the Tobruk–al-Dhaba rail line seven times. One time, when the line at Sidi Barrani was being blown, there was a sole SAS survivor. Corporal John Sillito managed to walk 200 miles back across the desert to British lines in eight days, with neither water nor food.

Now as part of D detachment, three jeeps were assigned eight men from the Greeks under Alexandris for operations in the Agadabia region between 19 November and 12 December. They didn't see combat; the Germans were in full retreat. Being trained, readied for action and then held back must have disappointed the Greeks in the same way Stirling and others in LAYFORCE had felt. In another aborted operation, sixty men were tasked, under the command of Lieutenant Colonel Emmanuel Fradellos, in taking part in a seaborne attack on El Agheila. That operation was also called off just before Christmas.

No sooner had they absorbed the SBS and the Greek Sacred Squadron, than the SAS lost most of the French. De Gaulle ordered them back to Britain and all, except Jordan and a small contingent, left Suez on 10 December. Two weeks later, Jordan took the remainder out of Kabrit to the base at Bir-Guedaffia, where Stirling arrived with a group of twenty men in eleven jeeps around 15 January. The Greeks, too, would be on the move again.

Meanwhile, Jellicoe had spent much of the second half of 1942 back in England because of the problems with his knee but was itching to get back into action. In January 1943, he succeeded. With the backing of

Mountbatten, the Director of Combined Operations, he received a very useful passepartout: 'Captain, the Earl Jellicoe is urgently needed back for operational duties in the Middle East. Please give him any help you can.'[252] The Foreign Office allowed him to carry dispatches, and he travelled to Lisbon and then Gibraltar, where he went on a pub crawl, met up with some American pilots who were ferrying Flying Fortresses and managed to get a lift. The next morning, he was in Heliopolis.

Stirling immediately asked Jellicoe to take D Squadron westward to Tripoli to organise raiding from there. Sutherland was also ordered to a new location, in his case Beirut, with fifty men. Initially, he bucked at the idea, but then Stirling put him in the picture:

> You're not going [with the rest of the SAS on continued North African missions], and I'll tell you why. You, George Jellicoe and Tom Langton have unique small boat operational experience. You will be needed soon to carry out raids on the soft underbelly of Europe. You are much too valuable to be wasted elsewhere.[253]

Stirling was already thinking of the front moving northwards to Italy and Greece.

Around 25 or 26 January, Jellicoe and Tsigantes moved base from Egypt to Libya to attack Axis forces in the rear as they pulled back to Tunisia. With forty jeeps, the two drove off with all the men. On the journey, they got to know each other better. Jellicoe enjoyed Tsigantes' 'universality' and the fact that he was 'loyal not only to his friends but also to his principles'.[254]

When they arrived in Tripoli they received the staggering news that David Stirling had been captured. He had at first managed to escape the Germans but was then picked up by Italian troops and was immediately heavily interrogated. Next to his cell was a 'British officer', a Captain John Richards. Starved of company, Stirling started talking, telling 'Richards', whose real name was Theodore Schurch, that he was C.O. of the SAS, the man Rommel had nicknamed the 'Phantom Major'. It was a coup for the enemy. Schurch had been with Oswald Mosley's Blackshirts in London's East End and had subsequently been recruited by Italian Intelligence. Stirling testified at Schurch's later trial and, after Joyce's execution, he became the last man to be executed in Britain for treason. Paul McCue told me that, despite having been hanged and buried in an unmarked but carefully recorded grave at Pentonville Prison, he is still commemorated on the Memorial to the Missing 1939–1945 at Brookwood Military Cemetery in Surrey and is also – very strangely for a traitor – 'Remembered' on the website of the Commonwealth War Graves Commission.

After four months of frustration and disappointment, Tsigantes now had to persuade Montgomery, no friend of Stirling and even less of Special Force tactics and demeanour, that they could be gainfully employed in the capacity for which they'd trained. Montgomery wasn't persuaded, an especially bitter pill to swallow given that Greek efforts to participate in the desert war had been further set back when the Greek 2nd Brigade was removed from the front. Tsigantes, with the help of the Greek Crown Prince Petros and Jellicoe, could do little else but appeal to the French. As a compromise, Montgomery allowed Tsigantes' men to join the Free French forces under General Leclerc. For a short interlude, Jellicoe and the Greeks would part company.

Within the SAS, 'chaos ensued' at the news of Stirling's capture.[255] The best thing for the SAS was that it was reconstituted. Jellicoe felt that such an outcome would be a good thing. 'It had become unwieldy' as it had grown a little too large, consisting, at this point, of 47 officers and 532 other ranks.[256] John Lodwick felt the same. It was the 'sensible way', as Stirling's persona and character ran through every sinew of the organization. Its men wore their wings and light camel-coloured berets with the Regiment's emblem with deep pride.

Stirling was, of course, decorated but he was, in Jellicoe's estimation, 'one of the most under-decorated officers in the British Army'.[257] It goes without saying that Jellicoe recognized Stirling's 'extraordinary levels of courage' combined with equally extraordinary powers of leadership.[258]

Part II

SBS Command

Chapter 5

Taking over the SBS

With its two original founders gone – Lewes killed, Stirling captured – the future of the SAS hung in the balance – its very existence as a unit, not just who should take over command. The SAS had always prided itself on its independence, and it looked like that was now at risk. The general opinion was that replacing David Stirling would be an almost impossible challenge. Initially, overall command passed to one of the Squadron leaders, Vivien Street, but he was replaced on 9 March by the former head of 51 Commando, Lieutenant Colonel H. J. Cator.

Stirling's brother Peter wrote that 'there is literally no one of the same stature and prestige to replace him.'[1] Mayne elicited an extraordinary level of admiration, but some of the men, like Reg Seekings, didn't think Jellicoe was up to it: 'Nobody ever thought of Jellicoe or anybody like that becoming CO of the SAS ... It was Paddy Mayne. Mayne was the man.'[2] Mayne's courage on the battlefield was legendary amongst the men and his fellow officers. David Lloyd Owen later commented that he knew of 'no other man who did more to deserve the Victoria Cross and who was so inadequately decorated for his exploits'.[3] Lance Corporal Denis Bell (No.11 Scottish Commando) wrote that Mayne, with whom he had served extensively, 'wasn't frightened of anything, nothing at all ... He wouldn't take any silly risks, but would rely on boldness, deadly accurate firepower and speed of action.'[4] Mayne might have been a superb man in the field, he did not, in Stirling's own opinion, necessarily have the political acumen for the job, even though, elsewhere, he would later write that he 'was exactly the man I wanted to succeed me in command of 1 SAS.'[5] While a certain irreverence was always welcome in the SAS, getting arrested for drunk and disorderly behaviour did not help relations with MEHQ, even if the word came down, when Paddy was in jail, that he was 'more use as an officer [than] to be broken to the ranks'. The Regiment's way is a distinct preference for a low profile. Stirling himself wrote about the two, at different times: Jellicoe, he said, was 'absolutely indispensable' and was 'much brighter than he appears at 1st sight'.[6]

The question now became 'what kind of unit is needed for a non-desert war?' Suggestions of keeping one amphibious force of around 150 men, the SAS Small-Scale Raiding Squadron, and another Commando-type unit, the SAS Commando Squadron, started to make the rounds; in fact, a consultative document written along these lines was sent to Mayne and Jellicoe for comments.[7] It was dated 8 March 1943. Mayne vigorously resisted the idea of Stirling's beloved SAS falling back to a Commando designation. Successfully.

On 19 March, the decision was taken to split 1 SAS. It would be divided into two almost equal parts – one squadron under Mayne maintaining its reconnaissance and sabotage roles, the other, under Jellicoe, taking on the more amphibious role that Stirling had always wanted with the retention and development of Roger Courtney's Folboat capability, always 'aspiring to branch out into sabotaging shipping and not just aircraft'.[8]

Mayne, still with the acting rank of Major, was given 250 men from the 1st SAS Regiment, itself only created the previous year on 28 September, now renamed the Special Raiding Squadron (SRS). In all, his strength totalled 280.[9] Most came from the A Squadron, which had arrived back in Kabrit from Lebanon in February.

The 2nd SAS Regiment, operating with the First Army, would come under David Stirling's brother, Bill. He had already taken command and would continue raiding operations in Sicily and Italy. That two Stirlings served in the SAS led to the joke: 'SAS really stands for "Stirling and Stirling".'

Bergé's forces had been handed back to French command and, with the two parachute battalions, would eventually become the 3rd and 4th SAS Regiments. His squadron had been incorporated into General Leclerc's Free French so that 'it could be used for operations aiming at outflanking the German right in Tunisia', where they fought in the battles for the Mareth line.[10] Already in February they'd headed off to north-west Africa.

Jellicoe, like Mayne now also promoted Major, took the men who remained from 1 SAS, 62nd Commando (SSRF) and fifty-five from the old Special Boat Section (SBS). In mid-April, the force was made up of 13 officers and 118 ORs but, with Maclean's arrival from Persia, another 4 officers and 100 ORs were added.[11] The Greek Sacred Squadron, *Ieros Lochos*, would also work alongside Jellicoe's SBS, although not incorporated into it.

The Special Boat *Section* commander, Courtney, had been declared unfit the previous November and repatriated to Britain in December 1941. Back training in Scotland and now a Major, Courtney raised a new SBS troop, the 2nd SBS, and was then succeeded by Captain Kealy when it was clear that he was burnt out, suffering from exhaustion. It was at this point that some of the men whose names would forever be associated with the unit – David Sutherland, Eric Newby and John Lodwick – joined. Newby would later write *Love and War in the Apennines*, an account of his escape through Italy; Lodwick would write *The Filibusters*; and Sutherland, 'a man who only spoke if he had something to say', would take over the SBS from Jellicoe at the end of 1944.[12] Like the others, he would also write about these days in *He Who Dares*.

In both the SAS and SBS, a premium was always placed on good language skills. Jellicoe's French had helped improve the liaison with the Free French and was one of the reasons Stirling wanted him on board. Another was Walter Milner-Barry, fondly known as 'Papa' because of his age, who spent much of his time helping to teach Greek to officers and ORs in L Detachment, which he joined in March 1943. Even men like Seekings apparently picked up pretty good basic Arabic by insisting on ordering food in the language. More than a few close calls were successfully avoided using the enemy's language.

To be on a par, both units, Mayne's and Jellicoe's, were renamed 'Squadrons', although even in their own early documents Jellicoe's unit was still confusingly called the Special Boat 'Service' rather than Special Boat Squadron.

Origins of the Special Boat Squadron

Although the SAS is the better-known of the two units, the first one that actually achieved success was the SBS in a raid on the Italian coast in June 1941 that blew up an ammunition train. The first SAS operation, that November, was a disaster.

The origins of the SBS are complex and controversial. SBS stands for many things: Special Boat Section, Service and Squadron. They are frequently mixed up, even in official records. Branches were started independently, within the Commandos, the Royal Marines and within David Stirling's SAS. The initials 'SBS' can refer to a number of slightly different organizations that were often 'cross-fertilized'. The original SBS unit was probably Roger Courtney's Special Boat Section, which was part of No.8 Commando's contribution to LAYFORCE. Jellicoe's new unit, formed in March 1943, was originally officially called the Special Boat *Service*, which by April 1943 had been changed to *Squadron*, to give it equal status, I think, with Paddy Maynes' SRS (Special Raiding Squadron). The new unit incorporated one of the two sections, the 2nd SBS. It should be said that, at the same time, in the same theatre, the Royal Navy was operating the Kabrit Canoe teams, while the Boom Commando Troop was being run by the Royal Marines. In 1947, the Small Raiding Wing of the Royal Marines was formed, to be renamed as the Special Boat Company in 1957 and the Special Boat Squadron in 1975. What the SBSA, the unit's Association, calls its 'lineage' is complicated but probably best recognises its mixed parentage.

Talents were recruited from far and wide. They were combined and pulled apart as duties and objectives changed. So it is not an easy task to trace the origins of the unit. It is easier – and actually more realistic – to cast the net wider and recognize the component parts that came together.

The squadron came into existence on 19 March 1943, although – even in its own documentation – it was still called a Service until the first formal mention on 7 April. Sutherland, Allott, Andy Lassen and Philip Pinkney all came to the Squadron via the Special Boat Section.

Roger Courtney and Tug Wilson were the founders of the original SBS, 'known initially as the Folboat Troop', part of No.8 Commando. Seeing that LAYFORCE would offer little potential to his force, Courtney transferred to HMS *Medway*, from which the small group operated as part of the 1st Submarine Flotilla.[13] Admiral Maud, Director of Combined Operations at GHQ, looked upon Courtney's section with interest: why not drop off saboteurs in the course of a normal submarine mission? A year later, No.2 SBS was formed in Britain as part of No.1 Special Service Brigade, again under Brigadier Laycock. Apparently, there was little in the way of unit identification. Lodwick (p.19) quipped that a clerk had looked at some documents with their stamp on it, asking what the 'Special Boot Section' was.

When Courtney was sent back to the UK because of ill health, the unit was taken over by Mike Kealy. It was through Courtney's unit that well-known names came into the SBS – David Sutherland, Corporals Duggie Pomford and Riley, Captain Ken Allott, Tommy Langton, Mike Alexander and Eric Newby.

Both units, the SBS and the SRS, would come under the command of Colonel Henry J. 'Kid' Cator, Commanding Officer of the Middle East Raiding Forces, reporting to General Headquarters in Cairo.[14] He was given a limited role – covering logistic support, training and discipline, but specifically omitting any operational control, which remained with Mayne and Jellicoe.

Cator's appointment couldn't have been easy for Mayne in particular. He was exceptionally well connected, since he was the Queen's brother-in-law. He was also a close friend of Geoffrey Keyes, the man who had Mayne removed from 11 Commando after another drunken episode. Mayne also had to accept that the nature of his war would change and that 'seaborne ops were obviously the key of the invasion of Mediterranean Europe.'[15] The core of the SAS went to Italy and then back to England for post-OVERLORD operations. With the war in the desert coming to an end, the SBS was assigned to the Aegean and Adriatic, the SRS to Sicily and Italy.

Essentially, what was left became the Special Boat *Squadron*. It was a tight group. First of all, as part of the old SAS D Detachment, it absorbed David Sutherland's Special Boat *Section*. Its ranks reflected that. The usually impeccably turned-out Sutherland became one of the new detachment commanders.

This is how the Dane, Anders Lassen, who had supposedly met Jellicoe when he was briefly back in London, came on board. Robert Laycock at Combined Operations HQ agreed to let him be seconded to Jellicoe's new SBS, since 62 Commando (also known as the SSRF, or Small Scale Raiding Force) had been disbanded. Lassen had received a field commission but he 'took his promotion lightly and never wore his rank badges or the Military Cross, awarded for his actions in Fernando Po, unless directly ordered to do so.'[16] His would be the only VC that either the SAS or the SBS would win during the war, and unsurprisingly Jellicoe described him as causing 'more damage and discomfort to the enemy during five years of war than any man of his rank and age'.[17]

Lassen's mother, Suzanne, wrote the first biography of her famous son. He had been away from Denmark for years and she had no idea what sort of man he'd become. Anders' younger sister, Bente, explained that she wrote about his life as a way to fill in the blanks. I read her account, probably when I was in my teens – around the same time I read Virginia Cowles' *The Phantom Major* – and still remember it vividly. Suzanne Lassen is still beloved by Danes, but mostly for her illustrated children's stories rather than the biography.

John Verney also joined, as did, from Persia, Fitzroy Maclean. He had a rather detached way about him which even David Stirling noted was misleading: he told Hermione Ranfurly that she should not be taken in 'by his rather pompous manner or his slow way of speaking – he is OK.'[18] Ranfurly had famously insisted on taking her butler to war when she joined her husband, Dan, and wrote about it in *To War with Whitaker*. At the time she worked for George Pollock, the head of SOE (MO.4) and could see the level of often political and counter-productive manoeuvring that went on between the various clandestine outfits. It was the documents she smuggled out that caused MO.4 to be subject to a major reorganization. After her husband was taken prisoner, she eventually ended up working for 'Jumbo' Wilson.

Then there was Milner-Barry. He had joined the SBS from the Transjordan Frontier Force, had worked in the Middle East with Shell Oil and was both an Arabic speaker and a diplomat.

Jellicoe moved the SBS into a camp at Athlit, 15km or so south of Haifa.[19] Initially, the SRS and SBS had shared a camp inland to the east, 'under the Golan Heights', overlooking Lake Tiberias (today's Sea of Galilee) when they moved from Kabrit to Palestine. This might have been what became the SBS 'winter camp', to which John House and Ian Patterson refer. The ORs were in tents; the officers in little cabins dotted around the mess hall. They also shared equipment: 'each group had 15 trucks and 5 jeeps.'[20] One of these jeeps was Jellicoe's and with it came a new driver, John House, an artilleryman and one of the original intake into the ranks of the early SAS. He and Jellicoe had been driving up to Haifa and were just passing a prison when Jellicoe spotted a beach across the dunes. 'The boss' (which was how John referred to him), 'declared the beach ideal for a camp.'[21]

On the way back they stopped again, this time at what John called a 'prison', where Jellicoe was able to persuade the 'Prison Governor' to let him use some of his civilian labour to help clear tracks and dig trenches. Mesh was laid down to help his trucks get across the dunes.[22]

It was a very different setting to Kabrit, with castle, Le Château Pèlerin, at one end of a long, golden beach, nestled under the slopes of Mount Carmel. Jellicoe joked that they arrived at their new camp on April Fool's Day, but they were actually there before that. Verney, Jellicoe's Adjutant, described the spirit of the Athlit days in *Going to the Wars*:[23]

> A lovely spring, an ecstasy of fitness and sense of mission … Days and nights spent tramping over thyme-scented Mount Carmel – in swimming across the Bay, in naked races along the sands, in landing canoes and dinghies on the rocks, watched only by a few tattered Arabs living with goats and chickens amid the ruins of the Crusader castle.

His account then takes a nosedive, describing the silhouette of the latrines. Almost everyone thought the place idyllic. Milner-Barry talked about it being 'a most beautiful site' with 'wild flowers of every kind'.[24]

Admiral Jellicoe's family at Government House, Wellington, during his term as Governor General. L to R: Myrtle, Prudie, Admiral Jellicoe, Gwendoline, Norah, Lucy. George Jellicoe is sitting on the floor. (*Author's collection*)

Jellicoe with Queen Mary, an occasional visitor with her husband, King George V, to the Admiral's Isle of Wight house, St Lawrence Court. (*Author's collection*)

George with his father, the Admiral, shortly before his death in 1935. He caught a chill attending the Armistice ceremony at the Cenotaph and died eleven days later. (*Author's collection*)

The SAS jeeps were fitted with an additional condenser and twin Vickers K machine guns, capable of 1,200 rounds a minute. (*Author's collection*)

David Stirling with some of his men (R to L: Lt. Edward Macdonald, Cpl Bill Kennedy, Pte. Malcolm Mackinnon, unknown, Cpl. Jack Sillito and L/Sgt. John Henderson. (*With kind permission of the SAS Regimental Association*)

LEFT: Jock Lewes, seen by Stirling as the co-founder of the SAS. RIGHT: Paddy Mayne took over the SAS when the SBS was split off under Jellicoe's command. (*Both photos with kind permission of the SAS Regimental Association*)

ABOVE: LRDG/SAS group photo showing Bill Fraser (1), David Stirling (2), Paddy Mayne (3), Jeff du Vivier (4) and Johnny Cooper (5). (*Courtesy Family of the late Lt. Col. Jake Easonsmith*). LEFT: The jump tower built by Jim Almonds after other training methods proved too dangerous. Steel was scrounged and labour supplied by the SAS, the nearby Royal Engineers and Italian prisoners.

Lord Jellicoe (5), Troop 2, 8 (Guards) Commando, commanded by Capt. Mervyn Griffith-Jones. Jim Almonds (1), Jim Blakeney (2), Bob Lilley (3) and Pat Riley (4), were known as the Tobruk Four.

Jellicoe – known as 'the Lord' or 'Curly – in the desert in the early days. (*Author's collection*)

The other SAS. ABOVE: Capitaine Georges Bergé, Free French SAS, led the raid on Heraklion airfield in June 1942. RIGHT: Colonel Christodoulos Tsigantes commanded the Greek Sacred Squadron, whose men fought to recapture the Greek islands in 1943–44 before the mainland could be liberated. Both became lifelong friends of Jellicoe. (*Author's collection*) Below: Tsigantes in a desert convoy with the SAS.

Bergé's Free French, England. L to R BACK: Contentin, Guegan, Le Goff, Audibert, Gauthier, Georges Royer, le Roy, Duccourneau and Cpt. Bergé. MIDDLE: le Gall, Léostic, Mouhot, Tourneret, de Bourmont, Belle, le Goas, s.Lt. Jacquier. FRONT Boutinot, Vidal, Jouanny, Guetry, de Bugnières, Mariage, Niot, and Carion. BELOW L: Augustin Jordan, 2i/c to Bergé. BELOW R: André Zirnheld, a philosopher and poet. One of his poems became the prayer for the French parachute service.

Jellicoe, post-war, with Cretan guerrillas. (*Author's collection*)

One of the twenty-two aircraft destroyed by the raiders on Heraklion airfield.

BELOW L: Jack Sibard, Free French Forces. (*Author's collection*) M: Jacques Mouhot, Kabrit, April 1942 R: Oberst Karl Meidert, German commander of the Heraklion airfield, June 1942.

ABOVE L: MO.4 officer, Major the Count Julian Dobrski (aka Dolbey), who parachuted into Rhodes at night, only admitting it was his first jump as he got up in the plane. ABOVE R: Colonel Turnbull, Jellicoe's CO in Raiding Forces. BELOW: The Italians and their new-found allies. L to R: Rear Admiral Mascherpa, the Italian Governor, Brigadier Brittorius, Commander Borghi, the Italian Chief of Staff, Turnbull, Lieutenant Colonel Li Volsi, the Commander of Italian Infantry Units. Back row centre: Captain E.H.B. Baker RN, Senior Naval Officer and on his left, Major Jellicoe, SBS.

Brigadier Tilney with General Müller after his surrender on Leros, 16 November 1943. Jellicoe escaped to Turkey with his men.

ABOVE: Lt. Col. Jake Easonsmith, LRDG commander, was killed by a sniper in Leros town (Platanos). RIGHT: Lt. Alan Phipps RN, killed on Leros defending Tilney's headquarters. (*Courtesy Jeremy Phipps*)

Jellicoe on the SBS command caïque, *Tewfik*. With him are Captain Chevalier (centre) and probably Lt. Petrakis, with whom Jellicoe had been on the Crete raid, June 1942. (This is sometimes thought to be Stefan Casulis, Greek Sacred Squadron, who was later killed in Lassen's attack on the Santorini garrison.) BELOW: Major Jellicoe briefing his men for a raid on Simi. On his left is General Kalinski(s), at the time of the island raids, Lt. Col. Andreas Kalinskis. (*Both photos with kind permission of the SAS Regimental Association*)

Andy Lassen, the only non-Commonwealth recipient of the Victoria Cross in the Second World War.

Adrian Seligman, Levant Schooner Flotilla.

Greek Intelligence officer 2nd Lt. George Pavlides, attached to the LRDG, arriving with some survivors at Farmakonisi, between Leros and Turkey.

George Jellicoe
and Patsy O'Kane
in Beirut, at the
Garrison Church,
on their wedding
day, 23 March 1944.
(*Author's collection*)

Life on board the caïques in one of the anchorage points scattered along the Turkish coast. (*With kind permission of the SAS Regimental Association*)

TOP L: Aris Veloukhiotis, ELAS guerrilla leader. TOP R: The ill-fated paratroop drop to reinforce Jellicoe's drive to liberate the city, Megara, west of Athens, October 1944. MIDDLE L: Major Ian Patterson MC. ABOVE: Jellicoe meeting with Archbishop Damaskinos, Athens along with Frank McKaskie (SOE) and Shan Sedgwick of the *New York Times*. (*Courtesy Alexandra Henderson*)

Athens Cathedral, October 1944. Left of George Jellicoe: General Spiliotopoulos, C-in-C of the Athens and African area and fully representative of the Greek Government before its return. To his right: The Mayor of Athens, Aristides Skliros, then Brigadier P. Katsotas, former CO of the Greek Brigade that fought at El Alamein, sent by the Greek Government from Cairo a few days before the liberation to act as Chief of Staff to General Spiliotopoulos. (*Author's collection*)

After a bitter 10-year divorce battle, Jellicoe's second marriage to Philippa was a happy one. (*Author's collection*)

Jellicoe was a very strong skier and would holiday in Courchevel, Verbier and for many years in Méribel, with Philippa. (*Author's Collection*)

In Washington, Jellicoe worked closely with (LEFT) Kim Philby, unconscious of his real loyalties. All the spies sent into Albania by the OSS and (RIGHT) Frank Wisner were betrayed. (*Courtesy Frank Wisner*)

Jellicoe with his children (L to R): Daisy, Johnny, Alexandra, Nick (the author) and Emma either side of George, David Lloyd, Zara and Paddy, at the time Viscount Brocas, now 3rd Earl Jellicoe. (*Courtesy Gideon Hart*)

LEFT: In 1960, Jellicoe became the last holder of the post of First Lord of the Admiralty and is here visiting an Oberon-class submarine, HM/S *Opossum*, in Gosport. He was particularly proud to have followed in the footsteps of his father, who had been First Sea Lord in 1917. RIGHT: Looking happy – and certainly relieved – after a carrier landing. (*Author's collection*)

ABOVE: Jason Mavrikis, Athens, 2004. (*Author's collection*) MIDDLE: Andy Lassen's bust in Copenhagen BELOW: With Jack Sibard, Heraklion airport commemoration. (*Author's collection*)

ABOVE: David Sutherland, David Stirling and George Jellicoe (*Author's collection*) BELOW: With Paddy Leigh Fermor, British Embassy, Athens. When he died in 2007, Jellicoe was the Father of the House of Lords and the longest serving parliamentarian in the world. (*Author's collection*)

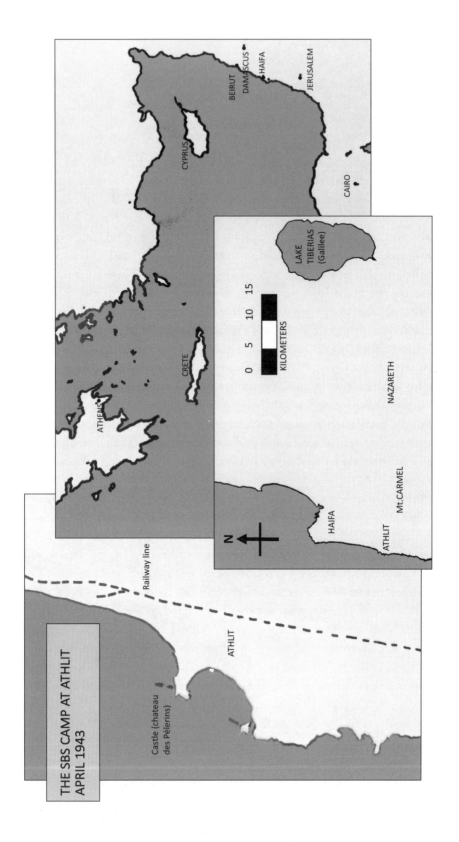

THE SBS CAMP AT ATHLIT
APRIL 1943

Castle (chateau des Pèlerins)

Railway line

ATHLIT

N

HAIFA

ATHLIT

Mt.CARMEL

NAZARETH

LAKE TIBERIAS (Galilee)

KILOMETERS
0 5 10 15

ATHENS

CRETE

CYPRUS

BEIRUT

DAMASCUS

HAIFA

JERUSALEM

CAIRO

The Folboat Section

A Forgotten Heritage?

Roger Courtney's SBS had nearly played a key role in LAYFORCE. Along with Lt. Cmdr. Nigel Wilmott, Courtney had made a detailed recce of landing sites on Rhodes before the assault was called off. He crawled ashore and got to within 60m of the German HQ at Hôtel des Roses. Later, his men, working with a Malta-based submarine flotilla, carried out successful small-scale sabotage. Like Stirling's brother Bill, Courtney had been at the Lochailort Officer Commando school as an instructor. His section profited from his peacetime love – canoeing. The first boats, the 'Cockle Mark I' folding canoes, were known as 'Folboats' or 'Folding boats', and the men trained to use them were 'Folbotiers' (Wynter, *Special Forces*, p.305). The Mark II, used on the Gironde mission, was rigid. The rubberized canvas boats were 16ft long, had a beam of 28½ inches and a draught of 11¼ inches. Fearing for his small unit's continued survival after the disbanding of LAYFORCE, Courtney took his group, which had by now grown to eight officers and thirty men, and transferred to submarines, where he could continue training. They used to scout ahead of commando raids or recce possible landing beaches and had been training for a raid on Pantelleria, an operation that never came to fruition.

When Courtney set up the Folboat Troop, with him went his 2i/c, Lt. R. 'Tug' Wilson (RA), Sgt. George Barnes (Grenadiers), Cpl. James B. Sherwood (RASC), Sgt. Allan (Royal Marines), Randolph Churchill, Cpl. G. C. Bremner, Cpl. White and Marine 'Wally' Hughes. Sherwood and Churchill had been RTU'd from No.8; neither had been physically fit enough. They trained on Arran, where No.8 also trained.

Wilson and Hughes were informally attached to the 10th Submarine Flotilla and then formally assigned to a submarine, *Utmost*. A series of successful raids was carried out – Santa Eufemia, the Saracino bridge in Italy in August 1941 and Navarino in Greece in December. After the loss of Crete, clandestine evacuations of New Zealand, Australian and British troops – 125 of them – were carried out by a single SBS canoeist, Cpl Bremner. Clandestine operations hugely supported SOE, delivering and extracting agents in enemy territory. Such experience would be useful again in Leros in 1943.

The most famous raid became a film, *The Cockleshell Heroes*. On 30 November 1942 canoe teams set out on the submarine *Tuna* with the intention of blowing up shipping sixty miles up the Gironde River in Bordeaux. The shipping was bringing rubber from Japan to Germany. There were only two survivors from the 7 December raid – Major H. G. 'Blondie' Hassler RM and his companion, Marine Sparks. Six men were caught and shot by the Gestapo. Hassler's group came together in Southsea in early 1942 but languished without support for most of the year. The successful December 1942 Alexandria harbour raid by the Italians, in which HMS *Valiant* and HMS *Queen Elizabeth* were both severely damaged, changed opinions. His unit, originally misleadingly named the Royal Marines Harbour Patrol Detachment, became the Royal Marine Boom Patrol Detachment (formally established 6 July 1942) and took part in the 1944 Leros harbour raid. Another group that came about as a direct result of Courtney's Folboat Section was Nigel Wilmott's Combined Operations Assault Pilotage Parties (COPP), set up in September 1942 to recce the TORCH beaches for the North African landings (8 November 1942). Later, COPP would be used on the Normandy beaches before OVERLORD (6 June 1944) and before the ANVIL landings in the South of France (15 August 1944).

Courtney's SBS was transferred out of Jellicoe's offshoot in 1948 to work under the Royal Marines. Despite the complex heritage, Oliver Warner concluded 'the SAS felt, not without reason, that if anyone was entitled to use the term Special Boat Squadron, it was them' (Warner, p.115). In 1950 the Small Raids wing of the Amphibious School was restructured and the Special Boat Section formed.

Despite the tough training, life at Athlit was special. It recognized the extraordinary nature of the brotherhood that had gathered together to wage war:

> In our pirate camp the usual tensions of army life, and of any organised communal life, were reduced to a minimum, we were there, all by our own fervent wish, and were free to leave any time we chose. No one tried to parade his authority – there was very little of that sort of authority to parade. Nor was there much place for the detestable concept of one-upmanship. There was no point in pretending, for example, that you could swim better than you did, when your capacity was daily tested and exposed, and when – the vital point – there was no advantage to be gained by that or any other similar pretence. We pretty soon came to know one another's physical and mental capacities, and with them our own. Strength and skill were respected, and a fair degree of both were essential, but everyone recognised that there were other qualities, such as a cool head, or a good temper, that might well prove more valuable.

On our type of operation the man who could make you laugh was more worth having than the bore who could only shoot straight … Life in the camp itself was such fun, and my fellow pirates so amusing and delightful. An atmosphere of Bohemian sociability reigned in our mess where high spirits and a conversational free-for-all usually made up for what the cooking lacked.[25]

The training was tough. It was also deceptive. It was designed to psychologically evaluate each man as a member of what would become a close-knit team. 'It was of the utmost importance when operating in small teams that every man could be trusted and would act as a member of the team.'[26]

Verney put Athlit's special feeling down to Jellicoe, 'the socialistic peer … [who] has long since changed his political allegiance. Jellicoe's stamina was legendary: 'his vitality exhausted even mine.'

House, Jellicoe's driver, maintained he was 'the untidiest man he had ever known'. His belongings and articles of his clothing would turn up all over the place. Verney agreed: Jellicoe 'littered the camp with his socks, shirts, ties and handkerchiefs. His trousers, when they were at last found, never had buttons.'[27] It was also clear that House had a soft spot for him: 'the Lord' was 'an easy and considerate man to work for'. He even did his own laundry but in a manner that I know was entirely true to his style: 'If it was his pants, he would wash them, and then put them under his sleeping bag with the fine hope that they would have the correct creases in them.'[28]

Jellicoe now organized his new unit into three detachments – L, M and S – initials chosen after their first commanders' names, Tommy Langton from Kabrit, Fitzroy Maclean from Persia and David Sutherland from Syria. Each detachment was 'made up of six patrols, each containing an officer, a sergeant, a corporal and nine troopers.'[29] Each of the patrols had two signallers. Fighting strength was around 230 men, but when the support staff, the 'base barnacles', were added in, the total number was considerably higher.[30]

Neither Langton nor Maclean stayed long. Langton was 'invalided' back to Britain ('a procedure which might in itself be described as a major health hazard' as Philip Warner wrote),[31] and Maclean's talents and language skills were again put to good use in Yugoslavia, where he went to advise Tito and his partisans.

Maclean's detachment was taken over by J. Neilson (Ian) 'Jock' Lapraik, a former lawyer. Physically he was a very fit man: he'd been both a runner and a swimmer. As a child, however, he'd had tuberculosis and had been crippled for years. That's what drove him to stay in top shape. He had been a PoW in North Africa and was lucky to have been sent to a hospital, from which he escaped. During an inspection of British prisoners by Rommel, he had been dispatched by the Field Marshal for immediate medical attention. The doctor who treated him turned out to be an old pre-war friend who dressed his wound so heavily that he was then sent to hospital.

Lapraik arrived with a tall New Zealander, Lieutenant Dion 'Stud' Stellin, nicknamed for his way with the ladies. Stellin, like Jellicoe's radio operator, Jack 'Zucky' Mann, was one of the few men who had been in all three branches of the Special Forces – SAS, LRDG and SBS – before joining Jellicoe. Mann, who'd been born in Cairo, was a natural linguist and joined up at seventeen as a radio operator. Because he spoke a little Italian, it wasn't long before he was recruited by the Intelligence service. He refused the task they had in mind for him: mixing with Italian prisoners. He felt his Italian wasn't *that* good. He joined the LRDG instead. The job was vital and required total concentration and peace: 'You have to listen for just one sound. It's double-coded so you have to decipher it. You have to take away the sounds of the other stations, the atmospherics – the wind and the crackles you hear … all sorts of noises.'[32]

Jellicoe 'held [his] appointment by right of being the most experienced officer at small-scale raiding, and probably the most daring.'[33] The men he assembled were special. Jellicoe specifically wanted 'self-reliant men with initiative and self-discipline, not the imposed discipline of the barrack square. Above anything else, I sought self-starters, men not dependent on an officer telling them what to do.'[34] It was exactly Stirling's philosophy: 'The man is the regiment, and the regiment is the man.'[35] Some became legends: Lassen, Lapraik, Porter Jarrell, the Canadian-American doctor (whom everyone called 'Joe'), Dick Holmes, Roy Trafford and the 22-year-old Liverpool Golden Gloves boxer, Duggie Pomford. Dick Holmes found himself in S Detachment's J patrol with George Munro as his sergeant and 'Nobby' Clarke as his officer.[36] Some had special talents that he wanted: David Williams had a 'marksman's badge' and was almost as good as Leonard Grant-Taylor, one of the instructors, a phenomenal shot who, at 'ten yards … would put six bullets through the middle of an Ace of Hearts.' With a pistol.

Then there was Jarrell, the medic, to whom Jellicoe offered the chance to train to be an officer, although he turned it down. Decades after the war, Jellicoe tried to help Jarrell, then living in France. He wrote to I. F. 'Tanky' Smith at the SAS Regimental Association, 'concerned that this very brave man is given his rightful due'. Jarrell had written to him and David Sutherland saying that authorities were 'unable to locate any records of my service with the British army in World War 2.'[37] I later met Jarrell's daughter-in-law, who was working in Geneva. Sadly, then, I knew little about what an extraordinarily brave man her father had been.

It goes without saying that there was a very special bond between these men:

> It had special ramifications for men who lived in small, isolated groups for such long periods, with almost no contact with the rest of the military. The raiders were, in many respects, perfectly content with their isolation. They had the sense of waging their own war with means and methods over which they had great control, and when they were not actively engaged they stayed in relative safety beyond the enemy's reach. When they did see action, they often felt safer behind enemy lines, where they could attack from the rear when it would be least expected, than if they had been on the front lines.[38]

Jellicoe was always more interested in performance and attitude than titles, rank or social background. He genuinely cared about people; actually he was fascinated by people, what made them 'tick'. He may have had a very relaxed persona, but underneath, it was performance that always counted – especially his own. It's what, I think, made him so special as a person. He didn't particularly care where the brilliance came from as long as it was there, recognized and nurtured.

The attitude formed a very strong bond. A feeling of being amongst an élite group that would be its own judge:

> Their filthy and often haphazardly assembled uniforms were in themselves symbolic, reinforcing the raiders' solidarity and accentuating their disdain for the rules that applied to the rest of the army. The same was true of the raiders' custom of always wearing their side-arms when they went into town on leave.[39]

Men like Holmes 'thrived' in Jellicoe's SBS: 'He hated mindless discipline and having no sense of control over his own destiny.'[40] The only one who stood apart and did not fit was Maclean. He seems to have been regarded with a certain degree of disdain. It was not that he was stand-offish; quite the opposite. He had learned from 'the time [he] spent as a Jock in the Camerons'.[41] It was more his 'spit and polish' approach which was so at odds with the seemingly relaxed intimacy that characterizes the style of Special Forces. The use of 'Blanco' for cleaning webbing, for example, was pretty much looked down on by most ranks and officers alike.

Jellicoe's own 'devil may care' attitude and focus on performance rather than looks, coupled with the beauty of Athlit, made the camp very special: '[Jellicoe] would turn up at grand parties in Haifa wearing sodden, muddy sandshoes or rush into the morning sea in the dancing pumps he'd worn all night.[42]

Athlit owed its character to Jellicoe's mix of intellect, perseverance and discipline. John Verney described this balance: 'Physically he was about as tough as the herculean sergeant, intellectually he could more than hold his own with the don or the M.P., and his vitality exhausted even mine.'[43] 'The socialistic peer' Jellicoe was, he concluded, 'an ardent burner of the candle at both ends'.

The informality could be deceiving: like its mother-unit, the SAS, men who didn't fit were 'RTU'd'. The ultimate sanction was invoked vigorously. One man, Lewis, under arrest for going 'into a Jewish village hoping to find a beer', tried to call Jellicoe's bluff and managed to get three of his mates to confront Jellicoe in support. All four were RTU'd. It was an early line drawn in the sand, to establish himself as a commander not to be crossed.

I can quite understand why he didn't want to be regular army. He loathed that sort of discipline and order, and 'being on parade'. Maclean was more a 'by the book' man and did not terribly care for Jellicoe's more relaxed attitude. Jellicoe actually may have thought that Maclean was trying to challenge him and what he was creating. Maclean would say, 'George is a splendid chap but he doesn't run a tight enough ship.'[44]

Maclean also thought 'a commanding officer ought to brush his hair occasionally.' I doubt 'Curly' would have appreciated the comment.

Maclean's bravery under fire and his sheer audacity, however, were never in doubt. After the Benghazi raids, Stirling had recommended him for an MC, although he had forgotten to post the letter. It was found on him when he was captured in January 1943. He hated paperwork and had a 'pathological disdain for red tape'; as Jim Almonds said, he 'strained every nerve to avoid administration in any shape or form.'[45]

Dick Holmes talked about the daily routine at Athlit. They would start off by swimming down the beach to the castle, run back, play basketball till lunch and then some more in the afternoon. Milner-Barry's diaries are full of endless sports activities, to the point where they become quite mundane. Each day would also 'invariably' end with a night march.

The training culminated in an exhausting 45-mile hike from the base to the shores of Lake Tiberias. In Holmes's words, 'We were so superbly fit that carrying a pack weighing 50–60lbs and marching 15 miles was quite a matter of course.'[46]

John House even joked that one of the new recruits turned out to have been a cobbler and was therefore a particularly prized addition to the unit: 'He fixed their boots by putting on two soles so that when one wore out, they merely removed that and underneath was a brand new sole.'[47]

They also spent a lot of time in Beirut. For Lodwick, Beirut was a wonderful experience: 'You can eat civilized French food, and people do not pester you … in winter you can ski down from the cedars almost to the city itself … in summer, if you have antiquarian tastes [Jellicoe had them] the ruins of Heliopolis are not far away.'[48]

The SBS men also trained in Jerusalem in a former police station. They called it the 'Killing School'. Here, they were taught how to kill, not at distance, but in a close-up, intimate way that would haunt many of them for years. Grant-Taylor put it bluntly: 'This is a school for murder. Murder is my business. Not a vague shooting of people in combat, but the personal, individual killing of a man in cold blood.'[49]

The importance of honing lightning reactions was drilled into them:

> Shoot the first man who moves, hostile or not. His brain has recovered from the shock of seeing you there with a gun. Therefore, he is dangerous. Next shoot the man nearest to you. He is in the best position to cause you trouble.[50]

It was how Paddy Mayne or Lassen would kill. Here they were also taught the 'double tap': never to shoot in bursts, but to 'tap the trigger so as to fire fast, accurate, single round shots'.[51] In the National Archives there's an interesting page highlighting German and Italian army weapons training. They trained on all sorts of British, American, German and Italian weapons: the Italian Beretta MAB 38 machine gun, the American M-1 carbine, the German Luger P08 or the MP42 machine pistol known as the Schmeisser. Two evenings a week, Fridays and Saturdays, were set aside for night firing exercises. Thursday mornings saw shooting with a silencer. [52] Grenades would include the standard British Mills but also the German Model 24 *Stielhandgranate*, nicknamed the 'Potato Masher', or little Italian grenades known as 'red devils' that were favoured by SBS because of their lightness ('though smaller and less lethal than the Mills bomb, the advantage of the Red Devils was that you could carry more').[53]

Each month, they would have a session in which anyone could air grievances. At one of them, Jellicoe set the tone:

> If you get drunk and can't make it back to your tent please don't pass out on the roadway. Last night I had to get out of the car no fewer than three times to move bodies out of the way before I could get into camp.[54]

The 21-year-old David Sutherland first met Maclean at Kabrit when the latter introduced himself as 'godmother to the French'.[55] It was his way of saying he was the liaison officer.

Anders Lassen, the Dane from an old aristocratic family, was, in Jellicoe's words, 'the most extraordinary person [he had] ever met'. When he met with Mike Langley, Lassen's biographer, he reinforced the point: 'Nothing is more important to me than my memory of Andy Lassen.'[56] Lassen was, above all, 'a fascinating mixture – quiet, sensitive, poetic at times and deeply sentimental, especially about children and dogs.'[57]

Some, like Dick Holmes, who described Lassen as 'the most arrogant of them all', clearly didn't like him. Others, like David Sutherland, would strongly defend him. His former commander responded sharply to what Holmes had written, saying that Lassen was 'far more than a pure killing machine'. He was a 'tactical genius ... very intelligent, highly experienced and completely fearless'.[58]

Special Forces offered a natural home for Lassen. The handsome blond Dane had grown up in the outdoors, hunting and living rough, constantly challenging himself, toughening himself, preparing himself – unknowingly – for the short life that he would lead. He'd trained many of his fellow countrymen in the Commando training camp at Achnacarry, surprising many of them by his lethal skills with bow and knife – and, of course, with a pistol. He was almost as good with his left as his right hand. Lassen was as efficient a killing machine as Mayne: 'ruthless, cold and calculating in action'.[59] Suzanne Lassen, however, recounted a different story. On the Paros raid (in April 1944), Lassen had talked to a new member of the squad, a Sergeant Waite, advising him to kill with a gun rather than a knife: 'I have at times been forced to use my knife', he confided. 'It's terrible.'[60]

Mary Henderson (née Cawadias), who met him on Liberation night in Athens, was completely captivated: 'He was a handsome, statuesque, towering, straw-blond, cold grey-eyed Dane with a deep, cavernous voice.'[61] His eyes could be especially frightening, sometimes as 'dead as stones'. Adrian Seligman talked of his 'godlike beauty' but at the same time threw in a quip about Lassen's false teeth turning up under a pillow, 'quite the wrong pillow from a diplomatic point of view'. (He had lost his front teeth misjudging a running jump on to an MTB.) Seligman recounted how a 'very deferential Arab servant, in fez and jellaba, arrived at the base with a small tissue-covered parcel. In it were Andy's teeth.'[62] Lassen even openly boasted that he'd slept with the maids ('Two out of three') when he was a London guest of the Danish Ambassador, Count Edward Reventlow.[63] He was utterly disdainful of authority and, his men would find out, ruthless.

Another time, Lassen had been with his men and running late for an RV on an exercise. He simply stepped out into the road, stopped a French military truck and threw the stunned Senegalese driver to the ground. 'It took all of George Jellicoe's charm and diplomacy to calm down the furious French military', although Sutherland was right there having to deal with the situation in person.[64] Mike Morgan summed it up: Jellicoe could get 'the very best out of his men – especially the brave, but often unpredictable Anders Lassen'.[65] When Sutherland told Sergeant Nicholson that he would have a new officer, Lassen, he was told, 'Keep an eye on him. Restrain him'.[66]

Lassen, like Stirling, loathed any sort of administrative duty. As much as Lassen's attention to the details of reconnaissance was highly regarded, his inability to write concise after-action reports was equally well-known. They would be as terse as '*veni, vidi, vici*'. Michael Holmes, Dick's son, quoted a typical Lassen report that his father had told him about: 'Landed. Killed Germans. Fucked off.'

Today, even if Andy Lassen's name is not well remembered in much of his native country, it is, daily, at the Danish Special Forces school. Cadet students running past his statue stop and salute, offering him a 'Good morning' before they tackle each day's exercises. It's a little-known but rather touching tradition that his younger sister, Bente, told me about over a memorably delicious lunch of herrings and schnapps.

When his country was occupied, Lassen's dislike of the occupiers grew into a deep hatred. It ran in the family. His first cousin, Axel von dem Bussche, was a German resistance fighter who'd tried to kill Adolf Hitler a year before the July bomb Plot. The hatred of the occupier might explain why, Bente continued, Andy developed such a strong empathy with the Greeks. He understood their plight, and the brutality and hardship which they had experienced, first at the hands of the Italians, then the Germans. Frants, Andy's elder brother, took up arms against the Germans on Danish soil as a member of the resistance. He was a courageous man, much maligned by those who had been lucky enough not to have suffered at the hands of the Gestapo as he had. He'd been injured and was caught, unable to run any longer. The ensuing interrogation was relentless, so when he felt that he'd protected his resistance colleagues for the necessary time, he surrendered the information which was sought – the address where they might be holed up. Frants gave them it in the confident belief that his friends would stick to the rules under which they'd always worked: never to go back to a location once used. But they had. For years Frants was cold-shouldered by his countrymen, some of whom had never done anything to defend their country or put their lives in the kind of peril he had. And what made it probably all the more painful was to be the object of shame in the shadow of such adoration for his dead brother.

However, there was also a completely different side to Anders Lassen. He could be a sensitive man. Seligman talked of his almost welling up with tears when he was unable to help feed a starving Greek family, or of being totally attached to his beloved dog, Pipo, a Maltese terrier. The dog had formerly belonged to the Italian commandant and would, apparently, only eat spaghetti at the start of the relationship with his new master. Seligman described Lassen's constant companion in scathing terms as the 'mangy and bug-ridden ... cur he had picked up in the back streets of Beirut'.[67] The dog had a habit of lifting his leg on any trousered target. Despite his 'pathetic eyes' that so appealed to Andy, the dog was 'by no means a pleasant shipmate in a 26-foot sailing boat, already crammed with men, stores and ammunition, on a ten-day voyage creeping from island to island under cover of night, hiding under camouflage nets among the rocks by day.'[68]

Porter Jarrell, the American medic with a Quaker ambulance unit, painted a picture of Lassen as a man struggling with inner demons, the complex and struggling character of a hero:

> It was as if a fever was burning inside him. He braved death and exposed himself to the greatest dangers. He was like a restless dynamo, loaded with energy. He had to do something to translate his thoughts into action. Even when he was on leave, it was as if he knew that he had challenged faith too much and had to fill these brief hours with the life that was about to run away from him.[69]

Lassen would protect his men to the death, even from British officers unaccustomed to dealing with the unique flavour of an encounter with SAS or SBS troops. Dick Holmes, who once remarked, 'Sometimes I love that man', recalled Lassen's dressing down of the officer who'd been trying – totally unsuccessfully – to make the men dig useless trenches and had been scornful of their appearance: 'My men don't have to be well dressed to be good soldiers ... now, if you've finished with my men I'll take them with me. We've got more important things to do than dig fucking holes!'

Lassen pointed out that the two sergeants – Dick Holmes and Dougie Wright – had both been decorated with the Military Medal and had both 'probably killed more Germans than [you have] ever seen.'[70] On another occasion, Andy was shot in the leg by one of his men. He was enraged, of course, but refused to report in sick as he worried that doing so would get the guilty Corporal into trouble.

Before he died in 2008, Wright talked to Gavin Mortimer. What he said was a little chilling – to contemporary ears at least:

> There was a lot of killing in the Dodecanese. Sometimes we'd bring one [a German] back for interrogation but mostly we'd just kill them. We didn't really have much respect for them.[71]

Mary Cawadias, Nico Henderson's future wife, remembered one of Jellicoe's officers talking about their adoration for him: 'We'd follow him anywhere – if he told us to walk across the sea, we would.'[72] To the best of her memory, Jellicoe's admirer was Ian Patterson, with whom he would bicycle the last miles to Athens as the Germans pulled out. Amongst this special band of brothers, an officer who didn't perform was ridiculed:

> The tone among the raiders was informal and, in many respects, 'democratic'. Just as in the rest of the military the raiders called the officers 'Sir'. But any officers who were not capable of winning the respect of the men, or seemed overly concerned with regulations and formalities, or who obviously had an excessively high opinion of their own importance, were mercilessly ridiculed, but always with a 'Sir' added at the end.[73]

With men like Bill 'Uncouth' Cumper, or Tony Drongin's 'Corporal Drongin to you, sir', you couldn't help having a special bond.

One of the two new officers from 62 Commando (the other, of course, was Andy Lassen), then in the process of being disbanded, was Philip Pinkney. He'd been ordered by his former C.O. in the desert to wear a tie for dinner and had dutifully appeared for dinner 'stark naked except for a beautifully tied tie'.[74] Luckily for him, the joke was appreciated. Pinkney's contribution to the unit was important, if bizarre. He'd become a specialist in survival foods and would quite happily munch on beetles 'in the spirit of scientific curiosity'. That sort of knowledge was never wasted in Special Forces but it could be pretty challenging. One day, he presented something he called 'Palestine soup'. It was concocted from all sorts of brush weeds as an emergency survival aid. Its key ingredients were clovers, dandelions, grasses and snails. Jellicoe wasn't put off. He would sit there, 'quashing objections by wolfing down his own bowlful and declaring the dish a surprise test of endurance'. 'A surprise test of the bowels, too', quipped Verney.

That summer, Pinkney would be shot, after being captured carrying out a bomb-planting in the Brenner Pass. He'd gone back to 2nd SAS and, despite having a fractured spine, dropped by parachute in July 1943.

Captain Milner-Barry, from the Transjordan Frontier Force, would become Jellicoe's 2i/c and often serve as his envoy, since the latter had 'a dislike of Personal Appearances'.[75] He was a very different character, distinctly conservative. He was in the bar of the King David Hotel in Jerusalem when war was declared, as he'd been working for Shell.

As you'd expect with any Special Forces unit, training was intense. There were the usual route marches and load-carrying, of course, but there was added emphasis on sailing, canoeing and submarine work. In May, they trained on the new Davis submarine escape hatch in Beirut, for example. Ken Lamonby was a keen sailor and put in charge of sea training in S detachment. Maybe because of his knowledge and ease in handling boats, the 23-year-old formed a friendship with Lassen. On one occasion, in Cyprus, Milner-Barry had organized training for SBS men to paddle ashore from the schooner *Apostolos* as part of their training. Friendly fire rained down on them from the local fort. It was a repeat of what had happened with some of Stirling's own over-realistic exercises.

When they were back on dry land, away from the front, the SBS was a law unto itself. It was no holds barred. 'Jellicoe's men could return from operations and go on leave amid a variety of nightlife unimagined in wartime Britain.' Very often the barman at the St Georges, Pierre Charitou, would be replaced by one of the SBS such as Captain Gordon Hogg, known endearingly as 'Le 'Ogg'.[76]

In Beirut, Andy Lassen had a girlfriend of sorts called Aleca, a diminutive for Alexandra. That didn't stop his roving eye. Jellicoe and the fair-haired Dane even vied for my mother, Patsy's, hand. That time, Jellicoe won out.

Jellicoe and Lassen would sometimes spend the evening in Tel Aviv, carousing in the bars. One time, Lassen, clearly extremely drunk, knocked his commanding officer out cold. One would have thought that 'clocking' your C.O. would bring about a pretty quick end to anyone's career, but Jellicoe 'knew Lassen was too valuable an officer to be lost on account of such a petulant outburst.'[77] Jellicoe confessed to probably having said 'something to rouse his Danish ire' and Andy could be very impatient and hot-tempered even if his disdain for authority was well-known. Consequently, Jellicoe found himself 'flat on my back'.[78] The SBS worked hard, and often played even harder.

Chapter 6

Frustrations of Failure – Sardinia and Crete, 1943

Many of the activities of the SBS in mid-1943 were addressed to concealing, after victory in North Africa, what the Allies' next target would be. Misinformation played a critically important role in persuading the Germans into reinforcing their garrisons in both Greece and Sardinia, rather than in Sicily where, in July, the Allies actually planned their next push. With Sardinia in mind, the SS *Sturmbrigade Reichsführer SS* and a new *Panzergrenadier* Division (the 90th) were created in July, while three Panzer divisions were moved to Greece.

As they had in June 1942, SBS operations would once again target the three most important airfields on Crete: Heraklion, Tymbaki and Kastelli. Sutherland, who would be leading the raids, knew Crete well as he'd raided Tymbaki the previous year when Jellicoe was raiding Heraklion with Bergé's men. Andy Lassen, 'the eternally pipe-smoking' Ken Lamonby and Lieutenant Ronald Rowe would lead the three patrols.[1] Lamonby, tasked with Heraklion airfield, would directly benefit from Jellicoe's on-the-ground knowledge but he was 'untried and untested in battle' and an odd choice as a team commander, not having been vetted by the sergeants.[2]

On board ML.367, the three raiding groups left Mersa Matruh for Crete in the early morning.[3] It meant that they could arrive just after nightfall, allowing the ML to start its way back still under the protective cloak of darkness. The team of fourteen SBS men was accompanied by two Greek SOE agents, Kimon Zografakis and Giannis Androulakis. Both had previous knowledge of the island: Androulakis had been an intelligence agent in Heraklion, while Zografakis had been on the 1942 raid. Once at sea, the raiders were briefed.

After midnight, on 23 June, they landed near Cape Kochinoxos. This gave them twelve days to get to their targets, lay up, observe and all raid in a synchronized series of independent actions. On the beach they were met by a local, Gregorius Hnarajkis, one of Paddy Leigh Fermor's men.

They set off carrying the equipment needed at the base camp, where Sutherland, his signals sergeant and others would stay. Leigh Fermor, known locally as 'Michaelis', was at the caves to greet them when they arrived.

Camp established, they set off on their separate missions, Lamonby and Lassen together for the first part. Almost immediately, one of Lamonby's men, Eddie Sapsed, was injured:

> [He'd] decided to explore during the afternoon and while attempting to jump from one rock to another misjudged his leap and fell about thirty feet on to some soft sand and suffered a sprained ankle.[4]

Taking turns, Sid Greaves, Nicholson and Holmes helped Sapsed.[5] Dick Holmes (known as 'Jeff', for reasons he never understood) ended up carrying his Lewes bombs for most of the night. With temperatures reaching 30 degrees centigrade, it was gruelling. On a map the distances might have looked small, but each mile was tortuous, curling around and up and down the harsh Cretan hinterland. Added to that was the heavy burden of '70–80lbs of personal kit, weaponry, explosives and water – a crushing load to carry in such heat and across such terrain'.[6] The loads were simply too heavy (the big radio batteries alone reputedly weighed over 70lbs).

After four days, the teams entered a gully at the end of which lay the small village of Apoini. This is where they split, Lamonby heading directly north to Heraklion, Lassen north-west to Kastelli. The radio operators stayed behind with the heavy MK2 sets. Runners from the local resistance would be used to pass messages back to Apoini. Establishing communications back to Jellicoe and MEHQ was already proving difficult:

> B and C sigs together as two sets much too heavy to carry. Sigs are being left behind ... Impossible to come up during day because of enemy. Will come up 2100 hours. Only one call for both sigs due to lack of time. Unable to establish com first time as hiding underground.[7]

Lassen's Kastelli Airfield raid

Lassen set off with 'one sergeant, two corporals, two radio operators and a Greek interpreter'.[8] He also had a new guide, Vasilis Konios. The jovial Hnarajkis ('Gregorius') stayed behind. He was known for his humour and for the strength of his handshake, so strong it would 'make you wince'.[9]As they progressed, new guides would take over. Konios was replaced by Cheritoc Karfopoulos. His name was so difficult, they simply nicknamed him 'Harris'.

Everywhere they went, locals hid them and fed them. Poor as their hosts were, they would more often than not refuse any payment. One day, they were given a large bag full of smokes. Their money was refused. Nicholson and Greaves even tried to leave their watches and their gold coins with one of the Greek SOE guides as a way of thanking him. Again, they were politely, but firmly, refused. Help from the locals increased the risks for both: locals, fearing hostage-taking, regularly hid in the vineyards when Germans were around.

For two days before the raid, they holed up in a nearby village, a perfect location from which to gather intelligence: the Stukas they heard were heavily guarded by three sentries sleeping in tents beside the field. Reports were that the garrison was a hundred-strong.

With Nereanos's help, the group found the cave they were to use as an LUP. Apparently, there were eight Ju.87s on the eastern side and five Ju.88s and some fighters on the western side. Lassen could see them clearly when he recce'd the field on 2 July. By each plane were posted the three sentries they'd been told about, and the perimeter was regularly interspersed with strong points. Tents had been set up beside the planes. Disguised as a local herding sheep, Lassen examined the airfield in the daylight with his guide, and when some of the sheep wandered towards the fence, he saw it wasn't electrified.

That night, 4 July, they crouched hidden in the vines. The attacks – planned for Nicholson and Greaves to enter on the east side where the ammo and fuel dumps were mainly located, and Lassen with Ray Jones on the west – would start at 2330. Lassen would create a diversion, while Nicholson and Greaves, guided by Nereanos, dealt with the dumps.

Lassen led the way, silently dealing with the first sentry, and then spotted another group gathered around a bonfire, singing. They didn't seem to notice him. Nor did the German sentry by the hangar. He and the next two Lassen greeted in German. The second one wasn't taken in, but nor was he fast enough raising his gun. Lassen shot him 'without so much as taking his hand out of his pocket'.[10] Now there was nothing for it; Lassen and Jones had to run. The alarm was raised, and immediately flares arced into the sky, turning night into day.

On the other side of the field, slightly later, Nicholson and Greaves penetrated the defences. Even though they'd been caught in the perimeter searchlights they froze, making no sudden movements, they still managed to get through unseen. Once in, they placed bombs on a light reconnaissance aircraft, an Fi.56, skipped the next plane, a Ju.88, as it was too well-guarded and moved on to another Ju.88. After placing two more bombs, they found a Stuka. As they were about to leave some more calling cards, a shot was heard from the other end of the field. It was Lassen's. Hearing the answering fusillade, Nicholson and Greaves froze for ten minutes; Lassen's 'diversion' had stirred up a hornet's nest. More Germans now arrived. Nicholson thought the other two had more than likely been shot or captured, so they decided to make their way out and make for the main base RV with Georgios. They were lucky to get off the field, which they did around 0130, but not before placing some more charges on another Stuka. As soon as they reached the raid RV they sent the runner back with orders to send the success signal.

Holmes always maintained that Nicholson and Greaves only found one plane on the ground; that it was because the signal to Sutherland had scrambled the number 'one', which came out as 'nine', that the raid was regarded as successful: 'On the strength of this, Nick (Nicholson) and Siddy (Greaves) had been awarded their MMs.'[11]

Still on the field, Lassen created as much confusion as he could, pretending to be a German officer and waving the enemy soldiers forward, away from him and Jones. It worked; trapped in the flames of exploding aircraft, even the fire engines caught fire. Jones now saw Lassen successfully bluff the Germans again. By the main gate, the Dane had been challenged and answered back so confidently that his orders to search elsewhere were once again obeyed. As Lassen was caught in the open in the searchlight's cold white beam, one German twigged who he was but couldn't fire fast enough. Lassen disappeared. Madly trying to find the gap they had earlier cut, the two raiders were challenged yet again. And again Lassen bluffed his way out. They retreated back on to the field, but this time Jones wasn't so lucky. In the firefight, he became separated.

As Nicholson's and Greaves' bombs were going off, Lassen went back in to try and find Jones. When he got out, he was on his own. He spent the next two days hiding up, first in a field of cabbages, then one of onions. On the second day, a farmer found him, came back that night and took him to his village. When finally reunited with Jones and Nereanos, Lassen had a raging thirst.

No wonder the Greeks admired Lassen so much. The new guide, Nereanos Georgios, compared 'Spiro', as they called him, to the stuff of legend:

> He was tall, slim and very agile, and looked like the knight 'Ipotis'. He worked like a machine and was so busy that he didn't realize how dangerous it would be to enter the aerodrome – it was like jumping into fire.[12]

Nicholson wasn't at all happy with Lassen: he'd ignored orders to destroy the Ju.88s first. True, his 'diversion' made it somewhat easier for the other two to plant their bombs, but Lassen's impetuousness had raised the alarm and they had to transfer their attention to the more lightly-guarded Ju.87s. Lassen thought he had blown up eight planes, but the Germans actually managed to remove many of the charges before they exploded. It must have taken quite some courage to remove charges without knowing when they were likely to go off.[13]

As Lassen made ready to leave he was accompanied by a dozen Cretans wanting to get to Egypt to help fight the Germans. On 5 July he signalled Sutherland: the 'success' message was flashed to Cairo and London, where the BBC was ready to launch an information campaign, partly to tout the success of the raids but also, importantly, to confirm that these raids were carried out by the British not local Greek resistance groups:

> Special message to the people of Crete. You have heard the communiqué that announces raids in Crete by British forces. You know these forces neither asked for nor received any assistance from local inhabitants. The Germans know this too … They know they will be punished for any outrages they commit.[14]

The message fell on deaf ears.

Lamonby and Heraklion

B patrol set off for Heraklion. It was only a dozen miles from Kastelli, but the march was just as gruelling. It didn't help that the team wasn't well-balanced. Holmes didn't get on with Lamonby. He thought him 'a handsome, well-built individual who carried on rather like a spoiled child, which he was. Except for Sutherland, nobody liked him.'[15] Even Lassen (equally disliked by Holmes) disliked Lamonby: he said that he 'assumed an air of self-importance' and had to be curtly reminded by one of the men that 'we don't have batmen in this unit'.[16] En route to the RV, Lamonby would run afoul of Holmes and Sapsed again. Both challenged his navigation and were correct. But it was very easy to become disorientated under these conditions; Holmes found that he and one of the other raiders and a friend, Billy Whitehead, couldn't agree on how many nights they'd been on Crete. It's surprising, then, that Sutherland assessed Lamonby so differently, saying that he had 'all that one admires in a young man – intelligent, adaptable and brave, with an earthy Suffolk sense of humour'.[17] It was only at a reunion after the war that Holmes put Sutherland in the picture of how badly Lamonby had led his men.

They laid up in a village, Ano Arkhani (today called Archanes) just south of the airfield. In front of their house, '200 German soldiers were drilling in the village square below.'[18] Holmes' mood improved:

> We ate eggs and chips, cooked by a very attractive Cretan housewife, while watching a group of Germans drilling on the streets of the small village of Ano Arkani(s). It made the food taste better.[19]

At the airfield, however, there were no aircraft. Their guide, Yanni, had warned them that it had been 'run down as a result of Jellicoe's attack' the previous year.[20] But the Greek also had some good news, and based on this new information, the group decided to attack a large fuel dump located at Pesar (Peza), a dozen miles away.[21] Aside from the 200,000 litres of aviation fuel, bombs were apparently also stockpiled there.[22]

At 2300 they could see the two targets. Holmes was ordered to hit the outer dump, where bombs were mostly stored, and then to act as lookout when the rest of the team went in to the remaining dumps with Lamonby. Holmes and Yanni crept forward to place bombs on the outside fuel dump, where rows of 40-gallon barrels, stacked three high, held around 4,000 gallons. A German guard with his dog was close by and he was joined by another. They were engaged in a nerve-wrackingly long conversation, and although their dogs had clearly picked up the scent, their obvious restlessness was, thankfully, ignored. As he waited, hiding in the dark, Holmes was 'surprised by how calm [he] was', not only about the dogs but also about the two-hour fuses that he'd just set. He hoped he had sufficient time. Once again, as he was about to slip off, the two guards came back, chatting interminably.

When he got back, Lamonby surprised him. Holmes tried to brief him on how to best get in but was brushed aside. Lamonby 'cut him short, saying that he was not going to attack the other dumps.' Holmes was livid; so was Sapsed, who openly argued with Lamonby for a quarter of an hour.

At 0110, Holmes' bombs went off. The dump went up in a huge fireball and, as the cartwheeling, exploding barrels rocketed into the night sky, burning fuel poured down over the hill, snaking towards the other bomb dump that Lamonby had earlier spared.[23] Next morning, locals confirmed that the second dump had also gone up. For Holmes, who'd been in Crete during the bitter defeat of 1941, it was a poetic justice of sorts. When he got back he was awarded an MM.

*　*　*

On 8 July, Lassen and Jones joined Lamonby at Apoini. The day before, Lieutenant Rowe's Tymbaki patrol had made it back to Sutherland's base. Lassen now heard about the German reprisals carried out after the raids and let Cairo know the terrible details:

> Sixty-two Greeks shot. Women and children imprisoned. Ten more will be shot daily until our capture. Greeks still helping at risk of lives … Suggest strong air attacks on barracks and daylight strafing if possible.[24]

By 9 July nothing had been heard at the main RV from either Lassen or Lamonby, although the next day, at dawn, Greaves and Nicholson made it back disguised as shepherds. With them were two prisoners.

Sutherland wanted to signal Cairo with the news of the raids and also wanted to get off Crete the next night, 11 July. The radios, however, were dead. The only hope was to go back and retrieve the heavy batteries that Lassen's patrol had used. Using two of them linked up together worked. Once again, Dick Holmes was the 'pack mule'. He carried both truck batteries (each weighed around 40lbs) on his back. The pick-up signal was duly sent:

> Request embarkation urgently night 11th–12th. Sigs as previously arranged. 12 extra to be taken off. Confirm time date. DUMP requests answer urgently.

The Germans repeated the harsh reprisals that had been carried out in 1942. Despite Yanni's leaving a Union Jack at the scene to show it had been a British raid, the Germans executed fifty-two civilians, threatening that another fifty would follow if the British did not give themselves up.[25] The Cretan guerrilla leader's reaction made many a Cretan's breast swell with pride:

> He said that if the British liaison officer was considering [the] surrender [of] the English commandos to save the hostages then he, Manoli Bandouvas, would with his own hand, shoot the British liaison officer.[26]

As they waited, two Germans stumbled into their hideout and were taken prisoner without a struggle. More the reason why Sutherland was furious was that the Cretans had tripped a firefight with the other two surviving members of a German patrol, concentrating searches on the coast. Reinforcements would soon be coming, and he ordered Lamonby to stop their firing. Once done, Lamonby continued to hunt down the others in the patrol.

When Sutherland got to the beach, Lamonby wasn't there, and neither could Sergeant Pomford and Nicholson find him. At around 0100 the caïques were boarded, slowly sailing along the shore, searching for him. Reluctantly, they headed back south and at 0300, just as the sun was starting to come up, headed off, along with a dozen Cretan volunteers who wanted to come back with them. Before they left, they unloaded spares for the guerrillas: grenades, explosives, ammunition and what food they could spare.

On the 17-hour sail back, the men chatted with the two German prisoners, Heinz and Ulrich, admiring their weapons. One was carrying a Walther G.43, a very new addition to German field weaponry. On 12 July, they arrived back in Mersa Matruh. Holmes, who earlier on had unseemly taunted the prisoners with his revolver, started on them again:

> I practised my pistol training pointing my big Webley at them and cocking and uncocking it just to keep my hand in. Viv, the signaller,

spoke fluent German and conversed with them from time to time and he said that they had expected to be shot.[27]

They were met by the Navy with bottles of beer. 'Oolie', as he was now called, and Heinz each got one, too. After an extremely good meal, they set off by road for Cairo. That night they slept on the roadside, waking the next morning to find that the two prisoners had cooked a bacon breakfast for them. They turned out to be 'pretty good cooks', Holmes admitted. Once in Cairo, they couldn't resist going to Groppi's, 'famous for its tea, ice cream and elegant staff officers'.[28] They must have been a sight:

> Believe me, the stares were justified as we had not shaved for three weeks nor even washed for at least two weeks so that we stank and we were carrying the oddest assortment of weapons ever seen in this establishment, including German pistols and Schmeissers.[29]

Holmes carried on, saying that 'in their haste' they'd forgotten about their German prisoners, who eventually followed them in. After a 'slap-up feed', Jack Nicholson and Sid Greaves took the two prisoners off for a beer. Inevitably, they were caught by some MPs, and Sutherland, as senior officer, was reprimanded. The scene could have been the closing sequence of *Ice Cold in Alex*.[30] Sutherland countered his accusers, saying that his prisoners were more likely to be co-operative after this treatment. Not everyone was upset: Turnbull praised Sutherland. The raid, he said, was 'one of the most physically exacting ever undertaken by Special Service troops in the Middle East', and Holmes, Ray Jones, Greaves and Nicholson were each awarded the Military Medal for their part in the raids.[31] Lassen received a second bar to his MC, the citation reading:

> Pretending to be a German officer, he bluffed his way past three sentries … Throughout this attack, and during the very arduous approach march, the keenness, determination and personal disregard of this officer was of the highest order.

Nicholson was annoyed, however – rightly, it seems – at the way the citation for Lassen made it sound as though the diversion was what really made for the attack's success: 'That was no diversion. It was a bungle.' Nevertheless, Sutherland had formed a strong bond with Lassen that would last till the young Dane's death in the last few days of the war, in Comacchio: 'Many times I turned to him for advice since he was invariably right. He never failed me and I hope I never failed him.'[32]

Later, it would be learned that Ken Lamonby had been shot by one of the two remaining Germans and had died in hospital. Years later, the mother of one of the Cretan hostages executed by the Germans, Joanni Manouras, wrote to Suzanne Lassen about the loss they shared. A photo of Anders proudly hung in her tavern:

> I know that by his death you have lost one you loved, I feel the sorrow of a mother, but you must be proud. For the tree of freedom has been watered with the blood of your brave son.[33]

The Sardinia Fiasco

John Verney, the new commander of of L Detachment, had been at Oxford with Jock Lewes. After three weeks of training, the SBS was moved to an 'unknown destination' in Algeria. Verney travelled with his new C.O. to Algiers and their new base at Philippeville (today's Skidada), where Bill Stirling's 2nd SAS was based.

At Philippeville, Jellicoe briefed the assembled officers on the planning for a series of raids on six Sardinian airfields where, Jellicoe said, roughly 200 bombers were to be found, 'each potentially capable of sinking a troop carrier, that is perhaps putting 2,000 men out of action before the Sicily landing'.[34] Like the desert raids designed to protect the Malta convoys, Operation HAWTHORN was to be another strategic use of Special Forces.

Jellicoe's plan was to drop the six teams on three separate nights – 30 June, 1 and 2 July. Five drops consisted of one officer and six men, while the sixth would establish an RV base on the east coast.

A number of tricky issues immediately surfaced. The first was the Prime Minister's son, Randolph. Unlike Stirling, Jellicoe at first refused to take him. He then appeared to soften by appointing him one of the team leaders but kept in touch with MEHQ to work out a way to remove him. A signal barring Churchill duly arrived. Working quietly behind the scenes was typical of Jellicoe. It was very effective.

The second issue was the men's health. Malaria was alarmingly prevalent. On 28 June, the men boarded the submarine HMSS *Severn*, and in the 'close conditions on the craft', the men who'd been infected, suffered without knowing why. *Severn* was unreliable: she couldn't dive below 250ft and, as it turned out, 'in full daylight the submarine was only thirty miles off the Sardinia coast and temporarily unable to submerge.'[35]

For these reasons, Imbert-Terry and Verney had to return to Algiers and were only able to rejoin the raid after being dropped by Halifax bomber the night of 7/8 July. Jellicoe was able to persuade the pilot of an existing Corsica-bound flight to alter his flight path to make the drop. They jumped without containers, instead strapping their 30lb rucksacks on their chests.

This saved time when landing but made getting aboard the plane impossible without being 'literally lifted' on.[36]

One of the first to land was Ian Brinkworth's team, north of Punto Foghe, on the night of 1/2 July. The first night, their guide, an Italo-American called 'Trench' Timparano, went missing. On 5 July, the team divided: Pat Scully stayed behind in charge of the kit, while Brinkworth went ahead to hit the airfield at Milis. When they didn't return, Scully concluded that Timparano must have betrayed them. They'd abandoned the raid after being challenged and had started heading back to the main RV. On the evening of 17 July, they were captured near St Vito. Scully and two others were captured separately.

Two other teams, 'Daffodil' and 'Bluebell', landed the same night as Brinkworth, the latter three and a half miles off.[37] Within days, two men in 'Daffodil' came down with malaria and three others were taken prisoner. It was the same in 'Bluebell': two men came down with malaria, one of whom died. The team's leader, Duggan, was left behind with a water bottle and 'bound [it] round his wrist where he couldn't miss it', but when the two raiders arrived at the airfield, no planes were found. They were captured at the RV.[38]

The only really successful raid – if one could call it that – was Imbert-Terry's. He and John Verney reached the Ottana target field and lay up observing; unfortunately, they discovered in daylight that they were way too close to the Italian sentries. That night, bombs were placed on Ju.88s by Imbert-Terry and three on other aircraft by his team. Getting out, they narrowly avoided running into more sentries. Their luck ran out after five days, and they were captured. Timparano had given the Germans all the details. Imbert-Terry managed to escape in December and was back in England on 25 December, 'thereby most unexpectedly fulfilling a self-imposed promise' to be back home for Christmas.[39]

Jellicoe only learned of the catastrophic raid from Pat Scully, who'd had been too ill to be moved from the prison in Sassari with the other SBS prisoners but had made his way back to rejoin the SBS after the Italian armistice. Jellicoe hadn't been allowed to go on any of the raids himself since he'd been briefed about Operation HUSKY ('because [he] knew the plans for Sicily').[40] Despite persistent badgering by Jellicoe, General Alexander would not change his mind and allow the young officer to participate in the raids.

Months before, in April 1943, a fully-dressed corpse was dropped into the sea off the Spanish coast. The body, dressed as a Royal Marine Major had a briefcase handcuffed to his wrist. Inside were letters from high ranking Allied officers and invasion plans for Sardinia and Greece. The Allied hope

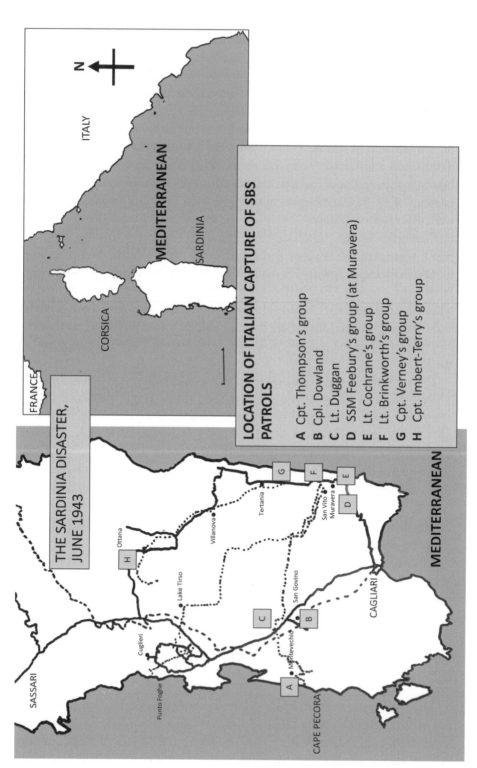

THE SARDINIA DISASTER, JUNE 1943

LOCATION OF ITALIAN CAPTURE OF SBS PATROLS

A Cpt. Thompson's group
B Cpl. Dowland
C Lt. Duggan
D SSM Feebury's group (at Muravera)
E Lt. Cochrane's group
F Lt. Brinkworth's group
G Cpt. Verney's group
H Cpt. Imbert-Terry's group

FRANCE

ITALY

MEDITERRANEAN

CORSICA

SARDINIA

MEDITERRANEAN

N

SASSARI

Punto Foghe

Ottana

Cuglieri

Lake Tirso

Villanova

Tertania

San Vito

Muravera

San Govino

Montevechio

CAGLIARI

CAPE PECORA

MEDITERRANEAN

H

C

B

A

G

F

E

D

Map Source: WO 218/174.

was that, via the local Spanish police, copies of the documents would end up with German Military Intelligence, the Abwehr. The film *The Man Who Never Was* told the story of one part of the fake intelligence jigsaw Dudley Clarke had constructed. The SBS raids were another piece of the same puzzle: its 'main purpose was as a decoy.'[41] If raiding the Sardinian airfields had helped create doubts about the Allies' next target and not just destroyed aircraft, then the raids could be judged a success. But they came at a high cost.

On 27 July, the submarine *Severn* with Jellicoe, Alex McClair, Jimmy Foot and Sergeant Sidlow on board, surfaced, hoping to pick up the raiders. They never appeared. The sub had seen 'a light flashing from the hill following which beach lights were switched on.' The team was 'obviously compromised'.[42]

Back at Athlit, Jellicoe reorganized the detachments. L Detachment had been badly reduced by the Sardinia operation, and with Langton invalided out, the new team leader was to be John Verney. The fact that he was a writer and a painter did not go down too well with the men. Maclean had been sent off to Yugoslavia to work with Tito, and M detachment was taken over by the 27-year-old 'Jock' Lapraik, a decorated officer who had won the MC in Abyssinia and an experienced one who had been with ME Commando throughout 1942. When he arrived with M detachment, they came in five trucks and four jeeps, the new commander in a staff car to which Jellicoe immediately took a liking. Before being sent off to Malta to train, Jellicoe commandeered Lapraik's prized transport.

With the capture of Sicily in August, the roles of 2nd SAS and the SBS were refocused. The SAS would concentrate on the Italian mainland and, since the Dodecanese islands were Italian territory, the SBS would tackle the Aegean, where their operations would be designed to stretch German nerves and resources.

Chapter 7

Prelude to Disaster –
The Dodecanese Gamble

On 7 September 1943, David Sutherland, Jock Lapraik and Walter Milner-Barry had all gone in to town to see Captain Hugo Ionides of the 1st British Submarine Flotilla and had spent most of the afternoon together, first lunching in Azzib and then going to Ionides' villa. There they'd continued working out details for one of Milner-Barry's submarine patrols against the Italian W/T post on Levitha, concluding that the patrol 'would remain at the S/M commander's disposal for the remainder of the patrol.'[1] Lapraik and Jellicoe had gone on to arrange for two SBS men to be aboard one of Lieutenant Seligman's Levant Schooner Flotilla (LSF) boats.

The LSF were there to carry out 'opportunistic raids' aboard their mixed collection of boats, MLs and HDMLs but more often local caïques (the HDML, the Harbour Defence Motor Launch, was the smaller version of the ML). The LSF caïques were designed to look as local as possible but they had powerful, silent diesel engines and were laid out to be easily camouflaged, so that they could pull into creeks and bays and lie up during the day. The 'main advantage of these craft was that they were available and cheap, and with their solid hulls and painfully lowerable masts, could lie up in near-invisibility close to the Aegean rocks'.[2] They had 'a certain Heath Robinson quality: the vessels were often powered by marinised 90 hp. Matilda tank engines with comms salvaged from Curtiss P-40 fighters.'[3] The new engine didn't give the boats more speed but allowed them 6 or 7 knots at half-throttle in 'comparative silence'.[4]

The Germans had their versions powered by twin Deutz high-speed diesel engines and usually carrying a crew of four or five Greeks, with a German NCO in overall charge, and eight or nine soldiers to man the guns and form boarding parties.'[5]

In the evening, Lapraik and Jellicoe joined up at the St Georges Hotel, Beirut. It was a beautiful spot, the dining terrace tucked on a headland with water on three sides. After dinner, around 2300, Jellicoe was 'tapped on the shoulder by a military policeman' and told he was wanted back at Raiding

Forces Headquarters.[6] He was ordered to fly to Cairo the next morning at 0630 and to be ready at the airfield at first light.

Before leaving, Jellicoe needed to spend some time with David Sutherland, who had come in on the same aeroplane he would take out to talk over details of S Detachment's planning. Jellicoe went back to the airfield early – it was already 0100 – and cat-napped before the flight. He was able to catch up on sleep by taking very short naps, and for the rest of his life was able to function well on as little as four hours a night.

He was met at the airport and taken directly by staff car to the Conference, which was due to start at 1000 at the GHQ offices at Grey Pillars. When he arrived he quickly shaved; he always found that this revived him. He then had some breakfast and heard that the meeting was to take place at the D.C.O. offices. When he finally found the office, the conference had already been going on for about half an hour.[7] Under discussion at the staff meeting (attended by, as he put it, 'a rather bewildered assortment of officers', Majors Dolbey and Barret, Lieutenant Commander Hailstones RNR, Group Captain Wheeler, Captain Fassenage and Brigadier Hayman from 'D' Plans, who joined a little later) was that the Italians were about to announce an armistice.[8]

Two months earlier, on 25 July, as the Italian front had started to crumble, Benito Mussolini had been replaced by Marshal Pietro Badoglio. By mid-August the Axis had been pushed out of Sicily and the drive up through mainland Italy was underway.

The end was inevitable. Using the Italian envoy in Lisbon, Badoglio let the Allies know that he needed more time before any announcement could be made. Although the actual document had already been signed five days earlier, on 3 September, the announcement had been delayed and was now planned for that very evening at 1900.

Jellicoe joined the meeting as they were talking about sending in an MO.4 agent to contact the Governor of Rhodes. It showed a remarkable lack of forward planning, since even two more days might mean the difference between success and failure. Jellicoe doubted the Italian Governor would take it seriously:

> What really amazed me was that this mission was going to go up in a couple of RAF 'crash-boats' and that the message was going to be delivered by an SOE operative, who was a peasant, I think ... (and, importantly) whose wireless had not been working for the best part of a month.[9]

Sutherland later commented that it was 'incredible' that 'a complicated diplomatic signal' should be even considered to be in capable hands with this arrangement.[10]

What seemed all the more incredible was that all this was 'being done at the last moment', as if the Italian armistice 'had not been anticipated', when, according to Gavin Mortimer, Brigadier Turnbull had already gone to Athlit on 13 August and given broad hints – without mentioning the destination – about what the mission might be. Milner-Barry also wrote in his diary that 'they were all to be engaged shortly depending on the political situation.'[11]

The RAF boats, based in Alexandria, would take at least two days to get there. Jellicoe was 'dumbstruck by the plan's vagueness'.[12] Later, he even said it was 'hair-brained'.[13] There was neither a plan for getting the 'Rhodes Mission' to the island nor for informing the Italian Governor, even though the Italians, who numbered around 35,000, were said to have very low morale, Jellicoe was told that no reinforcement could arrive before 15 September and that even then, they would not be 'assault loaded'. The only chance would be if 'token forces' were 'on tap', and that even then they would be 'exiguous' at best. He thought the whole thing 'rather a tall order', especially given that the Germans already had 'around seventy tanks or so there'.[14]

Eventually, he 'could not contain' himself any longer.[15] The discussion had just touched on the plans for Turnbull to head up the mission to go to Rhodes. Turnbull had also been late to the conference as he'd been in Gaza and was only able to arrive around 1130. Hesitantly, he added that, even though he was a junior officer, he didn't think the plan would work and suggested that someone be dropped in that evening:

> When all this dawned upon me, I just said I couldn't understand why on earth someone was not dropped in straight away that evening, and then they said, 'Would you care to be dropped in?'[16]

Jellicoe's suggestion to take in some men resulted in his being assigned the task of 'attempting to rally the Italian garrison on Rhodes to resist the Germans'.[17] On the other side of the conference table, an officer introducing himself as 'Major Dolbey' came forward, suggesting he accompany Jellicoe. Jellicoe asked him if he spoke Italian; Dolbey said that he could interpret, and since Jellicoe admitted he didn't, that was that. Dolbey, an MO.4 officer, was, in fact, a Polish aristocrat, the Count Julian Dobrski. He joined SOE in September 1940 and worked in the Italian and Aegean theatres. His languages certainly helped: he'd been educated in France, Italy and Switzerland and was a graduate of the University of Lyons.

The meeting came to an end around 1330. Over lunch at Shepheard's, Jellicoe talked through his misgivings with Turnbull, who was 'equally pessimistic'. Turnbull would follow once Jellicoe had established the initial contacts.

The Dodecanese islands, the '*dhodkeka nisia*' (twelve islands), are misnamed. There are, in fact, fourteen islands in the Southern Sporades island chain, but the name stuck as a political statement since twelve islands joined the protest against the Ottoman Turks as they revoked historic privileges. The islands had long been on Churchill's mind. Like Lloyd George, the British Prime Minister in the First World War, who was opposed by Haig, Robertson and Sir John Jellicoe, all trying to pull the Prime Minister back to focus on the Western Front and leave fronts like Salonika (Thessaloniki) alone, Churchill had 'an obsession with peripheral strategies'.[18] Churchill would have been called an 'Easterner' in the War Cabinet. Jellicoe remembered the way his father had talked about his battles in Lloyd George's War Cabinet. It was the same here: Churchill looked to expand fronts, in this case trying to bring Turkey into the war. Max Hastings talked about this 'fundamental doctrinal divide':

> The British liked minor operations while the Americans, with the marginal exception of MacArthur, did not. US strategic thinking, like that of the Germans, was dominated by a belief in concentration of force. The US Army undertook very few raids such as the British and Churchill in particular, loved – Vaasgo, Bruneval, Saint Nazaire, Bardia, Dieppe and many more.[19]

It was Churchill's 'driving force that impelled Middle East HQ to do something for which they were inadequately prepared.'[20] His ideas were opposed, not only from the Americans who distrusted his motives, but also from some of his own commanders, whose memory of the ill-fated Gallipoli campaign just 28 years previously was still fresh on their minds.

Ever since the Italo-Turkish War of 1911–12, the Dodecanese islands had been under Italian control, and 'three years later, France and Britain endorsed this shameless imperialist venture as part of the price for Italian accession to the Allied cause.'[21] The islands remained under Italian control in the Axis occupation of the Greek mainland and islands following Hitler's rescue of his ally in 1941.

Italy had spent more than thirty years building the area's military infrastructure, the most important improvements carried out between 1924 and 1936. In many ways, the island of Leros was a natural fortress – 'all the bays are commanded by heights, which are magnificent places for coastal artillery.'[22] These coastal batteries were powerful. There were

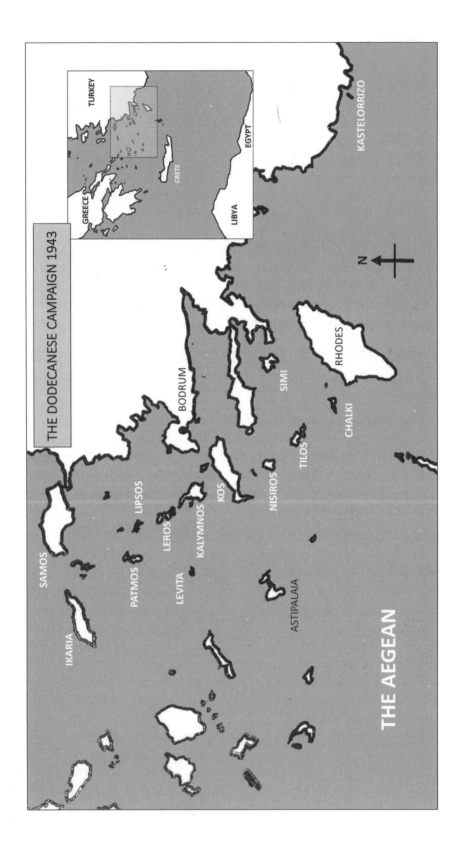

THE DODECANESE CAMPAIGN 1943

TURKEY

GREECE

CRETE

EGYPT

LIBYA

KASTELORRIZO

N

RHODES

SIMI

BODRUM

CHALKI

SAMOS

LIPSOS

TILOS

NISIROS

PATMOS

LEROS

KALYMNOS

IKARIA

LEVITA

KOS

ASTIPALAIA

THE AEGEAN

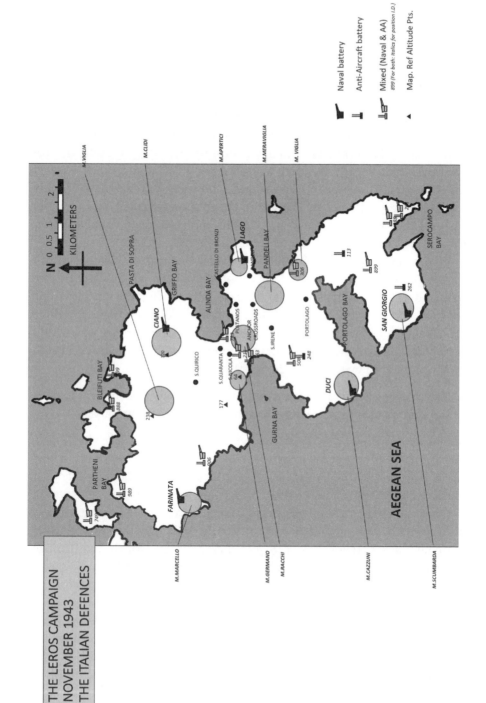

THE LEROS CAMPAIGN
NOVEMBER 1943
THE ITALIAN DEFENCES

N 0 0.5 1 2
KILOMETERS

M.VIGLIA
M.CLIDI
M.APERTICI
M.MERAVIGLIA
M. VIGLIA

M.MARCELLO
M.GERMANO
M.RACCHI
M.CAZZUNI
M.SCUMBARDA

PARTHENI BAY
BLEFUTI BAY
PASTA DI SOPRA
GRIFFO BAY
ALINDA BAY
CASTELLO DI BRONZI
LAGO
PANDELI BAY

FARINATA
CIANO
S.QUIRICO
S.QUARANTA
S.NICOLA
PLATANOS
ANCOR CROSSROADS
S.IRENE
PORTOLAGO
PORTOLAGO BAY
GURNA BAY
DUCI
SAN GIORGIO
SEROCAMPO BAY

AEGEAN SEA

Naval battery
Anti-Aircraft battery
Mixed (Naval & AA)
899 (For both: Italics for position I.D.)
Map. Ref Altitude Pts.

eleven 152mm guns, nine 102mm and fifty-eight 75mm. Of the fifty-nine guns in the thirteen more important batteries, thirty-seven were in service when the German invasion came on 12 November, even if many operated with obsolete fire control systems. So strong was Leros perceived to be that Mussolini reputedly called it 'the Corregidor of the Mediterranean'.[23]

Although Leros possessed an excellent deep-water harbour at Portolago (present day Lakki) and the island had also become a strongly fortified air and naval base, Rhodes, to the south-east, served as the main Italian naval base in the sector. Prior to operations, the 3rd MAS Flotilla, the 4th Destroyer Flotilla, the XXXIX Minesweeper Flotilla and other assorted ships were based there. (In terms of hulls, however, that was actually only a single destroyer, the *Euro*, along with eleven minesweepers, six MAS and two MTBs.) The *Euro* would be bombed and sunk on 1 October. After Leros, Kos, one of the next islands to its north, had airfields.

Why was Churchill pushing for a campaign that many felt would stretch his already limited resources? Many reasons have been put forward: that he wanted to find an alternative route to Russia, thus ending the terrible Arctic convoys; that he might be able to open up a 'back door' into Germany along the Danube; or that he might have thought it possible to open a route into Turkey at Izmir, allowing the Allies to support them if Germany decided to invade. Churchill rejected this specifically, writing:

> I have never wished to send an army into the Balkans, but only by agents and commandos to stimulate the intense guerrilla activity there.[24]

Maybe he hoped that the operation might be positively construed by Turkey, that it might subsequently be more inclined to enter the fray in the Allied camp. Taking back the Dodecanese from the Italians and holding them out to the Turks as bait might, he thought, accomplish this.

After the ill-fated Dardanelles campaign, Churchill was seen by many as obsessed with winning Turkey over to the Allied cause. In the year following November 1942, there were 128 meetings between British and Turkish government officials. The ratification of a programme of military assistance in May 1943 was one of the results.[25] Eventually, around £16m worth of equipment was supplied to Turkey in early 1943. All for nought.

In January 1943, Churchill tabled his views at the Casablanca Conference (SYMBOL). He received only grudging approval but, based on that, he gave the go-ahead to start planning an operation for 27 January 1943 under the code-name ACCOLADE: amphibious landings with three divisions and armour on Rhodes and Kárpathos. The inclusion of Major General Russell's 8th Indian division was called off when, in August, 'the shipping earmarked for the assault was sent to the Far East for operations on the coast of Burma, and the division was transferred to Allied Forces in the Central Mediterranean.'[26]

By late spring 1943, Allied attention was shifting towards Sicily (HUSKY) and the eventual invasion of mainland Italy. What Churchill was planning looked decidedly dangerous, a distraction at best, a strategic drain on resources at worst. By the time of the Quebec Conference (QUADRANT), American opposition had strengthened, and the planned resources, the 8th Division, for example, were moved elsewhere. Moreover, Roosevelt felt Churchill's Aegean plans were more aimed at British imperial aggrandizement than Germany's defeat. An operation which had, arguably, seemed feasible was fast becoming hopeless. It is surprising – in retrospect, maybe even astonishing – that the Commander-in-Chief for the Mediterranean had been kept in the dark about the planning. General Maitland Wilson had repeatedly stressed the need for more weight. The Supreme Allied Commander in the Mediterranean was known familiarly as 'Jumbo' because of his large girth. Churchill was no fan (he used to refer to the General as 'his jumbonic majesty') and felt that Wilson lacked verve.

As late as 31 August, Wilson complained to Eisenhower, 'Any enterprise against Rhodes or Crete except an unopposed walk-in is now impossible.'[27] Parish is quite critical of Wilson, saying that 'Churchill had given him thirty-seven days clear warning to be ready for this exact emergency.'[28] The problem might also have been Churchill: he just did not seem to hear what he was being told, enthusiastically signalling: 'Good. This is a time to play high. Improvise and dare.'[29]

The idea was to persuade Admiral Inigo Campioni, the Governor of Rhodes, to put his troops at Allied disposal and to hold the main airfield and the port in preparation for a larger invasion. Jellicoe was to combine SF elements with some regular army units on the island that would then use Rhodes as a jumping-off point for a rolling campaign through the Dodecanese islands. The only glitch was that he could not expect reinforcements before 15 September – at the very earliest.

Air cover was obviously going to be a major issue. Air Vice-Marshal Tedder was highly critical:

> One would have thought that some of the bitter lessons of Crete would have been sufficiently fresh in mind to have prevented a repetition …
> it seems incredible now, as it did then, that after four years' experience of modern war, people forget that air-power relies on secure bases, weather and effective radius of action.[30]

Cyprus was too far away for Spitfire support, and the Americans were adamant that the Lightning P-38 would not be made available. After four

days of service, they were withdrawn on 11 October.[31] By contrast, the
Luftwaffe could operate out of Crete, the Greek mainland (Megara, for
instance) and from nearby Rhodes and Kos.

While Jellicoe was being briefed, his men were alerted. Sutherland was
contacted just as he was sitting down for lunch at the OC in Athlit.

> The Italians have surrendered. Grab as many of your men as you can.
> Get them, weapons and equipment on board an ML in Haifa harbour
> and occupy the island of Kastelorizzo as soon as possible.[32]

With Milner-Barry's help, Sutherland was only able to find twelve men from
S detachment and another ten from M detachment. The depleted patrols
climbed aboard two 3-ton trucks and headed as fast as they could to Haifa,
20 miles away. Once there, Captain Stewart Macbeth's two M Detachment
patrols and Milner-Barry's two S Detachment patrols embarked on two of
Frank Ramseyer's MLs. While back at Athlit, Jock Lapraik organized the
rest of the SBS. All told, the forces amounted to around fifty men.[33] David
Lloyd Owen's LRDG forces would leave at roughly the same time, adding
another 130 or so.

The rest of the afternoon was spent getting prepared for the drop. It
wasn't easy to locate a suitable drop zone. Getting the appropriate kit and a
radio operator also had to be dealt with. And while Jellicoe was sorting these
out, Dolbey went off to MO.4 to tie up his own needs: codes, gold coinage
and weapons. Jellicoe arrived at the airport at 1900, Dolbey an hour and a
half later. He'd gone back to his apartment 'for a quick check of what might
have been left undone and a tidy up of his personal affairs'.[34] At 2100, the
van arrived with Kesterton, the radio operator, and they left for the airport
on the Mena road. However, en route he'd been 'seriously misdirected' and
arrived late. [35]

At the field, they found that the drop had been changed from the golf
course to another DZ 8km to the south. Dolbey joked, 'I was looking
forward to a soft fall on the greens.'[36] Then more delays: a dispatcher (the
man responsible for launching the jumpers) couldn't be located, and the
equipment had to be repacked.

Time was running out. At 0230, the Halifax finally rose into the night.
With a poetic sensibility, Dolbey recorded the moment:

> The black shape of the pyramids and the thousand twinkling lights of
> Cairo slide away into the night. Soon, when the moon fades beyond the
> western dunes and darkness is swept away by the ghostly desert breeze
> which heralds sunrise, we shall be flying over the red rocks set into the
> deep blue of the Aegean Sea.[37]

At 0530, the ragged outlines of Rhodes should have been visible below, 'but the low cloud gave them no sight of the island. They circled and circled, for a long, noisy hour, in increasing risk of scrambled fighters.' Jellicoe had wanted to stay on till first light, but the pilot was becoming increasingly nervous: 'No we can't, we'll be shot down.' When he later recounted the story to Mary Henderson, Jellicoe joked: 'The pilot had lost his way and spent the night flying all over Turkey looking for Rhodes.'[38] Jellicoe felt that the fault again lay with the disastrously last-minute planning: 'It was more a matter of faulty navigation due in large part to the fact that our mission was mounted at very short notice indeed.'[39]

Back they flew and landed at 0900. Then, at 1900, it was back to the same Halifax with the same crew and dispatcher (Dolbey remembered it as having been a Lancaster, but Jellicoe specifically talked about how relieved he was when he found they were going to be boarding a Halifax rather than an unarmed Dakota, the plane originally planned. It was not difficult to confuse a Handley Page Halifax with an Avro Lancaster – both were four-engined, both had rear fuselage guns and both were twin-tailed). By 1930 on the night of 9 September they were airborne again.[40]

After a short flight, Jellicoe, Dolbey and Sergeant Kesterton parachuted into Rhodes. It was just after 2145. Just as they were about to jump, Dolbey announced that, while he had done parachute *training*, he'd never actually made a jump. Aged forty-two, he was no longer a young man.

> I always remember at the very last moment, before Dobrski was going to go out, the first person, he said, 'Look I am afraid I told a lie about having been parachute-trained. I've never dropped. If, by any chance, I hesitate please give me a push.' Well he didn't need a push.[41]

Actually, Jellicoe might have been pretty understanding; he had 'always hated parachuting. It was very frightening. In those days parachutes sometimes didn't open.'[42] Dolbey ended up jumping first; his memories are a strange, ethereal mix of romance and adrenaline:

> A headlong eternity of nightmares and doubts as I fall downward. Ten seconds later I am floating. The night could be romantic … the rush of the scented breeze, the moon grinning over the low horizon, the sea of Odysseus so near … if it were not for the popping noises down below, for the odd bluish yellow spurts of flame and the occasional whine of a bullet which seems all too near.[43]

The drop did not go well. They landed in a 'wide stick', and Jellicoe said, with typical understatement, 'The next ninety minutes were unpleasant.' For Dolbey, the jump almost turned out to be fatal. As the three floated down,

Italians from an AA battery thought they were Germans. They had not been expecting an Allied drop. Indeed, nobody – not even Campioni – knew of the drop. Even when they reached the ground, the firing continued and was joined, according to Dolbey, by mortar fire.

Dolbey landed on the coastal road, hard tarmac, smashing his right leg 'extremely badly' and was then dragged over the ground. The wind had been blowing at around 20mph. Despite what must have been both extremely painful and frightening, Dolbey's humour is remarkable: after 25 yards, he detached the harness, 'the balloon of white silk floating away in best Scottish ghost style into the darkness'. When he came to a stop, the broken bone in his leg 'was sticking out through the skin in his thigh.'

Kesterton also landed badly, and one of his two radios was smashed. The other could not be found. When Jellicoe landed, 'a little further inland' (he later said it was about three miles from the intended DZ), he had to get rid of the papers with him to make his task easier.[44] He had 'strict instructions' that they should not fall into enemy hands. He ate the letter he was carrying from 'Jumbo' Wilson to the Italian Admiral.[45] Jellicoe did not, needless to say, feel that great after his forced meal. 'It was a heavily embossed official document and wasn't easily digestible.'

Jellicoe was relieved, however, that the fire was 'heavy but very inaccurate'. The first priority was for identities to be established: 'that the Italians were indeed Italians' and to convince 'the Italians that we were not Germans'.[46]

After around forty-five minutes, Dolbey heard people approaching and to his relief heard them speaking Italian. Once he was discovered to be British, the atmosphere changed completely:

> One corporal suddenly discovers that we are Allies and some obvious sign of hospitable welcome is overdue. Cigarettes, brandy, and two blankets on which to rest my leg appear. I am slapped on the back by each in turn, blessed, and assured by an admiring chorus that I deserve 'la Medaglio d'Oro'.[47]

Dolbey would, actually, later be awarded a Military Cross for his part in the mission. He now managed to persuade his captor's commander, Capitano Brunetti, to take them to the Admiral.[48] There were genuine apologies for what had happened. Jellicoe, Dolbey and Kesterton arrived at the Governor's Palace late 'in a very dilapidated lorry' but were able to arrange an audience with him.

The first meeting with Brunetti's superior didn't go well. He was 'not only a Blackshirt but also a martinet and could be relied upon to be unfriendly.' It did not take long before the Blackshirt Colonel 'for no apparent reason seem[ed] to be in a towering rage, [was] now cursing at anybody within reach but especially at my poor Captain Brunetti.'[49] The latter made it clear that his Colonel wanted to keep the three there till the morning but then took it upon himself to get a motorbike organized to take Dolbey to the Governor.

Dolbey finally arrived at the Castle of the Knights of St John at 0115, and after a short explanation with the Governor's ADC, was taken up, lying on a stretcher borne by four sailors, to see Campioni. The setting was palatial.

> The room is huge but well-lit … feel as though I had suddenly walked onto the stage of the last act of a Verdi opera. Staff officers in brilliant peacetime uniforms, capes of many colours, golden epaulettes and glistening swords move around as my stretcher is carefully grounded by the side of a red velvet covered armchair.[50]

After a 'frigidly polite' introduction, the Governor's demeanour thawed considerably, and a party was sent out for Jellicoe and Kesterton with his radio set and codes. Jellicoe was 'impressed with the efficiency of the Italian road blocks, but more so by the lethargy and obvious apathy of the columns of Italian troops which we passed on their march north along the coast road.'[51] They arrived around 0245 on the morning of 10 September.

Jellicoe's opening words – that he had had to eat General Sir Maitland-Wilson's letter – rather upset Campioni. Jellicoe found out that the Italian Admiral had only just heard about the Armistice and it had come as a surprise. He'd learned about it from the wife of a German officer (who herself had only heard the news on the radio) and had received nothing through official channels.

At 0900 the following morning, the conference resumed in Dolbey's room. Neither he nor Jellicoe was very impressed by Campioni or his entourage, which struck them as being 'rather of the yes type of officer'. Since Cairo hadn't replied, it was agreed that someone should get back to Cyprus to transmit the need to persuade GHQ 'immediately to take the risk of sending a small British force'. The choice was straightforward: 'We agree that being immobilized, I [Dolbey] ought to go'.[52]

My father always maintained that he introduced himself to Campioni as 'le *brigadier* Jellicoe'. He explained his mistake: '*brigadiere*' in Italian actually ranked him as a Sergeant. The more I think about it now, the more I think that it was yet another of his jokes against himself. Jellicoe's name and family were well-known to Campioni. That would have been the case with any naval officer, but 'the old admiral was a somewhat weak and vacillating character and it was therefore hoped that he could be influenced without too much difficulty.'[53] Although in considerable pain, Dolbey faithfully fulfilled his assigned role of interpreting for Jellicoe.

Though Campioni had more troops than the Germans, Jellicoe noted that they were dispersed over the island, while the Germans were concentrated around the main town, holding the middle of the island between the divided Italian forces. They were grouped in 'penny packets and almost without transport'. Furthermore, the Italians did not have much transport, which could have redressed the imbalance.

With the exception of the artillery units or the Blackshirts (as on Samos), most of the Italian troops did not want to go on fighting. The Germans, on the other hand, were fresh and eager. For the most part, the Italian garrison commanders

> were middle-aged or even elderly senior officers whose service careers had been rewarded during recent years by appointments to these pleasant and sometimes delicious islands, where danger had been minimal, supplies from the homeland regular and of good quality, and duties easy enough hardly to disturb the even tenor of what resembled a happy retirement.[54]

The German commander, General Ulrich Kleemann, had just been sent to Rhodes by Hitler with around 7,500 troops of the newly-created *Sturm–Division Rhodos* 'when he suspected treachery from the Italian King'.[55] Hitler regarded the potential threat as very real: the Balkans was 'an area which supplied him with bauxite, copper and chrome and also denied a firm base for the Allies to bomb the oil fields in Ploesti.'[56]

Kleemann's troops belonged to Luftwaffe General Alexander Löhr's Army Group (*Heeresgruppe*) E. His men were 'full of fight' and were already positioned around the airfields at Marizza, Calato and Cattavia. The Germans had worked out an agreement of their own with Campioni on the night of the Armistice announcement (9 September), that their troops would not redeploy from their existing positions. Immediately, however, they broke their word and repositioned units, so that by midday on 10 September they had occupied the centre, with troops in Psito, Catavia, Calato and Marrizza. Jellicoe could not promise that much: immediate airborne landings, yes, but no major reinforcements for at least a week. Campioni allowed him to contact Cairo with an updated sitrep using the Italian W/T station. All the while, Jellicoe was trying, in his words, to 'put spine into the Italians', communicating through Dolbey, who was by now showing 'signs of collapse'.[57] Campioni told Jellicoe that he had ordered resistance and that fighting had taken place around Marizza. To Jellicoe, however, there were few 'visible sounds or signs of fighting'.[58]

Campioni was now starting to become nervous and told Jellicoe to maintain a low profile, to dress as a civilian and not to leave the castle.

Jellicoe's request to take a look at the situation on the ground, particularly at Marizza, was refused. Obviously, Campioni was disappointed by what Jellicoe was offering and couldn't be persuaded to support the Allied plan. Without immediate Allied reinforcements, he felt extremely vulnerable.

Jellicoe later defended the Italian commander, knowing the pressure he was under. Despite the man's obvious vanity, he liked Campioni. The criticisms that he later heard were 'unjust'. He was a 'perfectly honourable man' who had treated him 'absolutely fairly'. 'If I had been Admiral Campioni, I would have made the same decision that he did', he concluded.[59] Campioni was walking a tightrope: at one moment, the German commander was in one room, Jellicoe in another. He went on: 'I personally dissent from the view that Admiral Campioni was "lily-livered". I very much doubt myself, given the positioning and equipment of the German forces and their mobility, that any protracted resistance by the Italian forces in Rhodes would have served any really useful purpose.'[60] Given the predicament Campioni found himself in, the Allies weren't putting much on the table: 'They did their best since, as you know, all I was able to promise Campioni in the way of military assistance was a non-assault-loaded brigade in about six days time.'[61]

Colonel Kenyon (who came with Turnbull, Group Captain Wheeler and Major Palmer and had similarly reached out to Campioni) came to the same conclusions as Jellicoe, that Campioni's hands were tied: he 'knew something of Campioni's record and personality, and formed the opinion, to which I still adhere, that in a difficult position, he was playing an in and out game, and halting between two policies.'[62]

Jellicoe saw that some of Campioni's staff wanted to resist and he took his request for Allied bombardment of the Calato, Marizza and Catavia positions as a positive sign. He'd not been able to deliver his sitrep through the Italians but now tried on the second radio set, which had finally been found in the drop zone and brought to the Governor's Palace.

During the day, a number of German planes flew over: a couple of recon aircraft and five Ju.87s. They dropped some bombs and were answered with Italian AA fire. Kesterton said that he and the German Chief of Staff had only narrowly avoided ending up in the same air raid shelter. The firing 'continued long after their departure.' It was as though they were firing for effect and nothing else.[63] Dolbey even talked with a medical orderly who said that he could not understand the purpose of the shelling as 'the shells were falling in the sea.'[64] It was a show being put on for their benefit. By midday, Jellicoe was getting frustrated at the evident lack of action and went to see Campioni again. The latter re-affirmed that he needed a bombardment in the south, admitted that he was negotiating with the Germans, saying that he was playing for time, but agreed to the arrival of Colonel Turnbull that evening. He was to be flown to Simi and brought to Rhodes by an MAS boat, the Italian equivalent of a fast torpedo boat.[65] At 1345, after lunch, Dolbey left for Simi on another MAS. Once there, he had to wait till the evening (there were patrolling Me.109s in the area), when he was woken by the Governor with a 'telegram received from Rome stating that Italy had now also declared war on Germany'.[66] Dolbey had to wait till morning before he could finally get away. Turnbull's aeroplane arrived at 0800, after which he left at 0930, and arrived back in Limassol at 1215. Nobody from GHQ was there to meet him, so he organized for the Staff Intelligence Officer, Captain Gianotti, to take Campioni's letter in person to Cairo that evening.

By 1700 on 10 September Campioni had completely changed his tune. Jellicoe had been sleeping and was woken by the Governor who was now extremely agitated, saying that he had heard that the Germans were about to attack in Rhodes town, that Jellicoe should leave and that the planned arrival of Colonel Turnbull should be cancelled (he had gone to Simi on 9 September in a captured Italian seaplane so as to be quickly available should Jellicoe need him).[67] Jellicoe initially resisted, saying that he didn't yet consider his own safety at risk. He changed his mind when he heard from the Governor's A.D.C. that an agreement with the Germans seemed to have been reached. Meanwhile, Campioni continued the charade, insisting that he was playing for time and that it would be better if Jellicoe and Turnbull were 'to remain handy' in Simi or Kastelorrizo rather than stay on Rhodes.[68]

Before he left, however, Jellicoe was able to obtain detailed plans of the island's defences and minefields. They were not as useful as first thought:

> In the event, the Italian plans of their own minefields were so inaccurate as to be valueless. Reliance on them was to cost the allies several ships before they realized their inaccuracy. This may have been by design – for Campioni was perhaps playing both sides against the middle – or it may have been due to inefficiency.[69]

Around 2000, 'shortly after dusk', Jellicoe left Rhodes, carrying a picnic basket and several bottles of Rhodes wine and accompanied in MS 12 by Campioni's Deputy, Lieutenant Colonel Ruggero Fanizza.[70] Just before dawn on the morning of 11 September, their MAS reached Kastelorizzo.

The day before, 10 September, Sutherland's SBS had also arrived and occupied the little island. They had come in on two of Frank Ramseyer's MLs, 349 and 357. With them were men from Macey's Raiders (No.8 Special Boat Commando) as well as the LRDG. Separately, Turnbull arrived with other HQ elements – AA gunners and RAF signallers – from Paphos on Cyprus. As they came close, they had signalled the two Italian forts at the entrance to the port, but 'perhaps owing to mediocre translation, a few rifle shots were fired at us, one of which slightly wounded a naval officer.'[71]

An intelligence officer went ashore to straighten things out. The decision was taken to 'take the bolder course of sailing straight into the port', in daytime on 10 September, rather than 'go in like a thief in the night.'[72]

The next day, Jellicoe's MAS came in over water that was 'as calm as a mill pond', SBS men lined up on the jetty.[73] Jellicoe and Kesterton disembarked, followed by Fanizza, who promptly fell in the water in what Jellicoe described as an 'undiplomatic tumble'.[74] Sutherland's men couldn't disguise their mirth. It might have been funny but it was bound to make an enemy of Fanizza if he wasn't one already. Although he got the identity of the victim wrong, Holmes' account set the scene nicely:

> It was an Italian admiral, about five feet tall, the whole left side of his uniform a rainbow of decorations, his boots glistened in the early morning sunshine and his smile was expansive to say the least … Unfortunately, he was long on aplomb but short on legs and fell in with a splash.[75]

Sutherland later said that Jellicoe 'looked physically and mentally exhausted' but temporarily revived with a whisky and soda.[76]

Leros was valued for its harbour and heavy coastal guns, while Kos was only considered important because of its airfields. But without Rhodes, the whole venture appeared to be still-born, even if opinions were divided. Jellicoe always maintained that 'the Dodecanese could have been held if we had gained control of the airfields on Rhodes.'[77]

At the time, Milner-Barry thought that a way to retain the islands could be found: 'We certainly did not realize at the time that without the capture of Rhodes itself, the remaining islands were virtually untenable.'[78] Maybe that was why, despite the disappointment of Rhodes, Jellicoe went on with what Lodwick called a 'contemptibly small' force, the equivalent of a single SBS detachment and several MTBs, to prevent the rest of the Dodecanese islands falling into German hands. LRDG commander David Lloyd Owen, however, felt very strongly that the die was cast:

> I believe we made our first of many blunders in so impotently failing to assume control of Rhodes. The failure to get the airfields on the island should have been the signal that those Aegean operations were doomed to disaster unless Turkey could be persuaded at once to come on the side of the allies. [79]

On Kastelorizzo, Jellicoe was too late to find Turnbull. The Brigadier had just flown in after Sutherland's and Milner-Barry's two-patrol force had landed but had then left again.

After a quick breakfast, Jellicoe got back on the MAS bound for Simi to try and catch up with Turnbull. It was still very early morning and the scene looked 'particularly delightful'. As they headed out, 'two peculiarly sordid looking motor caïques' arrived. They turned out to be those of Captain Chevalier and Commander Londos, both of whom were unaware of the armistice.

Now Campioni got 'windy' and signalled the MAS on which Jellicoe had just left to turn back. Jellicoe was annoyed but persuaded the boat's skipper, Commandante del Viso, to ignore Campioni's order and continue for Simi. Satisfied that this was where he was heading, an exhausted Jellicoe went to sleep. When he woke he found that he was back in the small port; Fanizza had countermanded his orders while he slept. He was furious but assumed that he had made an enemy of the Italian when Fanizza had seen him smiling quietly at his earlier immersion.

The good news was that Turnbull's Rhodes party had also returned after Captain Wheeler had been refused permission to land (Colonel Kenyon had somehow managed to get ashore and talk to Campioni). Jellicoe was now able to brief Wheeler and catch up with David Sutherland. Back in Cairo, General Maitland-Wilson received the news:

> At 1715 on 11th September, information reached me that Campioni had lost heart, had refused permission for us to enter the island and did not wish to have any further dealings with us.

That evening, he got further news from Turnbull that the Italian garrison had capitulated to Kleemann and that subsequently, the entire garrison had been taken prisoner.

David Sutherland later wrote in his *War Diaries* that the Allies had lost the bigger prize: Rhodes. He felt that, had they mustered the forces, it might have been a very different outcome. He was 'certain' that two battalions of infantry and twenty-four anti-tank guns would have provided 'sufficient forces' if in the south a diversion was created by 200 Special Force troops and two companies of paratroopers. He argued that the Germans had little air cover at this point and that Kleemann's forces were busy trying to hold down the airfields. It would have needed, to his mind, something like '24 MLs and 24 Dakotas (or the equivalent)'.[80] Sutherland thought that this would have been a far more worthwhile gamble.

The next day, 12 September, the British on Kastelorizzo set about taking stock of their situation and working through the organization of their new forces (the new additions were '12 assorted Italian auxiliary vessels', three MAS boats and two seaplanes). During the day, the LRDG also arrived. In the evening, Turnbull announced his intention to send Sutherland on to Kos and Jellicoe to Leros.

That night, together with Kesterton and Lieutenants Gross and McKenzie, Jellicoe slept well on the MAS's deck, and as dawn broke on 13 September, the two boats found themselves off the south coast of Kos. Sutherland took ten men although he said that he had little idea how they might be received or whether these were there.[81] They need not have worried. As they approached through the narrow harbour entrance, Sutherland was touched by the joyous welcome of the local Greeks:

> Their enthusiasm was almost startling in its exuberance and we were not altogether unthankful when time came for us to depart suitably equipped with grapes and, surprisingly enough, champagne.[82]

His men celebrated with the locals. Jellicoe, Sutherland and the men were regaled with flowers. 'The enthusiasm and joy of the inhabitants was touching in its spontaneity.'[83] Stefanos Kasulis, 'a young man with [a] classical nose, serious eyes, prematurely greying hair and a sensitive mouth which rarely smiled', made a speech in the town square.[84] The crowds were jubilant at hearing the words of their young compatriot.

Despite their abject poverty, the locals feted them with wine and roasted a whole pig (Sutherland, who seemed to have an extraordinary memory for food – his accounts are peppered with gastronomic references – said that it was red wine and *tagliatelle verde*.[85]) Jellicoe was not unaware of the sacrifice and honour this represented. It made a lasting impression on him. He often talked about the starvation he had seen in Greece and once told me he had 'never seen children thinner or more unkempt'. Greece's economy was in freefall, inflation so out of hand that its currency had, to all intents and purposes, disappeared. A cigarette cost 7½ million drachma; an egg 40 million.[86] Small wonder, then, that many SBS took to redistributing supplies to the Greeks, often earning rebukes from their fellow officers.

Only staying on Kos 'long enough … to verify the peaceful intentions of the local commander', Jellicoe continued on to Leros in the same MAS (MS 12).[87] Once on Leros, Jellicoe found the Italian commander, Rear Admiral Mascherpa, to ascertain his intentions.[88] Jellicoe wanted to make a full reconnaissance and choose suitable landing and disembarkation points as quickly as possible. A British mission had already visited the island a few days before and persuaded the Italians not to co-operate with the Germans.[89] (It struck me, when I heard this, just how disorganized these various missions were. One hardly seemed to know of the other's presence.)

On the way, a *Malteme*, 'a sharp Aegean wind', started to blow, and it became an extremely rough crossing. As they braved the storm, they were getting soaked, and the MAS was finding it difficult to make any headway. The Italian skipper commented on the weather: '*C'est grave*'. Ten minutes later, it became '*C'est pire*'. As soon as he landed, Jellicoe went to meet Mascherpa who, to Jellicoe's deep displeasure and suspicion, was accompanied by the same Colonel Fanizza who had already tricked him at Kastellorizo. He had found Mascherpa's welcome 'friendly' but he was now distrustful. He found Fanizza a 'difficult and odious character'.[90] Nevertheless, Jellicoe was able to send Turnbull a sitrep and then select landing sites with the aid of the Admiral.

The two of them had gone off in his staff car while Gross and McKenzie looked more closely at the Italian garrison. When they got back they quickly ate and drank, then flew that night in a seaplane, an Italian Cant, back to Kastellorizo. Jellicoe was dead tired and, after reporting to Turnbull, slept 'very soundly for fourteen hours.'

At the same time, back on Kos, Sutherland was able to 'guide down a company of the 11th Parachute Battalion on to the salt pans along the northern coast near Marmeti'.[91] (This was probably Marmari, just south of the salt pans.)

Two days later, 15 September, David Lloyd Owen arrived on Leros with additional LRDG mobile reserves of the Y.1. patrol. He'd been ordered to Kastelorrizo by Lieutenant General Anderson, who astutely added that the 'most likely role will be a move into Kos and Samos.' On the evening of 11 September he sailed from Haifa in a little flotilla of three ships, one Greek, the others British and French. 'Thus began, in a tragically vague way, the Aegean campaign.' They arrived two days later but were immediately ordered north to Leros. Leaving Kastelorrizo, he complained that the 'lack of reliable information was disgraceful'.[92] Like Jellicoe, he felt that the Aegean venture had been undertaken with minimal planning. And like Jellicoe, he'd had a very bad crossing: 'It was a cold, wet ride and most people were horribly sick.'[93]

Major (acting) Alan Redfern, one of the Rhodesian LRDG officers, had gone ahead by seaplane to also meet with Mascherpa but had been held up when 'the aircraft's Italian crew proved very unenthusiastic and contrived to collide with a Short Sunderland flying boat whilst taxiing.'[94] It strikes me as odd that the LRDG and the SBS were making contact with Mascherpa independently of one another, a repetition of the lack of co-ordination that was seen when both Kenyon and Jellicoe met with Campioni on Rhodes.

Admiral Mascherpa, 'parading resplendent as though to receive royalty', came to meet them.[95] As the Italian Governor took him around the island's defences, Lloyd Owen was unimpressed: 'There was no depth in the defence, and no provision had been made for a reserve to counter-attack any enemy that might land.'[96] Lloyd Owen was not comfortable with his new-found allies, the Italians. The order he received to have his men salute former enemy officers was not passed on. The Italian Admiral had made his chef available to the LRDG and LSF boys billeted in the Navy House.[97]

When the German assault finally came, everyone was pressed into service, including the cooks. Seligman was also conscripted into the front line, going up to Alinda Bay with his motley reinforcements to where the SBS and a Buffs mortar company were located. He had 'a little gang consisting of two naval ratings, a REME technician, two infantrymen (one a corporal) and two Italians'.[98] The Italian cook didn't take well to the idea: 'I am a cook, Signore, not fighting and dying.'[99] A Sten gun in his stomach persuaded him to think again. The LRDG immediately put the Italians (including, much to their distaste, officers) to work in large parties strengthening what and where they could.

A few weeks before, Seligman had flown into Leros on a Walrus flying boat. He was not used to flying and it was a hair-raising approach as he came into Portolago. He and his companion were entertained royally by the Italians, being served champagne by what he thought were waitresses but were actually 'inhabitants of the three *"palazzini"*, one each for the officers, NCOs and men, thoughtfully provided by a discerning government.'[100] It was an insight into the nature of the Italian occupation.

*   *   *

From 10 to 17 September, Jellicoe's men worked their way through to the other islands – Kalymnos, Samos, Simi and Astipalaia.

The initial British forces that went in immediately after Jellicoe's mission to Rhodes were 160 SBS, 130 Long Range Desert Group (LRDG), the Levant Schooner Flotilla, a Company of 11th Battalion, Parachute Regiment and elements of the Greek Sacred Squadron (*Ieros Lochos*) and SAAF (South African Air Force). Gradually, these forces were to be reinforced as elements of the 234th Infantry Brigade came together under the command of Major General F. G. R. Brittorous.

Brittorous was an extremely unpopular commander on Leros – more 'spit and polish'. He 'embodied almost every deficiency of the wartime British army ... obsessed with military etiquette, and harassed officers and men alike about the importance of saluting him.'[101] It was all the more surprising, given that he'd just gone through another siege on Malta.

Following his orders, fifty LRDG were sent to the outlying island of Levitha, 20 miles or so to the west of Leros. It was a badly planned mission that cost the unit two officers and thirty-nine ORs. Easonsmith and Lloyd Owen watched the disaster unfold as they 'stood on the highest point of Leros from which they could see the air attacks.'[102]

Almost immediately, Brittorous also managed to alienate Mascherpa by announcing that all Italian troops were subordinate to him. It might have worked on paper but was hardly the best or most diplomatic move when a close working relationship was needed. Brittorous was eventually replaced by Robert Tilney, who arrived on 5 November. By then it was too late for the newcomer to gain a really close appreciation of the situation on the ground, and the changes he made turned out to be fatal.[103] He threw Brittorous' troop deployment out the window, deciding that it was better 'to plan a defensive action based upon the existing Italian dispositions.'[104]

With Rhodes in their possession, the Germans moved fast. By the 19th, Karpathos, Kasos and the Italian Cycladic and Sporadic islands were in German hands. More alarmingly, German air cover was considerably strengthened. Their air strength reached 360 aircraft.[105]

The sense of urgency, however, wasn't present everywhere. If you look at the SBS operational diary, there are brief mentions of Jellicoe's flight to Cairo by 'special plane'. He got back to the islands by parachute, in a solo drop over Kos; as he put it, 'It wasn't the easiest way to get back.' A note adds that two patrols of S and M detachments were to 'proceed to naval docks, Haifa at 1615 hrs to embark on M.L.s for unknown destination', while the 'remainder of SBS continue normal training.' But it seems incongruous to read now that the remaining SBS men enjoyed 'a dance of Khayat beach' on 15 September and 'cricket against the RA in Haifa' on 19 September.[106]

Chapter 8

Prelude to Disaster – Kos, Simi and Samos

L ike Kastelorizzo, the 28-mile-long island of Kos lies only a few miles or so from the coast of Turkey. Its airfields made the island important: Antimachia, a second, smaller airfield at Lambia (though still under construction, it could only really be used as an emergency strip) and finally, the salt pan field at Marmari.

On 13, 14 and 15 September 1943, British reinforcements arrived, first the paratroops, then infantry. On 13 September, a small group of Lapraik's M detachment arrived to secure the airfields and the next day, the first Allied aeroplane landed at Antimachia, a Beaufighter from 46 Squadron, off-loading an RAF signals team to help guide in the stream of Dakotas and additional Beaufighters that followed during the day. That night, 120 men – A company of the 11th Parachute Battalion – took off from Nicosia, almost 400 miles away, and dropped at 0145 the morning of 15 September, just north-west of Kos town. The infantry – Lieutenant Colonel Kirby's 1st Battalion of the Durham Light Infantry – came later that day, and two days later, on 17 September, A and B companies of the 2nd Battalion Royal Irish Fusiliers joined them.

With the job done on Kos, Sutherland was ordered by the island's new commander, Lieutenant General Anderson, to move on to secure Samos, where his group – now numbering around twenty-five – arrived the next morning, 16 September. The Blackshirts' garrison was 1,500-strong and must, Sutherland thought, have taken a 'poor view' of his tiny party.

Sutherland's party waited just long enough to be relieved by a Battalion of the Royal West Kents before moving on to Kalymnos. Two weeks later, on 1 October, it was decided that the small island, just south of Leros, would 'make an ideal base for all raiding forces in the area, the SBS and the newly arrived and retrained LRDG, with Colonel Turnbull and the Raiding Forces HQ in Leros.'[1] With the LRDG was a young Captain, Moir Stormonth-Darling. Sutherland left the island with Jellicoe and Milner-Barry on one of Ramseyer's MLs.

The success that Jellicoe had in establishing a foothold on Kos (and Simi) was due partly to Ian Lapraik and David Sutherland; but it owed an enormous debt to the navigational and camouflage genius of a young lieutenant, Adrian Seligman, who had the standard camouflage nets for the caïques of the Levant Schooner Flotilla redesigned with a darker grey scrim to better work against the rocky island shores. He had the good fortune to meet Maurice Green, a man he considered to be the 'co-founder' of the LSF, who also happened to be a specialist in camouflage. Another friend, John Reid, flew his Beaufighter over a camouflaged caïque to test its effectiveness. The nets were even weighted to lower them into the water below the boat's hull. Seligman also invented a new type of navigation procedure for the younger officers, developing something that he called 'silhouette navigation' to make the task easier but just as precise.[2] His methods allowed Lassen's men to 'come like cats and disappear like ghosts', as a captured letter from a German garrison commander put it.

Kos was quickly reinforced by two battalions, one each from the Queen's Own Royal West Kent Regiment and the Royal East Kent Regiment, known as the 'Buffs'. Additionally, there would also be around 680 Durham Light Infantry, RAF personnel and, from the Italian troops, another 3,500 from 10th Regiment, 50th Infantry Division (Regina).[3] The evening of the 14th, another 120 parachute troops were dropped by Dakotas of No. 216 Squadron.[4]

Air defence was provided by South African pilots of No.7 Squadron SAAF, along with the RAF's No.74 Squadron. There was also a Bristol Beaufighter Squadron (with four planes: two day-, and two night-fighters), a Wellington torpedo bomber Squadron, a Hudson general reconnaissance squadron and a number of specially outfitted photo-reconnaissance Spitfires. This gave the Allies 260 aircraft, 144 of which were fighters.[5]

The problem with most of these aircraft, however, was their endurance. The only planes with any long-range capability were the Beaufighter and the American P-38 Lightning. But the P-38s (which were only made available by the Americans for four days) could only remain over the Aegean islands for around 20 minutes after expending most of their fuel en route from the Gambut airfield outside of Benghazi. Similarly, many of the Beaufighters had to fly 350 miles before they could even fight. For the aircrews, it was exhausting.

Wasting no time, the Germans started softening up Kos. The 17 September bombardment was devastating. The airfield at Antimachia became useless when 'butterfly' bombs – originally designed for anti-personnel use – were dropped from Ju.88s, peppering the runways. Immediate resources were poured into the alternative airfield, Lambia. It became operational on 21 September, when Spitfire sorties were renewed. But, out of an original total of twenty Spitfires, Kos was down to four by 26 September.

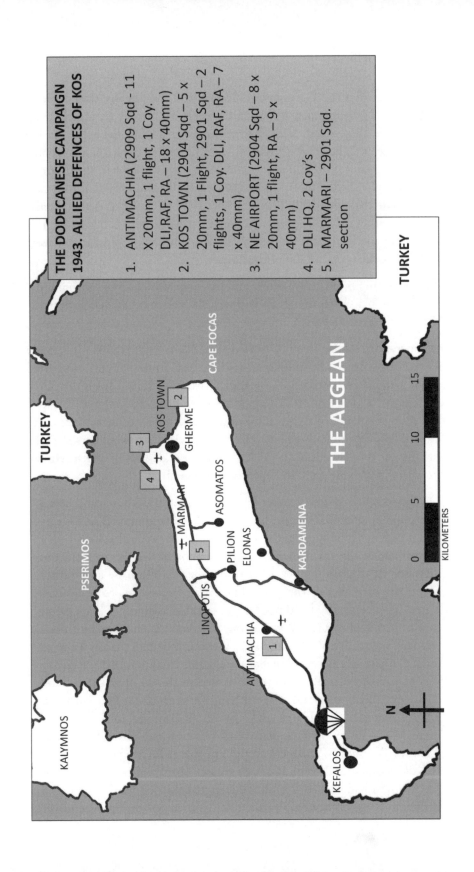

THE DODECANESE CAMPAIGN 1943. ALLIED DEFENCES OF KOS

1. ANTIMACHIA (2909 Sqd - 11 X 20mm, 1 flight, 1 Coy. DLI,RAF, RA – 18 x 40mm)
2. KOS TOWN (2904 Sqd – 5 x 20mm, 1 Flight, 2901 Sqd – 2 flights, 1 Coy. DLI, RAF, RA – 7 x 40mm)
3. NE AIRPORT (2904 Sqd – 8 x 20mm, 1 flight, RA – 9 x 40mm)
4. DLI HQ, 2 Coy's
5. MARMARI – 2901 Sqd. section

TURKEY

TURKEY

KALYMNOS

PSERIMOS

CAPE FOCAS

KOS TOWN

GHERME

MARMARI

ASOMATOS

LINOPOTIS

PILION

ELONAS

ANTIMACHIA

KARDAMENA

KEFALOS

THE AEGEAN

N

0   5   10   15

KILOMETERS

It was clear that the Germans would not wait long before they came in by sea. From 21 September, for around a week, no further air attacks were carried out as they marshalled their resources, readying them for the big attack. In the early hours of 3 October, coming ashore from a small armada of ten ferry lighters, two minelayers and other assorted vessels, the German attack was unleashed. The first wave landed at the small town of Marmari on the north coast at 0500. The attackers went in as light as they could. They had neither medical equipment nor stores with them. They had to rely on an enemy medic to care for their wounded. The conditions for operating were horrific: he soon ran out of the basics:

> The operating room grew steamy and the floor was cluttered with piles of foul and bloody clothing, while the wash basin was clogged with the sludge of plaster of Paris.[6]

The operation, codenamed *Unternehmen Eisbär* (Operation Ice Bear) achieved early success. By midday around 1,200 German soldiers, supported by light armour and artillery, were already working inland from the north and the south-west. Around 1330, paratroops (*Fallschirmjäger*) were dropped to the west and south of Antimachia and, supported by continued air cover from Rhodes, were quickly able to seize the airfield, even though most of the pilots managed to fly out in the nick of time. Guy de Pass, a South African pilot with No.74 RAF Spitfire Squadron, reported:

> On the morning of 3rd October I awoke at about 0430 hours and heard the sound of aircraft above me but didn't take much notice. The aircraft continued to fly around and I heard in the distance the sound of a motor launch. By this time, I was very apprehensive. Shots from the direction of the landing beach strip were heard. We arose and moved off in the direction of the road. The firing became more persistent. Flares were being fired and mortar fire could be discerned. It appeared to all of us that the island was being invaded and that enemy troops were in the vicinity. We began to run towards the main road as we were unable to put up any sort of defence and considered that the best policy was to join up with the main party of British troops. It was still fairly dark with plenty of cloud. I saw Flying Officers Bates and Norman, F/Sgt. Maxwell, Sgt. Harris and a South African and joined up with them. When we reached the main road, we saw a jeep driven by a South African. We piled in and went straight to Kos. The people in the hotel at Kos, a Major and some RAF Regiment chaps did not believe that the invasion had started. I took the jeep and warned British HQ, the Bofors gun battery and all and sundry. I then handed the jeep over

to an RAF Regiment officer who wanted to go to Kos aerodrome to collect some of his men. We pilots of 74 Squadron did not know that a party of our ground crews had landed by air on the previous night on Kos aerodrome, and by 11:00 hours, we had boarded an Italian boat in Kos harbour and set sail for Leros. On the way out, we ran into some German boats so we turned for Kefalcha on the Turkish coast eventually reaching Kastelorizzo and Paphos by high speed launch.[7]

At Piso Thermae on the south side, the Germans landed a battalion. Fourteen were killed. By midnight, after a series of 'brilliant but violent actions', the Germans controlled most of Kos except for the docks area, 'upon which they focused searchlights and sniped and bombed everything that moved.'[8]

At 0545, 3 October, the *Küstenjäger* Coy. was landed in Kamara Bay to support the paras. Now the second airfield, Lambia, scarcely operational for two weeks, was taken, and with it the last hope of any air cover was gone. Now German fire started to fall directly on to Kos town.

From Kalymnos, only a mile or so to the north, Sutherland and Milner-Barry watched the lightning German onslaught. It was over before they could even react. Jellicoe, also there watching the attack then went directly back to Leros.

After a final radio message went out ('Kos town untenable. Intend continuing to fight elsewhere. Destroyed wireless set.'), the British surrendered. They had been completely outnumbered.

At this point, Lloyd Owen, who was already off the island, got a message from MEHQ telling him to use the LRDG to 're-take' Kos. As he put it in his memoirs, this was 'one of the most brainless and preposterous orders I have ever received'.[9]

The SBS role now changed, from direct fighting to extracting troops from the island. Some tried to swim over to Turkey. Most wouldn't make it, but there's a story of one group getting the whole way across. Geoffrey Searle, an ML captain, recounted:

> I was ordered to go by night to Bodrum in Turkey to collect a party of Durham Light Infantry who, I was told, had escaped by swimming the eight miles between Cos to Turkey … the water was warm and somewhere near the middle is a large rock showing just above water line where it might have been possible to have a rest. [10]

Another escapee was a South African medical officer from the Marmari team who decided to swim the 5km gap between Kos and Turkey. He nearly got there, saw a boat flying what looked like a Red Cross flag and climbed aboard, only to be recaptured. He was unlucky: 'She was a German-

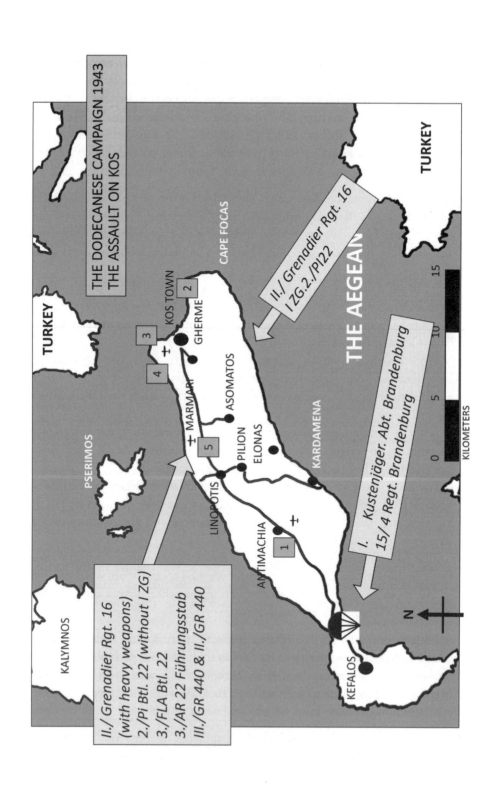

THE DODECANESE CAMPAIGN 1943
THE ASSAULT ON KOS

TURKEY

TURKEY

THE AEGEAN

KALYMNOS

PSERIMOS

CAPE FOCAS

KOS TOWN

GHERME

MARMARI

ASOMATOS

PILION

ELONAS

LINOPOTIS

ANTIMACHIA

KARDAMENA

KEFALOS

II./ Grenadier Rgt. 16
I ZG.2./PI22

I. Kustenjäger. Abt. Brandenburg
15/ 4 Regt. Brandenburg

II./ Grenadier Rgt. 16
(with heavy weapons)
2./Pi Btl. 22 (without I ZG)
3./FLA Btl. 22
3./AR 22 Führungsstab
III./GR 440 & II./GR 440

N

KILOMETERS

0   5   10   15

controlled Greek vessel with a German armed guard on board, flying the red and white German Sea Transport pennant.'[11]

Sutherland sent Milner-Barry back to delay the German advance as much as he could, while a local Shell-Mex representative helped organize the evacuation. Milner-Barry managed to collect the stragglers, some British and around fifty or so Italians. LSF Lieutenant McLeod used L.S2 to ferry himself, Kasulis and twelve men, including three signallers, to search for any more stragglers. Some tried building rafts, but these sank and they had to swim back to Kos. After three days, they were taken across to Turkey by caïque. Milner-Barry went back again, on the night of 8/9 October and found another eighteen soldiers. Not content with that, he went looking for more and was able to find Lieutenant Colonel Browne and forty officers and sappers. He took them off on the night of 31 October. In the end, he managed to evacuate a total of 'sixteen British officers and seventy-four NCOs and men, together with a very large number of Italians and a few brave Greeks'.[12] Not surprisingly, he was soon hospitalized suffering from sheer exhaustion.

Altogether, a total of 1,388 British and 3,145 Italians became PoWs. For many of the Italians the penalty was as they had feared. The Italian Commander, Colonel Felice Leggio, and many of his officers, following Hitler's orders, were summarily executed.

The hesitation shown by some Italian commanders was wholly justified by the manner in which Italian prisoners were treated by the Germans. One of the worst incidents must have been the mass execution of men from the 33rd Mountain Infantry *Aqui* division, which had surrendered on Cephalonia during the German operations to take control during Operation Axis (*Fall Achse*). The commanding General, Gandin, and around 400 officers and 4,500 men were executed. During the Leros operations, some eighty-nine officers met a similar fate.[13] A week after the British withdrawal, Lassen would go back to snatch some prisoners. Just because they'd taken the island didn't mean, in his eyes, that the Germans should feel safe. The Germans losses had been minimal – just fifteen killed and seventy wounded.[14]

On 16 September, British forces arrived on Samos. A local government was set up under the island's Bishop Ireneos, 'the most authoritative and highly respected personality on the island'. In the mountains, the *Andartes* guerrillas had established a reasonable control and on 30 October the island was reinforced by the Greek Sacred Squadron.[15]

Like the other islands, Samos was now pounded by bombers. Some 170 Germans who'd been tricked into surrender on Leros arrived by transport at Tighani and were being taken across the island on their way to a prison at

Vathy when the news of their arrival leaked. The whole route was lined with Greeks jeering them.

The news of what had happened to the *Aqui* division on Cephalonia travelled. No Italian wanted to take a chance. Despite the panic, the SBS ferried as many people off the island as possible, across to the mainland. Lassen and Nicholson were the last off. With Lassen came a new friend for Pipo, another mongrel, this one befriended on Leros. The 2,500-strong Italian garrison couldn't hold off the inevitable; it surrendered on 22 November.

Simi

On 17 September, as evening light was fading, Jock Lapraik brought the first SBS troops to Simi in two caïques. They had little idea of what to expect when they got there but were alarmed when, after shutting their engines off and waiting, silently drifting on the moonlit waters, the stillness was broken by a bell starting to toll, followed by another and then a whole symphony of bells. They weren't sure if it was a welcome or a warning.

The uncertainty made them edgy, so Lassen, who had only been able to leave Haifa on 12 September with Lapraik, and Douggie Pomford were sent ashore in a Folboat to find out details of the garrison, its size and whether it was German or Italian.[16] They rowed ashore. 'Three big strong Irishmen … Sergeant Sean O'Reilly, Patsy Henderson and Corporal D'Arcy' were aboard the same caïque.[17] Lassen had been in a British Military hospital in Nazareth recovering from yellow fever brought on by severe liver problems and was not well. Nevertheless, he couldn't bear the idea of missing out on the action. He'd had other things on his mind. He'd been thinking of his homeland a lot since he heard the news of the scuttling of the Danish Navy.[18] Like his brother, Frants, he wanted to go back and join the resistance to fight the Germans. In hospital, he had been 'a bundle of nerves'; 'everything which he was not allowed to do, he wanted to do, and his nurses had to keep on their toes if they were to look after him.'[19]

Lassen and Pomford were jubilantly greeted by the locals. The news flashed around the island, and soon word reached the Italian commander. Despite his 150-strong garrison he decided not to risk a confrontation, although not many of the SBS trusted him. Lassen also wanted to know if the harbour was going to be deep enough for the caïques to enter. He put the question to some of the Greeks on the quayside but became impatient. Startling the Greeks, he jumped in with full kit and then came back up to the surface confirming that the depth was all right; Lapraik's caïques could proceed.

Lapraik's forty men were divided into four patrols. Lassen took one and went up to an old school building on the high ground above the harbour entrance. Still deeply suspicious of the Italians, Lassen managed to get a radio installed without their knowledge at the monastery of St Michaels. It overlooked the bay at Panormiti on the other side of the island. The task was made easier by the abbot: Chrysanthos intensely disliked the Italians.[20] Lassen, however, was not in good shape. He'd badly burnt his legs when throwing petrol into a latrine to sterilize it. Porter Jarrell wanted to send him back to Athlit, but the stubborn Dane refused.

Lapraik wanted to use Simi as a base for his six caïques. A close bond had formed between the Greek fishermen manning the boats and the SBS. Two fishermen, the brothers Marco and Anastazia Costandi, had become very close to Lassen. Marco's pride would not let him accept the gold sovereign with which Andy had offered to pay them. After the war, Suzanne Lassen met with Marco; he still carried a letter signed by her son, addressed to Commander Frank Ramseyer. It was a letter of recommendation of 'Captain Marco of the Simi caïque *Anullak*' signed 'Captain A. Lassen'. It was a treasured possession.

Lapraik now received some early, but very welcome, reinforcements from the RAF: twenty officers and ORs from 74 Squadron, en route to Kos. He made it clear that while the mission was a limited one, they should be under no illusions about what to expect:

> So far, however, you have worked hard and well without moaning so keep it up but remember, be quick on the job and keep on your toes because if you don't you've —— had it, believe me.

Because of its proximity, Lapraik wanted to use Simi as an island base for reconnaissance on Rhodes. Using the caïques as productively as he could, he wasted no time. They used Marco's to explore some of the outlying islands in 'broad daylight' looking for Germans. Though they did not find any, Lassen brought back a 20mm Breda from Alimnia which he set up outside the Simi school. The view from the Italian gun's new emplacement was impressive; it completely dominated the harbour, and its missing footplate was quickly fixed by the local blacksmith.

Douggie Pomford likened their island-hopping expedition to sight-seeing 'Breakfast on Piscopi, dinner at Alimnia, tea at Calchi with Major Lassen running the whole show all the time.'[21]

Lassen was assigned the fortification of Calchi, lying adjacent to Rhodes. 'About a week after [the] expedition' rumours came back that the Germans had landed there. Lassen, with Porter Jarrell, the American medical orderly, went to have a look. He needed Jarrell's help: the backs of his burnt legs were in shocking condition, and Porter bandaged them up. The Germans did not know that the SBS were operating out of Simi but they did know that there were enemy agents on the island as they had picked up radio transmissions. These were coming from the monastery at Panormiti, and the Germans were desperate to find their source.

After landing provisions for the locals, Lassen now wanted to frighten the twelve Italian Carabinieri enough that they would fight the Germans instead. He used the next couple of days to reinforce the island's defences and give these policemen some additional training.

On 21 September, 'Stud' Stellin was clandestinely landed on Rhodes, getting ashore through a small gap in the Villanova minefield (opposite where today's airport is located). While his first trip was only five days, the second lasted three weeks. Elsewhere, one of the GSS officers, 2nd Lieutenant George Pavlides, as well as some of the Rhodesian LRDG recce'd Kalymnos.

Eastwood escaped after being captured, and Stellin very nearly met with the same fate. He'd been trapped and only got out by being hidden under straw on a cart being used to carry a happy couple to their wedding. Stellin never forgot the courage of the local priest, Papa Lucas, who arranged his escape, and went back after the war to visit him.

On 2 October, after Kos had fallen, Lapraik and Lassen returned to Simi. They already knew the 'lay of the land', but Lapraik didn't take kindly to the lack of discipline in some of the troops whom he would be leading, particularly the RAF:

> For the benefit of the RAF. As you have recently arrived in this area you are naturally unaware of the military situation in general, and in the island in particular, and consequently your actions seem peculiar under the circumstances. Our situation may be compared with that of Singapore when the Japs were only a short distance away and advancing rapidly, i.e. owing to our great strategic importance there is no doubt whatsoever that we shall be attacked. It is merely a question of whether it is tomorrow, or the next day or the one after. Let there be no doubt about it, they will come; therefore, we must be prepared. Consequently, it is essential that everyone be absolutely on their toes 24 hours a day. When the guard is called out, it will be out in seconds not minutes as was the case last night. When ordered to stand to, they will be downstairs and in the bushes like bats out of hell. Everyone must be absolutely on the job all the time no matter what task he is given. We are all doing strange jobs at the moment. We weren't trained as island defenders any more than you were but we have to carry out the task all

the same. When you realize that the next island to this, Kos, has been attacked, and almost wound up by the Germans we can understand the gravity of our position so for ––'s sake let's get our fingers out and get weaving and we'll show these ––s what we are capable of.[22]

Although a lawyer by training, Jock Lapraik's language was anything but judicial.

At dawn on 7 October, the Germans attempted to bring in their troops on board three caïques. The RAF had been on guard duty and had failed to sound the alert, so approximately 120 Germans were able to make an unimpeded landing in Pedi Bay. The Germans made quick inroads in the confusion and occupied a mountain ridge. Lassen's first priority was to find out what was going on. He separated his men into groups of three and he and O'Reilly went off to recce. They did not know what danger was awaiting them when they ventured into Simi town.

Three Stukas supported the German troops. A Breda was manned by an RAF Flight Sergeant, an armourer called Charlie Schofield. His shooting attracted the interest of a couple of the Stukas and he would win an MM for his determination to stay at his post to fight them off. Adding to his difficulties, there were no sights on the Breda and the flash eliminator had burnt off. His citation spoke of his actions and a little about the man:

> FS Schofield is short-sighted and his spectacles were broken by the vibration of the gun. He was also wounded in the arm but continued at his post until the wound turned septic two days later. He was then put into hospital.[23]

One of the patrols was led by Lieutenant Charles Bimrose. It was hit by machine gun fire from the ridgeline overlooking Simi town and then caught in an ambush. A 'potato masher' (stick grenade) wounded one of his men, a Seaforth Highlander, William Morrison, but Bimrose was lucky to escape with only slight injuries to his arm and made an immediate charge at the enemy positions, killing two and wounding a third. He briefed Lassen on what he'd found.

Determined Bren gun fire from Lassen and Laprik's men on School Hill saw the Germans off by 0800. Even though they held Simi town's northern areas, they had not taken the time to study the town's 'labyrinthine' layout.[24] Lassen had and knew it like the back of his hand. He simply outsmarted them:

> Lassen held his men back so as to draw the Germans in, and then the trap was sprung. Time after time as they tried to storm the ancient fortress of the Kastro, the German troops were ambushed, Lassen himself stalking and killing three at very close quarters.[25]

O'Reilly was in awe of Lassen's innate skill. At one point he said that Andy had 'smelled' Germans on the other side of a wall, while he had 'no idea there were Germans in the neighbourhood.'[26] The Germans often gave themselves away, their heavy hob-nailed boots loudly clattering and scraping over the stone steps, while the SBS were able to move silently in their rubber-soled boots.

As successful as Lassen was in the narrow streets, the Germans, reinforced by around another 100 soldiers coming across from Rhodes, landed on other beaches to the north. Lapraik sent Lassen and his 'Irish patrol' (Sean O'Reilly, Sid Greaves, Dick 'Jeff' Holmes, Douggie Pomford, Les Stephenson, E. R. 'Hank' Hancock, 'Gippo' Conby, Patsy Henderson, Doug Wright and 'Joe' Porter Jarrell)[27] forward to 'bolster' the small Italian garrison of around 140 men. Jarrell and Hancock were the only ones who weren't either Irish Guards or Southern Irishmen.

Heading south to make higher ground, they succeeded by 0600 in starting to push the Germans back. A German sergeant and two privates were quickly captured, while three others were killed. Lassen stood behind the Italians, his gun aimed at their backs, not allowing any further retreat. That, and their immediate success, renewed their spirit to fight.

By 1300 the Italians were starting to make progress moving up from the southern, lower slopes of the town, and by 1500 the Germans were retreating back to their ships. The German commander had 'withdrawn his men to the spot where they had first landed', and evacuation – first the wounded – started.[28] All the way back through Pedi Bay they were mercilessly picked off by witheringly accurate Bren gun fire. At 1600, a large landing craft full of reinforcements was seen just below the mountainous position where Lassen had placed the 20mm Breda. While Doug Wright, renowned for his ability with a Bren, opened up, the firepower from Lassen's 20mm was decisive. Eventually, one of its shells ripped through the deck of the German craft. That was the final straw, and the Germans retreated. At the same time, British caïques took to the waters using their own weaponry with savage results. The German vessels were raked with fire, Lapraik's men 'targeting the entire length of Pedi Bay' with heavy fire from Bren guns sited under the Kastro.[29]

One SBS patrol 'counted 30 Germans wounded and 16 killed.'[30] Six others were captured, and many of those who escaped wouldn't survive: up in the hills; the Greeks decapitated them if they were caught.[31] The SBS had suffered one KIA and two wounded, the Italians, ten wounded. Corradini, Simi's Italian commander, assembled his men. He was so pleased that, in front of them, he theatrically grabbed a handful of air-dropped propaganda leaflets and, with a satisfied look, went off to the WC.

Reports suggested that Kleemann was 'furious'. The next day, 8 October, he ordered a sustained air attack. Ju.87s screamed down out of the skies to avenge the ignominy of the previous day's hasty retreat. The bombing was 'largely indiscriminate and designed to terrorize the island's population'.[32]Around 0600, the town's hospital was hit. Inside, No.74 Squadron's doctor, Hank Ferris, had been caring for the many wounded Greeks and was himself injured. Two planes were shot down, but one SBS man, Lance Corporal Robert McKendrick, and twenty civilians were killed.

At midday, Lapraik's HQ was also hit. Lapraik escaped unscathed, but two of his men, Tommy 'Bish' Bishop and Sid Greaves, were trapped beneath rubble. The only way Greaves could be reached was if Bishop agreed to have his own foot amputated. He did so willingly. While still under attack, Jarrell Porter, aided by Harris and working by candlelight under the rubble, amputated one man's leg to release the other. Jarrell was awarded the George Medal, the citation reading that he 'worked for 27 hours, without rest to the point almost of collapse' exposing himself to extreme personal risk.[33] It was fruitless. Jarrell managed to free Bishop, but he died soon after he emerged; when Greaves was pulled out, his body, too, was lifeless. For Jarrell it must have been sickening. Harris, who'd been unable to assist in the operation because of his broken wrist, praised Jarrell: 'A fantastic bloke, with his Red Cross on one shoulder and a machine gun on the other … They hadn't a hope in hell but we thought that we had to try something.'[34]

It's not surprising that Jellicoe considered Jarrell 'one of the most admired figures in the SBS'. When Jarrell died in 2001, Jellicoe said he felt he had lost a 'dear friend'.[35]

The headquarters would be hit again. On 8 October, at midday, a Stuka launched a second, successful attack. Three of the defenders – an SBS trooper, LAC Guy and the Detachment cook – were killed while Ferris worked tirelessly for more than thirty hours, trying to extract two SBS men who were buried in the rubble. He succeeded, but they both later died. Ferris was decorated for his gallantry.

The SBS was starting to lose more men. But it was also very clear that the enemy was paying a high price.

The local population's hatred of Fascism didn't limit itself to the Germans. They'd been under Italian occupation for years. 'The Fascists on Simi had been bastards, dyed-in-the-wool nationalists who beat up Greeks for not saluting the Italian flag.'[36] It was very difficult for Allied officers who hadn't been through the experience to understand the intensity of the hatred. Lapraik had to make it clear that the Germans were the first priority. Other scores would have to wait before being settled. Jarrell was horrified by the poverty of the Greeks. The Italians were held responsible for their plight, and even though they had decided early that they would not resist the English, they were not seen as trustworthy, at least not on Simi: 'Between the Greeks and Italians strong friction existed; on the surface, relations appeared reasonable enough, but behind the back of the English the Italians threatened the population with all manner of reprisals if the English were to leave the island again.'[37]

The hatred that occupation brought with it has never really died. One of Lassen's Greek officers was Jason Mavrikis, then a young Lieutenant from the Sacred Squadron. He and his wife Virginia became close friends with Jellicoe after the war. Once in Crete, after visiting the *Fallschirmjäger* cemetery at Maleme with my father, I talked to him about reconciliation. I can still see the quick flash of anger in his eyes. He would have none of it. What had happened on these islands was too terrible for him ever to forgive.

Lapraik had even thought of keeping a force on Calchi, the nearest island to Rhodes' western coastline. He had recently reinforced it, but because it was so rocky, they hadn't been able to dig in. His refusal to give up the fight earned him yet another bar to his MC, his third – and a hospital bed. On 10 October, Lapraik was ordered off Simi. The order was immediately countermanded, but two days later, 12 October, it was back in place. He would return to the small island later in November. Then he launched an aggressive attack on the garrison – 'a German major with 18 men and 2 Italian captains commanding 60 Fascist militia, as well as 10 other soldiers from the island's police force'.[38] Most of the garrison were killed or wounded, and the dockyard was destroyed by fire.

After they'd left, Lassen received information from the abbot that more Fascists had been sent to the island to reinforce it. The radio then went dead: Chrysanthos and his nephew had been killed by the Fascists. They'd long suspected him of being the source of the clandestine wireless transmissions. Jellicoe gave his permission for Lassen to go back and avenge the execution, and Lassen would return to Simi a week later; eight Fascist solders were captured and the W/T put out of action.

Chapter 9

Leros – The Ignominy of Defeat

Sutherland had no great affection for Leros, saying it resembled 'a large cowpat trodden on by two feet'.[1] However, over more than thirty years of occupation, the Italians had installed 'a series of formidable coastal batteries' defending the island, which boasted one of the few deep-water harbours in the area, Portolago (Lakki, as it's now known).[2] Lakki reeks of its past. The town was built almost entirely by the Italians in Bauhaus style.

This was a difficult time. Italian officers were never sure whom they could trust, even if on islands without a German garrison it was easier. Both Mascherpa and Campioni were later shot by firing squad in Parma on the order of the Fascist Republic of the North.

The new British commander, Brigadier Robert Tilney, boasted that the only Germans to set foot on Leros would be PoWs. He wanted to block landings on any beachhead developing; the result was he thinly distributed his forces among the potential landing areas. Leros was divided into three defensive zones – north, south and central – which his infantry units – Douglas Iggulden's 4th Royal East Kent (the Buffs), Maurice French's 2nd Royal Irish Fusiliers and the 1st King's Own Royal Regiment – would defend. Jellicoe's SBS and Redfern's LRDG would form fast-reaction mobile forces. The battalion of Italian *Regina* Division troops 'hardly featured in the battle' even if the anti-aircraft and shore batteries played a significant role. But with no air cover, his plans were probably doomed.[3]

On 26 September, the Germans commenced the air bombardment as part of the softening-up for *Unternehmen Taifun* (Operation TYPHOON), the air and sea assault on Leros. Ju.87s screamed down, dropping their bombs, after a two-hour flight from Megara and Argos. In the port, Ju.88s sank the British destroyer HMS *Intrepid* (commanded by the unforgettably named Commander Charles de Winton Kitcat) and the Greek destroyer *Vasilissa Olga*. *Intrepid* was hit twice and towed to shallow waters, where she capsized and sank only after repeated hits. Fifteen of her crew died. *Olga* went down with her commander, six officers, sixty-five crew members and eight civilians. The Allies had no planes with which to counter. This date, 26 September, remains a day of remembrance on Leros, the most important day of commemoration of the Dodecanese campaign.

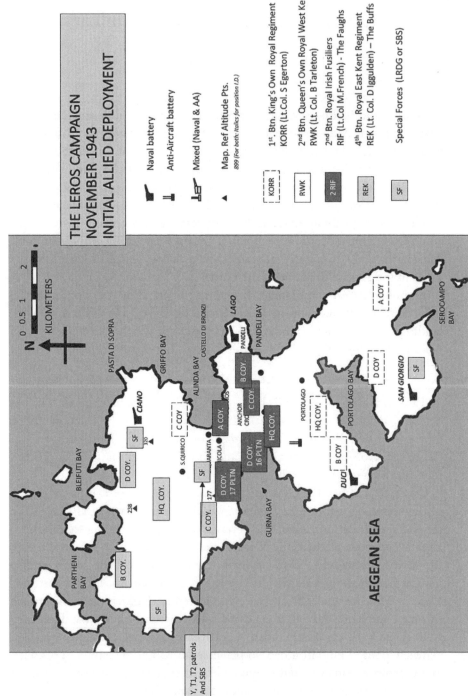

THE LEROS CAMPAIGN
NOVEMBER 1943
INITIAL ALLIED DEPLOYMENT

Naval battery

Anti-Aircraft battery

Mixed (Naval & AA)

Map. Ref Altitude Pts.
899 (For both: Italics for position I.D.)

KORR — 1st. Btn. King's Own Royal Regiment
KORR (Lt.Col. S Egerton)

RWK — 2nd Btn. Queen's Own Royal West Kent Regiment
RWK (Lt. Col. B Tarleton)

2 RIF — 2nd Btn. Royal Irish Fusiliers
RIF (Lt.Col M.French) - The Faughs

REK — 4th Btn. Royal East Kent Regiment
REK (Lt. Col. D Iggulden) – The Buffs

SF — Special Forces (LRDG or SBS)

N
0 0.5 1 2
KILOMETERS

AEGEAN SEA

PARTHENI BAY
BLEIFUTI BAY
PASTA DI SOPRA
GRIFFO BAY
ALINDA BAY
CASTELLO DI BRONZI
CIANO
238
320
S.QUIRICO
JARANTA
PICCOLA
LAGO
PANDELI
PANDELI BAY
ANCHOR CROC
PORTOLAGO
PORTOLAGO BAY
SAN GIORGIO
SEROCAMPO BAY
GURNA BAY
DUCI

B COY.
D COY.
HQ COY.
C COY. 177
D COY. 17 PLTN
C COY.
A COY.
D COY. 16 PLTN
HQ COY.
B COY.
C COY.
B COY.
HQ COY.
D COY
A COY
SF

Y, T1, T2 patrols
And SBS

While one contemporary account had it, that 'no Italian aircraft batteries opened up on them, no doubt fearing that they would become targets themselves', the facts don't support this. The toll from Italian AA of German aircraft was significant.[4]

It's clear that there was very little time left. From 30 September, Jellicoe started shuttling back and forth between Leros and Athlit, organizing and cajoling to get reinforcements. Supplies came in by any means possible. Seligman recalled that 'consignments of jeeps and Bofors guns, smothered in non-floating grease and lashed on top of the boat's casings with steel wire rope' came in aboard the submarine *Severn* in mid-October.[5] The jeeps would be worth their weight in gold.

Throughout October and into November, the terrifying and incessant aerial bombardment continued, taking a heavy toll on Allied shipping in and around Leros. While in Tobruk, Jellicoe might have joked about the Stukas, but it was different now. He admitted he was terrified. The change, he said, was partly due to tiredness, but more to the weight of responsibility he now bore.

Churchill fumed. Back in London, the daily litany of bad news from the Aegean dominated these dark days. General Sir Alan Brooke, never one of Churchill's greatest admirers because of his constant interference in the military's conduct of strategy, wrote:

I am slowly becoming convinced that, in his old age, Winston is becoming less and less well balanced! I can control him no more. He has worked himself into a frenzy of excitement about the Rhodes attack, has magnified its importance so that he can no longer see anything else and has set his heart on capturing this one island even at the expense of endangering his relations with the President and with the Americans, and also the whole future of the Italian campaign. He refuses to listen to any arguments or see any dangers![6]

The bombing was incessant but for many of the troops it wasn't anything new. Three of the four infantry battalions on Leros had been on Malta.

After more than a month, during which the island was supported with minimal or no Allied air cover against the roughly 1,000 German air sorties, the skies suddenly cleared. It was an eerie but welcome break, like the final hushed moments before the onset of a summer storm. Like on Kos, for an entire week, till 6 November, there was no bombing. The German focus was now on the logistics of the landings, getting the landing craft they needed.

Much-needed ammunition and supplies were dropped by parachute to Jellicoe's men. Sometimes the 'chutes would fail to fully deploy, the loads instead continuing to hurtle earthward and smashing. One reason was that the RAF was switching from nylon to cheaper calico 'chutes. Experienced soldiers could tell the difference because the new 'chutes would make an audible 'flapping' sound. It was pretty dangerous, and 'Nobby' Clarke very nearly received a direct hit from a full crate of ammunition.

Finally, on 11 November, Jellicoe came back with the news they'd all been waiting for; he'd been at a Brigade briefing and got back around 2030. In the small band were people whose names would come to mean so much over the next few days: Captains Blyth and Holt, Lieutenant Balsillie, SQMS Evans, Sergeant Workman, Corporals Dryden and 'Hank' Hancock. Four Greeks were also with them.

The same evening, Jellicoe took the time to jot a short note to Ronald Watler, one of the men who had served with him since North Africa and had also been on Kos: 'Many congratulations on extricating yourself for the second time'. He ended by adding that he hoped he would have 'a prosperous time' in Turkey or where he might find himself with Sutherland or Chevalier.[7] In the grim circumstances, it struck me as an odd thing to write.

By now, Jellicoe was doubtful that the island could be held; he sent David Sutherland off to contact Lieutenant Commander Croxton of the Royal Navy to work out evacuation plans: 'We know the Germans are going to attack Leros tomorrow. There is no point in both of us being here. I suggest you leave tonight for Turkey.'[8] Sutherland left with Stefan Kasulis, Harold Chevalier and seven ORs.[9]

The new LRDG commander, Jake Easonsmith, felt the same, ordering Lloyd Owen to return to Haifa on 5 November. Easonsmith was held in high regard by his 2i/c: 'He had a guile which was almost uncanny in his ability to foresee how the enemy would react.'[10]

He knew that disaster lay ahead … He [Lloyd Owen] was being ordered off Leros so that at least there would be someone to ensure the continuation of the LRDG.[11]

The preparations would prove invaluable, for both the SBS and the LRDG. Jellicoe and Blyth spent the night at the Brigade Reserve Company's HQ. They knew each other well; Blyth had formerly been the Adjutant of Stirling's SAS. The rest of the SBS took up positions in a nearby dried-out depression.

Leros – Day 1. Friday, 12 November

Early in the morning of 12 November, the invasion of Leros was launched.

Somewhere around 0300, the invasion craft were spotted by British MTBs as well as an Italian MAS, MS.555. But nothing was done with the intelligence. In the confusion, the ships were assumed to be British. Two hours later, around 0530, more reports came in; Lieutenant Commander Monkton. ML.456, 12 miles offshore, had first spotted German destroyers escorting LCIs at 0456. Monkton requested assistance, but none was forthcoming. It was 'an inexcusable failure'; the British could have leveraged their strength at sea even if they lacked air cover.[12] Without support, Monkton did what he could: he engaged the enemy. When his badly damaged launch limped back into Alinda Bay, six wounded – and one man who'd been killed – were off-loaded. He then went back out, only to be shelled by friendly shore batteries south of Leros, in the small channel between Telendos and Kalymnos,

German vessels of Oberleutnant z.S. Weissenborn's western assault group ran into the minesweeper, BYMS.72. The British ship was quickly captured after she failed to identify the other craft as German and, what's more, was taken in by their English-language signal: 'Hallo! What ship?' She had replied that 'she was a British minesweeper and was looking for a quiet place away from the danger of Stuka attacks on Leros.'[13] She dutifully followed Weissenborn straight into a trap. Years after the war, Adrian Seligman met Kapitän Loetzmann, who'd been the German commander. He laughed when he realized that Seligman had seen the mysterious ship turn away after a signal had been sent from Navy House: 'That was when my four years at an English public school came in handy. I was able to read your signal.'

Loetzmann had signalled BYMS.72: 'Take no notice of that fool flashing [actually that was Seligman] ... it's an Italian trap ... follow me.'[14] It was audacious and it worked. Overhead, incredibly, a substantial British bomber force (three Hudsons, seven Baltimores and four Wellingtons) had not even managed to land a single hit, although 'this disruption meant the enemy landing was delayed till 6 a.m.'[15]

David Sutherland was at sea. He'd left at midnight and headed for Gümüslük, a small harbour on the Turkish mainland. He, along with Kasulis and Chevalier, was just passing Kalymnos when the enemy was spotted.

Generalleutnant Friedrich-Wilhem Müller had divided his landing task forces. Three *Kampfgruppen,* independent task forces. Three would attack from the eastern side of Leros: *Kampfgruppen* von Schädlich, von Saldern and Dörr; one from the west, *Kampfgruppe* Aschoff. They would be supported by airborne elements, *Kampfgruppe* Kühne, and by the *Kriegsmarine* and *Pionierlandungskompanie.*The latter consisted of the *III Infanterie Regiment 440, II Infanterie Regiment 16, II Infanterie Regiment 65* of the 22nd Infantry Division, the *Fallschirmjäger* battalion and the 1 *Küstenjägerabteilung* of the Brandenburg Division. Air support would be provided by Ju.87 Stukas from *I Gruppe, Stukageschwader 3* based in Megara and the *II Gruppe, Stukageschwader 3* based in Argos and Rhodes. *Kampfgruppe 51* with Ju.88s would be available for air bombardment.

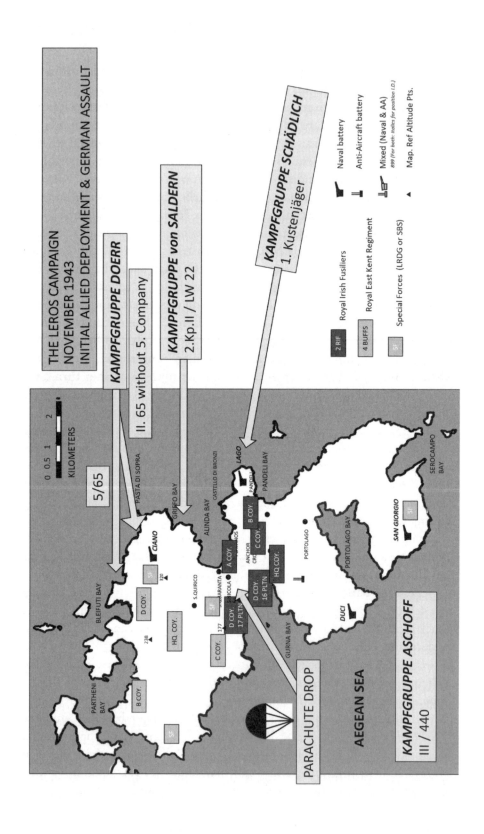

THE LEROS CAMPAIGN
NOVEMBER 1943
INITIAL ALLIED DEPLOYMENT & GERMAN ASSAULT

KAMPFGRUPPE DOERR
II. 65 without 5. Company

KAMPFGRUPPE von SALDERN
2.Kp.II / LW 22

KAMPFGRUPPE SCHÄDLICH
1. Kustenjäger

Naval battery
Anti-Aircraft battery
Mixed (Naval & AA)
899 *(For both: Italics for position I.D.)*
Map. Ref Altitude Pts.

Royal Irish Fusiliers
2 RIF

Royal East Kent Regiment
4 BUFFS

Special Forces (LRDG or SBS)
SF

5/65

KILOMETERS
0 0.5 1 2

PARTHENI BAY
BLEIFUTI BAY
PASTA DI SOPRA
GRIFFO BAY
ALINDA BAY
CASTELLO DI BRONZI
LAGO
PANDELI
PANDELI BAY
CIANO
320
238
S.QUIRICO
CARANTA
NICOLA
A. COY.
LINOS
ANCHOR
CK
B. COY.
C. COY.
D. COY.
16 PLTN
HQ. COY.
D. COY.
HQ. COY.
C. COY.
177
D. COY.
17 PLTN
GURNA BAY
DUCI
PORTOLAGO
PORTOLAGO BAY
SAN GIORGIO
SF
SEROCAMPO BAY

B. COY.
SF
SF
SF

AEGEAN SEA

PARACHUTE DROP

KAMPFGRUPPE ASCHOFF
III / 440

At around 0600, the landings started. On the east side, the attacks focussed on three landings between Palma and Grifo Bays in the north and to the south a thrust at the base of Appetici, around the corner from Pandelli Bay. The defenders pushed the northernmost attack, at Blefuti Bay, back, but to the south the defence was only partly successful as a company-sized force managed to get ashore, while at Grifo and Appetici successful landings were made by sizeable numbers of assault troops.

From their positions on the western side of the island, the SBS could hear the firing coming from Blefuti and Mt. Clidi. But nothing could be seen.

Around 500 troops landed in the north, the northernmost landing being Dörr's, at Pasta di Sopra and Palma Bay.

A landing even further north, at Blefuti Bay, was attempted but turned back. One ferry lighter and two assault craft were sunk before they retreated, having been hit by 25–pounder fire from Blacutera. At Pasta di Sopra, the Germans landed men from the *II. Gren-Regt.65* less two platoons from the *5.Kompagnie* and from the *II.Lw.Jäger-Rgt.22*, the *2.Pi.Btl.22* (minus one platoon). Men from the *6.Kompagnie, II. Gren-Regt.65* suffered heavy losses when an LC blew up. Two platoons from *II. Gren-Regt.65* were dropped at Palma Bay but suffered heavy casualties (both wireless operators were lost) after being targeted by LRDG Captain Olivey's Bren guns.

In the middle were von Saldern's assault groups concentrated on two bays – Alinda and Grifo, right under the CIANO batteries on Mount Clidi. Schädlich's 120-man Special Forces group attacked at the furthest point south and landed under the forbidding, towering cliffs of Mt. Appetici, where four coastal guns were located. On the western coast, the Germans turned away and went back to Kalymnos after three attempts, when fire from the Italian DUCCI and SAN GIORGIO batteries ranged the convoy of three *Marinefährprähme* (naval ferry lighters) on their way to Gurna Bay.

The convoy was being escorted by two captured Italian boats and was fired upon by the two batteries situated, respectively, on Mt. Cazzuni and Mt. Scumbarda. The first attempt was at 0645, and a second was made three hours later in which 'at least eight men' were killed and another forty-nine wounded.[16]

As news of the northern landings came in, all Tilney asked was: 'Is anybody doing anything about it?'[17] It didn't bode well.

Despite all the warnings, not everyone seemed that prepared. For some, the news came with almost poetic delivery. Marsland Gander, the *Daily Telegraph* journalist on Leros, was sleeping when he finally heard about the landing: a cockney orderly, 'who spoke in a quiet, unhurried voice, half apologetic at disturbing our rest, and betraying not the slightest sign by his demeanour that anything unusual was afoot' remarked, "The German invasion fleet has been sighted, sir" … It was so like a butler's entrance that I had expected him to add, "Shall I show them up, sir?"[18]

The German aim was to cut the island in two, and to do that they needed to dominate the high ground: Mt. Clidi (320m), Mt. Rachi (105m) and Appetici (181m). That would help isolate the British HQ at Meraviglia (204m), where Tilney was based. Meraviglia is where Maurice French had wanted to concentrate, not, as Tilney was doing, to disperse men everywhere.

The Germans would use a parachute drop in the centre of the island, then clustered on the slopes of Mt. Rachi between the two prominent bays of Gurna and Alinda to dominate the area, the bridgehead from which Müller would divide the defending troops. That very night, Jellicoe had moved the SBS into positions where they might best help fight off the anticipated drop, right behind a Buffs' position, overlooking the eastern end of Gurna Bay.

Initially, German preparations for the parachute drop didn't go well. After taking off from the Tatai airfield near Athens, the paratroops were less than three minutes from the DZ when they received a recall signal. All forty aircraft carrying the 1st Battalion of the 2nd Parachute Regiment (2FJR) had to pull up and turn around. Two Arado seaplanes flew across the formations, firing red flares, 'a pre-arranged signal to abort the mission'.[19] Müller had heard about the failure of Aschoff's western attack and wanted to give Kühne's men a more secure drop zone. He decided to wait until von Saldern's progress on the east of the island was more firmly established.

From his OP on Point 320, using some Italian, tripod-mounted glasses, Captain John Olivey had a panoramic view of the action all around him. The fifteen men of X.2 were, for the most part, Rhodesians from S patrol. He could look right down into the picturesque Bay of Gurna to his south-west, where the small chapel of San Isidro sits, reachable at low tide by a walkway that runs out across the water; or, directly to his south, to Alinda. The four 6-inch batteries he and the Buffs were protecting had been carefully sited, but the Italians didn't think any troops could threaten the CIANO battery from below the steep slopes but two guns had been hit by Stukas. However, the remaining guns could not be brought to bear on what would be a key landing beach for the Germans.

It was only about 2,000m from where Olivey was dug in to Jellicoe's SBS. The small bays to Olivey's north-east, where Dörr's group would land, would prove theAchilles heel of the northern defence.

In the early hours, 22-year-old LRDG signalman Gordon Broderick reported back to Olivey that 'a fleet of barges and other craft could be seen heading into a dead field of view beyond Mount Vedetta … The enemy's objectives were obvious, the cove below us and the dead ground behind the hill to our N.E.'[20]

An LC was hit just before it rounded the headland, blowing apart in a 'ball of flame'. Others quickly followed, however, and a beachhead was established on the north-eastern corner of the island. Once on the difficult rocky shoreline, the troops set to work, quickly building up their tenuous hold by bringing up mortars to clear the way forward and upward.[21] Olivey asked the Italian gunnery commander to take out some of the 88mm mortars that the Germans had brought ashore, but the latter insisted that he 'should not protect himself and proceeded to fire at a barge slipping through towards Partheni Bay.'[22]

Around 0900, troops arrived to reinforce Olivey and the small Italian garrison, and very quickly CIANO itself came under mortar fire. Olivey had been in the thick of it, pleading with the men falling back to hold firm and dig in alongside his own LRDG troops. To his north, another landing at Palma Bay, just below Blefuti, was pushed back.

The assault by Schädlich's *Brandenburger Küstenjäger* on Mt. Appetici was one side of a two-pronged threat. Appetici and Castle Hill were threatened from both sides – from the coastline directly below the steep slopes, but also from the south, from Pandeli Bay. Below Appetici, the crack German *Küstenjäger* jumped from their boats 'out of sight and virtually unopposed by the Italians above', but they lost their 'entire stock of spare ammunition'.[23] Suffering engine trouble, the I-Boot had fallen behind and had only just managed to land its troops before being hit.

The Germans were held off by A Coy. RIF even if they weren't able to push the attackers back off the steep shoreline. By 0930 the *Küstenjäger* had managed to capture two of the four LAGO batteries, where they only had to contend with small-arms fire. A platoon was sent from Pandeli Castle to help the Italians. The fighting was fierce, and the battery commander, Sottotenente Corrado Spagnolo, was badly wounded and died later that day, although the two higher guns, under the command of Capitano Ernesto Nasti, continued to fire. The *Küstenjäger* 'had achieved their immediate aim of silencing the battery before the arrival of the second seaborne wave into Ormos Ag. Marinas with the heavy equipment.'[24]

Some Italian troops fled down towards Platanos and the RIF lines. There, Ted Johnson, a 21-year old Lieutenant with no battle experience, was ordered up to Appetici by his company commander, Major Ben Barrington (who was sitting in relative safety back at the Meraviglia HQ).

Johnson's men fought their way to the top, attacking uphill on the steep slopes and continually being strafed and bombed by Stukas. When they finally got there around 1000, the remaining two LAGO battery guns had already been overrun. Barrington ordered him to re-capture them. The first he took without too much trouble, but as Johnson was standing beside his section commander, Sergeant John Caldwell, the latter was 'shot cleanly through the forehead.'[25] For a young officer with no combat experience, it must have been harrowing. Then strangely, when they got to the second position, neither German nor Italian troops could be seen. After the battery was secured, his men dug in.

That evening, however, he was ordered to withdraw to the Fortress HQ at Meraviglia at 1830. Understandably, Johnson was furious. Tilney, it seems, felt that the attacks at Clidi and Appetici had been contained and now wanted to reinforce Meraviglia. This was just one of many instances when the Brigadier countermanded junior officers who were probably better informed merely by being on the scene.

The Italians were also angry: they'd been left alone without support, and it was only after they complained that Tilney organized a night counter-attack under the command of Lieutenant Colonel Maurice French of the Faughs, with four companies, two each from the RIF and the KORR. The attack, planned for 2300, 'never took place due to communication breakdown.'[26] Other demands seemed to be more pressing. From the Bay, gunnery support came from the assortment of British and Greek destroyers, but one of their number, HMS *Dulverton* on her way to join the fight, was heavily damaged by a German radio-controlled Hs 293 glider bomb in the early hours of 13 November.

In the early afternoon, probably shortly after 1430, Ju.52s started coming in from the west over the sea. From his positions, Olivey saw them approach Gurna Bay and thought it was a 'low dark cloud close to the sea'.[27] Then it clicked; the 'dark cloud' was made up of Ju.52s flying 'in close formation' close behind waves of 'Jabos' (*Jagdbomber*) – Ju.87s, Ju.88s and Arado AR.196 seaplanes – whose attacks were designed to get the British to concentrate on getting into slit trenches rather than meeting the incoming threat.

'A warning had already been sent the previous day (10 November) that German air troops were assembling in Athens.'[28] While it did not take the SBS or the LRDG by surprise, it's clear that it was a surprise for many. As early as 18 September, *The Times* anticipated the German use of paratroops: 'Presumably the Germans will try to oust the allies by landing parachutists but it is hoped … that the allied forces will be sufficient to thwart the German efforts.'

The pilots were, Olivey later recalled with admiration, flying at 300ft. Before dropping their human cargoes, the fragile-looking corrugated-skinned transports would climb between 100ft and 150ft and re-arrange themselves into a line-astern formation. The low flight path was designed to give a jumper the best chance of survival: just enough time – 'a matter of around 5 seconds' – for the 'chute to open and the minimum time to become a target as he floated down in the agonizingly frozen moments before hitting the ground.[29]

From the thirty-five or so troop carriers amongst the fifty-odd planes, out tumbled Hauptmann Martin Kühne's 1st Battalion, 2nd Parachute Regiment *Fallschirmjäger*, twelve or so in each plane's 'stick'. Kühne was a seasoned officer and had taken part in the assault on the Netherlands in 1940 and Crete the following year.

When the DZ was reached, a klaxon sounded inside each plane for the troops to ready themselves. As they jumped out, they 'automatically assumed an X position' as they hit the slipstream.[30] This 'flat, spread-eagle dive' was known as 'the Crucifix'.[31]

They started landing close to Allied troop positions. The various British units – regulars and Special Forces – spread out, encircling what became the drop zone. Clockwise from the north lay: Jellicoe's SBS, B Company of the Buffs on the lower slopes of Quirico; the LRDG and C Coy. KORR at the CIANO battery, east of Platanos; A Coy. RIF (Faughs), D Coy. RIF (Faughs) clustered around the end of Gurna Bay (17 Pltn. around Germano and 16 to their south) supported by B Coy; RWK at San Giovanni. When the parachutists landed they were 'some 500 to 700 yards away on the slopes on the other side of the road'.[32] Almost immediately, an SBS trooper was hit and a Greek officer was shot in the leg.

It was a terrifying experience for the jumpers, known as *Springer*. As each parachutist hurtled towards the earth, dangling at the end of his harness, he must have felt totally exposed and at the mercy of the winds, the noise of his chute just like 'fluttering birds'.[33] Even if they were able to fire as they came down, it was difficult to guide the descent. The experience of Obergefreiter Walter Keller, a machine gunner in the *III. Kompagnie*, was typical:

> I was third out of the plane ... I suddenly felt something warm running down my right upper thigh ... my water bottle had been pierced by a 2cm Flak shot. A second shot caused it to come loose from my haversack ... I came down on the edge of a roof of a barracks ... I fell backwards on the ground, my machine gun still lying on the roof ... I pulled the rope and brought it down on its flash suppressor and crushed it. The feed tray cover had also shifted: in short, it was no longer working ... I encountered 10 Tommies who were just as bewildered as I was.[34]

Olivey ordered his men to concentrate their fire just below the aircraft, hoping that the young German soldiers would find themselves jumping into a wave of lead:

> As the first man jumped, everything on the island seemed to open up at once. Bullets flew overhead from our troops below. Everyone seemed to be firing. I am not sure that officers did not fire their revolvers. I had a Bren which got rid of three mags in no time.[35]

The Bren gun could take larger, 100-round magazines but it was very prone to jamming. The troops tended to use 'the more reliable thirty-round ones'. Even so, one KORR Bren gunner, Lemuel Bevan, said that 'in order to ensure that the magazine didn't jam, he put in only twenty-eight slugs.'[36] Bevan had come under Olivey's LRDG as part of the defence for the guns on Clidi when his own men had been badly cut down.

Its lumberingly slow speed made the Junkers an easy target. However, the defenders did not have a commonly accepted idea of where to concentrate their fire: on the ground or in the air, below the aircraft, at the falling parachutist or as he landed, or, as many of the SBS did, as they gathered around the weapons' containers. There was criticism of the 'inexperienced defending troops' who should have 'fired less at the paratroops in the air and more immediately after they landed, when they were at their most vulnerable and easier targets.'[37]

It was a grim spectacle: the Germans were very vulnerable in the air and on the ground. For some, the worst came once they hit the ground. Revd. Reg Anwyl, the Catholic chaplain, couldn't shake the horrifying images for the rest of his life:

> I could see the frenzied attempts of some of them to cut themselves loose and the fantastic movements of dead men carried away across rough grounds; some were still hanging from trees while others were still being pulled over walls and rocks beyond the landing ground.[38]

Adrian Seligman, acting as interpreter for Sutherland's men, remembered what he saw and described it in horrifically visual language:

> I have a nightmarish picture in my mind of their wriggling, jerking bodies, like grubs on fish hooks; others hanging limp, parachutes here and there torn by bullets or failing to open, their occupants hitting the ground with sickening thumps, and bouncing, like birds at a pigeon shoot ... bodies lay around everywhere – on power lines, in trees and bushes on the ground.[39]

Like the other dead, the bodies of many German parachutists lay scattered on the battlefield for days. A young Greek remembered picking through the German bodies:

We went to Rachi searching for food and found a dead soldier hanging from a tree. He had batons and machine guns and magazines. He must have been there for three days as there was a terrible smell. We pulled off his boots, washed them in the sea, and wore them.[40]

The worst fate was suffered by those who landed in the sea. One Ju.52 went down with all its crew and a full complement of jumpers. It might have been the same one that Lemuel Bevan had seen; he said that he 'could have shot a paratrooper who was still standing in the doorway waiting to jump but … held his fire as there was no hope, the paratroops were too low to jump and were doomed to die as the plane veered off and crashed in to the bay.'[41]

Even if they were lucky enough to reach the ground untouched, the ensuing fight was brutal: combat was immediate, intense and at lethally close quarters. Each paratrooper was equipped with small side-arms, and they were often forced to rely on these if they couldn't get to one of the weapon containers.[42] German parachute tactics called for extremely fast engagement. Once on the ground, 'the paras did not stop to dig in; mobility and firepower were the keys to success.'[43]

The SBS were expecting the drop and had prepared for it, but were under no illusions about the dangers. Jellicoe had a more personal appreciation of the courage and effectiveness of the German *Fallschirmjäger*. Although he did not fight in Crete in 1941, he had lost three close German friends, brothers who had been part of that élite attacking force. He and I went together to find their graves at Malame, where two, Wolfgang and Leberecht von Blücher, lie side by side. Leutnant Wolfgang, Graf von Blücher had led a small platoon of parachutists in the May 1941 assault. His men were pinned down by Black Watch machine-gunners when a rider was spotted galloping towards them. It was Leberecht, Wolfgang's younger brother. He died bringing his brother ammunition. Wolfgang was killed the following morning. The body of the youngest of the three brothers, Hans-Joachim, was never found.

At Point 112, the thirty-odd SBS had overnighted alongside 'three officers and 24 men' of the LRDG, including the 37-year-old Major (acting) Alan Redfern. There, they set up three Luftwaffe MG.15s on the hill overlooking the *wadi* with which to deal with any parachutists. The depressions were being used by the attackers to re-group and return fire from 1,000rpm 7.9mm MGs. The SBS men would shoot at the falling paratroops while getting to their supply containers first, looting all the useful supplies they could, especially 'concentrated food, the safety-razors, the chocolate'.[44]

Redfern sent Y patrol (T.1.) to his south to Germano and patrol T1 to 'the northeast side of the mountain'. Redfern, who now lies in the Leros CWGC cemetery, would be killed on the first day, machine-gunned around 1500 during a 'hasty re-deployment' that 'went badly' after these first contacts between the LRDG, SBS and Kühne's men.[45]

Around 1100, Keith Balsillie rejoined Jellicoe's men, having miraculously just survived a close encounter with the enemy at sea. Somehow he'd found himself amongst a group of landing craft who 'failed to observe that a small caïque had swelled their numbers.'[46]

The SBS sent out a number of patrols: Jellicoe ordered Captain Holt to take his team to scout around the Navy House, located on the western shores of Alinda Bay; Lieutenant Balsillie went with SQMS Evans down to Gurna Bay, behind them to their west; while Blyth took six men to the 'next hill' to keep engaging the Germans.

As the SBS began pulling back the three MG.15s, they started taking casualties. Corporal Walshaw was sniped: the bullet went through his neck killing him outright. Later, when they'd regrouped, Captain Holt went missing. He'd last been seen down near the Navy House fully engaged in a firefight. One of the Sergeants, Robinson, was also wounded, shot through the right foot.

The defenders couldn't but have mixed feelings: genuine admiration for the bravery of these young attackers but also relief that they were decimating them:

> Of the 470 paratroopers who emplaned for Leros, 200 were killed on the drop, either shot as they floated to earth or drowned in the Aegean. Another 100 sustained injuries as they landed on the rocky slopes of Leros. [47]

The parachute drop had taken a heavy toll. Many officers had been killed right at the start – Oberleutnant Othmar Lichy, a signals officer and Leutnant Schukraft, as well as medical personnel like Unterarzt Felix Katersohn. They were also out of radio link as no sets had been dropped. But, as Jellicoe commented, those that were left were 'very high class parachutists, very well trained'.

To their north, on the slopes of Clidi, the fighting was gruesome, and despite reinforcements from the King's Own (KORR), whose second in command, Major Tilley, had been killed, British troops had been pushed back by 1700. LRDG Signalman Broderick recalled that the Germans were almost upon them when 'a British officer (probably Major Tilley, the 2i/c) ordered his men to fix bayonets but he was shot and the order was not carried out.' Even if they were pushed back, it seems that only around thirty yards were surrendered.[48] Every foot was contested: 'as it got dark we were engaged in hand to hand fighting.'[49]

KORR had suffered heavy casualties in the counter-attack: there were so few left that they came under the command of the Buffs and as the Germans' final advance closed in, the LRDG destroyed one of the battery's guns.

Despite the Germans' heavy losses in the jumps, they had succeeded in establishing themselves on Rachi ridge, right in the narrow strip between Gurna and Alinda Bays, cutting the island in two. By around 1730, Mount Clidi and its important CIANO batteries were also under German control, even if there were still KORR soldiers holding out. On the other hand, not only had 'almost a third of the total seaborne assault ... failed to land', the assault troops that should have landed on the west had been at sea since early morning in conditions that were steadily deteriorating.[50]

Leros – Day 2. Saturday, 13 November

Around 0300 one of the four-man SBS patrols led by Captain Blyth returned to the main SBS positions above Gurna Bay to report that no Germans had been seen right through to the Navy House on the shores of Alinda Bay. Mt. Rachi, on the other hand, was 'strongly held' by enemy airborne troops.[51] By daybreak, Appetici was also in German hands, while below its commanding heights, in Platanos, German snipers moved amongst the buildings, targeting officers, like the LRDG's Guy Prendergast: 'If you were sensible, you wore as few badges of rank, as few indications you were an officer.'[52]

In the night, the SBS re-located. Despite being so few, several, like Dick Holmes, were ordered to Samos, leaving Leros in a 'decrepit old caïque that was capable of about 4 knots in good weather'.[53] It was only a couple of days before Holmes was ordered back, but by then it was too late.

Despite bad weather and rough seas, reinforcements from the 9./440 were brought in and German air cover continued: around 125 sorties would be carried out on the 13th.[54]

Some of the landings aborted on the first day now succeeded; where they ran into trouble because of the seas being too rough, the LCs were sent back to Kalymnos. Under Appetici, for example, Kampfgruppe Dörr was only able to land a single company.

Schädlich's additional Brandenburger *Küstenjäger* were initially held back, beyond range, while Ju.87s took over. Under cover of a destroyer-laid smokescreen, the fast assault boats returned. As one of the two boats approached a narrow beach on the north side of Pandeli, it was hit. Many got ashore and started the steep climb up Mt. Appetici. By 1100 all four LAGO battery guns were in German hands, sending British troops back in a disorderly withdrawal down to Pandeli.

Some 130 Germans managed to get to the top but, as they were crossing the open, rocky ground, their own aircraft failed to recognize them, swooped in and started bombing and strafing. None of their officers survived the first unsuccessful lunge and, after regrouping, they tried again, only to be bombed a second time, with heavy casualties. Their objective was switched to cutting off the Allied troops on Appetici rather than risking another frontal assault. The Germans encircled Platanos by moving around its south-east corner but remained unable to break the British line. For three days, re-supplied by air drops, the outnumbered *Küstenjäger* held their positions.

More troops landed just past Grifo Bay. At Pasta di Sopra, *Kampfgruppe* Aschoff finally got additional troops ashore under heavy fire, linking up with the thirty or so troops from Grifo. The fire was so heavy that Oberleutnant Steinman had to threaten his own helmsman; at pistol point, the poor man was forced to turn back towards the shore. As they approached, men had to abandon ship and swim 200 yards ashore after their LC was hit. Marsland Gander had been watching: 'Soon the vessel was a roaring furnace. Then it blew up with a mighty explosion showing that its chief cargo must have been ammunition.'[55]

The second paratroop drop was delayed till around 0645. There was a 'good deal of wind', Jellicoe recalled.[56] They were dropped under exceptionally difficult circumstances: a 40mph wind was blowing, and of 'the 200 who actually left the aircraft not more than a dozen ever went into action', according to one report. The report may have been exaggerated, but the overall impression was not.[57]

This time, the Ju.52s arrived individually. It's uncertain why, since it made the fifteen planes easier targets, allowing fire to be concentrated on each individual plane as it came in. The graphic detail of Gander's writing leaves little to the imagination:

> One of the slow troop carriers, hit fair and square, went flaming down into Alinda Bay, a horrifying spectacle, with one solitary parachute visible, dragging behind it the doll-like figure still attached.[58]

Other parachutists were dropped over the sea: their 'white silk parachutes, like huge water-lilies, floated across the water until they, too, sank.'[59]

The weather forced two of the Ju.52s to fly so low that most of their paratroopers were badly injured on landing; their 'chutes simply had no time to open. They went down like Roman candles, canopies completely snarled. From one plane, not a single parachute opened. The whole stick was lost; something must have gone wrong with the static jump cord. One of LRDG 2nd Lieutenant Merv Cross's T2 patrol, Private Les Nichols, watched as more than a dozen men plummeted to their deaths within a hundred yards of his position at Point 112.[60] Another plane had to make a landing on the water, a couple of kilometres off Palma Bay. All twelve men – the entire stick – were still on board. Unteroffizier Andreas Hutter, an air gunner, was just able to swim to the shore. He survived but was promptly taken prisoner by the Italians. To save himself, he had had to leave men behind. He had little chance of saving the parachutists. He tried inflating a raft, only to find it riddled with bullets. Laden with heavy jump packs and no life vests, the German paratroopers flailed helplessly in the water, struggling to stay afloat before inevitably drowning.

Others landed on rocky ground and were immediately dragged across the jagged, bone-breaking terrain as British gunners mercilessly targeted them. They dropped all around the LRDG where Olivey's colleague and friend, Alan Redfern, would die.

Around Appetici and Clidi, each side struggled to dislodge the other. From both, the high ground dominated Alinda Bay. There, one of the German ammunition re-supply barges had been hit and set on fire.

Nevertheless, despite strong gains, von Saldern's men couldn't break through to Appetici's LAGO battery from the north to link up with the waiting *Küstenjäger*.

The castle still held out and formed an effective barrier. Without the two forces joining up, the Germans did not have complete control of Alinda Bay and were therefore unable to bring heavier guns ashore. Moreover, it meant they couldn't suppress continued British naval bombardment.

By nightfall, however, German operations at Clidi had succeeded in gaining a deep foothold, and the British lost control of the CIANO batteries. The British had launched a counter-attack supported by a heavy barrage, but it was beaten back, and by the afternoon, Hauptmann Gawlich's fifty men were dug in. Now von Saldern moved troops south to San Nicola on the east, and around Quirico below Clidi on the south-west. They were pushed back by Buff troops at Quirico but slowly opened up the route through to the southern shores of Alinda Bay.

That night, Tilney, aided by enemy documents captured during the day including German recce photos and unit details, ordered the two battalion commanders, French and Iggulden, to deal with the two aggressive German incursions on Clidi and Appetici.

The British troop positions were re-drawn. Under cover of darkness, Jellicoe and Captain Ashley Greenwood, his LRDG liaison officer, went south from their positions beside the Buffs to organize the recovery of supplies from their former positions at Germano in two jeeps. Captain Bylth was in command. The next morning, they struggled back, with two fully laden jeeps.

At Appetici, the attack that had been cancelled seventeen hours earlier was now re-scheduled with three KORR companies for 1600. Nothing would have happened if it hadn't been for French who took the decision that 'having reached that far unobserved he had achieved the element of surprise for an attack'. He only sent back an HQ company and went ahead with his planned assault.[61] Tilney had been wavering and had actually tried to cancel any attack when German paratroopers had started mortaring the HQ positions on Meraviglia around 2200.

The Germans had effectively succeeded in cutting the island in half. In the north, Clidi was in German hands. Around Leros town, RIF soldiers blocking the road to Meraviglia were under severe pressure from the Germans at Appetici, even if Pandeli Castle itself was still under British control. For the moment, that prevented von Saldern joining forces with the *Küstenjäger* and the *9.Grn Rgt. 440* to make the final push on Meraviglia.

Leros – Day 3. Sunday, 14 November

Manpower wasn't Tilney's problem (he had over a thousand men: 500 in the north, 400 on Rachi Ridge and 200 around Leros town, plus RA, RE and HQ staff). The problem was air cover. His men were pinned down by closely supporting and extremely well co-ordinated enemy air support. A stretcher bearer, Corporal Vic Kenchington, described the efficiency of the German dive bombers: 'the Stukas seemed to be lined up just like a "taxi-rank", awaiting the Verey lights and down they would come.'[62] The Germans launched the attack with 135 sorties, D+1 saw only ten fewer but now, after being hampered by the bad weather and high winds of the previous day, German sorties 'intensified dramatically'.[63]

Sunday started badly. The two-company KORR attack on Appetici was strongly countered despite a 10-minute, 98-salvo softening-up barrage from HMS *Belvoir* and HMS *Echo*. The British attack did not take place till 0230 – a full hour and a half later. At the first gun emplacement, the repeated British assaults were held off by 'skilful use of the new MG.42 and an almost continuous barrage of shells from German 81mm mortars'.[64] At dawn, the British were driven back with heavy losses: only one officer and seventy men remained alive. Around fifty-five British and forty-five Italians were taken prisoner.

One of those killed was Maurice French. Close to him, and also wounded, was a Faugh Lieutenant, Robert Austin Ardhill. He saw French 'firing from the shoulder when he was caught in the heavy fire and fell mortally wounded'.[65] Some thought the Colonel knew he was going to die. The Battalion adjutant, Captain Dougall, said that French had acted out of character just before the attack, saying, 'Goodbye, Dougie' instead of greeting him as he normally did, using the battalion's battle-cry *'Faugh a Balagh!'* or 'Clear the way!' (to let them attack).

Ardill was indignant. At one point, French had even been called back to HQ by Tilney, who was also busy redeploying some of his men. On the ground, it was totally confused. A West Kents soldier, Sid Bowden, summed it up: 'We did not know who we were taking orders from really, half the time.' Bowden's 'apparently aimless wanderings to and fro set a pattern which many other men experienced.'[66]

Keeping Appetici under pressure, the Germans pushed towards Meraviglia from their positions on Rachi ridge. While Bill Shephard, the new Faughs commander, organized the counter-attack on Rachi, Iggulden's men, supported by mortars, managed to re-take Clidi's summit in the early morning, taking forty prisoners from Hauptmann Herbert Gawlich's unit. The LRDG had helped in clearing out caves with grenades, sometimes a final one being thrown in without the pin pulled to allow the Germans to get out alive. Olivey, their commander, 'seemed to be constantly itching to take part in some action [and] borrowed a Tommy-gun' from Lemuel Bevanto to speed them up.[67]

After midday, the RIF took 'Searchlight Hill'. However, they couldn't dislodge the enemy from a nearby hill, even if 200 or so Germans were taken prisoner. Further back, on the coastal flank, Jellicoe sent out SBS patrols to recce and gauge the strength of German forces around Germano, and later that night, the SBS was partially withdrawn, although one patrol with Sergeant Workman stayed behind with anti-tank guns on Gurna Bay.

At dusk, on Tilney's orders, a naval bombardment rained down on the German-held hilltop, the display of firepower from two destroyers doing wonders to boost his men's morale; and with further naval shelling, CIANO battery was re-taken.

With night also came relief; the endless air attacks paused while men and supplies were shipped in and the wounded and German prisoners were taken out. Around 500 reinforcements from the Royal West Kents arrived from Samos, although their C.O, Lieutenant Colonel Ben Tarleton, would only join them the next day with two more companies. Some say this meant, 'leaving them at a disadvantage as they were no longer a coherent fighting unit.'[68]

After three days of intense fighting and endlessly confused manoeuvring, all the men – German and British alike – were exhausted. The defenders, however, were probably more so: they'd already suffered weeks of air attack. It was curious that each side harboured the same sense of hopelessness: to Müller 'it appeared impossible that we should ever win the battle. The destiny of the troops on Leros hung on thin thread.'[69] For the British it was the same: from Meraviglia, tell-tale signals sent out at 0327 and 0429 hinted at the same sense of desperation as naval wireless operators prepared for the worst: 'All radio messages destroyed. No code. Everything destroyed. Radio station continues working.'[70]

Leros – Day 4. Monday, 15 November

In the early hours of darkness, the last units of the Royal West Kents arrived with Tarleton. In Turkish waters, *Belvoir* had transferred the troops to fast MTBs. With no air cover, time at the dock was to be minimized. Gander watched as troops disembarked from *Echo*:

> Rapidly, methodically, wooden chutes were run down over the ship's side on to the wharf. Then heavily laden soldiers with packs, helmets, rifles and other weapons came sliding down on their rumps. They were so weighed down that many could not stagger to their feet, and the Italian dock labourers waiting had to help them up.[71]

Stepping ashore in the darkness and going straight into battle, not knowing where they were headed or what the land even looked like, must have been profoundly disorienting.

Echo had earlier passed by as Germans, struggling for their lives in the water, looked helplessly on. To the north of Alinda Bay, RN MTBs had caught several LCIs in their searchlights. MTB.266 had a novel approach:

> As we continued to zig-zag round the island one of the bridge look-outs called, 'craft bearing green four five, sir'. Straining in the half-light I could just detect three dim shapes … They were two of our own motor torpedo boats about to attack another German landing craft … There was a gigantic underwater explosion as one of the little attackers dropped a depth charge under the stern of the enemy craft. But we were not stopping for anything.[72]

But the LCIs were carrying prisoners and German and British wounded. One ran ashore north of Pasta di Sopra. Oberfeldwebel Walter Lünsmann recalled the scene on the stricken ferry (*Fährprahm*), saying that he

> instructed the people there, some of whom were wrapped in blankets, to disembark. The first two did not understand German, presumably they were English. The next ones refused or, perhaps, were unable to move. We carried the men off the boat in our ground sheets.[73]

On Clidi, Lemuel Bevan was amongst the KORR soldiers, fighting alongside the LRDG, holding out. Below Appetici, it was the same; above Pandeli, the

Faughs held the line. With his five men, Jack Harte was 'exhausted, had not eaten for two days and had long since run out of water.'[74] As they broke cover, intent on searching for something to eat, MG fire ripped them to shreds.

Tilney wanted to re-take Rachi, partly held by exhausted KORR troops to box in the enemy. He met with Tarleton, telling him that his orders would be delivered by runner as the net was overloaded, but more importantly, that his newly arrived troops wouldn't be supported by artillery 'due to the somewhat confused situation prevailing on the ridge at this time'.[75] The Germans were also having a tough time: when their own Stukas mistakenly bombed them, white warning flares were sent up, the only problem being that 'the Stukas understood this, but so did the enemy … so we continued to be under artillery barrage from a nearby hill.'[76]

Within 50 yards of the German positions, mercilessly mortared and sniped at close range, 'only twelve men had managed to reach their objective.'[77] Two officers and twenty ORs had been wounded. Multiple attacks had become bogged down because of the hopelessly mixed chains of command between Tarleton's two newly arrived companies.

That afternoon, the objective was finally taken. Both company commanders were wounded. KORR Bren gunners, whose help was needed to consolidate their tenuous hold, were not forthcoming; they wanted them to protect their own positions. The other enemy position was also taken – with twenty or so prisoners – but Tarleton was astonished at the stiff German resistance:

> An enemy mortar barrage opened up on this feature [Point 36], supported by automatic fire at surrendering Germans and advancing British alike … We were lucky to have reached our objective, but had no chance to consolidate possession of it.[78]

For one very brief moment, the German hold on the island's centre hung in the balance. After Mount Germano was taken, the RWK and Buffs linked up. In the small village of St Nicola a fierce battle took place, 'bloody hand-to-hand combat in the small, dark, scantily furnished rooms'.[79]

On Appetici, Pandeli Castle finally fell after two hours of intensive fighting. At 1614, Germans were seen entering the castle from Meraviglia.

It's now clear that a German victory was not a foregone conclusion; their own signals tell the story. 'The fighting is confused and information scarce, and changes in control by the enemy results in a confused crisis.'[80] Little real news of the unfolding drama was reaching SBS HQ. Back at Kabrit, Milner-Barry received 'cheerful' news from Leros and noted (in his diary entry for 16 November) that the LRDG 'reckon that the island can be held if Jerry lands no more reinforcements.'[81]

Leros – Day 5. Surrender. Tuesday, 16 November

With Pandeli Castle in their hands, the Germans now focussed completely on Meraviglia. From the castle itself, a distance of 1,000 yards, they could machine gun and snipe the defenders, and by late Monday, some German troops were already close enough to be 'within grenade throwing range'.[82]

A sense of impending disaster hung in the air. Around midnight, Jake Easonsmith, Jellicoe's opposite number, took an LRDG patrol to Platanos to evaluate the situation. Syd Jenkinson went with him. In the dark, a shot rang out. One German was close enough to Jenkinson for him to hear his verdict ('*tot*') when he rolled Easonsmith's body over with his foot. The LRDG commander's loss was very profoundly felt even though Guy Prendergast, his replacement, was a soldier of equal calibre. His body lies in the lovingly maintained Commonwealth War Graves Cemetery on the shores of Alinda Bay.

While British strength dwindled, German reinforcements piled in: 1,000 men from the 3rd Battalion of the *Brandenburger Küstenjäger* 1st Regiment landed on the other side of the island in Leros Bay around 0200, and another 280 landed east of Appetici together with heavy weapons. All the British could bring in was one more of Tarleton's companies, immediately sent in a forlorn effort to reinforce the Buffs defending Platanos. Most of their mates were dead, wounded or already prisoners.

At 0400 von Saldern, now the overall German commander on the ground, launched the final assault on Meraviglia. The exhausted German troops pushed themselves on with Pervitin (Benzedrine tablets), and by 0615 had climbed up the north-eastern spur of Meraviglia after Tarleton's units placed at 'The Anchor', a point located on the main Portolago-Platanos road a little to the west of Meraviglia, had been pushed back. The stand had been almost impossible: only two field guns remained in action with only ten rounds, and 1 KORR and 2 RIF were pretty well finished as functioning units, while 4 Buffs and 2 RWK were down to around 200 men apiece.

By 0800 the situation was so bad that Tilney sent in the clear (he no longer had code books) a signal describing the situation as 'critical':

> If you reinforce Leros we can restore the situation. You must, repeat, must provide air cover. It is exhaustion we are fighting not numbers.[83]

At 0825, after the signals were intercepted, they were translated, immediately copied and air dropped over attacking German positions with a message of encouragement: 'Now let's finish them off!' Tilney had, unwittingly, given Müller all the encouragement he and his men needed.

Tilney decided to move his HQ and ordered Prendergast to move the LRDG to Portolago, from where he hoped to continue the fight. Tarleton, still at 'The Anchor', went back up to Meraviglia to rescue as many of the radio sets as possible for the move to Portolago.

By now the enemy was 'just 130 yards south-east of the battery CP'. Two men were killed around 0815.[84] A small force led by Lieutenant Colonel Richie, along with two other officers and half a dozen men, was desperately trying to hold on. Richie, a Bisley champion, was a 'very fine rifle shot and personally shot a number of enemy.'[85] He'd already had a 'close brush' when he and a German fired at each other at the very same moment. On his second shot, he discovered his pistol sight was nothing more than 'a twisted piece of metal. The bullet had apparently hit the tip of [his] barrel and had been deflected past [his] face.'[86] He'd been holding two enemy soldiers at bay with some 'Little Reds' (Italian hand grenades) when he was joined by Alan Phipps armed with 'an enormous Webley pistol'. Phipps had volunteered to come ashore from his ship, HMS *Faulknor*, to help run signals for the Navy. Together with Captain Ramsay, Lieutenant Horton and the Italian commander, the four hunted two Germans:

> Richie could not see what actually happened but shortly afterwards the Italian limped back with a hand blown off at the wrist and [his] leg badly wounded by a grenade. Ramsay returned a minute later to say that the two Germans had withdrawn from the hill but that Lt. Phipps had been killed by a burst of SMG in his chest in the area of the gun pit.[87]

Back at GHQ ME, a message was sent at 1600 saying that evacuation would be organized for the following night. It was too late. British resistance had already collapsed.

At 1630, fresh III./Brandenburger troops under Oberleutnant Max Wandrey took possession of the hill top. Tilney was still there. He called out for anyone speaking German to present a white flag. The unfortunate volunteer was badly wounded before his captors understood that they wanted to surrender.

On his way to Portolago, Prendergast looked around and back up at the Meraviglia ridgeline and saw 'what appeared to be the whole of the HQ staff lined up outside.'[88]

Meanwhile, Jellicoe, as confused as others were about Tilney's plans, decided to go to see the Brigadier himself:

> I worked my way through to Brigade Headquarters with a small party consisting of Sgt. Workman, Cpl. Dryden and L/Cpl. Allen. However, it would have been quite impossible to have

got there by jeep as the trip involved more or less crossing the German positions.[89]

Frank Ramseyer took him by jeep 'as far as the Navy House at the crossroads between S. Nicola and S. Quaranta'.[90] There he ran into a D Coy., Buffs' officer, Major Ewart Tassell, and the two exchanged what information they had. Tassell recalled what must have been a very brief meeting:

> Anyway, at the end of the enlightenment, he said, 'Well, I better get back' and then he turned round and walked back to the Germans, just like that. Extraordinary bloke, really.[91]

Jellicoe's own memory was a little shaky about the episode. In a 2001 interview with Tony Rogers, he remembered that it was actually Tilney who sent for him and that he couldn't get through in daylight as there were too many Germans.

He continued by saying that he 'walked towards the entrance of the headquarters and there at the door I was met not by our Brigadier but by a German officer (full colonel I think he was).' As he entered he was saluted by the German guards. There he finally saw Tilney, now a prisoner. He turned to Jellicoe and said:

> George, I do apologize. When I sent for you I didn't know that we'd be captured by now. Incidentally, your friend Alan Phipps is missing and I don't know whether there's any chance of finding out what's happened to him.[92]

Jellicoe immediately spoke to the German officer, asking if he could try and find Phipps. Without hesitating, the German agreed: 'Fine, if you give me your parole.' Jellicoe went out in the dark:

> I must have spent the best part of an hour looking for Alan Phipps but I couldn't find him. I found four or five quite badly wounded people. I was glad I had morphine on me and I was able to inject them, including one or two Germans, and then went back and surrendered my parole. Then we were all marched back down to the little port of the west of the island.

One can only imagine the desperation of his search repeatedly rolling bodies over in the dark, looking into the faces of the dead. But not Alan's body. It was never found, but where he died eventually was. A post-action report by Lieutenant Horton talked of his bravery and the circumstances of his death:

> I was assisting this officer and two others to retake and defend a gun position on the slopes of the island HQ Mount at about 1000 hrs.

Shortly after the site had been taken, Lt. Phipps was hit above the waist, apparently in the neck and chest … I should like to comment on the outstanding bravery of this officer, who initiated and led the attack on the position advancing across open ground exposed to fire. It was due to his leadership only that the position was retaken. [93]

In 2009, the historian Tony Rogers was on Leros and searched where Jellicoe also probably had, beside Gun No.4. Nothing was found there. Rogers then went to the cliff edge that bordered the gun position's northern side and looked over. His friend, Andreas Galanos, spotted something on the ground and handed it to him. It was a naval button. It could only have been Alan's. Rogers gave it to Phipps' son, Jeremy, in 2011. Jellicoe often talked – with great sadness – of never having found Alan's body. I wish the button had been found before his death in 2007. It would have meant so much to him.

It wasn't until May 1945 that Phipps' action was gazetted by the Admiralty and he received a posthumous MiD, an 'exceedingly rare' occurrence.[94]

Shortly after surrendering to Wandrey, Tilney left Meraviglia by jeep, accompanied by Captain Baker and two German officers, going to Portolago to ask Mascherpa to surrender the Italian troops. When Müller landed at Agia Marina at 1800, the Italians in Portolago were still fighting.

The news of Tilney's surrender didn't reach all units. Some Buffs continued fighting well through the night of 16 November into the next morning, as did the last of the Regia Marina batteries. As 'signal lights' announcing the surrender arced through the skies, many shared their feeling of incredulity: '*Non vi crediamo, viva l'Italia, viva il Re*' (We do not believe you, hail Italy, long live the King).[95]

Troops were completely exhausted. Ted Johnson recalled his first moments of capture:

My own company was decimated … we were down to five men, three soldiers, another officer and myself. We realized there was no point in carrying on. We had no ammunition and no grenades left, so we destroyed our weapons and walked down the hill with our arms up.[96]

Mostly, the Germans appreciated how hard fought the battle for Leros had been and treated those surrendering with professional respect even if the Italians weren't always so lucky. There were, of course, exceptions: Obergefreiter Walter Keller recalled an incident when German troops had disobeyed direct orders after taking the surrender of some Italians on the second day: 'Anyway, the rest came out. One was an officer and our Gruppenführer (Oberjäger Franz) Prokov said "Mensch, that's an officer, we will have to hand him in".' The Italian pleaded for his life, making them understand that his wife was pregnant. This time it worked: 'What good will it do if he gets shot? It's not like it will do us any good ... So, we told him to put on an ordinary soldier's uniform.'[97] Relieved and grateful, the Italian took off his watch and gave it to Keller. Around seven Italian officers were shot before Hitler's order was countermanded.

After the march down to the port, Jellicoe felt that his parole had been honoured. He told the Germans that his men would never surrender without hearing it from him, so they needed to let him go to them. The bluff worked.

Jellicoe got back to his own SBS and some of the LRDG, saying that he personally had no intention of surrendering. He was angered at what he called Tilney's 'Anglo-German Peace Conference' and announced that those who wished to leave the island with him should prepare immediately. There were probably around seventy or so men.[98] They were to take seven days' rations and destroy any secret documents they still had.

At 0245, they set off for Parteni Bay, found a waiting caïque and boarded her around 0315.[99] Jellicoe had taken precautions when he became increasingly certain that Leros would eventually fall. He and Frank Ramseyer had 'selected a number of places around the island from which the Navy had been briefed to take off escapers.' Parteni Bay was one.

Escorted by one of Ramseyer's MLs, LS.7, they left for Lipsos, a small island just north of Leros, and when they got there at 0600 they thought it better to 'lay up for the day'. Their presence was obvious: 'Local inhabitants insisted on walking around our positions and giving away our hideouts.'[100] Greenwood himself had only just made it. Along with ten men, he arrived by jeep at the embarkation point just as LS.7 was leaving. Obligingly, she turned back to pick up the late arrivals.

Eventually, Jellicoe's group escaped, first landing at a small Turkish fishing village, Gumusluk, and then sailing further to Bodrum, where they arrived on 18 November. From there, they were allowed to continue via Aleppo aboard a train made up of 'cattle-trucks pulled by a dilapidated railway engine' dressed as civilians.[101] While they were on a subsequent train to Haifa, friends back at base heard that they were returning and decided to come and get them. They stopped the train by driving a truck on to the tracks and hauled their friends off. Ranfurly met Jellicoe in Cairo a few days later, on 24 November: he was with an Italian, 'both dressed in Turkish civilian clothes'.[102]

Anyone who could get away did so. Over the next four nights, the SBS went back to Leros aboard LSF boats to rescue as many as possible. Lawson, the LRDG medic, and '36 other LRDG and 80 or 90 of other units with several officers' were some of the many escapees.[103] He and Guy Prendergast divided up the men and used different escape routes.

After Portolago, Prendergast had continued on to the battery at Monte Scumarda and, only finding Private Lennox, another LRDG man, the two teamed up and set off after filling their packs with rations and water. The following day, Captain Dick Croucher, Ron Tinker and three others joined them. Starting to run low on rations, Prendergast decided to look for a boat in Serocampo Bay. He didn't find one, but a local family took him in, fed him and promised to leave a patched-up boat on the shore the next day. The next day's strong wind and high seas, however, would have swamped them in minutes. In the distance they saw a small craft and decided to risk sending a flashlight signal. It was seen by an SBS man, George Miller, sent out by Jellicoe from Turkey that same night. Not wasting a minute, Miller decided to risk it and go ashore himself. Prendergast and his LRDG team got off.

John Olivey also got away. He hadn't heard about the surrender and woke up on the morning of the 17th hearing German soldiers singing and seeing seaplanes in the bay. Earlier, he had asked Jellicoe, 'How long I had to hold the fort. He told me until our casualties were higher than the enemy's, which seemed fair enough.'[104]

Not yet concerned for his own escape, he wanted first to spike the guns but then found he had no matches. He went back to the CP at Pt.320 and promptly ran into two Germans, whom he shot, then got away quickly and went north. This time, his luck didn't hold out. He found a house where the bed made up with cleansheets. It was too much to resist and he woke up in it to find two German officers who took him prisoner. He would be paraded through Athens with other prisoners from Leros but eventually escaped and was back in Cairo the following April.

Another SBS officer, Keith Balsillie, managed to escape in a rowing boat. Suffering from severe dysentery, he'd been left behind.

Captain Ashley Greenwood, Jellicoe's LRDG liaison officer, volunteered to stay behind to look for stragglers, going back to some of the batteries where he knew other LRDG were hiding. He managed to get a further eleven men out, including the Bren gunner, Ron Cryer:

A couple of miles from shore, it started to get light, so we decided to pull into a small island which had plenty of scrub on it … we all got ashore and hid in the small bushes and there were German aircraft flying round all the time but they didn't spot any of us in the bushes. When it got dark that night we all got into the boat and it took us most of the night to get into harbour at Bodrum.[105]

All told, around 250 managed to escape. By the end of November, 11 LRDG officers and 58 LRDG ORs had returned out of the 123 on Leros at the time of the surrender.[106] To the south, on Samos, Dick Holmes, who had 'waited on board for a couple of hours' in the expectation of going back to Leros, was told of the surrender and ordered to disembark.

During the 54-day campaign, the Germans had dropped 1,096 tons of bombs in 984 air raids.[107] It had been incessant.[108] Despite disparaging talk of the Italians, their AA gunners actually exacted a heavy toll on German aircraft. In total, they 'fired more than 150,000 rounds during the 52 days of aerial bombardment and were responsible for the destruction of more than half of the 92 Luftwaffe planes lost in combat' in Leros operations.'[109] It was a sizeable share of the 346 plans lost in the whole campaign.[110] Coastal batteries sank a ferry lighter and two LCs; MTBs, another ferry lighter and an LC.

The Germans had suffered 520 casualties;[111] 3,200 British and 5,350 Italian were captured, while 41 per cent of the British raiding force had been killed or wounded: 1,109 soldiers.[112] In the Alinda Bay cemetery there still lie the bodies of 251 Allied servicemen, 187 of them British; and while the Germans also had a cemetery on Leros, the bodies were eventually exhumed and taken back to Athens. Pauline Bevans described the little details that continue to bear witness:

> One could still make out the walls, steps leading up to the cemetery and the marble base of the former cross of sacrifice, which looked like an altar. This area was carpeted with a deep layer of pine needles and when I ventured there I found someone had placed a wreath on the base of the cross of sacrifice.[113]

Despite the carnage, there were moments of chivalry. Shortly after dawn on the fourth day, Easonsmith's 23-year-old Rhodesian signalman was killed. As Cliff Whitehead's body was being lowered into its rocky grave, a lone Stuka screamed down to attack. With no cover in sight, the eight-man patrol was completely exposed. But the pilot must have understood: 'at the last minute [the Stuka] pulled away without strafing or bombing, circled overhead several times, waggling its wings and disappeared.'[114]

The cost of the Leros campaign was enormous. In England, Churchill raged: 'The American Staff had enforced their view; the price had now to be paid by the British.' He had been told by Eisenhower that the Americans could not support the Dodecanese venture, but it was a wholly unfair criticism of an ally who was more focused on the larger theatre of war, on what they considered was 'doable'.[115]

Not unreasonably, the Greeks had been pushing for more involvement. The British were oddly schizophrenic: Greeks had proved themselves worthy and reliable allies, but Churchill still hoped for some sort of deal with Turkey. The Dodecanese represented a bargaining chip to lure her into the war, but when it became clear that the Turks weren't 'buying', British attitudes started to shift. Nevertheless, the 'go-ahead' was only finally given on 28 October, and by then British reticence had already deeply insulted many.

Tsigantes's *Ieros Lochos* was ordered to reinforce Samos where, since mid-September, Sutherland had brought in 25 SBS. While the battle on Leros raged, Lassen, Roger Wright, Joe Jarrell, Nicholson and Holmes went back over. The 'Sacred Greeks' as the SBS called them, were given the main role. Two hundred were dropped in two hours, the first under the 'middle aged and deaf, but gallant ... born leader of men', Colonel Andreas Kalinskis, the second under Tryphon Triantafyllkos.[116]

The drop, on 30/31 October, took place in strong winds: twenty-one were injured, five badly.[117] Tsigantes, delayed in Cairo, found the only way he could be with his men was to jump with them. He'd never made an actual jump before and received most of his instruction during the flight. This was typical of him. He'd avoided the training jumps, saying 'If I am to break my legs, it has got to be on Greek soil.'[118] On the flight over to Samos, he sat next to David Sutherland and, just before jumping, he turned around with an inquiring look:

> 'Sutherland, is that enemy fire coming toward us?'
>
> I reply, 'No, Colonel, those are sparks from the engine. It's old and needs decarbonising.'
>
> With that slender reassurance he jump[ed] into the void and disappear[ed]. It was Colonel Tsigantes' first parachute jump.[119]

Positions were quickly established and more troops came in by ship.

With the Germans' victory on Leros, *Ieros Lochos* reinforcements were held back as the Germans now turned their full attention to Samos:

> The fall of Leros ensured that of Samos. The Greek garrison was withdrawn from the island. Excluding Kastelorizo, no fragment of the Dodecanese now remained in British hands. Since all islands were now hostile territory, all were fair game for raids.[120]

On 17 November, the island's two towns were heavily bombed, Samos in the north-east (especially the port area of Vathy) and Pythagorio in the south-east: 'In Vathy, a fifth of the houses were razed to the ground, while Tigani was almost completely wiped off the map.'[121] The British garrison commander could do little else but surrender and withdraw: on 19 November the evacuation started. British troops, 300 or so GSS, 800 guerrillas,

12,000 refugees and General Mario Soldarelli's 6th Infantry division (the *Cuneo*) were all pulled out through Turkey.[122] The Italians were considered 'politically too unstable to be trusted to help the allies'.[123]

Despite the ferocity of Luftwaffe attacks, the evacuation was a success. Most of the ships sailed at night to avoid attack. The Germans expected the evacuation to be organized from Tighani; ships actually left Vathy escorted by two MTBs. On the first night, 1,000 left, a further 1,200 on the second, and on the third, 'thirty-seven heavily laden caïques reached safety' across the waters in Turkey.[124]

Lassen played a key role in organizing the massed caïque exodus. He and his men stayed behind on the island, thinking to continue a guerrilla war, but were soon also ordered to leave. They marched down to the docks at Vathy, heads held high, in tight order. Lassen wanted to be sure that the Greeks did not feel that the British had given up on them.

Even though Turkey was nominally neutral, an unofficial agreement had been reached allowing the British to use their waters with discretion. But the Germans' success on Kos and Leros gave the Turks pause. More bribes became necessary, and when Lassen's men arrived, they had to travel through Turkey in disguise to get back to Haifa via Aleppo. 'A kind English lady who lived in Smyrna' found suitable clothes for Anders and his men.[125]

German control of the Aegean islands would last and be maintained with an iron hand till war's end. On the mainland, in the small town of Kalavrita in Corinth, all 1,346 males, fifteen and older, were executed in the main town square. Even in the relative safety of Turkish waters, the SBS had to be careful. The Germans had spies all around and were increasingly pressuring the Turkish Government to withdraw any remaining support of Allied troops on Turkish soil or in their waters.

The Dodecanese campaign losses were substantial; it would take over a month to collect the dead. During battle there'd been no time, and as the bodies started to swell and rot in the heat, the pervasive smell of death was intense. More than seventy years later, Thassos Canaris recalled, tears welling up, the awful sight and smell of these bloated, blackened bodies pervading the islanders' daily lives.[126] Allied shipping losses were particularly heavy – four cruisers damaged, six destroyers, ten coastal vessels and minesweepers and two submarines sunk. The RAF flew over 3,500 sorties and lost nearly half the aircraft deployed – 113 out of 288.[127]

It's extraordinary that there were no VCs awarded, and only one DSO, 113 MCs, 8 MMs and 48 MiD. Astonishingly, Maurice French's name was missing. In January 1946, Tilney wrote a rather feeble explanation to Diana French:

I recommended him for a posthumous Mention in Despatches, which is the utmost one can do for one who died in circumstances where the award of the Victoria Cross is only foregone for the lack of positive evidence to support it.

Jellicoe briefly met with Churchill in Cairo after he'd left Leros and gave him his report. No doubt some of Churchill's fighting spirit burned fiercer after hearing of the exploits of Jellicoe's pirate band, but the days following Tilney's surrender must have been particularly dark and a bitter pill to swallow. The operation's inherent dangers had been anticipated by Eisenhower, as it had by both the Mediterranean Theatre Naval and Air commanders-in-chief.

A new officer now arrived in the ranks of the SBS: 29-year-old Major Ian Patterson. He reached Azzib in October, along with thirty-seven new recruits, all from the Royal Marines. Patterson already had extensive experience under his belt as he'd been 2i/c of the 11th Parachute Battalion and had fought on Kos. He'd approached Jellicoe looking to join his band. When Jellicoe offered him L Detachment he replied that he was hoping for more. 'I'm not sure that would suit me', was Jellicoe's terse reply. Persisting, Patterson said that he was very used to independent command.

Jellicoe could not hide his irritation: 'If I don't like you, you'll go.'[128]

This may not have seemed a very auspicious beginning, but their partnership would become, over the coming months, a very close one. Patterson was a tough perfectionist: he was responsible for having had around fifty men – and an officer – RTU'd. Sutherland did the same with officers that his men didn't trust. Holmes complained to him about two new officers not taking the Folboat training seriously, treating it as a 'lark': they were both RTU'd. 'The Regiment doesn't need officers like you', snapped Sutherland sharply.[129]

Patterson's men were soon transferred to Athlit, where Milner-Barry, along with Sergeant Pat Scully, now recovered, put the new recruits through their paces. Despite Jellicoe's definite preference for younger officers in the field, Milner-Barry, known as 'Papa' amongst the men, worked closely and effectively with 'the belted Earl'. He was very diplomatic and would often step in to represent Jellicoe in negotiations with the Turks, although not surprisingly he wasn't successful in getting them to agree on much. If caught on Turkish soil, British soldiers were still likely to be imprisoned, and both Jock Lapraik and Lodwick spent time in Turkish jails, Lapraik three weeks, Lodwick a few days in Bodrum.

At the end of 1943, two more officers appeared: Lieutenants John Lodwick (later to write *The Filibusters*) and James Lees. Lees had been on

Leros as an Intelligence Officer with the RWK and had earned an MC after he, along with a private, had cleared a house of snipers. He was described by his fellow officer as being 'modest and unassuming to a fault'. He had been a close friend of Steve Hastings while at Eton and had met him again in the desert.[130] In March 1945, he died 'in German hands' after being wounded by a grenade (Lodwick's report that he had been shot was incorrect).[131] Another SBS man, Harold 'Leo' Lyon, was right behind him when it happened and temporarily blinded. In an extraordinarily generous and moving act of reconciliation, his mother, Lady Madeline, apparently found the purported killer, an 18- or 19-year-old Italian Fascist, Tenente Roberto Comotti, with the help of a nurse, Maria, and the German doctor, Dr Wasmuht. It seems that the German had given Comotti Lees' signet ring. Lady Lees not only forgave him, she invited him to the family home and to unveil the memorial to James at the graveyard in Lytchett Minster, Dorset. Comotti may or may not have been his killer but he became a symbol. She wrote: 'I want you to know that I do not hold you responsible for what happened at Villa Punta and I entirely forgive and want you to become part of the family.' One of his own men paid tribute to Lees: 'I don't think the lads ever got over the death of Captain Lees. He was the finest officer and man I ever met in the armed forces, and we had some damn good officers in our unit.'

Lodwick's background was colourful: he'd been a journalist, was serving with the French Foreign Legion when captured during the fall of France and escaped back to Britain through Spain. Dick Holmes did not have a good word for many and said that 'Bombhead', as Lodwick was nicknamed, was 'disliked by everybody' and that he 'took himself off to the *Tewfik* to bask in the magnificence of Jellicoe's smile.'[132] Even Joe Jarrell seemed to share his disdain. He discovered Lodwick's diary while they were both based on a large caïque, the *Takiarchi*. Excerpts would be read out loud, much to the amusement of the men. It may have been unjust: Jellicoe wrote the introduction to *The Filibusters* and seems to have held him in some regard.

On 26 November, Jellicoe arrived back at Athlit and a few days later, Lassen and Holmes arrived from Samos.

Chapter 10

Terror in the Islands:
1944 Aegean Operations

At the end of December 1943, the SBS was briefed on its new role. After Leros, many were demoralized, but now they were ordered 'to make the German occupation an uncomfortable and precarious tenancy of short rations and sleepless nights.'[1] To Dick Holmes that simply meant, 'terrorize the Germans'. Strategically, however, Jellicoe's island operations were designed to keep German troops pinned down in the Mediterranean. Operation OVERLORD, the invasion of Northern Europe, was just six months away. With only a hundred or so men, the task would need cunning.

Kleemann was reinforced and distributed additional men around the islands. Leros and Samos received 6,000. The German did what he could to placate the Greeks; it was difficult enough for his occupation troops without needlessly disturbing a hornet's nest.

Turnbull 'separated the Aegean into two sectors. The GSS concentrated on the northern islands (Samos, Icaria, etc.), leaving the south Aegean (Dodecanese, Cyclades and Crete) to ... the SBS.'[2]

For the next thirteen months, from March 1944 to May 1945, Tsigantes' Greek Sacred Squadron 'participated in, organized and executed, co-operating with Allied Raiding Forces, 33 raids and 207 patrols on 50 islands.'[3] He split his considerably larger forces into three units led by Andreas Kalinskis (1st Raiding Section), Tryphonas Triantafyllakos (2nd Raiding Section) and Pavlos Dimopoulos (3rd Raiding Section). Dimopoulos had been recruited in 1942, then served as a Platoon Leader in the first unit of the *Ieros Lochos* to go into action in North Africa at the start of 1943. Because of his very large ears, he was nick-named *'Aftias'*, the man with the 'big flying ears'. Within a month, the unit's strength would be doubled.

The keys to island operations were mobility and stealth. The Levant Schooner Flotilla gave Jellicoe's men that and more: they kept them supplied and provided refuge when needed. Adrian Seligman, the commander, was 'powerfully-built and dark in countenance, with a lantern jaw and generally aquiline features, [but] he had, by contrast, a surprisingly effeminate mode of speech. The total effect, nevertheless, was of keen intelligence and strong will.[4] He was a very colourful character: in a small boat loaded up with a piano and accompanied by his 17-year old wife, he had sailed the world.

At Jellicoe's disposal was Seligman's 30-boat-strong fleet and 'over forty anchorages on the Turkish coast ... between Kastelorizo (south) and the tip of Samos (north)'.[5] Jellicoe established his roaming command on the 180-ton schooner LS.31, the *Tewfik*. Usually she lay anchored in the port of Deremen (Degirmen buku Deremen) in Turkish waters, at the end of the strip of water between the two peninsulas of Bodrum to the north and Datca to the south, next to the Kos channel. *Tewfik* 'had temperamental engines and rolled in the sea like the swing of a pendulum' but below her decks, she could carry 4,700lbs of explosives.[6] She was a 'home away from home'.

The SBS men lived aboard *Tewfik* and a sister schooner, *Takiarkis*. Life was cramped, the only exercise canoeing and swimming. The after-cabin was a 'mess room, ops room and bunkhouse rolled into one'.[7]Aboard were the usual names – Lassen, Stellin, Jarrell – but there were also some new ones: Freddie Crouch, a 26-year-old ex-policeman from London's East End and Donald Grant, a war reporter with *Look* magazine. In one of his first reports he described his shipmates:

> They were the scruffiest band of soldiers I had ever encountered, carrying an assortment of weapons which they cleaned meticulously... water is tight and no one ever takes his clothes off at night. There is considerable variation in uniform but all are dirty, greasy and torn.[8]

It wasn't unusual for there to be considerable amounts of alcohol on board. Enemy supply vessels were prime targets. Seligman described how, one day, the cook 'appeared with a bottle of Lanson '38. The words *Nür für Wehrmacht Offizieren* [For Wehrmacht officers only] were overprinted in red on its label.' After a raucous evening, some of the boys went ashore and started 'slinging rolls of loo paper like streamers up into the pine trees.'[9] Given that they were trying to keep a low profile in Turkish waters, the boats had to leave hastily.

Some of my favourite photos of my father are from his time on *Tewfik*. In one, he is sitting at breakfast with a young Greek second lieutenant (in one account identified as Petrakis, but I think more likely to have been Kasulis). Another SBS officer, Harold Chevalier, can be seen in the background. Jellicoe is wearing a V-necked sweater, his bushy black hair is dishevelled, and on the table sits a huge teapot and a large tin, recognizable as Tate & Lyle's treacle. Thirty-five years later, Jellicoe would become Tate & Lyle's Chairman. The teapot was a Jellicoe staple. John House, one of his drivers, talked about the 'enormous metal tea pot which would be on the go all day, the tea a bit stewed at the end'.[10] Reports and intelligence would constantly stream in, helping Jellicoe's men plan.

Each 20-ton caïque was heavily armed – usually with two .50 Brownings on each wing, two twin .303 Vickers and a 20mm Oerlikon cannon. The engines had been replaced with those from old Australian Matilda tanks, their 90hp capable of achieving 7 knots, but more importantly, at low speeds being almost completely silent.

Patterson's L Detachment was to lead the reign of terror on the islands. In some sense, the terror had already started: on 22 November, Lapraik hit Nisiros, destroying its W/T and capturing a number of caïques in German hands. The next day, the W/T on Tilos was similarly dealt with.

Calchi

On the last day of January, Lassen led a raid on Calchi, landing with O'Reilly, Corporal Smart and a Greek officer/interpreter, Lieutenant Katsikis (the normal patrol was made up of 'one officer in charge, one sergeant, seven riflemen and usually two signallers').[11] They brought large quantities of supplies for the local population – flour, pasta and bully-beef. Before anything else, medicines were also delivered, for there was widespread malaria and typhoid amongst the severely undernourished locals. Jellicoe admired Lassen's humanity:

> Andy had a quality which over-shadowed even his outstanding physical and moral courage and which will always stand out clearest in my own memory; that was his sympathy for those who were less fortunate than himself and the love that he inspired in them.[12]

After dropping the supplies, they went to find suitable prisoners. It was a bit of an anti-climax: the Italian soldiers were so frightened that they wouldn't come out, so Sean O'Reilly kicked the door in, ending the almost-comic stand-off: 'I took the Italians prisoner and with them, one typewriter, one shot-gun, six rifles, a wireless receiver, two Beretta machine carbines and a telephone.'[13]

They spotted a German E-boat silently gliding into the harbour. One of the Italian prisoners was persuaded to shout across to the German crew, inviting them to come ashore for a drink. As Lassen's men carefully inched into position, the silence was suddenly broken: Sean O'Reilly had tripped and had shot Lassen in the leg. Lassen cursed him – 'You Irish dog'. Concentrated fire was directed at the Germans, wounding two of them. Eventually, the boat was captured, and the engineer, only lightly wounded, restarted her engines and got her underway, partly under tow by Seligman aboard ML. 1083.

Lassen, however, was fretting. He didn't know whether to report his wound. It could be bad for O'Reilly, but if he said it was enemy fire, 'they will give me a wound stripe or something foul like that.'[14] He decided it was best say nothing. Aboard, a bonus was discovered: four pigs. Back at Deremen, the prisoners were handed over for interrogation to Sergeant Priestley, a South African who, as Lodwick said, was 'not conspicuous for those qualities of mercy popularly associated with Englishmen'.[15]

Lassen's wound turned bad and he had to be hospitalized in Alexandria. He'd long since forgiven O'Reilly but was upset at the SBS doctor who had not been able to deal with it. He brought his dog Pipo with him. At first, the dog was banned, but Lassen's good looks soon got it re-admitted, before the little mutt was taken home by 'Beba', the wife of a decorated naval officer, Hugh Stowell, RNVR. Lassen had 'shoved' the dog into his bed to 'keep him quiet'. Stowell had been on Leros with Jellicoe but got away on 15 November, the day before Tilney's surrender. With him he took 177 German prisoners in one of the captured F-lighters over to Haifa. George Jellicoe would be Stowell's best man at their marriage.

In January, S Detachment went to Lebanon for ski training. Jellicoe was probably delighted; the men less so. And because Sutherland was still recovering in hospital, Walter Milner-Barry got the detachment for which he'd been waiting for. At the end of February, he took over Sutherland's detachment.

He, Stefanos Kasulis and twenty-three other men arrived at Port Deremen on 8 March. More followed: Lieutenant Keith Balsillie, 'Nobby' Clarke and twenty-four more ORs.

Two weeks later, on 23 March, George Jellicoe got married in a small ceremony at the Garrison church in Beirut. None of his officers or men knew about it until John House, his driver, told them. They were, he admitted, 'a bit annoyed'.[16] John had known all about the CO's new lady, an Irish girl called Patsy O'Kane. He'd often driven Jellicoe on the six-hour trip to Beirut, where she worked. Jellicoe's pace – between running the Squadron and his romance – was hectic:

['The boss'] came on a Monday morning and said that he had to drive to Beirut that afternoon, come back the next morning and return again on Thursday as he was getting married.[17]

Patsy, known as the 'toast of Beirut', was stunningly good-looking. She, Anita Leslie and Anita's cousin, Lilah Fortescue, shared a flat. Patsy and George were photographed with Anita on their wedding day, Anita looking stylish in a dress she'd borrowed from my mother.[18] My mother had recently arrived from Shanghai, according to Penny Perrick, 'with a trunkful of glamorous frocks', though I somewhat doubt that this would have been possible; she was, after all, coming from a Japanese PoW camp.[19]

John had tried to smarten up the jeep, putting a clean blanket into the back. A brigadier inquired whose jeep it was, and John was genuinely a 'little hurt' when the officer commented on its 'dilapidated' state. The brigadier then very graciously said that Jellicoe and 'Lady Patricia' could use his 'clean and beautifully polished Chev' and he would get it back at the St George hotel, where the reception was to be held.

Jellicoe looked presentable but had arrived at the church having only changed from his battle-dress at the last minute (John had been sent to get a new uniform for himself and pick a new one up for 'the boss'). Lassen, just released from the Alexandria hospital, was an usher, as was one of the LSF officers, Martin Solomon: 'a cheerful pink-faced youth, exuberant and full of fun, he had earned a DSC when in command of an MTB at Tobruk ... Under point blank fire from German tanks surrounding the harbour, [he] had laid a smokescreen down on both sides of the bay, which allowed other ships to escape, he and Geoffrey Searle [ML.355] having been the last ships to leave.'[20]

Pipo was also present but wandered off and got lost. Lassen offered O'Reilly seven days leave to find him. The Irishman spent the first couple of days drinking before getting round to searching for the errant dog. He eventually gave up and brought back a dog that looked somewhat like Pipo. Lassen wasn't pleased. A week later, it was Stud Stellin's turn, and this time Pipo was found.

The photo of the young newly-weds – the 26-year-old Jellicoe and Patsy, one year older – is one of the few I have of the two of them together. It was a marriage to which Jellicoe's mother, Gwen, was strongly opposed. She had tried everything she could, 'even appealing vainly to Churchill to intervene', as she had always hoped her son would marry into a very high station.[21]

That evening, a wild shindig was held. Lassen got extremely drunk and the next morning, in utter embarrassment, couldn't find his false teeth. They were eventually presented to him by a very 'demure' Arab servant.

After the ceremony, Jellicoe and his new bride slipped away and sped out to the airport to board a squat Lockheed Hudson bomber, into which Patsy had to be 'very inelegantly man-handled'.[22] After a lightning honeymoon in Cyprus, Jellicoe returned to the war. Patsy recalled that in those days on Cyprus she lost her engagement ring while swimming. She watched it as it sank, dancing from one side to the other in the gentle currents, glinting all the way down in the crystal-clear sea, till it was lost from sight. It was an ill omen. Within ten years, they were living apart.

Nisiros

In March, reports had it that Kleeman's Kos supply barges would stop en route at Nisiros, and a hit was planned by Jellicoe and Patterson.

Patterson got there before the Germans arrived, and one of his men hid in the docks, waiting. He overheard some of the other Germans talking of their intention to take some local orphans to Rhodes. Patterson now planned an ambush as the Germans would be divided between those at the docks and those going to the Orphanage. There, the Mother Superior agreed with Patterson's plan: she would take the children up the mountains to hide them.

Now dressed as a priest, Patterson led the unsuspecting Germans into his trap. As soon as his men opened fire, two enemy soldiers were killed, seven others injured and the rest of the patrol taken prisoner. Patterson had a lucky escape: his gun jammed and he only got away when one of his men shot his assailant.

Patterson's attention now shifted to the Germans at the dock. When the first patrol hadn't returned, they'd sent some men to investigate. Their warnings were too late: they were gunned down, and grenades were lobbed at the docked barges. The Germans quickly surrendered and were taken back to be interrogated but, in Turkish waters, further barges were spotted.

One of them was armed with a 3-inch gun. Patterson jumped aboard and, manning a twin Breda, laid down a withering fire, but not before the 3-inch had claimed two sailors' lives on their own ML. Heavily outnumbered, it was now Patterson's turn to run: he and his men jumped overboard and swam ashore.

Patterson was decorated with an MC. 'The operation would not have been successful save for the careful planning of this officer, his resourceful improvisation on the spot at considerable risk to himself.'[23] The citation was not published to protect security. He had killed or captured twenty-two enemy and captured two enemy assault craft.

Milner-Barry's command now came to an end: on 26 March, Sutherland was back and immediately given orders to destroy the radio station on Scarpanto.

Alimnia

An SBS patrol arrived on Alimnia on 7 April. L.24 wasn't well enough camouflaged, and when four German caïques arrived at the anchorage five hours later, she was spotted. The patrol was already ashore and the boat was surrendered. The SBS team was then picked up by the E-boat carrying naval prisoners, Tuckey and four sailors, over to Rhodes. Bill Blyth was sent off to Athens for interrogation. It saved his life. The rest ended up in Thessaloniki, were tortured and executed.

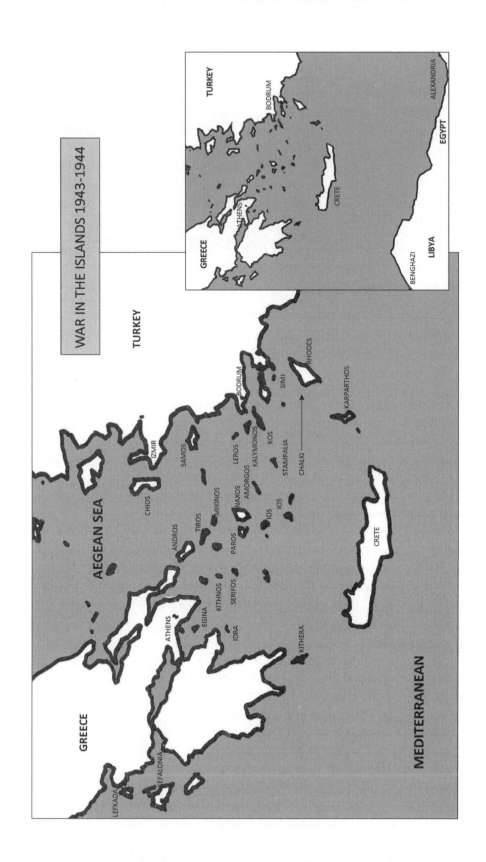

WAR IN THE ISLANDS 1943-1944

GREECE

AEGEAN SEA

TURKEY

MEDITERRANEAN

LEFKADA
CEFALONIA
ATHENS
EGINA
IDRA
KITHNOS
SERIFOS
KITHERA
ANDROS
TIROS
MIKINOS
PAROS
NAXOS
IOS
IOS
AMORGOS
CHIOS
SAMOS
IZMIR
LEROS
KALYMONOS
KOS
STAMPALIA
CHALKI
SIMI
BODRUM
RHODES
KARPARTHOS
CRETE

GREECE
ATHENS
BODRUM
TURKEY
CRETE
LIBYA
BENGHAZI
EGYPT
ALEXANDRIA

The fate of the men of the Alimnia patrol is remembered in the small Anglican church of St Paul in Athens. Beside a plaque dedicated to Jellicoe, there is another one to those executed: from the SBS, Evans, Jones, 'Digger' Rice and George Miller; from the Navy, Tuckey and Carpenter.

In 1986 it was alleged that Kurt Waldheim, the future Austrian Prime Minister and General Secretary of the United Nations, counter-signed the death sentences. He died three years later, but it was shown that he was on leave at the time of the executions.[24] The incident removed a scab that had hidden much of Austria's self-examination of her role in Hitler's war.

Piscopi

On 9 April, a 10-man patrol which included an American journalist who insisted on 'wearing a tie throughout' revisited Piscopi.[25] They planned to ambush one of the frequent 3–10-man German patrols on the fourth day.

The local mayor was asked for help, and he invited the German officer, Leutnant Urbanicz, to visit. The next morning, together with his quartermaster and a clerk, Urbanicz approached the mayor's office; 100 yards behind them there was a private sauntering along with a mule and a dog. The ambushers called out for the Germans to surrender but 'unfortunately they made for their guns and when it was all over, the casualties were 4 Germans and 1 dog killed. The mule got off without a scratch.'[26]

They left the island that night after others, sent off in a Folboat to sink shipping, returned empty-handed.

Turnbull now planned to hit a number of the German W/T posts. These small posts had been set up by the Germans to monitor Allied naval traffic and were, as a consequence, important targets. In a single night, Lassen and Keith Balsillie would hit Santorini, Lodwick, Mykonos, and 'Nobby' Clarke, Ios and Amorgos. Sutherland joined Lodwick's raid.

Mykonos

Soon after Sutherland and Lodwick landed on Mykonos on 22 April, they hit the island's W/T station and in the morning, the small garrison of six Germans in the town house was attacked.

Instead of taking up the offer of surrender, the Germans fought back, injuring Corporal Conby with a grenade. They even tried to attract the attention of a flight of six Ju.88s passing overhead by firing a flare, but their efforts came to little: they were under heavy Bren gun fire. The Germans held out for four hours, and Lodwick began to lose patience and threatened to burn them out. The minute they emerged, 'about 500 Greeks invaded the house and stripped it of all its food supplies.'[27] The locals were starving. Sutherland had really wanted to 'lift' prisoners for intelligence; now his men found themselves protecting them.

Two days after arriving, they left – with prisoners, captured weapons and code books. The 6,000 gallons of petrol they'd liberated was distributed locally.

Santorini

Around the same time, Lassen's 19-strong team arrived on Santorini. aboard two caïques (LS.1 and LS.2). After Alimnia, there was a discernible shift in attitudes; for a while, the rules of war were put aside. Lassen's war of terror certainly worked – Lapraik said it 'put the fear of God into the men' – but it raised many issues: 'Jellicoe's plan of attack ... called for nothing less than the liquidation of the island's entire garrison.'[28]

Lassen himself had done a recce with a Greek named Photi and had also received information from one of the earlier captives, an Obergefreiter Adolf Lange, who had been stationed on the island for a year. Under Priestley's 'gentle' persuasion he had given very detailed information on the exact location of the roughly 60-strong garrison.

Lassen now sent Kasulis on another recce. After five hours they had found little, and Lassen's caïques moved on. Landing again, they went inland and lay up in a cave. Based on Kasulis' new information, Lassen divided his forces: 'Z' team (Balsillie and four men) would attack the radio station at Imerovigli; Patsy Henderson with two men would head for the house of the local German commander, Leutnant Hesse; and the third, Lassen's own 'P' team (Kasulis, Sergeant Nicholson and a dozen men) would deal with a barracks (where a large garrison was billeted) above the Bank of Athens.[29]

The attack was brutal. Lassen and Kasulis brought their teams in from each side of the house, allowing ten minutes to get into position. Two men were placed by each of the five doors to kick them when the whistle was blown. Just before 0100, grenades were tossed in on the sleeping soldiers and a merciless fire opened up. Lassen threw grenades while Nicholson hosed the place with his Bren. Nicholson later expressed remorse, saying that 'fighting beside Lassen' was 'one of the reasons I'm trying to forget the war'.[30]

Then it started to go wrong: O'Reilly's Tommy gun jammed and then Kasulis and Kingston were hit. Kasulis was killed outright, shot in the chest. Sergeant Frank Kingston, the medical orderly, was badly wounded. Sammy Trafford, Lassen's new bodyguard, was hit in the arm and Jack Harris, in the leg.

Warner wrote that 'of the original sixty-eight occupants, only ten survived', but the number seems inflated.[31] One Italian, a sergeant, jumped to his death out of the windows, 40ft on to the rocks below. Holmes was watching as the German prisoners came out. One was severely wounded and begging for a doctor:

> A huge bearded Greek came out of the house and yelled fiercely; 'You want doctor? Here's Doctor Thompson!!' and he opened up on the Germans with his Tommy gun and cut them down.[32]

Somehow Kingston still managed to toss some grenades at the fleeing Italians. In great pain, he was carried down, but the streets were so narrow that they could not take a stretcher. He had a 'magazine full of Schmeisser bullets in his stomach'.[33]

After the initial massacre, Lassen's group slowly added more prisoners to the eight Germans they held. As Balsillie took the prisoners back, Lassen went back for Kingston, whom they eventually laid on a door as a stretcher. They reached a house where a Greek doctor was found. As he lay there, Kingston asked the Greek if he had an internal haemorrhage. It was clear he was dying. When he finally passed, locals came and gently laid flowers on his still body.

Leutnant Hesse, the German commander, and his orderly had somehow escaped unharmed and now took revenge; at least five Greeks, including the mayor, were shot.[34] Lassen sent a written warning: he would kill any German left if there were additional executions: 'If there are, we shall return with 1,000 men and kill every German on the island.'

They were lucky to get away. The Germans did not immediately send reinforcements from Melos, but the following day, a sizeable aerial search was undertaken by four Ju.88s, two seaplanes and an Me.109. When they got to the shore, they still had great difficulty getting out to the boats as the wind was so strong.

Kingston's and Kasulis' death hung heavily over everything: when they got back to camp, flags were flown at half-mast. Lassen hit the bottle; in Photi's words, 'Captain Lassen drank two days of sorrow – like a father.'[35] Lassen then had the sad responsibility of breaking the news to Kasulis' young widow. He took Kasulis' gold watch and chain and gently put them in her hands.

Ios was hit a few days later, on 28 April, when 'Nobby' Clarke led a combined SBS and 6-man GSS unit that wiped out the garrison, destroyed a German caïque and captured 75mm munitions. As always, food was distributed. Two days later, on 30 April, the Amorgos W/T station was also destroyed, and on Naxos, Doug Wright's and Duggie Pomford's Bren guns completely overwhelmed the 18-man German garrison.

Paros, 13 May 1944

Lassen's men then targeted the airfield at Paros. Three GSS under Sophoulis joined the eleven-man raid on the night of 13/14 May. After landing, the team headed to the highest part of the island at Koromboli, but Lassen and Nicholson quickly got lost; Lassen didn't know the island well enough. A local promised to help them, but the going was tough: the radio operator was struggling under the heavy weight of his batteries, so Lassen, typically, shouldered the burden himself. It must have been a sight, the tall Dane racing up the mountains, the ever-present Pipo at his side.

As the team lay up in the day, resting, Lassen – again, typically – was out scouting, again that night accompanied by two others. When machine gun fire was heard and flares lit up the surrounding landscape, it was clear they'd been rumbled.

Back up in the village, Nicholson's men divided into three teams, attacking a house where a German officer was billeted. After some grenading, he was captured. Stupidly, as the officer – a 'valuable prisoner' – was being escorted through the village, other SBS opened fire, badly wounding him in the neck. The clacking of his hob-nailed boots had made it sound like a German patrol. The officer later died after a grenade was mistakenly thrown in a second incident. When they finally met up with Lassen, he said he'd abandoned his own raid as the field was too well-guarded. That's what had caused all the commotion.

Lassen's attack interrupted work on the new German airfield and resulted in the death of six or seven Germans, but he was unhappy with the results: the islanders, he complained, had 'not been helpful', and 'three additional companies were expected' to strengthen the airfield defences.[36] Despite the loss of the German officer, other intelligence – on the location of fuel dumps, AA and a W/T station – had been gathered while another station, at Marpissa, had been destroyed.

In mid-May, a problem-ridden thirteen-man patrol hit Kos. As the patrol's boats were being lowered into the water not far from Antimacchia, they were fired upon and mortared. Two days later, they tried again, but the radios had become waterlogged and wouldn't work, and plus, without the rations, the team was useless.

Two weeks later, on 23/24 May, Samos was hit by a thirty-man GSS force under Siapkaras, accompanied a British SBS officer and a British W/T officer; they wiped out the German garrison at Marthocampos, where another Greek, Karademos, led the attack, killing the island's Governor.

Chios, May 1944

On the last day of May, a strong combined force hit Chios; forty-nine GSS, under the command of Lieutenant Colonel Andreas Kalinskis and accompanied by a British SBS officer, knocked out shipyards and destroyed caïques and the cables for the W/T station. They were badly let down by local *Andartes* who failed to appear with pack animals to carry their supplies: only two mules appeared, not nearly enough to carry their batteries, mortar shells and ammunition. One of these two fell down a steep slope, losing all their reserves of food.

A bombing raid on the 184-man German garrison, designed to cover the Greeks' approach, was called off at the last minute. Three Greek groups were assigned a range of tasks: hitting the boat yards, destroying the W/T station and its cables, covering the force and dealing with the garrison itself. All thirteen caïques were destroyed. Finally, the German garrisons reacted, not with an attack, only with 'ill-aimed machine gun fire'.[37]After the boats had been dynamited, more explosions were heard, destroying the cables and the cable-house.

In two months of the terror raids, Sutherland's men had achieved a huge tally: fifteen caïques sunk, damaged or captured; three wireless stations captured and eleven destroyed; 25 tons of medical and food supplies distributed. Over the extended period of incessant assault from the sea, the Germans were obliged to transfer another 4,000 men into the theatre. They used up reserves the Axis could ill afford, troops that could have gone to northern Europe, bracing itself for invasion.

In mid-May, another large attack was planned against Samos. A week earlier (around the 11th), Turnbull had been in Deremen and had discussed attacking the island grouping adjacent to the Turkish coast – Ikaria, Chios, Psara, Lesvos and, of course, Samos.

A large force – made up of thirty GSS soldiers, a British officer, a W/T operator and even an American journalist – landed in the bay of Marathokampos on the southern side of the island. The Governor was killed, two soldiers were taken prisoner and another was shot.

On 30/31 May, another strong group, this time around forty-five GSS in three caïques, headed for Chios under the command of Kalinskis. The force divided into three units under Dimitriadis, Vafelopoulos and Strathatos and set about their tasks, destroying caïques and, more importantly, the shipyards and underwater W/T cables. Kalinskis had wanted an RAF raid, but his request was turned down; the local hospital would have been endangered. A week later, on 5/6 June, a smaller group came back – Strathatos and nine GSS men – which was successful in destroying a German observation post.

In June, Tsigantes recognized the Squadron as a Regiment, the GSR, numbering 1,084 men divided into three sections, two led by Giorgio Roussos and Katseas.

Up to this point, the terror had been reserved for the Dodecanese and Cyclades. The focus now temporarily shifted north to the Sporades, and one of the first islands attacked was Pelagos, where Bob Bury's target was a monastery housing a small local garrison. After the guard – disguised as a monk – was killed, the rest of the garrison was taken care of.

Back in the Dodecanese, a small mixed group of fourteen or so SBS and *Ieros Lochos* from the 2nd Raiding Squad (renamed the 'Aegean Contingent') went into Kalymnos. Two team members – Ken Smith and Bill Mayall – were asked first to recce the harbour and around Vathi on the eastern side of Kalymnos, gathering intelligence. Running into a couple of Germans, they shot one, and the other fell over a cliff. During the 29 June raid, nine Germans were killed and a further ten wounded, including their commander. The raiding group was large, consisting of twenty-two GSR raiders and fourteen SBS led by Jimmy Lees, now a Captain. The SBS lost one dead, two wounded.

A few days later, a larger group (fourteen GSR and ten SBS) came back with support from the Greek Sacred Regiment under the command of Kasakopoulos. It turned into a disaster. They were heavily mortared and, while retreating, had to leave behind three of their wounded.

Nisiros

Some smaller recces were planned on Nisiros, garrisoned by fifty Germans and another forty Italians. A patrol led by a Greek officer, with three Greek ORs, was landed from caïque AH.6. After they'd gathered the information they needed, the raiders left with a dozen new volunteers for the GSS. The language of their reports was telling: 'German supplies are poor'; 'no thought is given to food for the local population'; enemy morale was only 'fair'. Of course, they also noted shipping and patrol patterns as well as reprisals taken, and identified collaborators. Retribution would come later.

Leros. The Portolago attack, 14 July 1944

Simi should have been the next target, but the threat posed by two destroyers in Leros' Portolago harbour meant that they had to be dealt with first. Help was sought from the Royal Marines Boom Patrol detachment, so successful on the Bordeaux river raids two years earlier. On Leros, they repeated that success, sinking two escort vessels and damaging both the *Turbine*, a converted Italian destroyer, and the other destroyer so badly that they both had to go back to Piraeus for repairs. The raiders left 'pandemonium behind them. Explosions, flares, Verey lights, guns – everything was going off.'[38]

Simi, 14 July 1944

The Simi attack, planned for July, would be on a full scale: 158 troops of the *Ieros Lochos* would be supported by Jock Lapraik with a further sixty-six SBS. Because of the scale, Turnbull decided to take part personally.

His force was split into three groups – his own 'Main Force' (with Ian Lapraik as 2i/c) and two others: a Northern group and a 'West Force'. Twenty-three SBS and ninety-one *Ieros Lochos* would attack Simi town, where the German garrison occupied the castle.

By 2230 on 13 July the force was assembled. Just before 0200, the main force landed in a protected bay, ferried in on ten MTBs and an assortment of schooners and caïques. What should have been straightforward went sour when two Greek officers drowned, being 'heavily weighted in full equipment'.[39] Simi was going to be a daylight operation 'because the enemy was now "standing to" during the night, and "stand[ing] down" by day.'[40] The SBS forsook its traditional cloak of darkness. All three groups were ready to move just as the enemy were changing guard.

At 0645, Northern group launched their attack on the city's port and fortress. It 'was the signal for simultaneous attacks by all groups'.[41] Two German small patrol boats (*Kriegsfischkutter*) chose the same moment to dock. They were immediately heavily engaged from the surrounding heights and captured.

In the night, West Force climbed the ridge overlooking the harbour and, in the morning, raked the Germans below with mortar and Bren gun fire. The Germans announced their surrender. The two boats that slipped out were sunk by five waiting LSF MTBs.

The castle garrison stubbornly held out in the mistaken belief that relief was near. One of the EMS petty officers was brought to the castle by an RN lieutenant to explain that the whole island was in British and Greek hands. The Germans played for time but were cut short. At 1500, they, too, surrendered: 'They came down the rocks with white flags and their hands up. We marched them from the castle to the town and while this was going on, six German planes came over and began dropping bombs.'[42]

It was none too soon, for presently a group of Messerschmitt fighters flew over, strafing. They were just ten minutes too late. 'I radioed them five hours ago ... that's what comes of being late', the captured German commander complained.[43]

Stewart Macbeth's South Force (twenty-two SBS and thirty-six *Ieros Lochos*) were to attack the Monastery of St Michele and the village of Panormitis. The telephone exchange and weapons were destroyed and twenty-eight prisoners taken. Captain Charles Clynes's West Force (twenty-one SBS and thirty-one *Ieros Lochos*) attacked the caïque boatyard at Simi harbour.

Most Allied casualties were incurred during the garrison assault: around eight were killed or wounded (including the two Greek officers). The Germans and Italians lost twenty-one killed and 151 captured.[44] They also lost an E-boat, two barges and nineteen caïques (amounting to 970 tons). Prisoners were taken back on the two captured EMS boats manned by their own crews. That evening, most of the SBS and *Ieros Lochos* left, although a small group stayed behind to continue demolition work and distribute food to the islanders. The next day, the Germans came back to bomb the island.

Despite the casualties, the Simi operation was a success. It was also a turning point, for it 'marked the end of SBS intervention in the Aegean.'[45] Thereafter, island raiding was to be the responsibility of the *Ieros Lochos*.They had worked closely with the SBS for long enough to pick up much of their training.

*   *   *

The results that all these operations achieved far outweighed the minimal manpower that had been committed to the effort:

> So effective were the SBS efforts that the Germans had to keep six divisions in the islands ... The claim that some 230 men could tie down six divisions (about 90,000 men) may seem an exaggeration ... but the Greek islands with their ragged coasts, rugged terrain and almost inaccessible retreats were highly favourable to guerrillas cooperating with people who possessed local knowledge.[46]

The SBS, now defined as a Regiment, was relocated north to Bari in southern Italy, better placed to operate in the Adriatic and in Yugoslavia along with No.2 Commando. The reputation of the SBS island raiders travelled far. In Parliament, Churchill found himself under a rather strange attack by a Conservative, Simon Wingfield-Digby, the honourable member for West Dorset, who asked, 'Is it true, Mr Prime Minister, that there is a body of men out in the Aegean islands, fighting under the Union flag, that are nothing short of being a band of murderous, renegade cut-throats?'

Churchill replied menacingly, 'If you do not take your seat and keep quiet, I will send you out to join them!'[47]

Chapter 11

Athens on a Bicycle: Liberation, October 1944

Τhe German evacuation of the Peloponnese, Greece's rugged southern underbelly, and the movement of their troops to the north represented, ironically, a potential danger to the Allies. They worried that the military vacuum that this created could provide an opportunity that the communists would exploit to seize power. On 9 October 1944, Churchill and Stalin had sat down together in Moscow. In an extraordinary meeting, the two decided the fate of Eastern Europe, apportioning Western and Soviet influence. Churchill had prepared his position, allocating what he foresaw as the ideal split: Romania 90 per cent Soviet, Hungary and Yugoslavia 50/50, Greece reserved for the West. Churchill had written 90 per cent on Greece, and Stalin 'reached over and marked the document with a big blue tick.'[1] Greece guarded British interests in the Mediterranean, most importantly Suez. That summer, Thasis Hadzis, General Secretary of the EAM, decried what he saw as the betrayal of the movement to British interests.

In September, plans were put together to seize an airfield on the Greek mainland, partly as a base for air strikes against retreating German forces, but also to launch an operation to liberate and feed the starving population of Greece; it would be known, fittingly, as Operation MANNA. As there wasn't significant German strength on the ground, the operation was to be 'throughout executed (and circumscribed) by a rigorous economy of means.'[2]

The British commander on the ground, Lieutenant General Ronald Scobie, was prepared for the worst, fully expecting a communist coup to be staged at any moment. His orders were clearly to 'crush ELAS', the communist guerrilla forces.[3] There might have been respect for their fighting capability, but ever since the more Stalinist elements had welcomed the Germans in 1940, there was also extreme distrust. On Greece's northern borders were Soviet troops in Bulgaria and a very organized communist guerrilla force in Tito's Yugoslavia. Middle East Command would also be later warned by SOE agent Paddy Leigh Fermor that ELAS 'was preparing to take control in Free Crete.'[4] Churchill had always worried that Greece would fall to the communists and wanted to make a show of force, but few troops were available for the task; only Special Forces. It made navigating the labyrinth of Greek politics extremely difficult, as 'British military authorities were in no doubt that ELAS was the most effective armed force in the country, if it could be harnessed to allied strategy.'[5]

Jellicoe would have to deal with the danger that ELAS (*Ellinikós Laïkós Apeleftherotikós Stratós*) represented. The group's acronym, ELAS, had been carefully chosen since it closely resembled *Hellas*, the Greek name for Greece. In the planning stages, it was clear that the issue of how to deal with the Security Battalions would arise in Patras. Jellicoe said he had 'received strict orders before leaving Italy on no account to intervene in Greek politics and to maintain a strict impartiality.'[6]

There was constant tension between the hard-line communist partisans and the 'moderate' Royalist group, EDES. ELAS was the military arm of EAM, the National Liberation Front resistance movement, which controlled most of the Greek countryside. Despite Churchill's agreement with Stalin, contact between communist guerrillas on the Albanian border and Greece was frequent. When the communists were asked to allow democratic institutions back into Greece, many in the EAM leadership, including its Secretary-General, Thanasis Hadzis, reacted bitterly. Many ELAS members appeared to have been completely indoctrinated. According to Alf Page:

> Our so-called allies, the partisans, had been fed a load of propaganda. They insisted that the uniforms and Sten guns we were dropping to them were provided by the Russians and the west had abandoned the Russians to go it alone. Each time we'd see them they would ask how come the British couldn't afford to clothe and arm them, why was it the struggling Soviets who dropped them all their supplies – by crikey they got that wrong![7]

The British could easily get caught in the middle of these bitter feuds.

There was reason to fear ELAS: further south, in Kalamata, Aris Veloukhiotis had committed horrendous atrocities against non-communist fighters. Around 1,500 citizens lost their lives in local actions, even if the extent of the massacres may not have been fully known at the time. In one incident, in the village of Kleitso in the fall of 1942, Veloukhiotis had ordered the execution of a number of family men accused of stealing wheat. The guard later admitted it was he who had been the thief. In his report, Jellicoe claimed that he 'did not discover till later, ELAS had carried out horrifying massacres at nearby Kalamata and Pyrgos, slaughtering Royalists, bourgeois, Security Battalion men, anyone who was obviously anti-communist.'[8] Maybe it was because Veloukhiotis, whose legal name was Athanasios Klaras, had himself been tortured by anti-communist police; 'the brutality he suffered appears to have rubbed off on him.'[9]

In a completely random encounter on the platform of Den Haag railway station, I once met a young Greek. I had been asking directions and got into a conversation with him. He talked about the terror of Kalamata and of the appalling choice his grandmother had faced when asked by one of Aris' men, 'Which child do you want to keep?' She had four children and, like Meryl Streep in *Sophie's Choice*, could not make the terrible decision. All four were killed. But Aris, one of the ELAS commanders who would later refuse to surrender their arms to the British, still has supporters. At the time, Jellicoe himself said, 'Despite his considerable personal brutality, I found Aris a man of some charm.' A horrifying thought. No wonder, when he entered Patras accompanied by Aris, that Jellicoe 'detected an air of apprehension.'[10]

The Germans, of course, played on these antipathies. They 'established' the anti-communist Security Battalions, later to inflict terror on the local population.[11] They also played ELAS and EDES off against one another in the heightened political climate of 1943, when the Allies, as part of the deception to cover the Sicily landings, had encouraged Greeks to think that the liberation of Greece was to happen first. It pushed ELAS and EAM into planning the state takeover.

Scobie divided his forces into two groups, Jellicoe's for the advance up the western edge of the Peloponnese, another under Lieutenant Colonel Ronnie Tod, called Foxforce, from No.9 Commando to tackle the east. Foxforce incorporated one of Jellicoe's other units, M detachment, the Greek Sacred Squadron and LRDG elements. Jellicoe, now also a Lieutenant Colonel, was ordered into the north-western corner of the Peloponnese to occupy the airfield at Araxos just below Patras. In his group codenamed, much to his dislike, Bucketforce, Jellicoe had an odd assortment of troops: Ian Patterson's L Detachment SBS, two companies of the 2nd Battalion, the 2908 Squadron of the RAF Regiment (OC 2908, SL Wynne), one patrol of the LRDG (Z.1) under John Olivey, with whom he'd fought on Leros, a half troop of 40 Royal Marine Commandos and other assorted elements including a COPP group (the Royal Navy's Combined Operations Assault Pilotage Party); a force totalling around 450. According to one of the LRDG, Alf Page, some members of S.1., recently in Albania, also joined. Subsequently, the taskforce was strengthened by two companies of 2nd Highland Light Infantry (HLI). For the operation, Jellicoe split his command into three, under Patterson, Wynne and Bimrose.

Patterson's group of fifty-eight men (mainly made up of L detachment) was parachuted just south of Araxos airfield on 23 September.[12] It was one of the few occasions on which the SBS parachuted into an operation. While the landing went smoothly, Jellicoe reported that stores were scattered and, when finally located, were found to have been

> comprehensively looted by the Greek villagers. Strips of the red supply parachutes, however, worn as kerchiefs had considerable and salutary propaganda value when worn in attending meeting with the local EAM authorities.[13]

Supplies and jeeps came in aboard six Dakotas, and eight Spitfires were later brought in at Vouprasion (as it appears in Jellicoe's report, today called Vouprasio, 3km to the south). An advance group had gone in earlier, commanded by Captain Charles Bimrose, to make sure that the field was clear and had with it an MO.4 specialist, Captain O'Donnel, who would supervise the airfield's repair. Bimrose duly reported the airfield slightly cratered but empty of enemy forces. Enemy troops were, however, reported at the port of Patras. As soon as Patterson's group landed, he sent a force to the port of Katakolo, 100km or so to the south, to see if it could be used for Wynne's seaborne elements.

Despite the political guidelines, Wynne was asked by an American officer attached to MO.4 to intervene in Pyrgos and agreed. His action brought the trials to a temporary end.

On 24 September Jellicoe flew in on a Dakota with Milner-Barry and Tryphon Kedros, responsible for the Balkan Counter Intelligence Section, escorted by eight Spitfires. Since Araxos was still being repaired, they landed on 'the low ground NW of Matoki' (today called Metochi, south-west of the current airfield at Araxos). Allied aircraft would only start using Araxos around 29 September.

Down the coast, to the south at the port of Katakolo, the remainder of Bucketforce had landed under Wynne's command with two LCTs by the following day. The port facilities had been considerably damaged, but local Pyrgos ELAS promised to help get them repaired. Jellicoe went to Katakolo to inspect the facilities and then on to Pyrgos, where he ran into the Security Battalion problem first hand. Two weeks earlier, 'summary trials and executions of the surviving members' had been carried out and were still going on.[14] The way back from Katakolo , however, was a nightmare. The heaviest rainstorm in 'nine years' was turning the track he was on in to a quagmire. Instead of the usual hour-and-a-half journey, it now dragged on for eight hours. He joked that the Vouprasio Spitfire LG had been turned 'into a seaplane base within three hours.'[15] He may have joked then; years later, he recalled 'the danger to which we were exposed as we drove in our jeeps along the then rather narrow and graveley [sic] roads between Katakolon and Araxos and Patras.'[16]

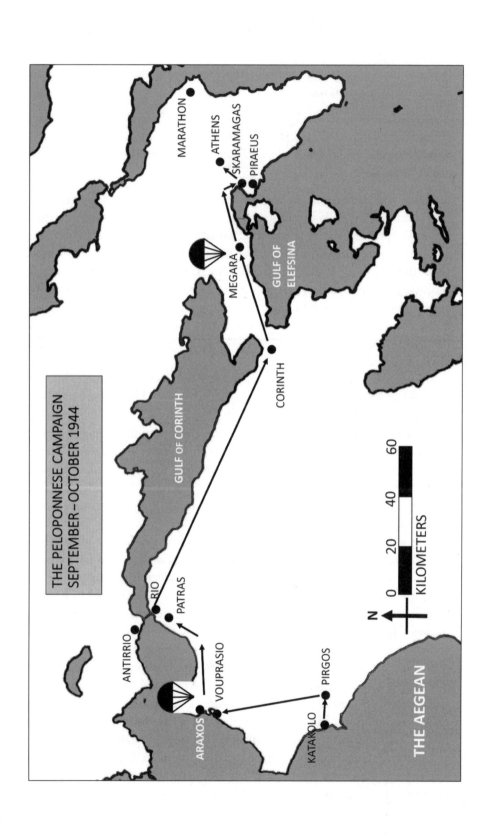

THE PELOPONNESE CAMPAIGN
SEPTEMBER–OCTOBER 1944

MARATHON

ATHENS
SKARAMAGAS
PIRAEUS

MEGARA

GULF OF ELEFSINA

CORINTH

GULF OF CORINTH

ANTIRRIO

RIO

PATRAS

VOUPRASIO

ARAXOS

KATAKOLO

PIRGOS

THE AEGEAN

N

0   20   40   60

KILOMETERS

Wynne managed to get his convoy through to Araxos by the morning of the 27th, even though at times his advance slowed to a crawl as the Greek population turned out en masse to welcome his troops. These were the first Allied troops on Greek soil since 1941. Alf Page remembered the welcome his LRDG patrol was given. He later recalled thinking, 'So much for this being a "Top Secret mission", as the whole town was there cheering us and throwing flowers.'[17]

The Germans in Araxos initially put up a fight but eventually retreated to the sea after they had mined the port. On 30 September, an E-boat and a minesweeper were spotted offshore, 'lying just outside the harbour.'[18] They were engaged with two RAF 6-pounders and two LRDG jeep-mounted machine guns.[19] Alf Page described how Olivey gave the Germans the impression that they were a larger force than the meagre 12-jeep group they actually were:

> We'd drive up the hills at night with our headlights on, turn them off and drive back down again, returning with lights ablaze to give Jerry the impression our numbers were greater than they were and encourage them to leave.[20]

In Patras, there was one battalion of German troops as well as two of Greek collaborators. Their 'activities were camouflaged under the bland title of Security Battalion.'[21] German strength was later estimated at 850–900 men, and that of the Security Battalions at 1,500–1,600. A direct assault by 350 – but more likely 60 – men was, in Jellicoe's words, going to be 'a tough nut to crack', especially since the Germans had good artillery, mortar and naval support.

Patterson first attempted to negotiate with the Germans. The SBS 'pride[d] themselves on always outwitting, rather than outfighting the enemy.' He went on ahead with the Swedish Red Cross representative, Herr Ornstroder, to try and broker a surrender agreement, telling the German 2i/c that his strong force would attack the next day if a surrender was not forthcoming by midday. The Red Cross added that the fate of trapped civilians had to be considered. The German commander, Kapitän zur See Magnus, buying some time, hesitated, saying that they needed permission from Athens.

Unknown to the Germans, they heavily outnumbered Patterson who, like Olivey's LRDG, would use mobility to give the impression of possessing a large force. At the same time, negotiations were opened with the Greeks – both with the Security Battalions and with ELAS. But now, with the airfield at Araxos stabilized, Jellicoe could turn his full attention to Patras. One of Patterson's officers, Captain Clarke, had already taken two patrols up the coast road to Patras to contact ELAS on 24 September. Patterson joined him the next day.

With the help of a local MO.4 officer, Captain Gray, Jellicoe started negotiations with the C.O. of the Security Battalion, Colonel Courkalakos. The Greek commander was suggesting that his men turn on the Germans to prevent damage to the harbour facilities at Patras. Courkalakos was 'fully cognisant of our numerical weakness, but almost embarrassingly anxious to extricate [himself] from an untenable and unenviable position.' [22]

Jellicoe was under increasing pressure: every day ELAS was being reinforced, and he felt the 'consequent danger of a general massacre in Patras, a town known to be strongly anti-ELAS.'[23] On 1 October, Jellicoe's final terms were handed to Courkalakos: he would 'accept no responsibility for the safety of any Security Battalion personnel who had not surrendered to the British forces by 0600 on 2 October. Any personnel, however, surrendering before that time were guaranteed safe custody and trial by the properly constituted Greek government.' Hopes were not high. Bets on the number that might surrender were made, and 'no estimate exceeded 300.'[24] However, by 2000 that evening SB forces started to surrender in droves, and by the 0600 deadline 1,600 had come over. Despite the agreement of the ELAS commander, Veloukhiotis, to withdraw his men so that incidents should be avoided, it had not been easy. Many SB officers initially refused to be disarmed, particularly those of the Psarras detachment, whose commander had been executed by ELAS. One of Olivey's LRDG Z.1 patrol, 'Ginger' van Rensberg, was shot in the stomach as the patrol was collecting weapons from some surrendering SB troops. Speed was needed to corral the new prisoners into a suitably protected enclosure and, because of the numbers involved, even Jellicoe was critical of the initial lack of appropriate administration.

After the Security Battalion's surrender, Patterson went into Patras with a mixed SBS/RAF group in five jeeps and two RAF Regiment armoured cars. It was only at the centre of town that the Germans engaged them. One L squadron member recalled, 'Patras became a bitter battle. We tried to penetrate the port and stop the demolitions. The Germans were being evacuated mainly by the port.'[25]

They had to withdraw after 'a considerable expenditure of ammunition.' With ELAS helping maintain fire from the eastern perimeter and Wynne's troops from the south, the Germans had been pinned down. Seven Germans were killed before they withdrew again.

During the night, Wynne's and Patterson's troops attacked 'Wireless Hill', the high ground overlooking the city. Against a well-dug in enemy, the RAF could supply two mortars, one a captured Italian model. After three hours of constant mortaring, the Germans withdrew. Left behind was an old 1908 75mm gun, and this was now seized and used against the German troops on one of the Siebel ferries in the port, initially, without great success, as the Germans had removed its sights.[26] At 0530 on 3 October, Patras was declared clear of Germans and Jellicoe, accompanied by Veloukhiotis, entered the city. One of the LRDG, Alf Page, said that he could 'remember the Earl, George Jellicoe from the SBS, and John Olivey going into the town and telling the German commander that if they didn't shove off we'd flatten the town, so the Jerries left.'[27] The fight had actually been considerably less cut-and-dried.

A tight curfew was put in place. Panayiotis Kanellopoulos, the representative of Papandreou's government, had arrived from Cairo to help. He was born in Patras and would play a significant role in halting the bloodshed.

On 4 October, Jellicoe received new orders requiring him to recce northwards towards the Corinth canal. He could not do so easily for he still had to protect civilians in Patras against ongoing communist reprisals. In his post-action report, he made clear how challenging this had been: 'The centre of military gravity immediately shifted from harassing Germans to the more difficult task of preventing civil disorder in a large Greek town freed after four years of German occupation.'[28]

Olivey advanced with Z.1, encountering only light resistance from the Germans, who retreated across the canal by boat. The only casualty in the patrol was when one of the jeeps hit a mine. Corporal Tighe, one of the two RAOC fitters, initially seemed to be unscathed but died a little later – 'with not a mark on him, it was very sad.'[29] By the small town of Corinth, the main bridge over the canal had already been blown. Monty Woodhouse, who had met up with Jellicoe in Patras, explained:

[Jellicoe's] task was to pursue and if possible cut off the retreating Germans, which was not easy because they were in a hurry and were blowing up behind them every bridge which we had not blown up in front of them.[30]

Back in Patras, however, the situation was not stable. Despite assurances to the contrary, EAM political police were making arrests. The 'rumours of lootings and forcible billeting of ELAS forces' persuaded Jellicoe to impose a curfew, restoring some semblance of order.[31] He then put Patras under the direct control of Major Carson of the 2 HLI who arrived with two patrols.

Jellicoe used both threat and diplomacy. Through an SOE agent he let Aris know that should any of the Security Battalion troops accused of having worked with the Germans be harmed once the Germans had gone, he would face British retribution.

It was tricky, because there were many more Germans there than us and there were also a number of anti-communist Greek security battalions, who weren't really pro-German but were definitely anti-communist.[32]

Jellicoe worked his diplomatic skills to the maximum. He brought the partisan leader, Veloukhiotis, together with Kanellopoulos in a ceremony at the town's cathedral on 7 October, the day earmarked to commemorate the liberation of the city. He'd earlier met with Aris, and it was clear that, even though the latter was not at all keen on participating, Jellicoe managed to persuade him by a mixture of threats and appeals to his vanity. He told Aris that the prisoners that he held – despite their being collaborators – should be considered 'under Crown Protection'.

In particular, Jellicoe made the tough guerrilla leader feel important, arranging a dinner in his honour:

A piper from the Highland Light Infantry was called to march round the table, playing Scottish tunes on his bagpipe. Velouchiotis, sitting next to me was perplexed. He turned anxiously and asked who was this kilted piper, and what on earth was the meaning of this display? I explained that he and his fellow men were being honoured, in the Scottish tradition, as very important persons. The hardened guerrilla was pleased![33]

The change of attitude by the SB was quickly evident:

Everything became very matey. Batmen spread a white tablecloth and we all joined in a lavish picnic with the senior officers of the Greeks … A promise had been made that the Security Battalion would be under our protection and we were ready to ensure that the ELAS guerrillas would not be allowed to murder them.[34]

In 2007, after Jellicoe's memorial service, there was a dinner at the British Embassy in Athens and that meeting came up in conversation. An old man stood up slowly: George Papoulios had been the Greek Ambassador in London and became a great friend and admirer of my father. He made it quite clear that Jellicoe's actions had saved a considerable number of lives. The British presence clearly acted to calm the situation, and it was conservatively estimated that 'between 1,500 and 2,000 people were saved' because of the restraint that it exercised.[35] To Jellicoe's knowledge, 'only one execution took place during the first week in Patras.'[36]

Members of the Security Battalions had been treated with extreme severity in the Peloponnese. What happened in Tripolis is illustrative. As the Wehrmacht's retreat created a vacuum, the Security Battalions took over, and the local commander, Colonel Papadogonas, resorted to extreme terror on the local population when talks with ELAS broke down. Eventually, he and his men surrendered to the British. All too often, locals exacted a terrible vengeance: in Kalamata, the former Governor of Messinia and officials were set upon by the crowds. Prisoners were beaten to death, others hanged from lamp-posts.

Jellicoe's actions in keeping a tight rein on ELAS were criticized by some senior British officers, and the comments made by the overall ELAS commander, General Sarafis, were sent on to him. It was obvious that Jellicoe found himself in an extremely uncomfortable position. However, Brigadier Davy, Commander of Land Forces Adriatic (LFA), supported him, as did General Scobie, the overall commander: 'Jellicoe already deals with local ELAS command and is most tactful … Agree with you that Jellicoe is indeed in a difficult position.'

He had a point. Jellicoe had actually kept the police under his own direct control. He'd even tightened the curfew when he found out that ELAS was shifting non-communists north while bringing in additional pro-ELAS forces to overwhelm the demonstrations. ELAS would turn on the British once Greece was liberated; EDES did not.

Official support was underlined by announcing Jellicoe's promotion to Colonel and his assumption of the rather pompous title 'Military Governor of North West Peloponnese' on 9 October. He later joked that he thought it 'a rather splendid title for a young man of twenty-six.' [37] His load was slightly lightened by being allowed to drop his civilian protection duties, handing these over to Kanellopoulos and the British Military Mission Commander, Colonel Chris 'Monty' Woodhouse.

The force moved further east and crossed over the canal just north of Corinth, on 7 October. John House recalled making the crossing 'on a sunken liner that was lying on its side and had been made into a rough road.'[38] After evacuating Patras on 3 October, the Germans had fallen back to the twin fortresses of Rio and Antirro, guarding the gateway to the Gulf of Corinth. Patterson's force chased the retreating German convoy along the coastal roads on the Gulf, covering them with harassing fire from their captured 75mm gun. The Germans did not know the origin of the fire and were 'periodically' putting up heavy AA fire. In his typical jaunty style, Jellicoe termed it 'a novel and exhilarating pursuit' which he was 'lucky enough to witness.'[39]

Arriving on the same day as his appointment, Bucketforce were too late to be able to dismantle the enemy's demolitions. While EDES guerrillas harassed the retreating Germans, ELAS were 'noticeably absent from these operations although they could very well have interrupted the retreating columns.' It turned out that the Germans had armed them 'in return for unmolested passage'.[40] After Jellicoe had been in Patras and seen how ELAS had behaved, he was quite sarcastic:

> The Germans had, as far as we discovered, met with negligible resistance as they drew in their outlying garrisons into Patras, and the ELAS 'investment' of the town was a polite fiction and consisted of small picquets on the main roads. ELAS activities, moreover, during the German evacuation of Patras were confined entirely to skirmishing on the last day. They incurred, I think, two casualties in all during the siege.[41]

Later, at Megara, Jellicoe found that ELAS there had acted in the same way:

> With German forces in the vicinity ... ELAS forces were noticeably inconspicuous but they began to filter in as the Germans withdrew and 24 hours after the evacuation of the town, it would be crammed with victorious though unbattle-scarred ELAS troops.[42]

His small force's advance was 'held up by a strong German flank guard' near the town.[43] Even so, Jellicoe had nothing but praise for the capability of ELAS troops: 'Their bearing, discipline and organization were remarkably good for guerrilla troops, and they had fought hard and savagely against Security Battalions in the Peloponnese.'[44]

Aris was guilty of doing just what he had accused Police Battalions in Patras of – working with the Germans. It also gave the Germans time to destroy the pontoons over the canal. Patterson got the troopers of L Detachment across using an old ferry, while Keith Balsillie took a caïque over to Piraeus, though he had too few troops to stop more Germans fleeing north.

Progress along the Gulf to Corinth was slow, hampered by the intense demolition work of a small, but determined German rearguard of fifty or so men. The demolition work on the canal itself could not be prevented. SBS troops entered Corinth on 7 October where 240 SB troops were handed over by ELAS. Wynne took another small group of 2908 RAF Squadron troops to Sparta to round up SB elements in Mistra. Another patrol under Captain Balsillie went forward and was ferried over the Gulf of Elefsina to Skaramagas.

Jellicoe handed over command of Bucketforce on 10 October before he headed to Megara, west of Athens. There, on 12 October, his advance group was reinforced by a company of the 4th Independent Parachute Brigade. Marsland Gander, the *Daily Telegraph* correspondent, had been with the paratroops as they prepared. He was able to report that the drop on to the flat plain under the lee of the high mountains was bad, accompanied by 'light shelling' of the drop zone. The 25-knot wind was gusting up to 40 knots and causing heavy casualties as parachutists were dragged off the airfield and on to the German-laid minefields. Two died and a number were badly injured. The decision for the drop to go ahead was a difficult one. It had been hoped glider-borne troops could be used, but the field had been too badly damaged: 'I think it was the correct decision because it was so urgent to get troops in to Athens', Jellicoe later said.[45]

If that wasn't enough, then Jellicoe faced what he described as 'the worst moment of his entire war'. One of the young paratroopers, about 400 yards away, was being dragged along the ground, trapped in his chute harness. Jellicoe thought that he could drive his jeep across and rescue the young man, halting his uncontrolled slide by running over his chute cords. Others were doing this; in fact, 'as the men landed, the Greeks – men, women and children – rushed to pull down the chutes.'[46] Alf Page remembered the drop:

> The 4th Para Battalion was to be flown in to reinforce us but there was a gale forecast and they were told not to make the jump, but given the bravado of the paras, they decided to jump anyway, with near disastrous results ... We rushed to the landing zone and spent half our time running over parachutes to collapse them before they re-inflated and dragged the injured or stunned paras to their death.[47]

John House said that the casualties were 'lined up on a path and during the night women came from far and wide and took care of them.'[48] But Jellicoe had decided that he could not place *his own* life on the line to rescue this particular paratrooper: 'If he drove himself over a mine, the mission would be in chaos. He let the soldier die.'[49] Monty Woodhouse remembered the drop but, erroneously I think, added that 'many of them fell into the sea, and some were carried under by their parachutes and drowned.'[50] I could find no evidence to support this claim.

My father never spoke to me personally about the tragedy or the terrible choice that he had to make. He talked about it to my brother Johnny, instead. And the circumstances in which they had that conversation reveal the man Jellicoe was. Johnny had been leading a ski-party and had been involved in an avalanche. One person had been killed. He was totally devastated and took much of the responsibility of that death on his own shoulders. Jellicoe realized that he could only pass on some learning in a real way if he revealed one of his own dark secrets. It helped Johnny overcome his demons.

With the arrival of the 4th Parachute Brigade, Jellicoe was put under the command of Lieutenant Colonel Coxon, who assumed control of all British forces north of Corinth.

When Jellicoe heard reports from Balsillie saying that he had not encountered Germans and had heard that they were pulling out of Athens, Coxon ordered Jellicoe into the city. Eleven of Patterson's men were temporarily put under Frank Macaskie's command to go ahead immediately. They arrived in Athens early on the morning of 12 October after disembarking at Skaramagas. Accompanied by Milner-Barry and the *New York Times* journalist Shan Sedgwick, who could help interpret, Jellicoe also arrived at Skaramagas.

The story goes that Jellicoe liberated Athens on a bicycle. Or that's what he would have had us believe. It sounded, and still sounds, very romantic. In fact, the march on Athens proved to be tortuous and deadly. His task, as in the Peloponnese, was to establish an Allied power structure in Athens before ELAS partisans could get a grip and establish a Soviet-style regime. ELAS did 'not know that Stalin, in his ruthless deal with Churchill, had sold them out in exchange for a freer hand further north.'[51] Jellicoe's SBS had to make the German retreat – which was in full swing – as difficult as possible. Already, on 2 October, a train had left Athens 'with prominent Greek collaborators, Italian Fascists and German civilians on board'. Among the passengers was the ex-Premier Logothetopoulos, whose wife was German.[52]

The threat from ELAS partisans who had already stopped fighting Germans was real. Jellicoe needed to get to Athens as fast as possible. Even though it was agreed that ELAS could not enter Athens until there was a legitimate government in place, they might just as easily have turned their guns on their non-Communist fellow countrymen in preparation for an attempted coup.

Aged twenty-six, Jellicoe was now made an acting Brigadier. John House's mother described what happened:

[Jellicoe] needed some additions to add on to his jacket to make himself look more impressive and official i.e. some red tabs to his collar. John took the job to his landlady of the previous night and explained (she could speak some English) what needed to be done. She could do it O.K. but had some difficulty finding some red material. She enlisted the help of her neighbours. How many shades of red are there? … Finally it was done and they made a very good job of it. John paid them the equivalent of ten shillings. Such excitement. It was the first money they had seen in years.[53]

Suitably fitted out, the two set off in a caïque with some guards. They got over to Skaramagas after dark on 12 October and were met by Ian Patterson roughly 10 miles south-west of the city. Jellicoe and he decided to make the last stretch to Athens on two bicycles which they had taken after the engagement with the German rearguard at Megara. Philip Warner said of the occasion, 'The liberation of the centre of ancient democracy by two men riding that most democratic of conveyances, the bicycle, was very appropriate.'[54]

All along the road they were met with a rapturous welcome from Athenians. Gander described it as 'the volcanic outbursts of joy and relief far surpassing' anything he had witnessed in France and Italy.[55] The shouts of *'Phetasane I Angli'* (The English are coming) could be heard all along the route.

Following behind them a few hours later in a column of jeeps and armoured cars were fifty-five SBS troopers from L Detachment. The next morning, Friday, 13 October, they arrived in the city. Alf Page recalled, 'They threw flowers and kisses on us and showered us with German occupation money, some of which I still have today.'[56]

Another L detachment member, R.A.L. Summers, said that an old woman shouted at him as they were being welcomed, 'You must take the flowers; they are all we have to give.'[57] The very next day, GSS troops landed in Piraeus. Unfortunately, as the sizeable fleet of one hundred or so small vessels approached land, a minesweeper and a number of caïques were lost to mines. The rest made it through in the mist covering the harbour. One of the newly arrived was a Greek naval Lieutenant, André Londos, one moment the commander of all the Greek vessels in the armada, the next a worried but excited father looking to catch a glimpse of his children on the quayside.

Jellicoe and Patterson went straight to the Hotel Grande Bretagne and parked their bicycles: 'a comic element to Jellicoe's arrival in the historic city; a touch of English eccentricity.'[58] There they met an SOE agent, Lieutenant Colonel Frank Macaskie, who had been hiding with Archbishop Damaskinos. It was Damaskinos who told Jellicoe that the German commander had disobeyed orders to blow the dam at Marathon. A photo exists of Jellicoe together with Damaskinos, Macaskie and Shan Sedgewick, the *New York Times* journalist.[59]

Macaskie had earlier gone over to Damaskinos' house dressed as a civilian and been asked by the 'teasing' archbishop: 'Where's your uniform?' When he pointed to his case he was told to put it on, and when he'd done so the two of them went out. There were cries of 'The Englishman!' and then he 'smiles back at them with affection. With the boundless affection he has for Greece.'[60] The atmosphere was electric. They had seen the swastika taken down and the Greek flag raised again on the Acropolis. 'The people are mad with joy,' as Tsatsos described it. 'They kiss each other. They weep. They wait for the English to come.'[61]

Macaskie had been highly nervous that ELAS would seize the initiative in Athens. One of the British Liaison Officers attached to ELAS, Nick Hammond, had been sending back disturbing reports that ELAS planned to take reprisals. But the ELAS troops that remained in Athens were, according to Monty Woodhouse, 'in handfuls rather than hundreds. Most of them belonged to the reserve ELAS, which was little trained and poorly armed.'[62]

It was at this point that Jellicoe put on his red tabs. Harder points out that he was first promoted to 'local acting colonel' but that

> this was deemed insufficiently senior, so the colourful Brigadier Joseph Patrick O'Brien-Twohig, commander of 183 Infantry Brigade (Adriatic Brigade), promoted Jellicoe on the spot to acting brigadier, and gave him the red collar patch from his own uniform so that he could act with the requisite authority. Milner-Barry was promoted to colonel in the same manner.[63]

Later that evening, Jellicoe went to see the new commander, the former commander of Greek forces in Attica, the towering Major General Panayiotis Spiliatopoulos, and was photographed standing with him on the steps of Athens Cathedral. The General was strongly anti-communist, to the point of being 'regarded by ELAS as a collaborator', but when people found out who the young British soldier was, shouts of 'Yellicoe! Yellicoe!' could be heard.[64] He had been on the balcony early in the morning of the 14th along with Frank Macaskie, and 'for the rest of the day, Jellicoe, Milner-Barry and Patterson were repeatedly called back out ... to wave to the crowd and make impromptu speeches in a mixture of English and Greek.'[65]

On 15 October Athens was once again a free city. After the clashes of the previous weeks, it was now the time for 'parties and politics.'[66]

It was also the right moment for the Greek government to return. On 17 October, the government-in-exile sailed into the port of Piraeus aboard the famous armoured cruiser, the fleet's flagship, *Georgios Averof*, having left Taranto two days earlier under a Canadian flag to rendezvous in the Bay of Poros. It was good timing for the new government, with Prime Minister George Papandreou at its head, to enter Athens on Wednesday, 18 October (Tuesday, apparently, was considered by the Greeks as a day of ill omen and to be avoided at all costs). The crowd roared in jubilation as troops of the *Ieros Lochos* marched in front of the hotel. The sight of their own countrymen was an electrifying boost to the flagging morale of the citizens who had endured years of deprivation. *Ieros Lochos* Force C commander, Lieutenant Colonel Messinopoulos, laid a wreath on the tomb of the Unknown Soldier, and his troops barracked in the buildings of what is now the Attica department store.

Lorna Almonds recounts a moment, many years after the war, when Jellicoe was in the back of a taxi in Athens in animated conversation with the Canadian CEO of Tate & Lyle, Neil Shaw, and there was a sudden exclamation from the cab driver: 'Yellicoe!' Jellicoe immediately knew who it was and jumped out of the taxi, hugging the man he called 'Zacharias.' They knew each other from the war. The friendships made in those days die hard.

Jellicoe never talked about his war years in a way that would either reveal his true feelings of loss or would inflate his ego. In William Waldegrave's words, 'He wrapped everything in a fog of extreme self-deprecation.'[67]

There was a service led by Damaskinos at the cathedral, where a Te Deum was sung. My father remembered 'with great clarity' the moment when 'the Primate of Greece sprinkled a shower of rose petals on the bowed heads of three or four of us young British officers.'[68] Flowers and garlands were showered on the British troops with great cries of *Zita Hellas! Zite Anglia!* (Long Live Greece! Long Live England!).

That night, the SBS slept in splendid luxury at the Grande Bretagne. They were joined by local Greeks for a massive celebration. Macaskie came in carrying armfuls of rations. Mary Henderson described him straining under the weight of 'tins of bully beef, which to us were like caviar, butter, marmalade, jams, biscuits, Lea & Perrins sauce.'[69] It felt like Christmas had come early. At the party was Hermione Ranfurly, who got talking to a journalist (probably the *New York Times* man Shan Sedgwick), who was giving her the 'lay of the land', mentioning that Jellicoe was now feted in Athens and that the Greeks 'clap whenever they see him.'[70]

At the party, Jellicoe met Mary Henderson for the first time, or, as she was known then, Mary Cawadias, when he saw her in deep conversation with Andy Lassen. The Dane had just arrived from Piraeus and had his notebook out. Apparently, he was taking down details of collaborators as she spoke. In the midst of the celebrations, Jellicoe wondered if the Dane was putting together an execution list. Lassen might also have had his eye on a 'buxom girl with a lustrous mop of chestnut hair, curved, new-moon eyebrows, a full and pouting mouth and large, innocent blue eyes'. Henderson warned that she had been an inmate of the Haidari concentration camp and that she was probably trying to get close to Jellicoe. Cawadias had been imprisoned by the SS and sentenced to death. Her father had been the King's physician and she had received her medical education in London so was suspected by the Germans of British sympathies. Cawadias said that the girl had apparently offered to '"serve" the commander of the SS camp.'[71] Henderson didn't elaborate on what happened to her.

Jellicoe intended leaving Athens for Thebes early the next morning and he asked Cawadias for her help as an interpreter. She immediately accepted and joined the SBS on the next stage north. Cawadias would later marry an Englishman, Sir Nicholas 'Nico' Henderson, and return with him to Athens as the wife of Her Majesty's Ambassador to Greece.

Chapter 12

The Final Act: Thessaloniki

Cawadias offered her help as a guide as well as interpreter, which Jellicoe accepted, and on 17 October 1944, the 950-strong renamed 'Pormforce' set off again. Behind the main force, fifty SBS followed 'in 15 jeeps and four trucks'.[1] The going was slow: every bridge that could be blown had been. In every village, the men were feted, although poverty was everywhere. None of the villages had electricity and few had running water.

Jellicoe met with Major General Sarafis, the ELAS commander, at their GHQ offices on 23 October. There he was told by Jellicoe that the British intention was to cut the Germans off 'on the Florina road'. Sarafis was unconvinced and told hm that he believed 'his small detatchment was not strong enough to cut off the German withdrawal.'[2] Jellicoe demurred and asked for ELAS support in repairing bridges. An ELAS officer, Captain Venetsanopoulos, was assigned to him as liaison.

After Larissa, the group crossed 'the plain of Thessaly westwards towards Kalambaka, and there turned north past the Meteora monasteries of Grevana … We succeeded in overtaking the Germans at Kozani.'

It was hoped that the German forces (around 3,500-strong) that had been retreating north from the Trikala-Metsovo area could be blocked south-east of Kozani. Sarafis asked Jellicoe to secure the bridge but in his memoirs wrote that he stopped his group in Grevena (reached on the 25th) for 48 hours, rather than move towards Servia just south of the Haliacmon bridge.

On the 28th there was some short but intense fighting at Kozani.[3] Patterson led a full-frontal assault on the town, partly defended by SB units, while Coxon skirted around, taking other troops on to Florina. Patterson noted the 'bad marksmanship of the enemy', but the toll was heavy: fifteen men were lost.[4] In pouring rain, the SBS moved forward to the town's outskirts but were pinned down by heavy enemy fire for two hours. The Germans successfully withdrew, but the SB was heavily mauled by ELAS troops, 'who spent less ammunition attacking Germans than they did against Greek collaborators and against Royalists.'[5] An EAM report not only downplayed the Allied role, it actually reported that 'the British did not fire a single shot against the Germans who were pulling out.'[6] Sarafis himself said that the pursuit wasn't continued by the British 'because of bad weather'.[7]

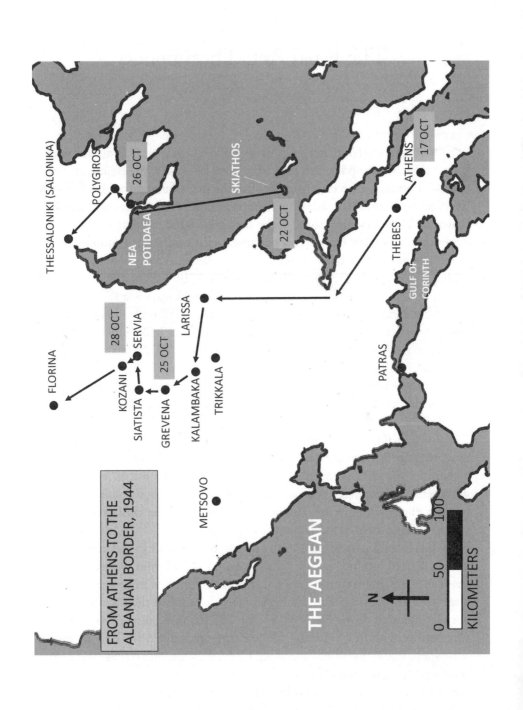

FROM ATHENS TO THE ALBANIAN BORDER, 1944

THESSALONIKI (SALONIKA)

POLYGIROS

26 OCT

NEA POTIDAEA

SKIATHOS

22 OCT

17 OCT

ATHENS

THEBES

GULF OF CORINTH

PATRAS

LARISSA

28 OCT

SERVIA

FLORINA

KOZANI

25 OCT

SIATISTA

GREVENA

KALAMBAKA

TRIKKALA

METSOVO

THE AEGEAN

N

0   50   100

KILOMETERS

It was pretty much the other way around, although Sarafis seemed more concerned about continuing the chase into Yugoslavia, which the British didn't want. On 28 October, at a meeting with Scobie, he was told to halt his troops and not to cross the Albanian, Yugoslav or Bulgarian borders.

North of Kozani, they went on to Florina, which was captured by John Olivey's LRDG. A German column was caught with 'devastating results'.[8]

The small railway town, immediately to the west of Thessaloniki, was where they stayed for two weeks after Jellicoe received a signal 'instructing us not to go into Yugoslavia or Albania, presumably as a result of a pact with the Russians.'[9] Milner-Barry did, however, cross over and met up with David Sutherland's force. The Greek campaign of liberation was, effectively, over. Years later, on one of his many post-war trips to Athens, Jellicoe spoke about the deep meaning these years still held for him. I always felt these sentiments, so eloquently expressed then, to almost be a part of my father's DNA. He had seen too much death:

> It is indeed my hope that on this day when we commemorate and celebrate the liberation of a city which means so much to all of us – it is my hope that we will dedicate ourselves afresh to doing all we can, in however small a way, to make this Europe and this world of ours a safer, happier and better place.[10]

When Lassen arrived, the Germans weren't immediately to be found. ELAS had been left in charge. The Germans were busy blowing up ammo and petrol dumps in their retreat. Even though the German garrison numbered close to 300, Lassen went in and decimated them: enemy dead numbered sixty; the SBS lost not a single man. Some questioned Lassen's brutality, but it had worked.

Lassen's orders were to recce north up to Thessaloniki while leaving half his force at Skiathos.[11] Newly promoted Major, he followed Jellicoe's departure from Athens on 22 October.

His orders were not to enter the city but to secure a small airfield nearby at Megalo Mikra. He decided that he would, instead, take the city. He left behind a sizeable number of men: mostly camp followers, cooks and the like. That done, he embarked 'Scrumforce', forty men and his beloved jeep, on one of two caïques, one commanded by a Royal Marine, Lieutenant Alec McCleod, the other by Lieutenant Martin Solomon, 'a man who would play a key role in the coming action, which at times would do justice to a Hollywood script.'[12]

Solomon was 'short, chubby and forever cheerful'. He and Andy had hit it off, and Solomon was 'a particularly close friend'.[13] For a Cambridge-educated actor's agent, he was no mean soldier: he had won the DSC at

Dunkirk and a bar as an MTB commander in the Mediterranean, two years later. He is reputed to have commanded one of the last MTBs out of Dunkirk on which he carried a French General, who awarded him the Croix de Guerre en route to Harwich.[14]

As they rounded the island of Skiathos, the lonely lament of bagpipes could be heard drifting across the waters. It was one of Lassen's camp followers sending the small band on its way. After four days at sea in waters that were some of the most heavily mined in the Mediterranean, Lassen's men made land at Nea Potidaea on 26 October, 60km south-south-east of the city.

Here, Lassen, Sammy Trafford, Martin Solomon and Jason Mavrikis ('more or less permanently' transferred to the SBS as his translator) set off in Lassen's jeep for an 80-mile recce.[15] The war correspondent, Richard Cappell, talked of the audacity of it: Lassen 'had sailed up when the Germans had no notion of any British within a hundred miles.'[16] Indeed, even local Greeks mistook them for Germans.

That night, after they'd stopped around 2100 for a rest by a forest from which German voices could be heard, they crept silently forward and took three prisoners for interrogation at Potidaea. What they learned was disturbing: the Germans were busy levelling the city's infrastructure, destroying anything of value. Two ships had been sunk in the harbour entrance, other smaller ones right beside the quays to make unloading hazardous if not impossible, while the sea wall was having holes blasted in it – fifteen so far. The Germans had two tanks, six SP guns and were around battalion-strength.

Lassen felt there was no time to lose. He knew that a 9,000-strong force was on its way but sent a cable saying, 'If you do not get here fast we intend to take Salonika ourselves.'

The following day, Lassen's force moved closer aboard caïques. At the same time, Lassen and Mavrikis, disguised as chicken-sellers, entered the city to recce on the ground. They roamed freely, gathering information and questioning locals when they could. It became clear that the German force had been considerably depleted through desertions and that the eastern part of the city was fairly clear of enemy. It was obvious from their actions that the Germans wanted to get out and save their skins: in one instance, locals had been offered the safety of the power station in exchange for money. Lassen contributed some of his gold sovereigns on the spot, although the German demolition team was bargained down from £100 to £15.

Lassen immediately sought aid from ELAS at Polygiros but found their commander, Colonel Papathanasion, completely unhelpful. At this stage of the fighting they were more prepared to let someone else do the work: the guerrillas 'were concerned only with their own manor', while national forces 'saw the war as a whole.'[17] Nevertheless, Lassen gave him a 'stiff tongue-lashing', and the ELAS were 'shamed by his words and stung into action.'[18] As Lassen talked, Mavrikis answered their questions as to why Lassen was so interested in information on a certain area around the port of Kavala. He lied, saying, 'A very large Allied convoy with an armada of warships and at least three Army divisions has just set sail.'[19]

He even elaborated on the lie, knowing that the information would leak, and said that the force consisted of the 34th and 57th Infantry divisions, as well as the 5th Airborne Division. The planted information was aimed just as much at the Russians as the Germans. Stalin needed to be discouraged from any designs on Greece.

Now, Lassen started putting his bluff into place. His jeep was used to transport a PIAT to various parts of the city and launch grenades 'in a high arc' to look like artillery shelling. Through the Swiss Red Cross, an ultimatum was issued to the German commander: evacuate Thessaloniki immediately or face annihilation. When the latter came back with a request for 48 hours' delay, Lassen doubled down: evacuate now or the threat would be carried out.

That evening, Solomon and M Detachment's 2i/c, the 6' 3" Captain Jim Henshaw, set off in Andy's jeep to ambush a supply truck and use its driver to carry a message demanding the surrender of a coastal gun emplacement that 'blocked their advance'.[20] They took some prisoners but suddenly found themselves confronted by heavy German forces. Solomon sensibly waited overnight before returning to reclaim Andy's jeep.

Now Lassen decided that action was required. He needed to create the impression that a large Allied force was fighting its way through the city towards the Germans. He needed transport for his troops and found the perfect mode: four bright-red fire engines. In the front one rode Sammy Trafford, 'Bren gun in one hand and an improvised bridle in the other, looking like a Hollywood Injun chief leading his braves into battle.'[21]

As they reached the main square, the local EAM leadership were busier making speeches of self-congratulation than thinking of their city. While the ELAS guerrillas peeled off, Lassen's men continued. From the docks came the sound of explosions; it was clear that the Germans were carrying on the destruction of the harbour facilities. Lassen gave the order that the fire engines should create as much noise, accompanied by as much firing as possible. At one point they came across a clearly-guarded *Triebstofflager*, a fuel dump, which they hit from two sides with massive fire. In minutes, more than sixty Germans were dead or wounded. The next morning, the Germans started to evacuate. Lassen turned to Solomon and said, 'England's prestige has been saved. Now we can have a bit of a fling.'[22]

Solomon said that he might 'never again have so much power or enjoy anything so much. Dictators for a week.'[23] With Thessaloniki under his control, Lassen sent Jellicoe a short signal: 'I have the honour to report that I am in Salonika.' The story has it that while in Thessaloniki, Lassen insisted on driving his beloved jeep into the hotel where he was billeted and even (it is alleged) had it put into one of the freight elevators for safe-keeping.

Jellicoe, sensing that he needed to play a careful game with a subordinate who had actually acted against orders, sent a careful response to Lassen – 'Give your estimated time of arrival Athens' – as though he was being recalled for reprimand.[24] Lassen had 'turned a reconnaissance of islands into an exploit that could be done justice only by Hollywood ... the capture of the great seaport of Salonika on four fire-engines.'[25]

There had been some tension between the two; 'his otherwise accommodating boss [Jellicoe] threatened to demote him unless he did as he was told.'[26] Lassen had been complaining about the number of seaborne operations.

Jellicoe briefly joined up with Lassen in Thessaloniki after Florina and then went back to Athens. Once back in the capital, he spent some time getting rid of the carefully tailored red brigadier tabs, 'cursing the little stitches that had been used to sew them on'.[27]

Nine days later, the main force of 9,000 troops arrived. Had it not been for Jellicoe's band, it is not entirely impossible that ELAS might have replaced the Germans in Athens. It would have had incalculable consequences for the history of post-war Greece.

George Theotakis, the writer, worried that 'it only needs a match for Athens to catch fire like a tank of petrol.'[28] Peace didn't last long at all; just a couple of weeks. On 3 December, demonstrations took place on Syntagma Square after EAM had walked out of parliament. The police opened fire, and after ten demonstrators were shot, fighting broke out between ELAS and the British. Scobie was ordered 'to act as if you were in a conquered city where a local rebellion is in progress.'[29] British 25-pounder field guns were brought into action against the communists in Kaisariani, while overhead, the RAF flew strafing missions over ELAS positions. The conflict would continue for another four years till 1949; this was the *Dekemvriana*, in which ELAS and the Sacred Band fought each other. With considerable foresight, Papandreou had lobbied to keep the Sacred Band and the 3rd Greek Rimini Mountain Brigade from disbanding to support his fight against EAM and ELAS.

Chapter 13

War's End

Jellicoe's war in Greece was now over. In December 1944 he handed over command of the SBS to 24-year old David Sutherland, announcing, completely unexpectedly, that he was going to attend a Staff College course at the Middle East Staff College in Haifa from January. He was having breakfast with Milner-Barry and Sutherland on 6 December when the two of them confronted him. They extracted a promise that he would come back to the Squadron after the course, to 'lead the unit to the Far East to fight the Japanese'.[1]

He had seen many of his close friends die. The latest casualty was Ian Patterson, his 2i/c, killed in an air crash near Brindisi. The Dakota on which he was travelling slammed into a mountain top near Troia, 25 miles south-west of the airfields at San Severo/Gioa del Colle.[2] He had risen from a rather baby-faced 21-year-old junior officer to a battle-hardened veteran of the SAS and SBS and had 'brought to the task breadth of view, administrative competence, courage and humanity'.[3] David Sutherland had already taken over the 2i/c role, his own role as commander of S detachment being taken by Captain Clarke.

I never really knew much about my father's achievements from his own words or through the stories that he recounted. More came from friends and old military comrades. He never even really talked to me – or others – about the war in a real way, of its terror, sadness or even boredom (although I doubt that he ever allowed much of that in his busy life); of the friendships made and the lives lost, or of individuals betrayed. He talked about it more as if it had been another *'Boy's Own'* yarn. His self-deprecating style was to always downplay his achievements, and the story of the 'Jellicoe Inflatable Intruder' is typical.[4]

> The only serious military distinction I ever achieved was having a new type of assault boat named after me. It was called, I am ashamed to say, the 'Jellicoe Inflatable Intruder Mark One'.[5]

In November, Jellicoe had gone back to London, where he'd met Mountbatten, heading Combined Operations, and his scientific adviser, Solly Zuckermann. He was asked to design a rubber raiding boat (they'd been using German boats as they didn't have good enough ones themselves). The new design had later been produced in great quantities – the docks and harbours of the Middle East were 'inundated with them' – when the need for them was long past. He did later say that he thought the naming was 'rather impertinent'. Then he laughed. The whole idea caused him great amusement. He also went to see Churchill and, though he said that he 'had lost his attention entirely', clearly made enough of an impression to be immediately invited to spend the weekend at the Prime Minister's country residence, Chequers.[6]

It was remarks like this that made George Jellicoe so loved by those whose lives he touched. Rarely could he be accused of 'band-standing'. Just the opposite. Nevertheless, the war had been the highlight, the '*glanzpunkt*' of his life.[7]

After Athens had been liberated, Jellicoe's war started to slow down. A surprising correspondence took place between him and his old commander, David Stirling, still a prisoner in Colditz castle. Apparently Stirling sent Jellicoe a message through the 'underground' saying that, while he was anticipating the end of the war in Europe, he was putting together a group that would go east to China and fight with Chiang Kai-Shek. He said he wanted Jellicoe as his staff officer.

Rumour had it that Winston Churchill had heard about the scheme and applauded the idea and, supposedly, that was why in January 1945 Jellicoe travelled to Haifa to attend a staff course in preparation for the new assignment.

I never heard my father mention this, which was odd. He knew my deep interest in twentieth century Chinese politics, in which I was well-read. Maybe Stirling had heard about Jellicoe's new wife, Patsy, and that she had been born in Shanghai. Certainly, Stirling seemed interested in going east and had talked about the idea with Hermione Ranfurly in May 1945.[8]

With the end of the war, Jellicoe went looking for other work. One could imagine that for a man who had lived his life on the edge and seen so many of his friends die, it was not going to be an easy transition. I would imagine that, as for many people, the war ended with a mixture of feelings: jubilation and relief at the fact that he had made it; sadness and regret for the ones who hadn't. The start of a very long list included Peter Pease, Alan Phipps, Mark Howard, David Jacobsen, Andy Lassen. The deaths of Pease, Howard and Jacobsen were particularly difficult for him. They had been, in his words, 'three of the closest friends I have ever made'.[9]

The glamorously good-looking Pease, part of Jellicoe's Winchester crowd along with Howard and Jacobsen, had been a fighter pilot during the long summer of the Battle of Britain. He was having an affair with Peter's sister, Pixie, as well. Mark Howard's younger brother John, then a Major, had led the glider attack to secure two vital bridges across the Caen Canal and the River Orne in the early hours of 6 June in Normandy in 1944. It had been Howard's own choice of the Coldstream Guards that persuaded Jellicoe that it should be his choice too. Jellicoe must have received word of Andy Lassen's death at Comachio through the grapevine. Like many others, he must have been devastated that Andy, who most thought totally indestructible, had been killed in the war's closing days. Lassen's exploits were such that Tsigantes even made him an honorary member of the *Ieros Lochos*, writing after his death that Lassen had the right to wear the GSS emblem 'for courage, perserverance and zeal displayed during the war of liberation'.[10] Then there was David Jacobsen, an old Etonian who had joined 'the Territorial part of the Rifle Brigade', the Tower Hamlet Rifles, and was someone with whom Jellicoe had often golfed and through whom he had discovered his love of opera. He was also 'much more politically aware' than Jellicoe and might have been the source of Jellicoe's growing political awareness in these years.

Howard was killed in Normandy before the bloody fighting in the bocage. Jacobsen was killed in North Africa, in the first great retreat from Libya, when the truck he was riding in was ambushed at Derna aerodrome in 1941. Pease's Spitfire was shot down over Maidstone on what would become Battle of Britain day, 15 September. Richard Hillary's book, *The Last Enemy*, is dedicated to Pease's girlfriend, with whom he fell in love.

After the war, one of his other Cambridge friends, Archie Wavell, was killed in Kenya in 1953 during the Mau Mau uprising. He was thirty-seven.

In Jellicoe's 1939 diary (the only one of his that I know of, as he didn't regularly keep a diary), he compiled a list of some family members and friends, writing below, 'I shall be very sad if any one of these should die in this war.' I think he was sad about their loss till the end of his life. He often talked of these friendships. From Cambridge days, he'd mention Mark and Peter most, and from the war years, Andy. He kept many of Peter's letters.

Jellicoe transitioned back into civilian life by taking a position as second in command of the United Nations Relief and Rehabilitation Agency (UNRRA) in Klagenfurt, southern Austria.

The agency, established in 1943 'with impressive foresight at Roosevelt's behest' to prepare for what was already anticipated to be a gargantuan task, relocating Europe's millions of refugees, began operations in the Balkans and then, in 1945, was extended to cover the rest of Europe.[11] Already, by the end of May 1945, almost a million people had been sent back to their homelands. The Agency's approach was to try to go beyond food and shelter and to provide DPs (displaced persons) with 'opportunities for counselling, education, recreation and even political activity'.[12]

Germany had been packed with armies of forced labour. Around eight million people had been transported there to work in her factories and farms. Added to that there were, it is estimated, '4.8 million *internal* refugees'[13] and another 275,000 prisoners of war amongst the British and American troops.

'Germany in 1945 was one huge ant's nest. Everyone was moving. This was how the Eastern territories of Germany looked like'.[14] Everywhere in Europe there was starvation on a massive scale. Lowe estimates that calorie intake averaged around 2,750/day at the start of the war but had fallen to 1,412/day by its end.[15] Two countries in particular were on the point of food collapse. One was the Netherlands, where average daily intake was a staggering 400/day, 'half the amount received by the inmates of the Belsen concentration camp'.[16] The immediate post-war years in Greece were remembered for starvation on a mass scale, although the country had already suffered dramatic losses through starvation in the first year of German occupation. Woodhouse put the death toll at 400,000.[17]

Rape, theft, murder and destruction were everywhere. 'Central Europe was reverting to the dark ages.' [18]

The psychological problems were equally staggering. It was referred to as 'Liberation complex', 'a great and sullen suspicion ... towards all authority'.[19] UNRRA recognized these special psychological needs, while many of the military support units could not comprehend them. UNRRA camps would often have their own police forces and courts organized by the DPs. It was a way in which to give the feeling of self-determination back to people who had been treated worse than cattle for years.

Just before Christmas 1945, Jellicoe arrived in Vienna, where he stayed, delayed by flu. In Klagenfurt, he found himself responsible for the well-being of around 25,000 displaced persons: Russians, Ukrainians, Poles and around 1,500 Jews. The familiar UNRRA red flag that hung outside their headquarter buildings was often mistaken for the Soviet banner and for many of the Eastern Europeans it caused a good deal of panic at first.

Jellicoe eventually 'fell afoul of the British authorities on occasion, as when he helped Jews in the refugee camps to make their way to Palestine in defiance of official policy.'[20] Unlike almost all the other refugees, they did not have a country to which to return. It was, all in all, a nasty business. DP status, in general, was looked down upon rather than empathized with:

> It is clear from the official reports of the time, as well as the many memoirs and diaries written by ordinary soldiers, that the allied authorities were far more wary of DPs than they were of Germans.[21]

'Liberation complex'[22] made many DPs sullen, cynical and apathetic. For many of their liberators, it made helping them even more difficult.

The Russians regarded most of their DPs as traitors. Some were. Some had fought with the Germans; but the majority who had not were regarded as having committed treason by allowing themselves to be taken alive. Many returnees would pretend to be Polish to avoid the bullet or work camp that would be waiting for them on their return. This was particularly the case with displaced Cossacks, whose story was told by Nicholas Tolstoy; he believed that Harold Macmillan had 'entered into a criminal conspiracy with V Corps commander, General Keightley, allegedly with the intention of sending 70,000 Cossacks and Yugoslavs to a certain death.'[23] Macmillan was completely aware of what the risks were, even though he told Keightley to comply with the Russian demands. He himself said in his diary that handing them over would be to condemn them to 'slavery, torture and probably death'. However, he went on, 'To refuse is to deeply offend the Russians, and incidentally break the Yalta agreement.'[24] Of the three million prisoners the Soviets took, 'more than a third died in captivity.'[25] Russia had lost 27 million people. The nation seethed with hatred of anything German.

Not everything in Vienna was work. Jellicoe loved skiing and so took every chance he could to go up into the Alps. He spent a lot of time in Davos but found that it was 'full of old Nazis'.

With the war over and Europe struggling with the challenges of peace, Jellicoe now pondered his own future.

Part III

The Cold War

Chapter 14

The Cold War

Jellicoe now set about achieving his pre-war goal: entering the diplomatic service. Had the war not intervened, it's what he would have done. His first attempts to join were unsuccessful. Failure was an unusual experience for Jellicoe but it didn't deter him. He doubled his effort, tried again, and this time he was successful. On 10 September 1947, Jellicoe joined the Foreign Office as a Foreign Service Officer, Grade 8, starting as the Third Secretary in the German Political Department based in London.

Returning to 'civvy street' must have been difficult after the last five adrenalin-fuelled years. One disappointment was discovering that most of his personal effects had not been properly stored by his mother when he left home. His father had given him a large collection of stamps, many from early colonial days and including a few 'Penny Blacks'. As he opened the albums, a shower of shreds gently floated to the ground, the stamps having been long since been devoured by moths. The collection had been priceless.

The war had both prepared him and spurred him on. He had found himself in many difficult situations in which diplomacy had been the only way out, particularly in Greece. And it was also in Greece in the early 1940s that he witnessed the danger that the coming Cold War would bring. As he fought his way up the Peloponnese, Jellicoe had seen the darker, more ruthless side of communism.

It wasn't long before he was included in some high-level activity, joining Ernest Bevin's mission to Moscow at the very end of the year, in preparation for the fourth Meeting of the Council of Foreign Ministers. Clement Attlee, the new Labour Prime Minister, had selected Bevin as his Foreign Secretary. It was a position previously almost exclusively reserved for the old boys of Britain's élite public schools, but Bevin was a trade unionist; he'd been a founding member of one of the most important unions, the Transport and General Workers Union (TGWU), in 1922. He was also an anti-communist, not necessarily for political reasons as much as out of anti-semitism, since he saw many communist intellectuals as being part of a 'Jewish conspiracy'. He'd apparently taken part in the 1926 General Strike, but not as a leader. Jellicoe's father, then Admiral of the Fleet Earl Jellicoe, had been on the other side; he'd enlisted as a special constable although he was already sixty-seven.

The Moscow meeting with Stalin and his Foreign Minister, Molotov, had been set up without Bevin's knowledge. He was, quite understandably, 'furious'.[1] It turned out to be one of the last meetings before the Cold War opened its next super-charged chapter, a year before the Berlin blockade. The issues were extremely complex, and common ground was extraordinarily difficult to find. Questions about the level and speed of German reparations payments, the political structure of the new country and the fate of their prisoners of war dominated the discussions.

Molotov complained about the 81,000 German PoWs in the British zone helping reconstruction and mine clearance. Apparently, the Russians, who admitted that there were close to a million German PoWs in Russia (many would stay there till the mid-1950s, and even die there) thought the British were building a new military force in secret.

Stalin played along with the West and Bevin in particular. Bevin was 'at a loss how to deal' with him and, for some, acted with 'surprising naivety, taking Stalin's replies at their face value'.[2] He wasn't alone: President Roosevelt can, arguably, be criticized for having done the same.

Jellicoe enjoyed working with Bevin, and the feeling was mutual, Bevin enjoyed Jellicoe's spirit. On one occasion, Bevin had been unable to join a meeting, and Jellicoe, a Third Secretary, found himself alone in a negotiation about the border between Poland and Germany, dealing with a Field Marshal. Bevin sent through a message saying that he could lend a hand if Jellicoe felt the need. Typically, Jellicoe turned it around offering his help to the experienced politician and diplomat: 'Thank you for your kind offer. I'm fine. But do let me know if *you* need any help.'[3]

There were also opportunities for Jellicoe to watch the Kirov. Ballet became a lifelong love.

Bevin wasn't well at the time and died not many months later. His doctor was with him on the trip, and he wasn't allowed to fly. As a consequence, Jellicoe boarded a train from London's Victoria Station for the long journey to Moscow. With him was Cy Sulzberger's uncle, Arthur Hays Sulzberger, the legendary publisher of the *New York Times*. En route, the two men stopped off for a while in Paris and then went on to Berlin, where they visited Hitler's bunker, and Warsaw, where they saw the charred remains of the ghetto.

Washington. The web of spies

In March 1948, six months after joining the Foreign Office, Jellicoe was sent as Second Secretary to Washington, where Sir Oliver Franks was ambassador. Jellicoe was just shy of his thirtieth birthday, a young man determined to build a reputation.

With the defeat of Nazism, the wartime alliance had broken apart and the Cold War intensified. Jellicoe's own experiences with ELAS and, to a much lesser extent and more indirectly, with Tito's partisans in Yugoslavia, put him in a position to bring hands-on credibility rather than academic learning to his job. The Berlin blockade, an aggressive move by the Soviets designed to test Western resolve, was in full swing.

The change in Western views of their former ally, the Soviet Union, was profound and total. During the war the Germans had tried, albeit unsuccessfully, to exploit this division, for example by publicizing the Katyn massacre, in which 4,000 Polish officers had been executed by the Russians in 1940. But the British simply could not believe the German claims, or at best 'Britain and America chose to ignore this evidence of Stalin's methods.'[4] At the 1943 Tehran Conference, where the 'Big Three' met to discuss war strategy, Roosevelt was persuaded by Stalin that he should stay at the Soviet Embassy. Naively, he did so, and Stalin was able to listen each morning to a precise transcript of his ally's overheard conversation. Nobody thought that 'Uncle Joe' would stoop so low. Even towards the end of the war, he cold-bloodedly allowed the Germans to wipe out Warsaw after he'd encouraged the Poles to mount their 63-day uprising. He halted his armies on the eastern bank of the Vistula and even prevented the British supplying the beleaguered city by air. In February 1945, the Big Three met again at Yalta, in the Crimea, and Roosevelt again played into Stalin's hands, allowing the disagreements between himself and Churchill to be exploited. It was, in any case, difficult to discuss the future of Eastern Europe with any degree of realism, since the Red Army was already occupying much of the territory that they would gradually consolidate into the 'Communist Bloc'. Stalin promised that Poland would have free elections, and Churchill, who was about to be voted out of office, and Roosevelt, who would be dead less than two months later, both believed him.

On 25 April 1945, American and Russian soldiers met on the Elbe River. The war in Europe was, effectively, over and the final surrender was signed in Rheims in the early hours of 7 May 1945. The mood had changed by the time of the last of the great Allied conferences at Potsdam. One of the British delegation, Hugh Lunghi, called it a 'bad tempered conference'.[5] Truman, the new American President, thought that he was holding a trump card in the atomic bomb. He told Stalin that the US had developed a new and formidable weapon, without saying what it was. Stalin already knew what it was, but didn't let on. The Manhattan Project had been betrayed long ago by the Rosenbergs and Klaus Fuchs. Four days after the end of the conference, Hiroshima was bombed.

When Churchill visited America in 1946, he coined the expression that would come to characterize the Cold War:

From Stettin in the Baltic to Trieste in the Adriatic, an Iron Curtain has descended across the continent.

Clark Clifford, the presidential adviser who would later become embroiled in a financial scandal, noted that the speech was not well received at the time and that Churchill's position was regarded as being too harsh.

Jellicoe was now to be sent to Washington as the Foreign Office representative 'in a four-man committee running the Albanian operation'; disaffected DPs were being sent back to work as spies and saboteurs against Enver Hoxha's Stalinist regime: 'I was the FO representative in the committee because I was the Balkan specialist in the Embassy. I remember meetings in Frank Wisner's office.'

Wisner, a former Wall Street lawyer, had become the Central Intelligence Agency's Chief of Covert Operations at the end of 1951.[6] Under Dulles he had created a group in 1949 deep 'in the State Department bureaucracy under the purposefully dull name' of the Office of Policy Co-ordination.[7] It became a key driver of espionage management. Within three years it had a network of forty-seven overseas offices and employed 300 staff.

Jellicoe quickly rose to Second and then to First Secretary. George and Patsy Jellicoe were living at the time at 2541 Waterside Drive, a lovely red-brick townhouse, surrounded by trees, on the bend just behind Massachusetts Avenue, known as 'Embassy Row'.

The Washington embassy was a den of spies. Later, they would first be known as the 'Cambridge Three': Donald Maclean, Guy Burgess and H.A.R. 'Kim' Philby all worked there at one time or another, as did Anthony Blunt, the keeper of the Queen's art collections, whose real purpose in life would only be uncovered later. When Jellicoe arrived at the embassy, his office was directly opposite Kim Philby's, and the office next to Philby's was occupied by Guy Burgess. Jellicoe and Philby would 'sit together reading the telegrams on the operations' progress'. Jellicoe said that it was Philby 'who made all the operational decisions. I was just there to give political guidance, from the diplomatic point of view.'[8] Of Philby, he said:

> I liked Kim very much – and Aileen. I remember him coming to Patsy's and my house in Waterside Drive quite often. I found him very convivial – the same word he uses about me – and very intelligent. [9]
>
> We looked at the telegrams together and discussed the operation generally. But it was very much under his control operationally. He did it all very professionally.

Philby did indeed find Jellicoe a 'convivial soul'.[10] They would work through the SIS and FO telegrams together, Philby on the operational side, Jellicoe on the diplomatic. Philby's intellect probably appealed to Jellicoe as much as his affability. He was also extremely well-connected:

> He was far from being a mere namedropper; he could talk interestingly, often brilliantly, about his celebrities, and indeed about many subjects.[11]

Kim Philby had been under Soviet influence since 1936, when he went to Germany. The next three years, from 1937 to 1939, he spent in Spain. The Soviet defector Walter Krvitsky later told British interrogators in October 1937 that his country's intelligence services had sent a 'young journalist' to Spain. Philby had worked for *The Times*. In 1933, when he went to Vienna to work with anti-fascists, Philby met a young girl, Litzi Friedman. He fell in love and through her was introduced to the world of left-wing politics. 'Philby had already been intellectually convinced by communism, but Friedman radicalised him.'[12] When the two got to London, Friedman introduced him to another communist friend from Vienna, Edith Tudor-Hart, a photographer. She was working with Soviet Intelligence and it was she who recommended Philby's recruitment. She also reassured Philby – or *Söhnchen*, his code name – about the morality of the 1939 Soviet-German Non-Aggression Pact. Philby may well have been highly dubious about the ethics of the pact after what he'd seen of the impact of Nazism in Austria.

For much of his career, Philby lived with the burden of his true identity. What must have gone through his mind as he watched the Germans advance on Moscow at the end of 1941? One reconnaissance battalion actually reached the town of Khimki, only 8km from Red Square. Had they reached the city, files that could have revealed his identity might easily have been found. In June 1950, he had come across a reference in the Venona decrypts (messages decoded by the U.S. Army Signal Intelligence Service, later the NSA, from the NKVD, KGB and GRU sources) of a 'particularly important' spy code-named 'Stanley'. This person was identified as someone who had operated in the UK since 1945. 'Stanley' was Philby. The head of the Venona project, Meredith Gardener, was later to comment that when Philby visited the Americans' decoding centre at Arlington Hall Station in Virginia, he had shown an unhealthy interest in the details of the work.

Both the FBI and MI5 were also looking for a mole in the British Embassy code-named 'Homer' (or 'Gomer' as the mole was known in Russian). For some reason they were convinced that this would be someone like Elyesa Bazna, the British ambassador's butler in *A Spy Called Cicero*, someone at a junior or clerical level. 'Homer' was actually Donald Maclean, the son of a former Cabinet minister and a member of the Reform Club.

Philby's affability and social connections gave him an extraordinarily effective protective cloak. It was the reason he even managed to befriend the CIA's head spy-catcher, James Jesus Angleton, a committed Anglophile:

> Philby was impressed both by Angleton's grasp of intelligence and his appetite for food and drink ... Angleton had few close friends, and fewer confidants. Philby had many friends, and had refined the giving and receiving of confidences to an art form. They fitted one another perfectly. [13]

Jellicoe worked on operations planning with the CIA and often attended meetings in Frank Wisner's office. At the CIA, Wisner had been working on a plan to slip back into communist Albania a group of agents who had been picked up while they had been DPs. The tightly-knit planning group included representatives of two foreign services – Robert Joyce from the State Department's Policy Planning Staff under George Kennan, and Jellicoe, the Balkans specialist and British Embassy's First Secretary. 'In 1951 and 1952 some sixty of these "Pixies" infiltrated by sea or air. They were almost all killed or captured.' It seemed obvious that there was a leak, and Wisner 'had arrived at Philby as the most likely culprit.'[14] But rather astonishingly, Wisner continued with the operation. His reasoning has yet to surface.

When Guy Burgess turned up in Washington at Philby's house, 5228 Nebraska Avenue, in August 1950, Aileen, Kim's long-suffering wife, almost had a second breakdown. She'd nearly faltered when Guy stayed with them in Istanbul and she knew when his request for a bed 'for a few days' arrived that they'd never get rid of him. When he wrote to Kim he declared, 'I have a shock for you. I've been posted to Washington.'[15] Burgess was a slob, and Aileen's friends commiserated with her, knowing how bad he was:

> I thought of the cigarette ends stuffed down the back of sofas, the scorched eiderdowns, the iron-willed determination to have garlic in every dish, including porridge and Christmas pudding, the endless drinking, the terrible trail of havoc which Guy left behind him everywhere. [16]

John Philby, Kim's eldest son, also talked of Burgess's ceaseless smoking, his 'dark, nicotine stained fingers' and of his nail-biting.[17]

Burgess was a known commodity: he was 'an outrageous figure on the London scene, a homosexual, well-known for his brilliant wit and scandalously drunken behaviour'.[18] The Jellicoes did not care for Burgess. Patsy talked of his habit of turning up late, usually drunk. He had, on one occasion, got into a fight with a colleague from the FO outside the RAC, then fallen down its marble entrance steps. Patsy summed him up as an 'awful show-off. He knew everyone and would tell you ... no one liked him because he pretended to be so grand. He dropped names to be important.'[19]

Burgess had, like Philby, worked as a journalist. But unlike his fellow spy, he'd used his journalism to better advance his contacts within the British establishment. They would later pay extraordinarily large dividends. He was an Old Etonian, 'the son of a former Cabinet minister, a product of public school and Cambridge, a member of the Reform Club'.[20] He joined the BBC and then became producer of *The Week in Westminster*, a responsibility he'd held till 1944. For three years (from 1939 to 1941), he'd doubled up by working for MI5, helping the Service develop propaganda.

But what he was actually doing in the embassy no one was quite sure. No one really wanted to have anything to do with him; his reputation was that bad. Dennis Greenhill, later to become the Head of the British Foreign Office, said that it had been intended that Burgess should work for Hubert Graves, who had the oversight of Far Eastern issues. But Graves had 'refused to have anything to do with [him]'.[21] Burgess was then handed back to Greenhill, but that didn't work either. Burgess 'expressed at once a total disinterest in the Middle East', Greenhill's area of focus.[22] But he did become a member of the Far Eastern Commission, a group set up to make sure that Japan fulfilled its post-war obligations. Here he saw a great deal of confidential information, though 'not anything startling'.[23]

One of the roles that Burgess did play, however, was that of Philby's courier, taking information from Washington to New York, where Philby's Soviet controller, Valeri Makayev, was based. He'd done the same when Kim was in Spain in 1937.

Burgess disappeared in 1951 with Donald Maclean. The two drove away immediately after Maclean's thirty-fifth birthday and fell off the radar. Harold Acton summed Burgess up wonderfully: he was 'to win notoriety as one of the "Missing Diplomats", though nobody could have been less diplomatic.'

Donald Maclean was Head of Chancery and, with Jellicoe, held one of the eleven Second Secretary positions. He'd arrived in Washington in 1944, would remain till 1948 and had already, apparently, talked openly of his interest in communism in his recruitment interviews.[24] He was Jellicoe's boss. Both Patsy and Jellicoe liked him. Patsy, in fact, found him 'extraordinarily nice', and Jellicoe would regularly play tennis with him.[25]

A key influence on the young Maclean was a Londoner, a Jewish East Ender, Kitty Harris. She was thirteen years older and had already been working for the Russians for almost twenty years. She'd spent time in Canada and had even worked with the communists in Shanghai. They 'met' in 1937, and Maclean would regularly bring Foreign Office papers back for her to photograph. By 1938 they'd become lovers and, when Maclean transferred to the Paris embassy, she was, surprisingly, allowed to come with him. But Maclean's ardour started to cool, and when he met his future wife, Melinda, at the Café de Flore in 1940, he fell for her immediately. She later seemed surprised that Maclean had defected, something that she was perhaps better able to successfully carry off as she was 'attractive, but also prim and spoiled ... delicately good-looking, and carefully groomed'. But when the same friend who introduced them to each other in Paris in 1940 later met the two in Moscow in the 1950s, she 'jumped down his [Maclean's] throat' when he said 'something that implied faint criticism of the Soviet Union'. Maclean had seen this side of Melinda, an ideologically committed woman who 'doesn't mind mixing with communists even though her parents are well-off.' Maclean said that he and she 'spoke the same language'.[26] Maclean told Harris that when Melinda had wanted to break up with him, he finally took a gamble and told her what he really did. She apparently decided there and then to support him (and when he was made Head of Chancery at the Embassy in Cairo, she did so actively. She would take the messages to his Soviet contact's wife at the hairdresser). They got married in June 1940 and then, as France fell, moved back to England.

Philby found out that the Washington Embassy mole-hunt had cast suspicion on Maclean. He had to get a warning to him, anxiously thinking that he could easily crack and give the game away for all. To friends and acquaintances there was no longer that calm, debonair manner about him. He was drinking heavily, he would stutter as though under stress, and his hands would tremble. Burgess passed Philby's warning to Maclean in London, after he was asked to leave Washington because of his antics. On 25 May 1951, Burgess and Maclean disappeared. Melinda played dumb, calling the Foreign Office and asking if they knew where he was. In September 1953, she joined him. She drove with her children to Lausanne, where she disappeared, then flew from Austria to Moscow. Five years later, Maclean re-emerged in Moscow. Philby later wrote that Maclean was an asset too valuable to sacrifice: 'It was essential to rescue Maclean ... no question was raised about his future potential to the Soviet Union.'[27] Maclean tried to integrate into the Soviet way of life, learning Russian, earning a doctorate and then specializing in economics at the Foreign Ministry. In March 1983, aged sixty-nine, Donald Maclean died alone after a bout of pneumonia. Melinda had tired of their Moscow life, had a brief affair with Philby and then went back to live in New York.

Philby's association with Burgess definitely damaged his reputation, and in 1955 he resigned from MI5 after he had been investigated for, although not charged with, espionage. The head of the CIA, Walter Bedell Smith, had demanded his removal, but 'the general view in SIS itself was that Philby had been sacrificed on the altar of American jealousy and McCarthyite bigotry.'[28]

The machinery of American espionage planning seemed to be impervious to the obvious:

> Incredibly, Wisner continued to order agents dropped into Albania … agents reported progress … and asked for more help. Wisner sent more, although his counter-intelligence people worried that the 'fist' – the individual style and pattern that distinguishes telegraph operators – didn't seem quite right. It wasn't: the agents had been rolled up or turned.[29]

Philby went back to working as a journalist and wrote for both the *Economist* and the *Observer* on Middle East issues. Even though Harold Macmillan, then Foreign Secretary, had told the Press that Philby was innocent, another Soviet defector, Anatoli Golitsyn, someone who had worked with him, now spoke out against him.

One of Philby's friendships had been with the Oxford don, Hugh Trevor-Roper. After he defected, Philby wrote to his old friend saying how much he missed their discussions. Trevor-Roper's reply said what many of Philby's former friends must have felt:

> Discussion needs common ground on which to stand, how deep down soever it may lie; and where could we find such ground now? Probe as I may in search of it, the solid rock which I once imagined proves but a continuation of the spongy quagmire of double-spoken words.[30]

Meanwhile, the Jellicoes were feted everywhere they went, meeting Jack Kennedy, Richard Nixon and J. Edgar Hoover. Patsy maintained that she once confronted the anti-communist witch-hunter Senator Joe McCarthy:

> He said he didn't really know how many Communists there were in the State Department but reporters needed a number so he made one up. I asked how that differed from Hitler's Big Lie and he was not best pleased with me.[31]

During his time in Washington, Jellicoe made some important new friendships. One was with Nico Henderson, who was serving as First Secretary. Jellicoe had first met Cawadias in the first days of Athens' liberation and had asked Henderson to take his old friend many a letter. Nico did so, and ended up asking for her hand in marriage. He'd gone to the Washington embassy the year before, after working as Assistant Personal Secretary to the Foreign Secretary. Another great childhood friend was also in Washington: Tim Marten. He'd come to work on the NATO treaty. Tim would often stay with the Jellicoes at the Isle of Wight estate. One time, the two of them caused considerable embarrassment when George V and Queen Mary visited the Admiral; none of the apples that had been so carefully nurtured for the royal couple survived a concerted attack by the two boys.

On his thirty-first birthday, 4 April 1949, Jellicoe attended the signing of the North Atlantic Treaty, which his old boss, Ernest Bevin, signed on behalf of the United Kingdom. Anglo-American relations were at a crucial point: the Western Allies were increasingly nervous about Europe's susceptibility to communism; the spectre was knocking on the doors of France, Italy, Greece and Albania. NATO's role, as Lord Ismay, its first Secretary General, would have it, was 'to keep the Russians out, the Americans in, and the Germans down.'[32]

It was against the backdrop of the complete destruction of European industries and economies that the US pushed for European economic recovery. A revitalized German economy was central to that vision, and the Russians, with their constant and exorbitant demands for German reparations in the form of industrial stock, were acting completely counter to this. The Organisation for European Economic Co-operation (OEEC) – the forerunner of the OECD – channelled the substantial American cash injection of Marshall Plan funds through its offices in Paris. The creation of the European Steel and Coal Community (ESSC) was aimed at sharing critical resources. This new organization was the forerunner of the European Economic Community (EEC) and the European Union (EU). It was during these years that Jellicoe became a committed European.

Work continued at a fast pace. The fourth session of the United Nations General Assembly was on the horizon. With the forming of the Warsaw Pact in 1955, the new battle lines in the Cold War became even more starkly drawn.

My brother Paddy, the current Earl Jellicoe, and his elder sister Zara Lison were both born while Jellicoe was in Washington. Patsy occupied her time – and also generated a small additional income for the two – by painting portraits of people and of their Washington homes. She kept some of them in her bedroom till she died. They were scenes from P Street in Georgetown, beautifully light watercolours of the dappled sunlit street. They should have gone to the two children born in Washington. Sadly, they didn't.

Brussels. The heart of NATO

After Washington came Brussels. On 10 September 1951, Jellicoe was moved to the Belgian capital to serve as Head of Chancery and then, in 1952, as the new Chargé d'Affaires. He'd initially gone without Patsy, as she was looking after the children. He took a small apartment near Frère Orban. Living in the apartment below was Ronnie Grierson, who had been the only Austrian officer in the SAS (he was born in Austria under the name of Griessmann and would later be a colleague of Jellicoe in the bank, S.G. Warburg).

Just before leaving, Jellicoe had an encounter with John Julius Norwich, who had just joined the Northern Department in which he was First Secretary. As he came in, Jellicoe jumped up and pulled up a chair for him.

'There', he said, 'it's important to make a good start. No one's ever going to do that for you again.'[33]

With the founding of NATO, Brussels' role in Europe gained importance (the NATO Pact was actually based on the 1948 Treaty of Brussels).

Many new friendships were made, among them with Baroness Renée Lippens, who'd worked in Belgian SOE and later became my godmother. Another new friend was Louis Camu, the resistance fighter turned banker, who, like Mary Cawadias, had been imprisoned by the Gestapo. When Julian Dobrski (the Major Dolbey with whom George had parachuted into Rhodes) moved to Geneva with his wife Nikki, he bought 'Les Sapins Rouges' on the golf course at Crans-sur-Sierre, and Jellicoe would often be invited to ski and meet the Dobrskis' other guests. One was the famous American diplomat and historian, George Kennan. He was known for his hawkish views outlined in the so-called 'Long Telegram' of 22 February 1946, but thought the West could avoid a military confrontation with the Soviet Union, which it could economically outrun and outlast. Core to his thinking was his recognition of an 'instinctive Russian sense of insecurity', which would naturally lead to a 'patient but deadly struggle for total destruction of rival power'. Nikki stayed in the Valais until her death a few years ago. Jellicoe's mother, Gwen, was persuaded to buy an apartment there, clearly pandering to her son's passion for skiing. She soon sold it. While Jellicoe was in Brussels, Group Captain Peter Townsend joined as Defence Attaché. The handsome Battle of Britain fighter ace was in the middle of the ill-fated affair with Princess Margaret.

In the summer, Jellicoe received a letter from Derek Hoyer Millar, the Foreign Office Parliamentary Secretary (FOPS), saying that he could no longer talk with Philby. Jellicoe, of course, toed the line but he was angry about it since Kim was a friend:

I was outraged. It struck me as McCarthyism at its worst. It was an order so I obeyed it, but I didn't like what I was doing. I truly believed him innocent. I was completely deceived by him.[34]

It was at this point, in London in 1953, despite my own arrival as the fourth child, that Jellicoe's marriage to Patsy O'Kane sadly started to fall apart. While Jellicoe was with Tim Marten, skiing the Haute Route from Chamonix in France to Saas Fee in Switzerland, Patsy was bedridden in London. Although born in London, I was baptized in Brussels.

Jellicoe liked the ambassador, Sir Christopher Warner, despite his constant corrections of Jellicoe's policy drafts. The two shared a common belief in the value of a European union of sorts and would frequently communicate their views to London. Janetta Warner became one of Patsy's greatest protectors and provided constant moral and financial support in the early years after the breakdown of her marriage

On 5 March 1953, the 'Man of Steel', Joseph Stalin, died. For a brief moment, the autocratic power that had been vested in one man was fragmented. A committee made up of Bulganin, Beria and Kaganovich held the reins of power until the new Soviet leader, the former political commissar who had fought at Stalingrad, Nikita Khrushchev, emerged. A summit meeting was planned between the three leaders: Macmillan, Eisenhower and Khrushchev.

In September, Jellicoe came back to London, where he became No. 2 in the Northern Department, responsible for the Soviet desk. His job was to monitor everything known about Soviet intelligence and military matters. His boss from the FO chaired the all-important Joint Intelligence Committee, a body which reported directly to the Cabinet Defence Committee.

Baghdad

In January 1956, Jellicoe was transferred to Baghdad as First Secretary and held an important role as the Deputy Secretary-General of the Baghdad Pact. He was one of five representatives, from Pakistan, Iran, Turkey, the United States and the UK.

Patsy should have moved to Baghdad to join him. She only made one fleeting visit and – despite her later deep interest in Middle Eastern culture and art – never spent any time in Baghdad. I still have my old British passport stamped inside with the Iraq visa that marked the year. Jellicoe was, in fact, living with a woman who was twenty years younger. Her name was Philippa Bridge but she'd been born a Dunne, the younger sister of two brothers, Thomas and Martin Dunne. Although her father, Phillip Dunne, had also been in 8 Commando, she and Jellicoe did not meet until many years after the war. Philippa had heard the name Jellicoe but had always, she maintained, associated it with the old Admiral, never with his son. She had married very young, but the marriage fell apart. Her parents had both been very much against it in the first place, but she'd insisted and couldn't be budged. Her husband, Christopher Bridge, was ex-Coldstream and knew Jellicoe. He, too, had been in the desert war, where he'd been badly injured after his tank had been hit.

How the pair came together was another story. Geoffrey Keating had been Montgomery's official photographer. He was a kind man but always seemed to be trying to make new connections and would act very much as a social fixer in order to expand his circle of acquaintance. Philippa had been introduced, and he asked if she'd like to join a dinner party at which Jellicoe would be one of the guests (Keating probably knew Jellicoe through his friendship with Stirling or Shimi Lovat). At the dinner, Philippa was struck by his looks, although Jellicoe, she said, was far too busy flirting with most of the girls to really take notice of her. When Keating gently laid more bait for Philippa, saying that he was hosting some Middle Eastern friends and would she like to join the party and bring someone, she replied yes and that person turned out to be George Jellicoe. I had always mistakenly thought that it was Gian Marina Gross who had made the introduction.

Keating's friendship with the Jellicoes, like many of his other connections, did not last. He was too pushy. Keating then turned his attentions to my mother and offered to lend me one of his cameras. I was an aspiring photographer, but I now think, maybe unfairly, that it was probably his way of trying to rebuild the link with George.

Jellicoe and Philippa had fallen in love and were now taking short holidays in Europe together. In February 1956, they went skiing in Courcheval and Cervinia and then spent time travelling in Lebanon and Syria. Jellicoe was now able to drink in all the beauty of those many historic spots he'd always loved so much but had not really had the time to appreciate in wartime.

Together, they visited Baalbek, the Krak des Chevaliers, the famous eleventh century crusader castle in Syria and, of course, Palmyra. Baalbek, situated in Lebanon's Bekaa Valley east of the Litani River, later became a Hezbollah stronghold, while much of Palmyra was to be destroyed by Islamic State (ISIS). Wherever they went, they enjoyed the simple hospitality of the land. They travelled over the desert, eating dates and lamb, near Shiraz stretching out carpets on the sands and contentedly sitting in the early morning coolness of the desert. It was a whirlwind of cultural pleasures. They visited the great temples and shrines of Persepolis and Isfahan and crossed the wondrous seventeenth century Sassanian half-bridge, half-weir, half-building at Pol-e-Khaju, before venturing into the wilds of Kurdistan. To cap it off, in the summer months they came back to Europe and spent idyllic days on Capri.

Philippa was swept off her feet by Jellicoe's charm and good looks. Much though she loathed flying, she took a flight to join him, drinking so much on board to calm her nerves that when she got off she almost tripped on the steep stairway. At the bottom, she collapsed with nervous fatigue into his arms, imploring him to marry her.

Philippa's parents were strongly against their marriage. It was clear that the Foreign Office would not look kindly on the relationship. In Baghdad, the ambassador was usually absent in the hot summer months, so when Philippa visited she was able to put up a believable charade of being Jellicoe's secretary. It was her father who had been deputized by Peggy Dunne to reason with Philippa. She still remembers the dread she felt about the impending meeting at her Rutland Gate flat. But it was only when her father was opening the door to leave that he turned around and said, rather meekly, 'I don't suppose you can be persuaded from marrying George Jellicoe.' Her mind was made up, and she replied that there was not the slightest chance of her retreating.

Philippa now joined Jellicoe in Baghdad for three months. It would be far more time than they had ever spent together in one place, and in September 1956, they left again for Kurdistan. In 1957, she came home in October. Despite the cool, dark, sunken rooms of the Turkish house they lived in, she found the summer months unbearably hot. Again they explored countries and sites throughout the Mediterranean, visiting Byblos in Lebanon, Side, Corycus and Amanur in Turkey, the ruins at Termessus, exquisite amphitheatres, the temple at Didyma and Pergamon's theatre. Jellicoe knew these sites well, not just from books. They went on to places which carried vivid and deep memories for Jellicoe: Port Tigani, Kos, Corfu and Patmos. Just as they arrived back in England, they read with horror that the boat on which they'd just been touring the Dodecanese had sunk.[35] It wasn't long, before they were off again: over Christmas they went skiing in Lech, where a longstanding friendship developed with one of the mountain guides, Kurt Wick.

Jellicoe lived on the banks of the Tigris, far enough away from the embassy not to feel it was around the corner, but probably only about five minutes away from the bridge under the shadow of which it was huddled. Between the house and the river was a shaded, tree-lined road, just wide enough for people to ride along its dusty track in the evenings.

They had been befriended by some local policemen who generously made their horses available; behind the house were woods, where they would often spend the evenings riding in the welcoming coolness. And if not riding, they went swimming in the wide, muddy waters of the river. Sometimes, as darkness fell, they would swim behind a boat rowed ahead of them, with candles lighting their way. For a young couple in love, such evenings must have been magic.

George Jellicoe – and Philippa when she was there – was very much taken under the wing of Seton Deardon and his engaging wife, Sue. Seton pictured himself as an Arabist: he had spent much of his career in the Middle East, knew its customs and spoke Arabic fluently. He introduced Jellicoe to the desert tribes. This was nectar to Jellicoe, who was delighted to develop a deeper understanding of Iraq and its many peoples. Jellicoe loved nothing better than to sit on the ground, on a kilim, and share food in the communal fashion. He was also close friends with the younger Michael Butler, a Wykehamist like himself. Sir Michael, as he became, would later be very influential in the European Community and a renowned collector of Chinese porcelain. In fact, they were literally surrounded by interesting people. Agatha Christie and her husband owned one of the houses next door, even if they were rarely there. A little further away, in one of the new, modern buildings, lived Nuri al-Said, the Prime Minister. Another of their friends was Nadim Pachachi. The handsome, westernized oil minister eventually married one of Philippa's American friends. He and Michael Butler were very much part of the social life of Baghdad, both seemingly always caught up in romantic intrigues. Another friend was Jock Jardine, from the famous Hong Kong family, who also lived in one of the many Turkish houses nestled against the banks of the Trigris.

There were constant local excursions, either to the other great river, the Euphrates, or closer by. Philippa remembered that she always felt safe then, that a woman could drive by herself without any threat, although Jellicoe was not above trying to unnerve Philippa when her western dress disturbed local Islamic sentiments. He encouraged her to disappear with some local women to be outfitted in a more conservative manner.

Jellicoe was not good at book-keeping. His mind was too untidy for that. He had a tendency to run up large bills and disappear. Amongst the papers from his London home, Chapel Street, there were old bills from Baghdad tailors and shirtmakers; even a 'painful letter asking for cash' written to Jellicoe in February 1958 under the letterhead of the Baghdad Pact Secretariat General.[36] It was for an electric fire he'd never paid for.

While he was in Baghdad, the Middle East erupted. In the early morning of 6 November 1956, a task force of 130 British and French warships stood off the Egyptian coastline. It was a massive armada brought about by the reaction to Egypt's unilateral declaration that the Suez Canal would now come under their exclusive control. Britain mobilized around 60,000 troops and moved them to the Middle East, in what was the largest airlift of troops since the war.

When Jellicoe was recalled to London, the couple took the time to drive back across many of the countries of the north-eastern corner of the Mediterranean. They passed through large swathes of Lebanon and Syria that will never be seen again in the way that they could. They revisited Baalbek, Pergamon and numerous temples. They drove along the southern Turkish coast up through to Bodrum. The trip was made along precipitous roads, often blocked with herding sheep, taking in the countryside and the people from all walks of life. Eventually, they ended up in Tunis, where they spent Christmas with Seton and Sue Reardon, who was now working, like Philby, for the *Economist*.

Back in London

The Suez Crisis nearly brought about Jellicoe's resignation from the Foreign Office. He was strongly opposed to British policy.

He fell back on what he thought would be friendly family connections and asked his cousin, Sir Nicholas Cayzer, for a job in the family business, British and Commonwealth Shipping.

> I know that, at 39, an ex-diplomat and an ex-temporary soldier may well be, in business a round peg in a square hole. All I can say in my favour is that I have no distaste for hard work and that if you were able to offer me a job I would not expect more than I was worth. I realize that, to start with, this would be very little.[37]

He had hoped to run the South African operations but, instead, for a short time, became a director of the two mainstream sides of the business: the commercial Clan Line Steamer business and the cruise line business of the Union Castle Steamship Company.

Family rivalries were strong, however, and Jellicoe believed that two of the cousins, Tony Cayzer and Bunny Rotherwick, joined forces to oppose his entry into the firm. He felt that they saw him as a potential rival and had, additionally, always begrudged his easy style. It might also have been that – at least in Tony's case – they felt protective of Patsy. The last straw for Jellicoe came on a company outing when he was completely isolated and ignored. He soon got the message; each day must have been a kind of purgatory. The treatment meted out to him has since been recognized as having been wrong:

There are many among the management of the family firm today who still speculate about what George might have achieved if it had embraced him in 1957.[38]

However, it was now that his affair with Philippa caught up with him. It hit the headlines of the gossip columns, even if Jellicoe's view was that 'half of London must know that I want to marry' Philippa. The media exposure wasn't good, and he was forced to resign from the FO in March 1958.[39] He was admonished by the Permanent Secretary, Sir Derick Hoyar Millar, who told him that he had to make up his mind. Such behaviour was not well regarded from a man in his position: 'You have a choice of ceasing your relationship with this lady or changing your job.' It was an easy choice for him: he decided on the latter.

Disappointed, he left the Foreign Office to look for new opportunities. Nevertheless, he felt that 'he never had an easier decision to make.'[40] He would not give up Philippa. But by now the family business was clearly not going to be the answer. The South African position had dried up, and Jellicoe turned his attention to politics.

Part IV

The Later Years

Chapter 15

Friends in War and Peace

Jellicoe lived life at a breathless pace. He was determined, in the midst of trying to make a living for his family, to make a difference to the lives of others. The war had evidently left a deep scar. He had seen so much death and lost so many friends that it was natural that his way through was to try and give back, to rebuild and nurture young, promising talent and to embrace life to the fullest.

A cousin, Mary Buckley, who had been married to Peter Buckley, the former CEO of Caledonia Investments, summed it up by talking of 'the lovely way in which he put lesser and younger people so much at their ease … with that lovely twinkle in his eyes.'[1] Many agreed. Jellicoe 'liked to nurture talent when he saw it' was how another parliamentarian, Lord Howe, described his affinity with younger people.[2] He was always accessible and would immediately put younger people at ease with his humour. He would sit at the House of Lords' Bishop's Bar and invite you to have a drink with him. Howe clearly missed Jellicoe's touch: 'Nothing prepares you for this place, the way of doing things no matter how good you think you might have been before you came to the Upper House.'

The constellations around which much of Jellicoe's personal and philanthropic life revolved started, of course, with his military service, and was reinforced by his years in the Foreign Office. Jellicoe had seen the impact of Stalinism at first hand, both on the ground in Greece and subsequently in Washington, soon to be embroiled in spy scandals.

Inextricably woven into everything was his deep love of the arts, history and, of course, women. He had loved many women. Two he married: my mother, Patsy O'Kane, and Philippa Dunne, the women with whom he shared the closest of companionship. They could not have been more different. Both were beauties and strong individuals. Patsy was the only child in a Scots-Irish family, intellectually brilliant but equally highly strung. Her father, the chief engineer at the Shanghai Electrical Company, adored her. Philippa's family were landed gentry, and she was extremely well-read but not an intellectual. Both were engaging women – Philippa because of her engaging warmth, Patsy because of her intellect. But Philippa turned out to be, in many ways, the perfect companion for George: warm-hearted and down-to-earth. She became his soul mate in a very real sense. They 'sparked' off each other in a way that Patsy never could. And Philippa knew when to let George have his way and when – and more importantly how – to rein him in when he became intolerable. Collette, his nurse in his last years, used the word 'cope'. His children became quite used to his bellowing through the house when something wasn't just quite to his liking. And when he spent more time at his country home in Wiltshire, Tidcombe, as his career slowed down, he became, if anything, more demanding.

Jellicoe, wrote another friend, 'was much more widely read than he pretended, in German and French as well as English; a connoisseur of pictures, music and the fine arts.'[3] Later in life, there was always music at Tidcombe. Jellicoe would work in a separate wing, his only companions great symphonies of Mozart and Beethoven, or Bach and Italian opera. If he wasn't writing or working through papers he might have been sitting in the drawing room, eyes closed, gently smiling, his hand rising and falling to melodic sounds. Now he's gone, so has the music. He and Philippa would regularly attend Covent Garden. In fact, the night that he went to see Edward Heath about the call girl inquiry he'd been at the ballet with Philippa. He must have shared these loves with Patsy, his first wife, as well. She'd been close friends with Margot Fonteyn, with whom she'd grown up in Shanghai.

The shelves at Tidcombe were filled with books from his father's naval collection and with his own interests in history, literature and archaeology. Jellicoe had not been keen on history until he went to Winchester. Initially, he had studied science but changed to history, at which he excelled, largely due to the efforts and dedication of one man, Harold Walker, who later became his housemaster of 'Cook's'. So close was their relationship that when Walker left the College, he invited his favourite student to come and select something from his rooms as a keepsake. When his house in the country was burgled in the 1960s, what probably upset Jellicoe more than the disappearance of some of his father's memorabilia was the loss of what he'd been given by Walker. Jellicoe ended up winning the Vere Herbert-Smith History prize, even though he said, typically, that he was 'not very bright' as a student.[4]

It was a terrible moment when he explained why he wasn't reading so much: 'It's simply because I read a line and by the time I've got to the next sentence I cannot remember what I've just read.' Both my parents possessed great intellects, and for both of them old age turned out to be cruel. For my mother, there was the additional burden of failing eyesight. When we buried my father, under one arm was tucked a bottle of Poire William, but under the other was tucked a paperback of Lermontov which my half-sister, Daisy, had lovingly put there. It was a touching gift for his journey into the afterlife. He and I both adored bookshops: Hatchards on Piccadilly, and when it was still there, Waterstones in South Kensington, or Heywood Hill on Curzon Street when he'd been into Trumpers for a quick trim.

Jellicoe first took his seat in the House of Lords in 1939 but it wasn't until 3 December 1957 that he took the oath and 28 July 1958 that he made his maiden speech. As was the custom when the House was addressed by former officers, he wore his Coldstream Guards full dress uniform. Fresh from his experiences in Iraq, his speech was entitled 'The International Situation: The Middle East'. Jellicoe spoke about the death of the King and Nuri. He and Philippa had last glimpsed the ex-Prime Minister having coffee at Fortnum and Mason in Piccadilly. While he was still on the cross benches, Jellicoe was able to talk of these recent events with first-hand knowledge.

Although he was 'not by nature a political animal' and had 'never been a wholly committed party man', neither was Jellicoe an ideologue. It did not take long for him to be hooked into the Conservative ranks.[5]

> This was the period of 'Butskellism', when the divisions between the parties were as indistinct as in the days of Blair and Cameron. Indeed, in the Lords at that time and subsequently it was often said that it was difficult to tell which of the close friends, Lords Shackleton and Jellicoe, was the Conservative and which Labour.[6]

When in Ted Heath's government in the 1970s, Jellicoe had to deal with the Civil Service Department. Its first political head was Labour's Lord Shackleton, his predecessor as leader of the House of Lords and Lord Privy Seal. Eddie Shackleton and George Jellicoe became close friends when Jellicoe took over the role in 1970. When Shackleton was inaugurated into the Order of the Garter, Jellicoe invited him to Tidcombe. He wouldn't take the Garter off for the whole weekend.

The reaction to Jellicoe's resignation on 24 May 1973, in the wake of the Lord Lambton call girl scandal (something I wrote about later), was not what one expected of a fallen politician. He received more praise than condemnation. Eddie, even though a close friend, spoke for his party, saying that he had been

> as good a leader of this House as we have known ... I don't think we can let him go – though happily this is not an epitaph – without expressing our very deep sorrow to the House and to the country ... with immense thoroughness, patience and personal sensitivity Lord Jellicoe fulfilled his role as Leader of your Lordships' House ... we

found him an admirable open-minded and wise colleague; my Lords, I believe that we and the country have suffered a grievous loss.[7]

Shackleton spoke of wider constituencies within the Labour party, talking of the 'regret his departure has been received [with] both by officials and by the trade union side'.[8] It was an unusual detail, but he acknowledged that Jellicoe had worked very closely with a number of union leaders to resolve the confrontational politics of the early 1970s. The General Secretary of the Civil and Public Services Association (CPSA), William Kendall, said, 'In our union we respected him as a tough, capable and fair negotiator.'[9] Eddie died when my wife and I were living in Maryland in the early 1990s. My father and I talked frequently by telephone, and I remember him saying that, in the course of one week, he'd lost three close friends, one after the other. Eddie was one. Confronted with death so close, he was sensing his own mortality. Another Labour politician, Richard Crossman, wrote that Jellicoe was 'among the bravest, ablest, most decent members of the Heath Government'.[10]

Jellicoe's circle of friends was wide, and while he had some close friends from his days at Warburg's, Paolo di Robilant, Ronnie Grierson and Raymond Bonham Carter, for example, his heart was not in 'The City'. One exception might have been Sir Neil Shaw, with whom he worked during his Tate & Lyle days. George and Philippa became close to him and his second wife, the Canadian sculptress, Pixie. Outside Ascot, Shaw built a large modern house, where the gardens had been remodelled by Sir Geoffrey Jellicoe, a distant cousin. Other friendships from T & L days included people like Colin Moynihan, who had been Jellicoe's Personal Assistant. Moynihan was later appointed Minister of Sport in the Thatcher Cabinet in 1987 and was part of the Committee for the British Summer Olympics.

Jellicoe's closest friendships, for sure, were with those with whom he had fought – David Stirling, Georges Bergé, Stephen Hastings or Carol Mather. In the 1960s, Jellicoe planned a trip with Carol Mather and Robin Fedden to climb up over the Atlas Mountains – spectacular scenery the whole way, from the desert floor to the high, snow-covered mountain passes. In the desert, the expedition set off from Tinerhir on donkeys, and the supplies were transferred to massive baskets from the car that Philippa had driven out.

Outside that circle, his friends were to be found more in the world of politics and diplomacy. Tidcombe would regularly host guests like Roy Jenkins or Peter Carrington. Carrington had been Jellicoe's mentor in the Lords, and the two were very close. Sadly, when I went to talk with him shortly before his death, it was clear that his mind was clouded. After a long lunch, he turned to me, just as his car was coming to pick him up, asking,

'And how did you know George, exactly?' He had been a handsome man, and I was genuinely sad to see the loss of such a mind. Years earlier, he had given a beautiful memorial speech at the Guards Chapel. 'Woy' Jenkins and Jellicoe were both lovers of the good life, but it was Jenkins' deep grasp of history that probably most engaged Jellicoe's attention. Other friends included the Bonham Carters (Laura and her husband, Hayden, are still friends), Jacob Rothchild and Sam Baring. Nico Henderson, of course, was a close friend from Washington days, and he and Mary rented the Jellicoes' cottage at Tidcombe for many years. In that circle would also be others like Anthony Parsons, Chris Patten, his political protégé, or Michael and Damaris Stewart, and from earlier days, Hoyveda, the last Prime Minister of Iran before the Shah's fall, and Mitsotakis.

Introductions were not always successful. A frequent visitor was the young, rather slick Iranian ambassador, Parveez Radji, one of Hoveyda's 'protégés'.[11] He was not a particularly likeable man. Philippa 'really disliked him', going so far as to say that she 'absolutely loathed him.' Parveez had worked his way into power on the coat-tails of his affair with one of the Shah's sisters, Princess Ashraf, and as the Shah's ambassador in London had to deal with attacks on his master from the likes of the British satirical weekly, *Private Eye*, which insisted on calling him 'The Shit of Iran'. Ashraf herself 'had near legendary reputation for financial corruption and for successfully pursuing young men'. She had been named Chairman of the United Nations Human Rights Commission, which appeared a supreme irony.[12]

The Jellicoes had first met Radji at a dinner at No.10. Philippa was seated next to him and Mrs Harold Wilson, and he did not say a single word to the ex-Prime Minister's wife throughout the whole dinner. Harold Wilson had been so angry that he left as soon as was polite to do so. Jellicoe had always liked Wilson and saw the slight that he'd suffered. On the night of the revolution which toppled the Shah, Parveez was with them in London at the flat. It was the first time Philippa had ever warmed to him.

Jellicoe had been on good terms with Hoveyda. He probably enjoyed his easy elegance, his worldliness and the fact that he always spoke his mind. One of the last meetings with Hoveyda took place at the Jellicoes' London flat in Onslow Square. It provoked sad memories. He had decided go back to what was an almost certain death sentence, although he might have rather naively thought that Iran's judicial system would exonerate him. When he got into the lift he briefly turned, saying, 'Goodbye. I doubt if we'll ever meet again.' He went back to Tehran the next morning. Jellicoe, with others, lobbied strongly but in vain to get a stay of execution.

Parsons, a man whom Margaret Thatcher described as being a mix of 'intelligence, toughness, style and elegance', was not prone to mincing his words, while Sheila, his wife, was even more outspoken. At diplomatic dinners, she would often cause more than mild ruffles, never being one to shy away from challenging Government policy. When Parsons once came down to Tidcombe to lunch, Jellicoe wanted to produce something special for him and asked Philippa to serve some of the caviar that Hoveyda had given him. To his horror, Philippa replied that she had thrown it out thinking it had gone off. It had been 'the best golden caviar. The type that only the Shah ate.'[13]

Leslie and Peter St Just and their daughter Laura were other regular guests, as were Janetta Jackson, who had been married to Robert Kee and then Derek Jackson, the nuclear physicist, and multiple Dunne relations (from Martin's and Thomas's families). And, of course, there was Sue Baring. She has remained Philippa's closest friend and became godmother to Jellicoe's last child, David Lloyd. He was unknown to most of both families till he was nearly in his twenties. Although he did not show it, Jellicoe was clearly immensely proud of David. 'You know my son', he told Collette one day, 'he's very clever.' Collette had no idea he even existed. Not many people did.

Guests at Tidcombe not only reflected Jellicoe's life and career, they also reflected Philippa's. One frequent visitor was 'Spider' Quennell. The tall, long-limbed beauty had been friends with Philippa's mother, Peggy, before she and Philippa also became close. Jellicoe adored Spider's wonderfully outspoken eccentricity, although in old age she became a more difficult character.

Gianmarina Gross and her three daughters, 'Bino', 'Niotti' and Talia had rented a cottage from the Jellicoes and felt, like the Hendersons who'd stayed under the same roof, very much at home. Nearby lived Michael Stewart and his wife, Damaris, as well as Bryan Moyne, whose large house and grounds at Biddesden set the stage for many summer evenings.

A house filled with as much entertainment as Tidcombe could only keep going with the right kind of help. Barbara and Tony Hunt have really become part of the family. We grew up with their children, Alan and David, both of whom now work in David's immensely successful forestry management company. Barbara grew up in the village of Tidcombe, where she had worked as a dairy maid. The pair's stalwart support of the family has always been heartfelt. And, most importantly, Barbara's cooking is renowned.

Jellicoe had a butler called Obidan. He was one of the most eccentric men I ever met. His twin brother had worked for the Italian Foreign Minister, Count Ciano, and so, for a short time, had 'Ob'. He would regularly entertain visiting lunch guests, toupé awry, with a routine that could well have been the inspiration for *La Cage aux Folles*. He was a superb cook – and a kleptomaniac. Nothing was safe, although if something was missing, you just needed to mention it and magically the item would reappear.

George Jellicoe's love of Greece ran deep, to his core. He loved the people, the land and its historical legacy. And he was loved by them:

> George Jellicoe had bonded with the gallant Hellenes in their hour of peril, which is why he will be remembered, alongside British philhellenes such as Monty Woodhouse, Patrick Leigh Fermor and others with admiration and affection by my compatriots.[14]

Paddy Leigh Fermor, the war hero and travel writer, was one of Jellicoe's closest friends. He was revered by the Greeks, especially Cretans. At the invitation of the Greek Government, George and Philippa had been asked back as guests of General Tsigantes on his yacht. Jellicoe and Tisigantes had been together in the desert, and the old general held my father in the highest esteem, saying that he was 'the bravest man he'd ever met'.[15] After sailing down the east coast and by Monavassia, Greece's eastern Venetian trading port, they headed west around the Mani, the Peloponnese.

The General's own life was not that straightforward. It's said that he'd had a child with his young niece, Kyria, an altogether unattractive relationship if this was true (it seems now that it was not). However, there was also a funny side to him, like the time he set fire to one of the sofas at Tidcombe. Left alone for a moment by his hosts, he'd made strenuous advances to a lady and, in doing so, dropped his cigar between the cushions.

While Tsigantes lay dying in his London hospital bed, Jellicoe went to see him. The General reminded him of a promise that had been made: that his body should be cremated and his ashes laid to rest in the churchyard at Tidcombe. He swore never to return to Greece while the Colonels held power, and Jellicoe had agreed to his last request. It caused a serious diplomatic incident as Tsigantes was revered as a military commander of the first order. The Ambassador, John Sorokis, did, however, attend the ceremony. As a result, my father's own final resting place is next to a gravestone dedicated to Tsigantes. When Greece finally returned to civilian democratic rule, an honour guard of *Evzone* was sent to bring the General's body back to his homeland with full military honours. They arrived in full regalia and, as they marched through the wooded avenue to the church, their traditional clogs (*tsarouchi*) clacked loudly on the uneven, chalky Wiltshire soil.

It was in 1965 that Jellicoe first saw Paddy Leigh Fermor's house in Kardamyli. The house is situated on a headland an hour or so south of Kalamata, overlooking a small bay. The land was gifted to Paddy by the Greeks. It is a magical place, lovingly built with pebbled terraces and shaded areas to pass the hours in conversation or lost in a book. At night, chatting and laughing, we all swam in the calm, warm waters, each swimmer leaving a twinkling trail of green fluorescence in the moonlight. The simple luxury of it is unforgettable. Paddy had wanted George to buy the adjacent land that ran down a small valley to a larger, longer, white-pebbled beach. It had none of the magic of Paddy's place, and I'm glad he decided not to agree to it.

Looking out across the bay from the stone table at the edge of Paddy's property, there's an outcrop of rocks to the right just beyond a stony beach. It was nicknamed 'Jellicoe's Leap'. The name came about after Paddy had eulogized Jellicoe in a letter to Damaris, the widow of Sir Michael Stewart, the former British ambassador in Athens. She had known Jellicoe most of her life and was a cousin of Tim Marten, Jellicoe's boyhood friend. Michael shared Jellicoe's love of Greece and, as a former artist, of Greek paintings. Ghika was a favourite of his.

> George did a tremendous high dive from a rock, which I'll always think of as Jellicoe's Leap, rival to Saphos in Lefkas. Put on my mettle, I stole there after they left and when no-one was about (in case of flunking at the last moment), described the same dread parabola. It wasn't as dread as it looked, but I wish I'd thought of it first.[16]

I hope, in years to come, it will continue to be known this way, as *his* rock, recalling the lifelong friendship between two great Philhellenes. It was my father at his best, his physical best that is. Sitting out on one of the terraces in the cool of the evening. He would recall their lifelong friendship. Paddy was just as dashing, extraordinarily gifted intellectually and strikingly handsome. But shirtless there was an incongruously prominent double-tailed mermaid tattooed on his left arm. I never quite fathomed how it got there.

The family holidayed many a summer at the house while Paddy took Jellicoe's house in Wiltshire in exchange. Many years later, I was there with George when age was starting to takes its toll. In 1997, he had been diagnosed with prostate cancer and the treatments drained his strength. Though it was rare for him to complain, he was in excruciating pain and urinating blood. Eventually, it got too bad for the local doctor at Kardamyli to deal with. Johnny and I laid him gently in the back of our station wagon and took him to Kalamata Hospital. He was in good hands. The hospital was modern and well-staffed, but Philippa decided to stay with him throughout the night.

No encounter with George, no matter how fleeting, would fail to create its own special energy. Jellicoe's short stay at the hospital turned out to be just the same. He shared the ward with a mixed bag, including one very elegant man with whom he was – when he had the strength to talk again – to strike up a brief friendship. They were both suffering the same symptoms. The other patient's situation was a little more complicated, in that his aged spouse insisted on occupying the only bathroom throughout the night. Philippa did her best to be patient. It turned out that the wife had taken the opportunity to wash her underwear. Large baggy black knickers and old-fashioned corsets were hung, dripping, on every conceivable purchase all around the small room, its more mundane purpose completely subjugated to this new role.

Finally released from hospital, George did anything but follow 'doctor's orders'. He never did. Instead, we went to a mountain restaurant. To start with, it was pretty quiet, but eventually the music started. Jellicoe couldn't resist. His cane was thrown aside in a quasi-biblical scene – the cripple walking, except he was dancing, energetically. As one description puts it, Cretan dances are 'light and jumpy, and extremely cardiovascular'.[17] It wasn't long before the elderly villagers were voicing hearty encouragement. Shouts of '*Houpa!*' echoed across the village square and up the valley, interspersed with peels of loud laughter and the clinking of glasses. He was clearly enjoying being back on centre-stage. We were all thoroughly enjoying having our hero back from the wars and amongst us again. I miss those days.

Some years later, we all went to the southern coast of Crete to stay in a small village only accessible by sea, west of Sfakia. In May 1941, the Allies had been evacuated from there under fire after a murderously exposed march across the island under the constant strafing and bombing of German fighters. My father swam in the blue-green waters on the waterfront of the small village of Loutro. But when it came to getting out, he simply did not have the strength to lift himself on to the slippery, shingled rocks. I could see his sense of frustration and the indignity he felt at having to ask for my help to pull him out.

When Paddy died, years after my father had, his house was left in the care of the Benaki Museum in Athens. Given the turmoil of the Greek economic crisis, it wasn't surprising that they were never able to do much, but the lack of initiative was, nevertheless, frustrating. There were so many people who would gladly have given their time. The house started to look badly in need of love. Window frames were rotting, walls collapsing and the house was open to vandalism and theft. Finally, in the spring of 2016, the Onassis Foundation generously stepped in and the finance for the restoration of the great writer's home was guaranteed.

For ten years (1983–1992), Jellicoe was a member of the Onassis International Prizes Committee. It was a rare honour for a non-Greek and, in fact, after his death, the exception was discontinued. One time, he needed a 'name' for an event in Athens. He finally went, accompanied by William Waldegrave, at the time a Foreign Office Minister and later Provost of Eton

College. Jellicoe had dangled the opportunity to Waldegrave of spending a weekend with his wife, Caroline, at Paddy's idyllic house.

Jellicoe's influence in Greece remained strong right up to his later years. He was asked by a new Greek Prime Minister, Konstantinos Mitsotakis, for advice on the formation of his government after the socialists had been ousted. In Waldegrave's eyes he 'was hugely admired on the democratic right in Greece (and, like Paddy [Leigh Fermor], equally hated and traduced by the Stalinist Greek left – fellow travellers, many of them, of the Stalinist Greek Communists whom George had helped keep out of power in 1944').[18] Jellicoe's support for all things Greek brought him membership of a wide array of associations. He was on the board of the London Hellenic College, Chairman of the Anglo-Hellenic League, a Vice-President of the Byron Society and a President of the Anglo-Cretan Veterans Association (1991–5). A commemorative dinner was hosted at the British Embassy in Athens, in part organized by Jason Mavrikis, for whom Jellicoe had campaigned for a honour. Sitting beside me was Mitsotakis.

At the Anglo-Hellenic League, his name is linked to the Steven Runciman Award, a literary prize for works published in the English language about Greece and Greek culture. The award was launched by Jellicoe in 1986 in memory of his beloved Cambridge tutor. Runciman had had an extraordinary career after Cambridge, where he'd already made a name for himself. Forbidden to keep a piano in college, he'd flouted the rule by buying an antique dulcitone, having amassed a large collection of silk gowns. He'd given piano lessons to Pu Yi, the last Emperor of China, worked as a press attaché in Sofia during the war (based on the recommendation of one of his former pupils, Guy Burgess) and even read the palm of George II, King of the Hellenes, divining his future. Jellicoe praised his time in Athens when he served on the British Council, saying 'I doubt whether the British Council has ever had a better or more influential representative.'[19]

At the House of Lords in 2007, along with others who had been closely associated with him, I spoke about George as a family man and a father. It was daunting company to speak alongside, consisting of, among others, Sir David Miers, a former British ambassador to Greece, and John Julius Norwich.

Years later, my brother Johnny was told about George's exploits in Crete. After he'd taken his O-levels, he was invited to stay with Mannousis Manousakis and Mitsotakis. The two Cretans were close friends, having spent the war years fighting together, and had built their houses close to each other overlooking the bay at Chania. They were on their way to a wedding when Johnny was approached by an old Cretan, who whispered quietly to him that every man in the group had actually killed another. He then said, 'Your father had such balls, such very beeg balls.' Johnny thought that a long-hidden episode of a sexual nature in our father's wartime past was about to become public and found himself slightly panicking. But it had nothing to do with that. It was his courage that was admired. Manousakis was a character. He would worry incessantly about being on time. He insisted on taking Johnny to Heraklion airport but drove the whole way in his old VW Beetle in second gear and arrived with four hours to spare. He would often call Tidcombe and leave memorably measured messages on the answer machine: 'This is Mannoouuuusis Manousakis from Chaneeeea, calling.'

Jellicoe did not talk very much about his wartime exploits. When he drove to Kardamyli with Waldegrave, the latter had tried, unsuccessfully, to draw him out, but 'George, like most real heroes, spoke little and wrote less about his war.'[20] When he was under attack by Stukas on Leros in 1943, it was an entirely different affair from when he'd been in Tobruk two summers earlier. In the desert, he'd treated the whole thing as a jaunt. He hadn't seen anything. In Leros he saw death all around him. He was exhausted. The kick of adrenalin wasn't there to counter the fear of feeling that you, and you alone, are in a pilot's sights.

Jellicoe's first real encounter with death was probably when his batman died. This was around the time of the November 1941 offensive that took the Guards 3rd Battalion right across the desert to Ajdabiya, at the bottom of the Gulf of Sirte. Jellicoe had come back from a patrol to find him dying, shot in the stomach. 'That was really almost my first experience of seeing somebody badly wounded and I remember how shaken I was by that.' He'd been hit by machine gun fire in an air attack.

While many Germans now visit Crete, there is no love lost amongst the old Cretan veterans – the few that remain – for their former adversaries. So it was all the more extraordinary that Mannoussis married a German; and that George Psychoundakis, the hero of *The Cretan Runner*, had for years tended the graves of German parachutists at the Maleme memorial on the western end of Crete, where the glider-borne troops had landed in 1941. It was an extraordinarily personal act of forgiveness.

In 1991, on the fiftieth anniversary of the invasion, I went to Crete with my father and Philippa. It must have been one of the last occasions, and a great number of veterans had passed away. We had a day with the Duke of Kent, patron of the Anglo-Cretan Veterans Association. We were supposed to be discreet, but the Greek police went to town. We roared through towns and villages, a long cortege of black SUVs, sirens blaring and windows darkened. If ever there was going to be a terrorist attack, this surely begged for it. George and I visited Maleme as he wanted to find the final resting place of the German brothers, the Blüchers, who had all died within days of each other in the May 1941 attack. I could sense a deep sadness overcome him. It felt like the opening scene of *Saving Private Ryan*.

George had been President of the UK Crete Veterans Association and joked with Georges Bergé that he 'had no right to this exalted rank, having as you well know, only paid a fleeting visit to that well-remembered island during the war.'[21] So I know he would have approved of, and would have supported, today's UK Crete Veterans and Friends Society, which continues to donate to local schools and causes, even if the veterans themselves have passed on. It's a lasting sign of respect from the veterans' families for what the islanders did to help them. Late in the summer of 2017, I was honoured to be invited by a group of Germans and Italians to Leros. We spent the week talking about the fighting – and the hopelessly lost cause – of the September 1943 Dodecanese campaign.

Jellicoe was also a patron of the Greek Archaeological Foundation. I would imagine that this role required a high degree of diplomacy, given the continued refusal of the British Museum to return the Elgin marbles. The British stance cuts deep into Greek national pride. There was a chance for an extraordinary national gesture at the time of the Athens Olympics. It would have created shock waves in the museum community but it would have won Britain pride of place in Greek hearts. Tourists are still asked to sign an electronic petition when they arrive at Athens airport.

Five minutes or so from the balcony of the Hotel Grande Bretagne, down the street from Parliament Square, is the small church of St Paul's. Inside, at the far corner on the left, there is a plaque on the wall of the church dedicated to Jellicoe that Jason Mavrikis, one of the early *Ieros Lochos* additions to the SAS, was instrumental in having placed. The two opening lines from Cavafy's epic poem of the Spartans' sacrifice were the ones chosen for the stone.

> Honour to those who in the life they lead define and guard a Thermopylae.
> Never betraying what is right,
> consistent and just in all they do
> but showing pity also, and compassion;
> generous when they're rich, and when they're poor,
> still generous in small ways,
> still helping as much as they can;
> always speaking the truth,
> yet without hating those who lie.
> And even more honour is due to them
> when they foresee (as many do foresee)
> that Ephialtis will turn up in the end,
> that the Medes will break through after all.

My brother-in-law, Colin Heber-Percy, a screenwriter and a Greek scholar, was the one to suggest these inspiringly beautiful lines. Only a foot or so away is another plaque. That one commemorates the SBS and Greek Sacred Squadron members of the Alimnia patrol that were captured in April 1944 and later executed by the Germans. Both Jellicoe and Sutherland attended its dedication.

The day Jellicoe's plaque was unveiled, we met in Athens at the British Embassy. There was a dinner with many notables and a ceremony at the church. The diplomat, George Papoulios, summed it up, saying, 'We Greeks will be forever grateful to him.'[22] When my father's memorial service was held at the Guards Chapel, I read these same lines, but in Athens I found myself completely overcome by the setting. Later, Father Malcolm at St Paul's worked very quietly in the background with the family to diplomatically replace the original tablet with one that had been corrected. That he made some unfortunate error in its wording should not diminish the kindness of Jason Mavrikis in organizing the work.

Jellicoe's early association with David Stirling made him a natural to take over the Presidency of the SAS Regimental Association (1996–2000). I have many fond memories of visits to the Regiment outside Hereford and of colleagues from the Association travelling with us when we were in Crete, Lieutenant Colonel Keith Edlin in particular. We met Keith for the first time when we RV'd at the ferry dock at Sfakia. He and a friend, Chris Dodkin, had just 'yomped' through the gorges. Keith and I remained in contact for many years, as indeed I did with Chris, who later took over from Keith.

Another memory was the opening of Jellicoe Road, afterwards standing under a shower of poppies at the SAS Clock Tower and, along with Philippa and Daisy, listening to the tributes to the Regiment's men lost in action. We remembered the eighteen SAS who were drowned when their Sea King helicopter went down in the Falklands conflict in 1982. All my own visits, however, were made after my father's death. It would have been more special, in many ways, to have been there with him and to have heard him talk about some of the people shown in the photographs that cover the walls. It was all the more surprising, given his connections and role within British Special Forces, that the Club which bears the same name took a whole year to get his photograph mounted on its staircase. In my opinion, it was a not insignificant oversight that he wasn't there in the first place.

It was Jellicoe's deep Special Forces connections that persuaded him to help found Hakluyt and Company in 1995 with Christopher James and join its Board of Directors (1996–2000). James had been both SAS and in the Intelligence Services. The company's work provides companies with strategic political intelligence as background information for business. Fitzroy Maclean was on the Board and asked Jellicoe to give them the benefit of his insights and connections, which he did, without remuneration.

Jellicoe's connections with the Free French were less well established. He maintained a regular correspondence with Jack Sibard (who sadly died in August 2019) and Georges Bergé and would occasionally see Augustin Jordan, Berge's 2i/c in the desert. One occasion was at David Stirling's memorial in 1991.

In 2002, he also became Patron of The Second World War Experience Centre near Wetherby in Yorkshire, and I was able to provide a photograph of Jellicoe in the desert that had not been seen before. He's holding a kit bag which looks more like a teddy bear.

When he was asked by Celia Sandys, Winston Churchill's grand-daughter, to talk to a group of American admirers of the great war leader, Jellicoe was asked to take them around Scapa Flow, Britain's most northern First and Second World War naval base sheltered amongst the islands of Orkney. Not unnaturally, Celia assumed that the close connection between his family name and Scapa Flow meant that the Admiral's son would know all there was to know about one of the Flow's landmarks, the Churchill barriers – especially since his own father was based at Scapa for the first two years of the Great War. Jellicoe accepted the invitation, not letting on about his ignorance, but in preparation for the tour he went up to Orkney and 'did a recce'. He did it well enough to be able to feign surprised satisfaction at seemingly remembering small things from his earlier times there. I remember, however, at the same time he was more than a little miffed that few of those whom he met in Kirkwall seemed to recognize the significance of his name. I have come to greatly love Orkney and admire the Orcadians. It is the place I associate most with the Admiral, rather than Southampton, his birthplace.

Mealtime conversations with Jellicoe, best with a few admirers gathered around the dining room table at Tidcombe, listening intently to his every word, were always engaging. 'Fizzy' might be the word he would have used: he was not a man to constantly repeat himself, he liked to explore new territory and learn. It was only when he was asked to talk about his war years that one would hear a well-rehearsed delivery. It was a way to avoid the pain that he undoubtedly carried within; his stories were full of humour, not sadness.

Chapter 16

Privilege and Public Duty

George Jellicoe saw 'public service [as] both a duty and a privilege'.[1] The words were those of Peter Carrington, his political mentor, and spoken at his memorial service at London's Guards Chapel in 2007. After he left the diplomatic service, Jellicoe's life continued to follow a richly tapestried path, leading him from politics to business and allowing him to hold numerous positions of public trust along the way. They included such diverse positions as the chairmanships of the Davy Corporation, Tate & Lyle, the British Overseas Trade Board and the Medical Research Council; and the Presidencies of the Royal Geographical Society and the London Chamber of Commerce. He would also serve as a director in companies as diverse as Sotheby's, Smith's Industries and the bankers, S. G. Warburg, and be elected a Fellow of the Royal Society and Chancellor of the University of Southampton. On his death, he was the oldest parliamentarian in the world and the last holder of the fabled office of First Lord of the Admiralty. He lived life – in all its richness, diversity and disappointments – to its fullest.

In 1961, Jellicoe joined the government as a junior minister for housing but within a year was named First Lord of the Admiralty, after which he took the far less glamorous position of Secretary of Defence for the Royal Navy. The ceremony was carried out to 'the perhaps inappropriately jolly strains of *HMS Pinafore* on Horse Guards Parade, when the Admiralty flag was lowered for the last time and the Lords Commissioners of the Admiralty ceased to exist.'[2] His father, Sir John, would have been proud of his son's career; he himself had become the First Sea Lord in December 1917. Jellicoe's mother, the Dowager Countess, was just still alive to see him become the political head of the Admiralty, a role he held for two years from 1962 to 1964. There's a photograph of her standing proudly between her son and her nephew, Admiral Sir Charles Madden. On her hat is a diamond-studded family brooch of HMS *Iron Duke*, the Admiral's flagship at the battle of Jutland in 1916.

The Sea in his Blood

George Jellicoe's other naval connections

George Jellicoe's strong naval connections were not just through his own father. The Admiral's grandfather had married Constantia, one of Admiral Philip Patton's daughters (others were married to other senior military figures: Mary to Admiral Sir Edward James Foote, Anna to Admiral Sir John Loring and Eliza to Admiral Sir Edward Down). Philip Patton's father had been a naval captain and his grandfather, Baillie Phillip Patton, had fought at La Hogue in 1692.

By the time he died in 1815, Patton had fought in nine great naval actions under the command of such men as Edward Boscowen (on whose flagship, HMS *Torbay*, he served in 1755), Hawke and Rodney. Patton became an Admiral of the Red and served as Second Naval Lord in the Admiralty under Lords Melville and Barham during Pitt's administration and at the time of the Battle of Trafalgar. During a period of involuntary retirement at his home in Fleetwood, Fareham, Hampshire, Patton wrote an Admiralty study on the need to reform the navy's treatment of the ordinary seaman.

Not all Jellicoe ancestors bore the name with honour. Two extremes would be Father Basil Jellicoe (b.1900) and Adam Jellicoe (b.1725). Basil Jellicoe was the Admiral's cousin, but much about the exact lineage still remains a little hazy. Basil always referred to John Jellicoe as 'uncle', but it may have been more a term of endearment than the exact relationship. Basil; was, however, a man of extraordinary philanthropic vision.

Adam Jellicoe, however, was someone who, like the illustrious Sir Bernard Brocas' son Bernard, brought the family name and its naval connections into significant disrepute. In 1781, Adam's financial support was successfully sought by a Gosport industrialist, Henry Cort. Jellicoe was the Deputy Paymaster of the Navy's Pay Office, and Cort had the contract for making the hoops for the Royal Navy's storage barrels. This was a substantial business opportunity, but he had also heavily over-invested in his Fontley mill and was short of liquidity. The London cartel that the Navy wished to undercut with the Cort contract retaliated and forced iron ore prices up. The result was that Cort was out by £10,000.

Adam Jellicoe agreed to lend Cort £20,000 at 5 per cent interest and in return for agreeing to bring his son, Samuel, into the business. What was not known to either Cort or Samuel is that Adam had used misappropriated naval funds to finance his investment. After six years, in July 1788, his crime caught up with him. On 29 August 1789 'Extents' were issued calling for his arrest and the return of £36,500. He never returned any money, but instead committed suicide. Curiously, his home was just doors away from my eldest sister's house in Highbury.

Of the £36,500, £9,000 was actually owed by the business. Somehow, his son, Samuel managed to raise this amount, paid it back and kept the business. What was quite unforeseen was that Cort himself was found to be legally responsible for Adam Jellicoe's debts. He eventually died penniless in London in 1800. The Government also seized the patents to Cort's revolutionary iron production.

The affair leaves a very bad taste, but I'm not entirely without some sympathy for Adam Jellicoe, even if his failure at the end caused untold misery for Cort. After his death, a note was found in his chest:

> 'Ever since I have had Public Money in my hands, it has been a constant rule with me to have the value of it in Navy Bills, &c. &c. in the Iron Chest, that in the case of my death, the Balance might be immediately paid in; I have never failed in observing this method, and have always had much more than my Balance by me, till my engagements, about two years ago, with Mr. Cort, which, by degrees has so drained me, and employed so much more of my Money than I expected, that I have been obliged to turn most of my Navy Bills, &c. into Cash, and, at this time, to my great concern, am very deficient in my Balance. This gives me great uneasiness, nor shall I live or die in peace till the whole is restored.'

Harold Wilson's stunning electoral victory in 1964 put Labour back in power, and George Jellicoe fell back on business to pay the bills. It was not a time he enjoyed and he clearly perked up when, in 1967, he was made Peter Carrington's number two as Deputy Leader of the Opposition in the House of Lords.

In June 1970, the large Labour majority that Harold Wilson had won in 1966 disintegrated. Edward Heath won back 77 seats for the Conservatives and ended with 46 per cent of the vote, giving the Tories 330 seats against Labour's 287. Number 10 had called Tidcombe but had not been able to speak to Jellicoe as he was in the pub celebrating the victory with Nico Henderson and some friends. Heath had already given him a position in his Cabinet. Reluctantly, Philippa had to give the pub's phone number but was nervous about doing so as Jellicoe had recently been in the news. He had been stopped about 100 yards from his London apartment in Onslow Square and breathalysed. He 'was in a frenzy of anxiety' about the consequences.[3]

Philippa called the pub to warn her husband. 'No.10 to speak to Lord Jellicoe' rang out the call from the barman, somehow making himself heard above the clinking of glasses and verbal cacophony. It was Ted Heath. The new Prime Minister merely wanted to tell Jellicoe that he shouldn't worry about the drink-driving issue. It was a rather fraught phone call for Jellicoe, who was trying to act nonchalantly though respectfully. I think most people would have been in a cold sweat at having a conversation about this particular subject, with the obvious question for Heath being whether Jellicoe's consumption of alcohol might be a continuing issue.

After Ted Heath brought him back into government in 1970 as his Leader of the House of Lords, Jellicoe initiated much-needed reforms in the Civil Service and, using his long-honed diplomatic skills, saw important legislation for the European Union through the Lords.

In 1973 George Jellicoe found himself in the glare of public interest when he was implicated in the Lambton affair and resigned from the Heath government. There was an entry referring to 'Jellicoe' in the notebook of Norma Levy, the prostitute's 'madame'. Jellicoe was quizzed about it and immediately admitted that he had had 'some casual affairs'. His name was there for a completely different reason, however, because it was merely an address; but he was not to know at the time. The Admiral's cousin, Father Basil Jellicoe, the great social reformer, had been largely responsible for the creation of Somers Town in London's St Pancras slums in the late 1920s. Jellicoe's father had actually opened one of the new housing schemes in June 1928, and it was named Jellicoe House in remembrance of Father Basil's works amongst London's poorest. The honour bestowed on one Jellicoe would bring down another.

He had had the chance to talk the whole affair over with Philippa when he was driven to the Fulham Road restaurant, San Frediano, where she was waiting for him. Jellicoe came right to the point and told it how it was. It was typical of Philippa that her first reaction was not to blame or get angry with him. It was to blame *herself*, saying that she probably should have been with him more rather than spending so much time in the country with the children. Then she thought about it further and immediately took the stance that the value of his integrity was paramount.

In situations like this Philippa was a rock and quietly gave her opinion. George listened and took his wife's advice, although I have no doubt that there was never any doubt in his mind about what he had to do: he offered his resignation.

Jellicoe was grateful to Heath for how he had handled the difficult situation. He left London, initially for Philippa's brother's house to escape the press, and later to the home he loved, Tidcombe, to reflect and plan his next steps. He set up a table in one of the enclosed gardens and under the shade of four cypress trees sat, pondered and wrote. He wrote of what had happened and the mistakes he had made, but he also wrote to friends and old colleagues, exploring his options. This was one of those letters, to Edward Heath:

> Now that I have caught my breath, I feel that I must write to thank you for the kindness and consideration which you have always shown me both professionally, as it were, and privately – and not least last week. In a situation of horrible embarrassment and difficulty you extended to me a degree of courtesy and human understanding which I shall never forget. Thank you for all that you did to take so much of the sting out of the most bitter moment of my life.[4]

Whatever one thinks of Heath, I am sure that Jellicoe admired his deeply meritocratic sense and his personal drive. He had brought Margaret Thatcher into a heavily public-school cabinet, where Jellicoe was amongst friends, with cabinet colleagues like Willie Whitelaw and Peter Carrington. Within the structure of Downing Street was the Central Policy Review Staff (CPRS), for which Jellicoe recruited William Waldegrave. Jellicoe had recommended Waldegrave to Victor Rothschild, supposedly asking whether the latter needed a 'messenger-cum-tea-boy'. He had been introduced through Waldegrave's father, with whom the son was having tea in the House when Jellicoe had mentioned that 'Victor's looking for some chaps.' His father afterwards quietly told Jellicoe, 'I am really not selling you a dud.'[5] When I met Waldegrave in 2017, he was the Provost of Eton College, his alma mater.

Out of Government, after a second resignation connected with the women in his life, Jellicoe took on the chairmanship of Tate & Lyle and joined the non-executive Board of Sotheby's, where his daughter Alexa's father-in-law, Sir Peter Wilson, was chairman. Wilson was reputed by some to be 'a man who had the ability to stand outside the elite into which he was born and to prey on it shamelessly.'[6] He 'gave the market a popular appeal it had never had before. He also transformed Sotheby's itself.' Wilson had been in MI.6. His code number was 007 and he was possibly Ian Fleming's inspiration for his famous character: suave, debonair and lethal. Like Jellicoe, Fleming had worked in Washington and, like my father, had unknowingly befriended Russian spies.Wilson, however, wanted Jellicoe on the non-executive board to add more weight to a group that was already excessively over-titled. It included Ann Getty, billionaire Gordon Getty's wife, Hans Heinrich 'Heinie' Thyssen-Bornemisza de Kaszon, Carroll Petrie and HRH Infanta Pilar de Borbón, Duchess of Badajoz.

His contributions to the country, nevertheless, continued to be significant: he helped re-write British anti-terrorism legislation, was a trustee of Margaret Jay's UK National AIDS Trust, raised money for research and, as President of the Royal Geographical Society, to support causes protecting the environment. The RGS was one of the real loves of Jellicoe's long life. One of his closest friends, Eddie Shackleton, son of the famous Polar explorer, had been a past President. The relationship he and Jellicoe had in the House of Lords has often been cited as one of the best examples of bipartisanship. Members of opposing parties, they shared interests in geography and both served on the Science and Technology Committee and as Chairmen of the East European Trade Council.

At Tate & Lyle, Jellicoe was clearly more comfortable. His work took him – and very often Philippa – to many parts of the globe, to plantations in Belize, manufacturing plants in America and buyers in Iran. Jellicoe had visited most countries – some extensively. In every case, he'd spend time educating himself in a country's culture, people and politics. Maybe it was the pull of learning from different cultures. Perhaps it was the diplomat in him. He would often combine an old, battered red Baedeker with some related literary work. It was a joy to travel with him. You would learn by just being around him. It was a sad day when he gave up the Chairmanship in 1983; the company's well-known logo, 'Mr Cube', was a welcome sight in the kitchen.

Rita Gardner, a former Chief Executive of the RGS, said that Jellicoe had a 'brilliant, natural astuteness about people'.[7] The fact that he 'just liked people' made him a very engaging listener. He very clearly understood what his role needed to be – a source of reassurance but also a supporter of change – and he played to that. In committee, he would always try to induce contributions from those who would not normally speak out. His 'wicked sense of humour' usually broke the ice. Having worked in government to protect the environment, he could talk with passion from personal experience, and with the natural humility of not being an academic but someone who wanted very much to understand the world in which he lived. It was only natural that this love of the countryside persuaded him to take on the Presidency of the Kennet and Avon Canal Trust. The 87-mile-long canal is now thriving, with canal boats, weekend canoeists, cyclists and runners. There was a time when it had been impassable.

Another job in which he excelled was the chairmanship of the BOTB in 1983. The British Overseas Trade Board was the Department of Trade and Industry's promotional arm supporting British trade and exports. It became more of a passion than a job. Surprisingly, the *Independent* newspaper mislabelled it as the British Overseas *Training* Board.[8] He fell into the job with gusto, loving the travel and meeting interesting people. Some of it was hard going, but he was rarely one to be put off. If he felt he was helping, he would push himself. Meeting with difficult and dour characters was merely a challenge to be managed. He would make it his business to find the spark that would bring them to life. Jellicoe enjoyed people and getting to understand what made them 'tick'.

When the Soviet head of state, Mikhail Gorbachev, and his wife, Raisa, visited the UK in December 1984, Jellicoe was asked to look after the couple. There is a photo of Jellicoe seated next to the Russian leader, instantly distinguishable by his port wine birthmark. The former Secretary General of the Soviet Union's Communist Party understood that his disfigurement was an electoral plus. It made him instantly recognizable, like Churchill's slurred speech, enhanced by the false teeth which he decided should be kept ill-fitting, as it was this that made his voice so memorable.

In one photograph Jellicoe appears to be sound asleep. He wasn't. After Gorbachev had finished speaking, he rose and delivered a 'first class speech'. In the early days, this tendency of 'appearing to fall asleep' was pretty alarming to others. Later, they knew what he was up to and that he would jump back into action. 'It was all pretend.'[9] The Jellicoes enjoyed meeting the couple. Philippa got on well with Raisa, taking her shopping, to Mappin & Webb, where she bought some gold earrings, and generally acting as her London tour guide. Meanwhile, her husband kept a more appropriate schedule, visiting the library where Lenin had started the revolutionary newspaper *Iskra* (The Spark) in 1903 and Marx's tomb in Highgate cemetery.

One member of the Royal Family who worked closely with Jellicoe in these years was the Duke of Kent. He complimented my father on his time at the helm: 'It couldn't have been a greater pleasure ... he was such an enormously distinguished public servant.' In fact, he received a knighthood, a KBE, for the contributions he made while at the BOTB. Like many veterans, the Duke said, Jellicoe 'never, ever spoke about the war.' He only discovered 'anything about his war record after [he'd] known him for about ten years.'[10] He'd been clearly impressed that Jellicoe had never 'blown his own trumpet'. It was a trait that he had picked up from his father, the Admiral.

My own favourite story about Jellicoe's foreign business missions was Nico Henderson's in *Old Friends and Modern Instances*:

> Leading a high-level British Trade delegation to Tokyo, he was called upon at the end of dinner to say a few words of thanks to his Japanese hosts. 'In speaking to you at this important juncture', he began rather heavily, 'I have to tell you that I am a much-diminished man compared with the person I was when I sat down at this dinner.' A pause followed.

Translations were whispered. The Japanese smiled. George continued: 'Yes, I took off my shoes at the beginning of the evening, and now I can't find them.' There was a longer pause and further translations. The Japanese smiled even more. They had heard tell of British humour.[11]

One of the last business chairmanships that Jellicoe took on was of a company whose name has now all but disappeared. In 1985, he became Chairman of the Davy Corporation. The company's name was closely tied to the famous Davy lamp which miners would once take below. There's a photo of Jellicoe dressed for the pit, with miner's helmet and lamp, grinning. When he had wanted to join the ranks of Labour, he told me that he'd been rebuffed with a polite but firm recommendation. 'First, go work down a mine, lad.'

As its Chairman, Jellicoe had also headed the Medical Research Council (MRC) to help the scientific body deal with Government. Jellicoe had no medical or scientific background but could master difficult, technical briefs and identify the major issues. Having limited technical knowledge made little difference. He used a Council meeting after a trip to Bangkok to win over his audience, startling the eminent group of medical practitioners with a supremely personal statement: 'My quack says I've got toxoplasmosis.' He then challenged anyone to tell him what that was. Nobody was able to answer. Jellicoe's humour was infectious. It was the time of Auto-Immune Deficiency Syndrome (AIDS), and Jellicoe had just come back from a trip to San Francisco, where he'd been staying with my sister Zara, to whom the disease, which had devastated the city's gay community, was also a deeply personal matter. After meeting with Margaret Thatcher and getting the support of Willie Whitelaw, he and Jim Gowans, the CEO, succeeded in getting important research fast-tracked and a public information campaign launched. The result was that the United Kingdom 'had the smallest increase of AIDS of any major European country'.[12] On 28 June 1988, George Jellicoe was made a Fellow of the Royal Society. He added the initials FRS to his list of military decorations with justified pride. Few non-scientists have been given such an honour: Eddie Shackleton, Samuel Pepys and Margaret Thatcher are some rare examples.

In his later life – after he'd retired – Jellicoe finally had time to devote to some of his other loves. Gardening was one. Gardeners seem to have a deep sense of time and, by what they do, a deep respect for nature and a concern for its protection. Those who work the soil think in seasons and years. They develop a special kind of patience. They remember particular patterns of weather. The only time I ever saw my father shed a tear was when his garden's great avenue of trees was devastated by the severe storms of 1987. Jellicoe called on the help and advice of a cousin, Geoffrey Jellicoe, the renowned landscape architect. He'd become famous for his doctoral work, published as *Italian Gardens of the Renaissance* (written with John Shepherd), and for *The Landscape of Man* and the visionary work on the *Motopia* urban planning project sponsored by Pilkington Glass in 1959. Geoffrey immediately reassured his cousin that the storm was a hidden blessing. And indeed it was. Under Geoffrey's skilful guidance, the gardens took on a reinvigorated life and identity. He reassured my father that what had happened was part of a natural cycle of nature and that what would come back would be even better. He was right, and my father was able to see how the garden bore witness to Geoffrey's vision. Jellicoe could sit in the dining room in one of the comfortable chairs in the corner and enjoy the afternoon sun, looking out into the garden from the comfort of his favourite perch.

Sadly, in later life, Jellicoe started to lose his faculties. At Tidcombe, the kitchen, with its warming Aga, is the house's heart. His nurse, Collette, once found him sitting by himself, staring up at the row of Gould Toby jugs lined up on the top of the old pine kitchen dresser. One was of his grandfather, the others were Churchill, Wilson and Joffre. Beatty's jug – probably purposefully – is missing from the group. Gould's design for Beatty placed a large shell at his side: more appropriate to his nickname 'Hellfire Jack' than the Admiral sitting holding a jug of his own with that inscription. It was a daily reminder of my father's heritage. He was pointing to each in turn, triumphantly exclaiming, 'I've outlived you, and you, and you'.[13] Sometimes, as the old boiler kicked into action, the gentle vibrations would remind him of his childhood. He'd think he was back in New Zealand, maybe on a ship with his father coming back to England. One evening, having dinner with him and my sister Emma, he turned to me, waving his wine glass rather flamboyantly and asking 'Of course, you two know each other?' One could do nothing but laugh at the sad absurdity of the moment.

George Patrick John Rushworth Jellicoe, 2nd Earl Jellicoe of Scapa, KBE, DSO, MC, PC, FRS died on 22 February 2007. At the time of his death, he was recognized as the longest-serving parliamentarian alive and was the Father of the House in the Lords, having sat there for 68 years. Unlike 660 of his fellow peers whose hereditary right to sit and vote in the House of Lords was removed in November 1999, Jellicoe remained there, having become, six days later, a life peer as Baron Jellicoe of Southampton. It was certainly an honour bestowed on a former Leader of the House of Lords but also, perhaps, on a man who had continued to devote so much of his life to the common good.

He died as he would have liked to: looking out over the garden he and Philippa had both so lovingly created. He had suffered a massive heart attack and died in the arms of a man who was as close as family, the gardener and groundsman, Tony Hunt. Tony and his wife, Barbara, had worked for the family for more than thirty years, Tony tending the grounds, Barbara managing the house. Now retired, they continue to live in one of the manor's cottages. He'd asked Tony and Collette, his palliative nurse, to take him to the window to catch his breath. In a different way, Collette had also been close to the Jellicoe family for many years. She had first worked for Lady Elizabeth Scott, who happened to be godmother to my aunt, Lady Norah Wingfield. Collette would visit her Irish home, Salterbridge, and eventually cared for her. Norah always wanted her to meet her brother, so much so that Collette was rather nervous about doing so; but when she did she immediately took to the man Norah called 'the wonderful lord'. She would bring great sensitivity to the care she gave my father.

It was fitting that this was how George Jellicoe should draw his last breath. He had always loved the simple beauties of his own English country garden at Tidcombe. That death came from a heart attack was ironic, for he was a past President of the British Heart Foundation. It was prostate cancer that really 'took the wind out of his sails.'

The last thing he would have seen were the trees and the green lawns of the home he loved. The garden was just starting to revive after the grey winter, and the first daffodils were pushing through. It was, we all felt, the most fitting way for him to leave us, the way he would have chosen.

He was buried on a typical Wiltshire winter's day: grey, blustery and chilling. In the graveyard of an eleventh century Norman church, a small group stood to one side as the coffin was lowered to its final rest. It was a simple service attended only by immediate family and a few of his closest friends.

Six uniformed members of the Special Air Service served as pall-bearers, coming to pay their last respects to one of the Regiment's early officers. Each of his children, his wife and his closest friends passed by the open grave, scattering soil on his coffin. I scattered some which had been sent all the way from Greece by Jason Mavrikis. He wanted George Jellicoe to lie close to the soil of the country for whose freedom he had fought. The name 'O-Tzellliko' drifted into my thoughts. It's how my father had often been called in Crete. Earlier, each one of Jellicoe's children had spoken, including a young man, David, the youngest of his children, who talked of his love for a man, his father, whom he had hardly known. The evocative words of the 'Viking Farewell' were read.

Unlike his father, who was a deeply religious man, Jellicoe was an agnostic. Turning to his carer, Collette, he once declared, 'I think I'd better keep an open mind, my dear.'

Notes

Introduction
1. 'almost as a folk hero…'. Elliot, *A Forgotten Man*, p.188
2. 'in so many fields from politics to business…'. de la Billière, personal correspondence
3. 'There are in fact four Georges'. Henderson, *Old Friends*, p.107
4. 'raised the wattage', Speech, Anglo-Hellenic, House of Lords, 14 Feb 2008, Viscount Norwich
5. 'Like most real heroes…'. Waldegrave, p.24
6. 'revered'. Leigh Fermor, *Remembering Lord Jellicoe*
7. 'deprived the Conservative party…'. *Guardian*, Obituary, 26 February 2007
8. 'largest engineering contractor…'. Almonds, *British Achilles*, p.226

Chapter 1
1. 'impotent pain and rage'. *Guardian*, Obituary, 26 February 2007
2. 'ashamed'. IWM, Jellicoe interview, reel 1
3. 'I'm absolutely certain that…'. Holland Interview, 2002, p.3
4. 'rat on the Poles'. IWM, Jellicoe interview, reel 1
5. 'they were allowed to uncover…'. IWM, Jellicoe interview, Reel 1
6. 'to assemble, organize, equip…'. Paget, p.152
7. 'two or three weeks, ski-ing…'. Holland Interview, 2002, p.3
8. Mather referred to the *Batory* as the *Baretry*
9. 'Our bones would be bleaching'. IWM, Jellicoe interview, Reel 1
10. 'About one fifth had only three days on skis…'. Mather, p.16
11. Jellicoe was at the Regent's Park Barracks in May/June 1940 (Holland interview (2002, p.3)
12. 'I suppose, Jellicoe, you want to have…'. IWM, Jellicoe interview, Reel 1
13. 'the name of which had been borrowed…'. Mather, p.31
14. 'inspired Roger Courtney …'. Mortimer, 'The Week', *Meet the SBS: one man strangled nine Germans with his bare hands*. 9 March, 2012
15. 'black tussled hair, his serious…'. James, p.87
16. Almonds. *Gentleman Jim*, p.23
17. 'felt fully entitled to poach his deer'. IWM, Jellicoe interview, Reel 1
18. 'earmarked'. Warner, p.12
19. 'a 10,000 ton, 17-knot converted…'. Lewes, p.151
20. The spelling was *Glen Erne* according to Cooper (p.10)
21. 'Our living conditions were…'. Cooper, p.11
22. 'He would stand, facing towards…'. Almonds, *Gentleman Jim*, p.32
23. 'Christ! He's so stupid…'. Holmes, p.186
24. 'I began to realize …'. McLynn, p.108
25. 'Truth to tell he was no good…'. Mather, p.31
26. 'much too outspoken and militant…'. Lewes, p.149
27. 'He would sit in Shepheard's Hotel openly…' McLynn, p.96
28. 'aggressive, headstrong…'. Mortimer, *Stirling's Men*, p.47
29. 'boisterous, xenophobic…'. Mather, p.51
30. 'a hard-drinking white hunter…'. Quoted in Mortimer, *SBS*, p.15
31. 'very crowded … this is practically no exercise…'. Lewes, p.151

32. 'The son of General Archibald...'. Malcolm, p.4
33. 'translate his needs to the family'. Malcolm, p.4
34. Jellicoe, SBS Reunion Speech 1996
35. 'In the closed world of the ship...'. Quoted in Malcolm, p.6 from Artemis Cooper, *Cairo at War*
36. John Jellicoe, 18 September 2016
37. 'lost almost three years' wages...'. Waugh, quoted in Harder p.74
38. 'an irresponsible and unremarkable...'. Mortimer, *Stirling's Men*, p.3
39. 'a couple of deep snifters...'. Mortimer, S*tirling's Men*, p.9
40. 'hint of impish humour'. Hastings, *Drums*, p.45
41. 'There must be a clown...'.Mortimer, *Stirling's Men*, p.3
42. 'arid plot named Geneifa Camp'. Mather, p.37. The Commandos arrived there 10 or 11 March
43. 'reached rock bottom'.Almonds. *Gentleman Jim*, p.32
44. 'very soon we will be performing...'. Lewes, p.155
45. 'in heavy seas was hell to sail in'. Ranfurly, p.151
46. 'who'd insisted on coming...'. IWM, Jellicoe interview, Reel 2
47. '...ended his days hunting ...'. IWM Jellicoe interview, Reel 2
48. 'good Australian ribaldry which...'. IWM, Jellicoe interview, Reel 2
49. 'The Stukas used to come over...'. IWM, Jellicoe interview, Reel 2
50. 'the ponderous presence...'. Mather, p.45
51. 'hair-brained scheme'. Correspondence Mather to GPRJ, 12 March 1991
52. 'Hardly looking up, (he) said to the agitated...'. Carol Mather's book in draft (p.40), Chapter III. The source was Rear-Adm. Morgan-Giles
53. 'a rotten navigator'. Mather, p.48
54. 'It was an absurd idea'. Holland interview, 2002, p4
55. 'in terms of casualties ...'. *Daily Telegraph*, Obituary, 30 April 2013
56. 'not particularly well-planned operations'. IWM, Jellicoe interview, Reel 2
57. 'looked after this young...'. IWM, Jellicoe interview, Reel 2
58. 'at 30 yards or so I didn't feel...'. IWM, Jellicoe interview, Reel 2
59. 'Nothing really... eighty miles....'. Holland interview, 2002, p.5
60. 'for not running away faster'. IWM, Jellicoe interview, Reel 2
61. 'explain to a slightly peeved...'. IWM, Jellicoe interview, Reel 2
62. 'rather sort of stuck-up and snobbish', IWM, Jellicoe interview, Reel 3
63. 'essential to leadership, judgement...'. Lewes, p.153
64. 'I don't like being shelled much...'. Lewes, p.181
65. 'But in the salient we were nobody's baby'. Lewes, p.189
66. 'blessed with a blade of cutting wit'. Mortimer, *Stirling's Men*, p.14
67. 'changed from parties operating on foot...' NA, SBS War Diaries, *Brief History of L Detachment*
68. 'When I have got my legs...'. Ranfurly, p.98
69. 'got very engrossed and had forgotten....'.Asher, p.26
70. 'This may be sort of plan...'. Mortimer, *Stirling's Men*, p.11
71. 'The unique opportunity', McLynn, pp.91–2
72. 'He had very quickly understood...'. IWM, Jellicoe interview, Reel 3
73. 'We really could not give [his scheme] ...'. Asher, p.40, quoting Mather, p.53
74. 'In effect I had to eat humble pie...'. Mather, p.82
75. Psychologically the parachute was...'. Stevens, p.18
76. 'I think Jock wanted to be sure ...'. Lewes, p.193
77. 'unfailingly obstructive...'. Mortimer, *Leap of Faith*
78. 'One of the reasons that the SAS concept...'. Stevens, *Originals*, 1985 interview
79. 'Stirling was away for most of 1941'. Lewes, p.205
80. 'Together we have fashioned this unit'. Lewes, p.191
81. 'a sort of HQ place'. Dillon and Bradford, p.23
82. 'An intelligent boy, kind, good...'. Malcolm, p.7

83. 'he had, I suppose, something...'. Asher, p.106, quoting Dillon and Bradford, *Rogue Warrior*
84. 'he was known in Arran to sit on his bed ...'. Mortimer, *Stirling's Men*, p.6
85. 'he replied curtly that his name...' Asher, p.44
86. 'As a teenager, he was able...'. Jellicoe, Bryanston speech, p.8
87. 'unpromising material for ...'. Dillon and Bradford, p.16
88. 'picked [him] and hit [him] one hell of a blow...'. Dillon and Bradford, p.20
89. 'There was no time to lose...'. Snelling
90. 'run amok with a rifle and bayonet', Dillon and Bradford, p.23
91. 'this commanding officer wasn't for hitting'. Dillon and Bradford, p.28
92. 'sulk phenomenally' McLynn, p.95
93. 'nothing of the rather clever...'. James, p.39
94. 'a natural gang-leader...'. Asher, p.100
95. 'Six stout Aussies had been laid...'. Hastings, *Drums*, p.48
96. 'more sensible and intelligent...'. James, p.143
97. 'had in common an insatiable...'. Almonds, *Gentleman Jim*, p.125
98. 'what you would call dour ...'. Mortimer, *Stirling's Men*, p.21, quoting Storie
99. 'I'd seen a film of these...'. Mortimer, *Leap of Faith*
100. 'Be it on your own head...'. Cooper, p.5
101. 'a wind like Emery paper...'. Langley, p.165
102. 'very unpleasant'. Holland interview, 2002, Background Notes, p.13
103. 'clouds of flies ...'. Maclean, p.156
104. 'very trim' James, p.33
105. Mortimer, *Leap of Faith*
106. 'pinched a load of bricks...'. Mortimer, *Stirling's Men*, p.16
107. 'Parfaitement reconnaissable...'. Forgeat, *Ils ont choisi*, p.131
108. 'Jock stood on the lecture...' Lewes, p.199
109. 'The basic unit would be a four...'. Stevens, p.17
110. 'There was a distinct whiff of the Foreign Legion ...'. McLynn, p.93
111. 'an idiosyncratic collection...'. Hastings, *Drums*, p.45
112. 'You were treated as one of a team...'. Stevens, p.34
113. 'the real engine room of any effective military organization...'. Stevens, p.111
114. 'In a sense they weren't really...'. Stevens, p.34
115. 'big-headed'. Mortimer, *Stirling's Men*, p.49
116. 'He did not bark orders...'. Cooper, p.9
117. 'wolf-whistled'. Fraser, *War Diary*, p.37
118. 'complete freedom to experiment...'. Lewes, p.162
119. 'wise ones buried their...'. Hastings, *Drums*, p.54
120. 'On one 60-mile march...'. Mortimer, *Leap of Faith*
121. 'wearing a detonator behind his ear...'. Malcolm, p.26
122. 'in fits'. Holmes, p.186
123. 'Apparently, with the eternal wisdom...'. Hoe, p.138
124. 'obsolete Vickers Valencia biplane'. Mortimer, *Stirling's Men*, p.9. Others (Hastings, *Drums*, p.47) refer to the first plane as being a Bombay
125. If you so much as glanced...'. Hastings, *Drums*, p.47
126. 'The men secured their "static lines"...'. Hunter, p.8. Fraser, *War Diary*, p.34 is more specific: 'the chutes were connected to a bar which ran along the bottom of the fuselage.'
127. 'really put a crater in the desert'. Stevens, p.16
128. 'We threw out a dummy made...'. Stevens, p.15, quoting d'Arcy
129. '...people on the ground heard...'. James, p.40
130. Dillon and Bradford (p.30) maintain that David Stirling was first out. Pat Riley, specifically said he should remember as he was behind him on that jump, the team's fourth jump
131. 'starting at 1,000 feet down...'. House, p.6

132. 'often drop man-sized depth charges...'. McLynn, p.102
133. 'canoe the 4 miles across the Bitter Lakes...'. House, p.6
134. John House (Jellicoe's driver), p.7
135. 'Few jeeps survived more than...'. Mortimer, *Stirling's Men*, p.56
136. 'The springs were breaking...'. Stevens, p.133
137. 'The jeeps 'drank petrol'. Stevens, p.135
138. Asher (p.136) states that the guns were spares from 'decommissioned Wellesley and Bombay bombers'
139. Ross, p.83
140. 'there to see the fun'. James, p.69
141. 'you just pulled the window back...'. Stevens, p.102
142. 'an Ordnance officer, whose...'. Lewes, p.215
143. 'You would love it here...'. Lewes, p.134
144. 'Small explosions punctuated the day...'. Lewes, p.216
145. ''Cos if things are going to start...'. James, p.200
146. 'best Royal Engineer officer in the Middle East'. Lodwick, p.33
147. 'Me? Uncouth? D'yer hear that?...'. James, p.202
148. 'Tell them we'll be paying a visit...'. Dillon and Bradford, p.30
149. 'four water bottles, a pound...'. Fraser, *War Diary*, p.36
150. 'where everybody met everybody'. IWM, Jellicoe interview, Reel 3
151. 'he had an appointment...'. IWM, Jellicoe interview, Reel 3
152. 'Very nice seeing you, George...'. Holland Interview, 2002, background notes, p.8
153. 'already achieved some...'. IWM, Jellicoe interview, Reel 3
154. 'she was hoping soon...', Maclean, Veronica. *Past Forgetting*, p.118
155. 'improve the administration ...'. Paget, p.163
156. 'rather lacked...'. IWM, Jellicoe interview, Reel 3
157. 'very great loss to the SAS'. IWM, Jellicoe interview, Reel 3
158. 'one of Stirling's finest officers'. Morgan, p.152
159. 'immaculate...in his clean shirt...'. James, p.93
160. 'seen as a huge vote...'.Almonds. *Gentleman Jim*, p.118
161. 'One day Peter Stirling woke up...'. McLynn, p.100
162. 'I dined with Peter Stirling at his flat...'. Ranfurly, p.122
163. 'dans l'ancienne alliance entre ...'. Forgeat, *Ils ont choisi*, p.16
164. 'Immense admiration'. McLynn, p.94
165. 'a marvellous commander...'. IWM, Jellicoe interview, Reel 3
166. 'irascible but keen-as-mustard'. Asher, p.99
167. 'excitable and mercurial', the other, a northerner, 'saturnine and phlegmatic'. McLynn, p.94
168. 'very powerfully built...'. Malcolm, p.24
169. 'Taller (5' 11"), slender, with ...' Malcolm, p.24
170. 'very, very free...'. Macintyre, *Rogue Heroes*, p.124
171. 'They have quite literally everything...'. Malcolm, p.25
172. Forgeat, *Remember*, p.15. Portier (p.41) quotes Stirling's strength being increased by '*la trentaine de Francais*' (thirty-odd French)
173. 'We must not only catch...'. Malcolm, p.26
174. 'Les hommes n'en peuvent plus ...'. Portier, p.46

Chapter 2

1. 'What went through ...'.Stevens, *Special Air Service Originals*, Defence Media Network
2. 'treated like men going...', Macintyre, *Rogue Heroes*, p.47
3. '...they used to flip on their backs...'. Stevens, p.64
4. 'by the time they reached the area...'. Marrinan, p.38
5. 'It was a night without any moon...'. Stevens, p.66
6. Mortimer, *Leap of Faith*. Stevens (p.68) quotes Dave Kershaw who said it was Keith ('then we discovered Keith with his damaged back, and detailed Corporal Arnold to stay with him')

7. 'set the back bearing…'. Cooper, p.23
8. 'only two could be located'. Eshel, p.47
9. 'flashes on the ground'. Mortimer, *Leap of Faith*
10. 'waist deep in a swirling…'. Mortimer, *Stirling's Men*, p.25
11. 'six of us were sitting there…'. Stevens, p.70
12. 'I shall always be indebted…'. Mortimer, *Leap of Faith*
13. 'kindly and with great amusement'. Mortimer, *Stirling's Men*, p.27
14. 'that they should never…' Asher, p.66
15. 'I think I'll wait here for a bit…' Dillon and Bradford, p.33
16. 'sensed throughout that he was…'. Dillon and Bradford, p.33
17. 'flat sand plains (*serir*), rocky plateaus (*hammada*)…'. Lewis, *Ghost Patrol*, p.4
18. 'especially when others had ridiculed…' Mortimer, *Men who Made*, p.260. The Mosquito army reference is from Lewis, *Ghost Patrol*, p.21
19. 'relatively light and fast and not…'. Lewis. *Ghost Patrol*, p.30
20. 'he and I entered into a conspiracy'. Stevens, p.78
21. 'If you're looking for a supply…'. Hoe, p.107
22. LRDG was 'reconnaissance', the SAS were 'raiders'. Dillon and Bradford, p.34
23. 'the irrational tenth…like the kingfisher…'. Maclean, p.95
24. 'It was absolutely essential to keep quiet…'. Stevens, p.77
25. 'not by open signalling…'. Stevens, p.78
26. 'a typical Foreign Legion outpost…'. Lewes, p.234

Chapter 3

1. According to Marrinan (p.42), it was a 37-man LRDG patrol in seven trucks
2. Eshel, p.48
3. 'three of his trucks down the coastal road…'. Marrinan, p.44
4. 'It was just after ten o'clock… Marrinan, p.44
5. 'about thirty off-duty German…'. Morgan, p.39
6. 'his continual use of…'. Marrinan, p.45
7. Ross, p.68
8. 'too generous at the petrol…'. Marrinan, p.46
9. 'At this stage of mobile warfare…'. Mather, p.84
10. 'Drinking songs turned to…'. Ross, p.69
11. 'brightly painted truck…'. Almonds, *Gentleman Jim*, p.92
12. 'an irresistibly jolly expression'. Asher, p.88
13. Mortimer, *Stirling's Men*, p.31
14. 'deep and very soulful eyes'. James p.41
15. 'a water bottle, a compass…'. McCrery, p.19
16. 'the tripwires were tripped…'. Wynter, *Special Forces*, p.311
17. 'one batch of CR.42s …'. Wynter, *Special Forces*, p.311
18. 'On the way back, we…'. Mortimer, *Stirling's Men*, p.32
19. 'ammunition crackling and exploding…'. Asher, p.91
20. 'parked snout to tail…'. Asher, p.91
21. 'It was as perfect a raid…'. Asher, p.94
22. 'to be blasted off his feet'. Mortimer, *Stirling's Men*, p.33
23. '…the LRDG shot a gazelle…'. Stevens, p.83
24. Ross (p.70) states that it was half the distance, three not six miles
25. 'It always fascinates me…'. Dillon and Bradford, p.38
26. 'there were signs of greater …'. Ross, p.70
27. 'That was rather a mistake …'. Dillon and Bradford, p.39
28. 'a very un-German-like brogue'. Marrinan, p.50
29. 'became known in the unit…'. Ross, p.70
30. 'The party regained their trucks…'. Wynter, *Special Forces*, p.122
31. Wynter (*Special Forces*, p.313) says that Fraser was dropped with 'four men'. I can only name three. He also misspells Jock Lewes as 'Lewis' and refers to 'a few German F.E.109s which I take to mean 'Me.109s'

32. 'The occupants were sleeping inside...'. Wynter, *Special Forces*, p.313
33. Sutherland says this was 30 December. He also identified the aircraft as a 'low flying Savoia' not an Me.110 (p53). Wynter (*Special Forces*, p.315) says that the first plane that attacked was a Messerschmitt and that, subsequently, two Stukas 'and a reconnaissance plane' (possibly Sutherland's Savoia) attacked
34. 'fiddling about with some...'. Asher, p.97
35. 'He'd bled to death...'.Asher, p.97
36. Wynter (*Special Forces*, p.316) says that the remaining LRDG (nine men) and Bob White walked back to Jalo. White never made the 200-mile walk
37. '...sighted a lone Messerschmitt 110...'. Wise, p.354
38. 'Back today with Pullable Beard ....'. Lewes, p.239
39. 'No one will stop by his grave...'. Almonds, *Gentleman Jim*, p.105
40. 'There is no doubt that any success...'. Wise, p.357
41. 'he was a very highly principled...'. IWM, Jellicoe interview, Reel 3
42. 'the man who was responsible for...'. Asher, p.98
43. 'serious, single-minded, systematic and analytic'. Asher, p.30
44. 'Stirling was the backbone...'. Mortimer, *Leap of Faith*
45. 'academically brilliant...exceptionally beautiful...'. Malcolm, p.11
46. '...your capacity was daily ...'. Quoted in Harder, p.166
47. 'by at least a division'. Mortimer, *Stirling's Men*, p.36
48. 'We must have looked a grim sight'. Mortimer, *Stirling's Men*, p.40

Chapter 4

1. 'Progress was slow...'. Wynter, *Special Forces*, p.126
2. 'passed within a few yards...'. Wynter, *Special Forces*, p.316
3. Hamish Ross, Mayne's biographer (p.71), points out that Mayne never got to state his own version of events. Virginia Cowles had picked the story up from Stirling directly
4. 'It was fairly common knowledge...'. Almonds, *Gentleman Jim*, p.119
5. 'Trezz beans' (*Très bien*). James, p.203
6. 'change the direction of SAS attacks'. Sutherland, p.55
7. 'I am becoming a Captain...'.Mayne to his sister, 8 February, quoted Ross, p.72
8. 'a wonderful man'. Stevens, p.91
9. 'Good to have you with us'. Sutherland, p.56
10. 'The party went into action with rum and lime...'. Dillon and Bradford, p.41. Diary entry, 26 March
11. 'Some of the people who know the South Downs...'. Ross, p.74
12. 'entrusted (Fitzroy Maclean) the task .... Marrinan, p.62
13. 'we might have been in the Highlands ...'. Maclean, p.168
14. 'damn fat'. Asher, p.109
15. 'Captain Churchill, we never...'. McLynn, p.104
16. 'He used to bring a case ...' Mortimer, *Stirling's Men*, p.48
17. 'there was no moon, but...'. Maclean,p.175
18. 'We were simply scorching along...'. James, p.70
19. 'We have just met with ...'. Maclean, p.175
20. 'He looked rather *douce* and benign...'. Lady Soames, Memorial Address
21. 'distinctive screech'. Maclean, p.173
22. 'I didn't waste any time in chucking...'. James, p.70
23. 'no more than a pin prick'. Asher, p.112
24. 'He was not a bad lad...'. (Dillon and Bradford, p.45). There is disagreement who was in the car. Dillon and Bradford maintain that it was Stirling, Seekings, Rose, Gurdon, Maclean and Churchill
25. 'partly because of an identity of aim...'. Warner, p.25
26. 'nervous energy, the quick movements...'. James, p.36
27. 'I know it must seem awfully rude of us to push off like this just as you arrive'. James, p36

28. The fifteen Free French SAS included the team leaders (Jordan, de Bourmont and Tourneret) and Gillet, Drezen, Jouanny, le Goff, Vidal, James, Prados, Guichaoua, Georges and Jean Royer, Geiger and Logeais
29. 'highly intelligent man'. Tiefenbrunner interview, *The Secret War*
30. 'average physique and a thinker…'. Lewis, *Ghost Patrol*, p.5
31. Two Luftwaffe pilots were interrogated in July 1942 and revealed that the SIG / FF raid had been expected for weeks before
32. 'il est allé chercher une clé'. Forgeat, *Remember*, p.75
33. 'half a ton of explosive'. Eshel, p.51
34. 'He was completely out of breath'. Tiefenbrunner interview, *The Secret War*
35. 'too dangerous'. Lewis, *Ghost Patrol*, p.100
36. Eshel, p.50
37. 'anaesthetic'. Marrinan, p.64. The only reference to Mayne's interaction with Brückner I could find
38. 'details of the coming …'. Lewis, *Ghost Patrol*, pp.103–4
39. 'after a sterling start…'. Lewis, *Ghost Patrol*, p.111
40. 'bien sévèrement gardé'. Forgeat, *Remember*, p.78
41. 'les "arrosèrent" copieusement …'. Forgeat, *Remember*, p.78
42. 'discipliné et respectueux à l'extrème…'. Forgeat, *Remember*, p.78
43. 'les Allemends ayaient appris …'. Forgeat, *Remember*, p.79
44. 'Vous serez fusillés! dès demain…'. Forgeat, *Remember*, p.79
45. Forgeat, *Remember*, p.119
46. 'un parcours pénible et épuisant'. Portier, p.59
47. 'was clear that they…'. Mortimer, *Stirling's Men*, p.52
48. 'constaté que l'explosion avait …' Forgeat, *Remember*, p.120
49. 'had learned to spaced their aircraft out on the airfields…'. Asher, p.113
50. 'ils n'ont pu détruire qu'un seul avion'. Portier, p.58
51. 'considered a crack shot (*un tireur d'élite*)…'. Forgeat, *Ils ont choisi*, p.21
52. 'the rollers creaked'. Asher, p.117
53. 'All right, Cooper, this one's mine….'. Cooper, p.52
54. 'a silly show of bravado'. Asher, p.117
55. 'Your average soldier's not bothered…'. Seekings quoted in Malcolm, p.29
56. 'making … horrible bangs on the beach'. James, p.35
57. 'a bull of a man'. Mortimer, *SBS*, p.20. Allott was known as 'Tramp' because of his consistently shabby dress
58. With Captain G. I. Duncan (Black Watch) would be CSM C. Barnes (Grenadier Guards), Cpl. Barr (HLI) and three Greeks (Wynter, p.409)
59. 'the place sounded like Crufts…'. Lodwick, p.34
60. 'experience'. Warner, p.26
61. 'first SAS seaborne operation'. Asher, p.124
62. 'at least 70 Germans…'. Gartzonikas, p.44
63. 'so heavily defended they just…'. IWM, Jellicoe interview, Reel 4
64. 'they had no intention…'. Gartzonikas, p.44
65. '…and second he knew Crete well'. Cowles, p.162
66. 'rather easy access…'. IWM, Jellicoe interview, Reel 3
67. 'Jellicoe at this stage of his …'. McLynn. p.108. McLynn actually talks about 'Berger' but he means Bergé. He also says it was July, but the raid on Heraklion was in June and Bergé did not come back. He was captured and ended up in Colditz with David Stirling
68. Portier (p.53) puts the date of departure as 6 June
69. 'en un lieu ecarté du port d'Alexandre'. Forgeat, p.92
70. 'getting a bit long in the tooth'. IWM, Jellicoe interview, Reel 3
71. Lt. Epaminondas Kontonyannis (1912–90). Jack Sibard gives the spelling as Condonyannis. Forgeat (*Remember*, p.89) spells it as Condoyannis. He probably got his account from Sibard. Portier names the 'capitaine de frégate' Kontogiannis

72. Lodwick, p.35. Not attributed to Jellicoe but more than likely the source of the comment
73. 'inquiet et déçu'. Portier, p.53
74. 'la plus dangerouse'. Sibard, p.16
75. 'Je dois vous signaler que j'étais…'. Forgeat, *Ils ont choisi*, p.63
76. 'had usurped Jonny Cooper's place…'. Asher, p.123
77. Forgeat, p.92. The shallow depth might have been a result of the submarine's age. Portier, p.53, cites the depth as having been 'à plus de quarantaine (more than forty) de metres de profondeur'
78. 'irrespirable'. Forgeat, *Remember*, p.92
79. 'J'ai constaté qu'il y a beaucoup des…'. Sibard, p.38
80. 'captured German rubber boats'. Lodwick, p.35
81. Mouhot put the distance at around 15km from Heraklion which, I think, is too great
82. 'always very nattily dressed…'. Lodwick, p.35
83. 'l'émotion de notre ami nous…'. Sibard, p.46
84. James, p.38
85. 'essential rubber tube for condensing…'. Mather, p.134
86. 'far too much heavyweight equipment'. IWM, Jellicoe interview, Reel 3
87. 'extraordinary rough-going…'. IWM, Jellicoe interview, Reel 3
88. 'le cheminement est extrêmement…'. Forgeat, *Remember*, p.93
89. Sibard's account, contrary to these reports, maintained that their disguises worked well
90. 'Il se fait passer pour un maquisard…'. Sibard, p.52
91. 'Lord Jellicoe a tenu à conserver…'. Forgeat, *Remember,* p.93
92. 'les cent pas'. Sibard, p.54
93. 'des pierres qui dégringolent bruyamment', Forgeat, *Remember,* p.94
94. Portier, p.55. 'Sagement, le commandant Bergé decide de reporter l'opération au lendemain'
95. '*Wasser bitte!…Nero, Nero*'. Forgeat, *Remember,* p.94
96. Lodwick, p.36
97. Lewis, *Secret Warriors*, p.4
98. Mouhot's account (Forgeat p.63) talked of triple engined Ju.82s, clearly a mistake
99. 'L'attaque est prevue pour ce soir …'. Portier, p.54
100. 'tête dans les jambes du précedent'. Sibard, p.69
101. '…thought that the patrol …'. Jellicoe, speech, Athens University Club, p.6
102. Lodwick (p.36) said the sentry 'spotted Jellicoe's large and curly head and wished to know what he was doing there'. More than likely poetic licence
103. 'stopped within a foot of his head' Wynter, *Special Forces*, p.412
104. 'ghastly, lingering, drunken'. Lodwick, p.36
105. 'me félicite de mon à propos'. Forgeat, *Ils ont choisi*, p.63
106. Godfrey Elliot, *A Forgotten Man*, p.187
107. 'L'allemand me pousse d'un pied…'. Forgeat, *Ils ont choisi*, p.63
108. 'avec son flegme britannique'. Portier, p.56
109. Lodwick (p.37): the total was eighteen aircraft – sixteen Ju. 88s and two other aircraft, one which was undescribed and about to take off with a Fieseler Storch parked beside it
110. 'Bravo Mouhot!. Grace …'. Forgeat, *Ils ont choisi*, p.64
111. 'The target was a fat and sitting bird'. Asher, p.131
112. Forgeat (*Remember*, p.89) wrote that the agreement was for the RAF to hold off bombing on the night of 12/13 June
113. 'les bras chargés de victuailles' Portier, p.56
114. 'There's something about that…'. Holland Interview, background notes, p.10
115. 'dancing eyes, and nervous, artistic hands'. Cowles, p.165
116. 'a certain Miroyannis'. Jellicoe, speech, Athens University Club, p.8
117. According to Lodwick's account (p.38), the informer was killed and his body thrown down a well ('later liquidated, and his body thrown down a disused well') Sutherland (p38) repeated the story

118. 'The Germans must have known that...'. IWM, Jellicoe interview, Reel 3
119. 'fidèle à sa reputation...'. Portier, p.57
120. 'He knew immediately...'. Holland Interview, 2002, Background Notes, p.11
121. 'contact with the local population...'. Asher, p.131
122. 'climbed two ranges of mountains...'. Lodwick, p.28
123. 'jaunty way of walking'. Sutherland, p.68
124. 'had begun scratching his back ...'. Sutherland, p.69
125. Patrick Leigh Fermor. *He drank from a different fountain*, online blog
126. 'Many of the population of S. Crete...'. Wynter, p.411. McCrery's book, *The Complete History of the SAS* (p.23), makes the claim that around '20 Cretan refugees' were taken off. I had not been aware of this but it is confirmed in Sutherland's book (p.69) and Beevor gives more detail
127. 'experienced deep-sea...'. Seligman, p.10. Seligman specifically refers to a boat called *Hedgehog* 'that Campbell used for landings and supply runs to Crete' (p.11). I doubt that Campbell commanded two boats, one called *Hedgehog*, the other *Porcupine*
128. *Satanas*, nom de guerre of Antonis Grigorakis, 'the greatest kapitan of them all' (Beevor, p.97)
129. 'seemingly little the worse for his savage...'. James, p.81
130. Sutherland, p.59. David Sutherland had recuperated at Tessa Whitefield's house
131. "We respected them. They behaved...". IWM, Jellicoe interview, Reel 2
132. *London Gazette*, 5 November 1942
133. 'spoke fluent German [and] managed...'. Wynter, *Special Forces*, p.322
134. 'the acrid fumes of burning paper permeated'. Asher, p.135
135. Figures differ: Dillon and Bradford (p.49) counted thirty-four – Mayne's twenty-two and twelve for the Blitz Buggy
136. '1,500 tons of supplies, including...'. Lewes, p.165
137. 'the lowest point on the continent...'. Mather, p.80
138. 'a treacherous area of *mish-mish*...'. Asher, p.137
139. 'Très ravine, tout en montées...'. Forgeat, Remember. P.133
140. 'a minefield blocking the entrance...'. James, p.107
141. Marrinan (p.73) says they stopped 'within half a mile of the aerodrome'. From here Stirling went off to set up the roadblock while Mayne attacked the airfield
142. 'Some of the fuses didn't go off...'. Hunter, p.18
143. 'Le capitaine Mayne semble être...'. Forgeat, *Remember*, p.133
144. 'Shoot low. Go for the petrol tanks' Asher, p.140
145. 'after three magazines the Vickers...'. Mortimer, *Stirling's Men*, p.57
146. There is some discrepancy over the numbers destroyed when Mayne went back on to the field with Stirling. Marrinan (p.74) states twelve rather than fifteen planes
147. Source Wynter (*Special Forces*, p.326). The author also states that in subsequent photo reconnaissance it was confirmed that 'in all thirty-seven aircraft had been destroyed' and that one was an unused Hurricane
148. 'The odds are so heavily against...'. Dillon and Bradford, p.50
149. There's confusion as to which of the Fuka fields Jordan was assigned. For Portier (p.63), it was Fuka-19; for Forgeat (p.140) Fuka-16, the satellite field to the west. Fraser, *War Diary* (p.66) states that Sharpe's RAF group targeted 'the satellite airstrip which lay near by'. It seems more likely that if Fraser took on Fuka-19 to the east, the logical field for Sharpe's group would have either been Fuka-17 (the main field) or Fuka-18, the southern field
150. The accounts from the same author, Forgeat, are confusing: in *Remember*, p.132, it was the reverse: 'les avions ici ne sont pas gardées' while in *Ils ont choisi* (p.98), the planes were 'très sévèrement gardée'
151. 'les tires sont trés imprecises non...'. Forgeat, *Remember*, p.132
152. 'bonne dizaines des minutes'. Forgeat, *Remember*, p.132
153. 'très sévèrement gardée'. Forgeat, *Ils ont choisi*, p.98
154. 'blown up nine planes for certain'. James, p.115

155. 'discovery had raised the alarm…'. James, p.115
156. 'You could just imagine their…'. Forgeat, *Ils ont choisi*, p.21
157. 'irrémédiablement touchés par…'. Forgeat, *Remember*, p.141
158. According to Fraser, *War Diary*, p.68, it was three Italian Macchi planes
159. 'the most easterly of…'. IWM, Jellicoe interview, Reel 4
160. 'against the advice…'. Asher, p.141
161. 'stuffed the radiator with plastic…'. IWM, Jellicoe interview, Reel 4
162. 'it smelt like a chicken coop!' Mather, p.84
163. 'saved us a very long walk…'. Hastings, *SAS in North Africa*, p37
164. Pleydell (James, p.149) thought the navigator's name was Corporal Preston not Stocker. He was also wounded: 'His leg was bandaged; a dirty old bandage through which the blood had soaked and dried in irregular dark patches.'
165. 'He looked as if he was exhausted…'. James, p.49
166. 'probably to take over second…'. IWM, Jellicoe interview, Reel 4
167. 'patted him on the shoulder …'. James, p.151
168. 'Son sang froid et sa calme …'. Forgeat, *Ils ont choisi*, p.129
169. Hastings, *Drums*, p.57
170. 'an expression of feeling…'. James, p.135
171. 'between two methods of defence'. Asher, p.141
172. 'were even fitted with…'. Almonds, *Gentleman Jim*, p.136
173. 'in proper sequence, tracer…'. Dillon and Bradford, pp.53–4
174. 'you could see tracers…'. Stevens, p.24
175. 'the inevitable Penguin'. James, p.159
176. 'tins of tobacco, sweets, pipes'. Mather, p.88
177. Almonds, *Gentleman Jim*. p.135
178. There are different estimates of the number used but Virginia Cowles convincingly illustrated the formation in her book, *The Phantom Major* (p.200). Jellicoe himself remembered 18, Caïtucoli uses 18, Mortimer (pp.59-60, *Stirling's Men*) uses 20 as does Almonds (p136) as the initial force led across the desert and then 19 within the text ('Stirling led the other 18 jeeps'). Asher (p.143) refers to 20 in the 'dress rehearsal' days before. The lowest estimate – 12 – was Hastings (*The SAS in North Africa*, p38, *Drums* p58) but it was written in 2003 and Steve Hasting's memory was probably struggling (he also misnames the only casualty on the field, naming L/Cpl. Robson as McKay)
179. Different rates of fire are used by various authors. I have used Dillon and Bradford, p.49
180. 'decreed live ammunition', Hastings, *Drums*, p.58
181. 'Every gun fired outwards…'. Cowles, p.201
182. 'best moments were at…'. Hastings, *Drums*, p.54
183. 'the desert so soft and silvery…'. Mather, p.96
184. 'le Simbad du sable'. Forgeat, *Remember*, p.149
185. 'He had a unique way of being…'. Almonds, *Gentleman Jim*, pp.120–1
186. 'Brighton beach' Cowles, p.205
187. Forgeat, *Remember*, (p.150) has a slightly different sequence. The element of surprise would have been lost: he maintained that fire was first opened on the landing aircraft, the airfield lights were extinguished and then 'deux minutes plus tard, le Major envoie la fusée verte pour assurer la formation en deux colonnes en U renversé'
188. 'It was blown to pieces…'. James, p.160
189. 'we just cruised around…'. Holland interview, 2002, p.9
190. 'It was like a duck shoot'. Mortimer, *Stirling's Men*, p.61
191. Asher (p.144) says it was an He.111 not a Ju.52
192. As with every raid there are disagreements on the number of planes claimed. In a study of wartime Axis airfields in North Africa, de Zeng, Henry L. (*Luftwaffe Airfields 1935–1945*, p.102) for example claims that '70+ years later states actual losses were 10 Luftwaffe aircraft destroyed and 11 more badly damaged, mostly Ju 87s from St.G.3'

193. 'within an hour of the attack there…'. Mortimer, *Stirling's Men*, p.62. Pleydell says that it only took 'wthin about 10 minutes' before planes were coming back in to land which seems like a far too short a time (James, p.161)
194. 'collars turned up against…'. Hastings, *Drums*, p.68
195. 'It wasn't the raid…'. Mortimer, *Stirling's Men*, p.62
196. 'A raid was like a booze-up'. Asher, quoting Paddy Mayne, p.140
197. 'We didn't worry so much…'. Stevens, p.140
198. 'the big problem in the desert…'. Stevens, p.141
199. 'at the last place we had…'. Thompson, p.44
200. 'centre of a water course…'. Dillon and Bradford, p.55
201. 'It was a curious burial, just…. Dillon and Bradford, p.56
202. Forgeat, *Remember*, p.153
203. Pleydell remembered it as six Ju.87s not four (James, p.161)
204. 'au cours desquels ils sont…'. Forgeat, *Remember*, p154
205. 'Mon pauvre vieux, je suis foutu …'. Forgeat, *Ils ont choisi*, p.132
206. 'Ça n'est pas le cas de vos hommes'.Forgeat, *Remember*, p.158
207. 'lying up…six hundred yards'. IWM, Jellicoe interview, Reel 4
208. 'You can't shoot me…'. Macintyre, *Rogue Heroes*, pp.146–7
209. 'the earl had done…'. Macintyre, *Rogue Heroes*, p.147. Jellicoe's IWM interview (Reel 4) doesn't mention the Baron's wife, merely that he had lunched with the Baron's parents in Bremen with Fritzi von Preussen
210. Dillon and Bradford, p.57
211. 'a figure scurried round…'. Andrew Rodigan to Jellicoe, 1 or 7 July 1990 and Jellicoe reply 7 August 1990
212. 'his heavily bandaged knee showing whitely…'. James, p.184
213. Hastings, *SAS Benghazi*, p.156
214. 'six separate groups of palms…'. Mather, p.133
215. 'two lakes of brilliant turquoise-blue…'. Maclean, *Eastern Approaches*, p.184
216. 'the heat haze made visibility poor'. Maclean, p.187
217. 'half of whom came…'. Mortimer, *Stirling's Men*, p.66
218. 'they did indeed start but got bogged down…'. Hastings, *SAS Benghazi*, p.156
219. 'was so perfect that he could be taken …'. Norén & Gyllenhal, pp.81–2
220. Hastings, *SAS Benghazi*, p.156
221. 'I hit them with my revolver'. Lodwick, p.49
222. Warner (pp.35–6) adds Cpl. Wilson to the group
223. 'with 10 water-bottles, some…'. Lodwick, p.51
224. 'very well and fit and enjoying life'. Correspondence Capt. T. B. Langton to Mr Watler, undated
225. 'a shifty looking Arab deserter…'. Hastings, *SAS Benghazi*, p.157
226. 'no great importance is attributed …'. Asher, p.161
227. 'with typical bravado, proclaimed…'. Mather, p.142
228. 'a dozen machine guns opened…'. Maclean, p.193
229. '…managed to pass through…'. Jellicoe to Mrs Almonds, 29 Nov 1942
230. 'within about forty to fifty paces'. Stevens, p.158
231. 'calme à son ordinaire'. Forgeat, *Ils ont choisi*, p.22
232. 'Il était resté à bord, à sa mitrailleuse…'. Forgeat, *Ils ont choisi*, p.23
233. 'a bullet had drilled through his…'. Asher, p.166
234. 'Corporal Drongin to you, sir'. Asher, p.167. Hastings (*SAS Benghazi*, p.157) remembers Drongin as a Sergeant Major and 'one of the toughest and bravest NCOs in the SAS'
235. McLynn, p.112, said that the Germans had been 'forewarned' of the raid
236. 'the main cause of failure was…'. Asher, p.173
237. 'In one day, twenty-five trucks…'. Dillon and Bradford, p.59
238. Source Dillon and Bradford, p.59
239. 'paraded round the town'. Stevens, p.163
240. 'The trouble came the next evening'. Hastings, *SAS Benghazi*, p.157

241. 'eye to eye' and had a 'very close alliance'. Asher, p.175
242. 'a lot of prima donnas'. Thompson, p.102
243. 'swallowed temporarily by the Stirling octopus'. Lodwick, p.47
244. 'a prosperous restaurateur'. Sutherland, p.132
245. 'the dashing, original and very…'. Leigh Fermor, Patrick. *Remembering Lord Jellicoe*
246. 'the private army of the Greek right'. Dinshaw, p.329 quoting Hugh Seton-Watson
247. Eleni Tsigante, interview
248. Interview with Major General (ret'd) Konstantinos Korkas, formerly GSS (WhiteFox Films, *Ieros Lochos*)
249. 'heated discussion'. Nikoloudis, p.2
250. 'I find your request arrogant in…'. Asher, p.178
251. 'always conscious that the fight …'. Dillon and Bradford, p.61
252. 'Captain Jellicoe is required …'. Thompson. p.257
253. 'You're not going…'. Mortimer, *SBS,* p.18 quoting Pleydell papers
254. 'loyal not only to his friends…'. Interview with Greek TV
255. 'Chaos ensued'. Lodwick, p.54
256. McCrery, p.24
257. 'one of the most under-decorated officers…'. IWM, Jellicoe interview, Reel 4, quoting Bob Laycock
258. 'extraordinary levels of courage…'. IWM, Jellicoe interview, Reel 3

Chapter 5
1. 'there is literally no one of…'. Asher, p.206
2. 'Nobody ever thought of Jellicoe…'. Asher, p.207
3. 'no other man who did more to…' Morgan, p.35
4. 'wasn't frightened of anything…'. Morgan, p.31
5. 'was exactly the man I wanted to…'. Dillon and Bradford, p68
6. 'absolutely indispensable'. Letter David Stirling to his mother quoted in Hoe, p.215
7. See MO3/3201/1
8. 'aspiring to branch out into sabotaging …'. Mortimer, *SBS*, p.16
9. Source Ross, p.93
10. 'it could be used for operations…'. Nikoloudis, p.6
11. Source Mortimer (*SBS*, p.29) and Lewis (*Secret Warriors*, p.163)
12. 'a man who only spoke…'. Warner, p.19
13. 'known initially as the Folboat Troop', Courtney, Introduction p.xx
14. Before he took over on 9 March 1943, Cator was preceded by Major Vivian Street, commander of 1 SAS B Detachment
15. 'seaborne ops were obviously the key…' Asher, p.209
16. 'took his promotion lightly …'. Warner, p.40. Gubbins' plans for the Fernando Po raid were strongly opposed by Sir George Giffard, the Army C-in-C West Africa and Vice-Admiral Algernon Willis, the Royal Navy's C-in-C South Atlantic. Giffard called them 'unnecessarily provocative' (Milton, p.134). Both the Admiralty and the Foreign Office, however, backed the plan. Lassen had been with March-Philips and Appleyard on the disguised fishing boat, *Maid of Honour*
17. 'who caused more damage and discomfort…'. Jellicoe, SBS reunion dinner, 1996
18. 'by his rather pompous manner…'. Ranfurly, p.159
19. Athlit was considered a 'summer camp', the 'winter camp' being on the shores of Lake Tiberias (Thompson, pp.257–8 and House, p.11). There is also reference elsewhere to Ian Patterson later establishing a new camp on the southern shores of the lake, at Samakh
20. 'under the Golan Heights'. House, p.9
21. 'declared the beach ideal…'. House, p.9
22. I am indebted to Paul McCue for the correction. It was actually a Military Detainment camp that had been built in the 1930s. The camp is now a national memorial site
23. 'A lovely spring, an ecstasy…'. Langley, p.164

24. 'a most beautiful site'. Milner-Barry, diary, 28 March 1943
25. 'In our pirate camp the usual...'. Verney, John. *Dinner of Herbs*, 1966. p.17 (p.11 Google online)
26. 'It was of the utmost importance...'. Lassen, p.62
27. 'littered the camp with his socks... Verney, p.18
28. 'If it was his pants he would wash...'. House, p.10
29. 'made up of six patrols, each...'. Holmes, p.186. I have seen slightly different – even if very close – descriptions: 'Each detachment had five patrols of one officer and twelve men of whom two were signallers' (document entitled 'The Special Boat Squadron', dated 5 July 1999, from Peter S-R)
30. Initially, it was four patrols per detachment. Warner (p.39) uses the figure of 230 men
31. 'a procedure which might in ...'. Warner, p.61
32. 'You have to listen for just...'. Sharman
33. Verney, John. *Dinner of Herbs*, p.18
34. 'self-reliant men with initiative...'. Langley, p.174
35. 'The man is the regiment ...'. Asher, p.51
36. With Holmes were Jack Cree, Billy Whiteside and Davey Fairweather
37. 'unable to locate...'. Correspondence, Porter Jarrell to Jellicoe 4 November 1998
38. '... it had special ramifications...'. Harder, p.250
39. 'Their filthy and often haphazardly...'. unpublished MSS
40. 'He hated mindless discipline...'. Lewis, *Secret Warriors*, p.165
41. 'the time (he) spent...'. McLynn, p.83
42. '...would turn up at grand parties...'. Langley, p.164
43. 'Physically he was about as tough...'. Verney quoted in Harder p.150. It's not quite clear who the 'don' was. It might have refered to Philip Pinkney. The 'M.P.' was Fitzroy Maclean
44. 'George is a splendid chap...'. McLynn, p.117
45. 'strained every nerve to avoid...'. Almonds, *Gentleman Jim*. ('pathological disdain for red tape', Morgan, p.21)
46. 'We were so superbly fit...'. Holmes, p.181
47. 'He fixed their boots...'. House p.11
48. 'you can eat civilized French ...'. Lodwick, p.40
49. 'This is a school for murder....'. Lewis, *Secret Warriors*, p.169
50. 'Shoot the first man who moves, hostile or not'. Lewis, *Secret Warriors*, p.169
51. 'tap the trigger so as to fire...'. Lewis, *Secret Warriors*, p.169
52. WO 218. Orders dated 29 July 1943
53. 'though smaller and less lethal...'. Lewis, *Secret Warriors*, p.175. Otherwise, they were known as 'Little Demons' (Langley, p.170)
54. 'If you get drunk and can't make...'. Holmes, p.185
55. 'godmother to the French'. McLynn, p.94
56. 'the most extraordinary person...'. Langley, p.10
57. 'a fascinating mixture – quiet...'. Seligman, p.127
58. Holmes, *Mars and Minerva*, 1992, pp.26–8, *Anders Lassen. The Man and the Myth*
59. 'ruthless, cold and calculating in action'. Morgan, p.55
60. 'I have at times been forced to use my knife'. Lassen, p.149
61. 'He was a handsome, statuesque...'. Henderson, *Xenia* p.106
62. 'very deferential Arab servant...'. Seligman, p.129. Quoted in Langley, p.160
63. 'Two out of three'. Langley, p.181
64. 'It took all of George Jellicoe's charm ...'. Sutherland, p.101
65. 'the brave, but often unpredictable ...'. Morgan, p.152
66. 'keep an eye on him...'.Langley, p.148
67. 'mangy and bug-ridden...'. Langley, p.159
68. "by no means a pleasant shipmate ...". Seligman, p.127
69. 'It was as if a fever was burning...'. Harder, p.254
70. 'probably killed more Germans... Harder, p.267 quoting Dick Holmes

71. 'There was a lot of killing…'. Mortimer, *The Week, Meet the SBS*
72. 'We'd follow him anywhere…'. Henderson, *Xenia*, p.107
73. 'The tone among the raiders…'. Harder, unpublished MSS
74. 'stark naked except for a …'. Warner, p.40
75. 'a dislike of Personal Appearances'. Lodwick, p.59
76. 'Jellicoe's men could return…'. Langley, pp.160–1
77. 'knew Lassen was too valuable …'. Morgan, p.56
78. 'flat on my back'.Langley, p.147

Chapter 6

1. 'the eternally pipe- smoking'. Harder, p.155
2. 'untried and untested…'. Lewis, *Secret Warriors*, p.173
3. According to Holmes, they boarded ML.367 (ML.361 is mentioned in other accounts)
4. '…decided to explore during the afternoon…'. Holmes, pp.159–60
5. Lewis (*Secret Warriors*, p.181) says Nicholson and Holmes helped Sapsed not Greaves
6. '70–80lbs of personal kit…'. Lewis, *Secret Warriors*, p.177
7. 'B and C signs together…'. Lewis, *Secret Warriors*, p.182
8. 'one sergeant, two corporals …'. Lassen, p.67
9. 'make you wince'. Lassen, p.67
10. 'without so much as taking his …'. Lassen, p.70
11. 'On the strength…'. Holmes, p.195
12. 'He was tall, slim…'. Lassen, p.69
13. Harder, Benaki Museum, Athens Lecture
14. 'Special message to the people.…'. Lewis, *Secret Warriors*, p.211
15. '…a handsome, well-built individual…'. Holmes, p.153
16. 'we don't have batmen in this unit'. Mortimer, *SBS*, p.58
17. 'all that one admires in a young man…'. Mortimer, *SBS*, p.75
18. '200 German soldiers were drilling…'. Lewis, *Secret Warriors*, p.189
19. 'We ate eggs and chips…' Holmes, p.161
20. 'run down as a result…'. Gartzonikas, p.46
21. Holmes, p.162
22. Lewis, *Secret Warriors*, p.200
23. It's hard to get an accurate figure on the amount of fuel destroyed. Seymour (p.209) puts the figure, for example, at 44,000 gallons
24. 'Sixty-two Greeks shot.…'. Lewis, *Secret Warriors*, p.213
25. A few months later, on 14 September, Generalleutnant Friedrich Wilhelm Müller, the 'Butcher of Crete', issued the infamous directive to the 22 Luftlände-Infanterie ordering reprisals to be carried out in the region of Viannos – all males older than sixteen and anyone found in the countryside were to be executed. 500 or so Cretans eventually shot and a further 200 taken prisoner. Most would end up as slave labourers. A terrible list of villages were burnt to the ground – Kato Symi, Amiras, Pefkos, Agios, Loutraki, Mythoi and Christos (Lewis, *Secret Warriors*, pp.223–4)
26. 'He said that if the British …'. Lassen, p.75
27. 'I practised my pistol training…'. Holmes, p.172
28. 'famous for its tea, ice cream …'. Warner, p.47
29. 'Believe me the stares were justified …'. Holmes, p.175
30. Holmes's account rings more true: after Groppi's, they went to sleep at the Kasr Nil barracks, where they persuaded the guard to allow their prisoners to stay with them. It was only the next morning, when they turned the two Germans in at Bab El Hadid, that the 'police sergeant started shouting at them and generally giving them shit' (Holmes, p.176)
31. 'one of the most physically …'. Mortimer, *SBS*, p.73
32. 'Many times I turned to him for advice…'. Lassen, p.77
33. 'I know that by his death you…'. Lassen, p.76
34. 'each [is] potentially capable of …'. Mortimer, *SBS*, p.45

35. 'in full daylight the submarine…'. Imbert-Terry, p.3
36. 'literally lifted'. Imbert-Terry, p.4
37. *Sardinia Operational Report*, WO 218/174
38. 'bound [it] round his wrist…'. Mortimer, *SBS*, p.52
39. 'thereby most unexpectedly fulfilling…'. Imbert-Terry, p.48
40. 'because I knew the plans…'. Thompson, p.258
41. 'main purpose was as a decoy'. IWM, Jellicoe interview, Reel 4
42. 'a light flashing from the hill following which beach lights were switched on'. Courtney, p.68

Chapter 7
1. 'would remain at the S/M…'. Jellicoe, *Rhodes Drop Operational report*, p.1, 7 Sept 1943
2. 'main advantage of these craft …' Kirk, p.95
3. 'a certain Heath Robinson …'. Sadler, p.167
4. 'comparative silence'. Seligman, p.13
5. 'powered by twin *Deutz*…'. Seligman, p.3
6. 'tapped on the shoulder…'. Langley, p.155
7. Jellicoe flew out from Haifa at 0630 and landed at Heliopolis at 0900 on 8 September
8. 'rather bewildered assortment of officers'. Jellicoe, *Rhodes Drop Operational Report*, p.2, 8 September 1943
9. 'What really amazed me…'. IWM, Jellicoe interview, Reel 5
10. 'incredible'. Sutherland, Appendix to Personal War Diary, 7-14 September 1943, p.3
11. 'they were all to be engaged…'. Mortimer, *SBS*, p.76
12. 'dumbstruck by the plan's…'. Mortimer, *SBS* p.80
13. 'hair-brained'. Jellicoe, Speech, Athens University Club, p.11
14. 'around seventy tanks…'. IWM, Jellicoe interview, Reel 5
15. 'could not contain' himself. IWM, Jellicoe interview, Reel 5
16. 'When all this dawned upon me…'. Peakman, p.26 from IWM, Jellicoe interview, Reel 5
17. 'attempting to rally the Italian…'. Mortimer, *SBS* p.80
18. 'an obsession with…'. Sadler p.160
19. '…The British liked minor operations…'. Hastings, *Finest Years*, p.404
20. 'driving force that impelled…'. Langley, p.156
21. 'Three years later France …'. Hastings, *Finest Years*, p.401
22. 'all the bays are commanded…'. Kampouras
23. Wikepedia does not cite a source
24. 'I have never wished to send …'. Hastings, *Finest Years*, p.410
25. Correspondence Ian Powys to Lord Jellicoe, 31 October 1999
26. '…the shipping earmarked …'. Thompson, p.262
27. 'Any enterprise against Rhodes…'. Hastings, *Finest Years*, p.403
28. 'Churchill had given Wilson…'. Parish, p.269
29. 'Good. This is a time to play…'. *SBS in the Aegean, September 1943*
30. 'One would have thought…'. Hastings, *Finest Years*, p.417
31. Churchill, *Memoirs*, Abridgement p.737
32. 'The Italians have surrendered…'. Sutherland, p.115
33. Pitt, p.88 Kindle LOC 19754
34. 'for a quick check of what might …'. Irvine, p.82
35. 'seriously misdirected'. Jellicoe, *Rhodes Drop Operational Report*, p.3
36. 'I was looking forward to a soft …' Irvine, p.82
37. 'The black shape of the pyramids…'. Irvine, p.83
38. 'The pilot had lost his way…'. Henderson, *Xenia*, p.108
39. Correspondence Jellicoe to R. Lamb 8 December 1992
40. Dolbey and Jellicoe flew back to Cairo West (Jellicoe, *Rhodes Drop Operational Report*, p.4) even if, in later years, Jellicoe maintained that they landed in Cyprus, a seemingly more likely destination

41. 'I always remember...'. Peakman, p.27

42. 'always hated parachuting...'. Holland interview, 2002, background notes, p.8

43. 'A headlong eternity of nightmares ...'. Irvine, p.84

44. 'a golf field 8 km south of the city', Maltoni

45. Wilson had a particular liking for American cars but was described by Anthony Beevor as 'even less politically sophisticated than most officers of his generation' (McLynn, p.113)

46. 'that the Italians were indeed...'. Jellicoe, *Rhodes Drop Operational Report*, p.5

47. See Irvine, p85, Citation text, p.91

48. Correspondence, Jellicoe/Fabio Sandi (Luciano Alberghini Maltoni's report in Rhodes, 3 June 2005)

49. 'for no apparent reason...'. Irvine, p.86

50. 'The room is huge but well lit...'. Irvine, pp.86–7

51. 'impressed with the efficiency...'. Jellicoe, *Rhodes Drop Operational Report*, p.5

52. 'We agree that being immobilized...'. Irvine, p.88

53. 'the old admiral was a somewhat weak...'.Smith and Walker, p.74 (1974 edtion)

54. '...were middle-aged or even...'. Sutherland, p.122

55. 'when he suspected treachery...'. Parish, p.269

56. '...an area which supplied...'. Jellicoe papers, Peter Stewart-Richardson papers, 5 July 1999

57. 'signs of collapse'. Jellicoe, *Rhodes Drop Operational Report*, p.6

58. 'visible sounds or signs ...'. Jellicoe, *Rhodes Drop Operational Report*, p.7

59. 'perfectly honourable man'. IWM, Jellicoe interview, Reel 5

60. 'I personally dissent ...'. Correspondence, Jellicoe to R. Lamb, 9 December 1992

61. 'They did their best ...'. Correspondence, Jellicoe to Ian Powys, 21 January 2000

62. 'knew something of ...'. *SBS in the Aegean September 1943*

63. 'continued long after...'. Jellicoe, *Rhodes Drop Operational Report*, p.8

64. 'the shells were falling...'. Jellicoe, *Rhodes Drop Operational Report*, p.8

65. *M.A.S.*, abbreviation for '*Motoscafo armato silurante*'

66. ' telegram received from Rome...'. Irvine, p.89

67. Read, p.13

68. 'to remain handy'. Jellicoe, *Rhodes Drop Operational Report*, p.9

69. 'In the event, the Italian plans...'. Smith and Walker (1974 edition), footnote, p.78

70. Fanizza wrote about his wartime experiences: *De Vecchi, Bastico, Campioni ultimi governatori dell'Egeo: uomini, fatti e commenti negli ultimi anni di pace e durante la guerra, sino all'armistizio con gli Anglo-americani* ('De Vecchi, Bastico, Campioni last governors of Aegeus: men, facts and comments in the last years of war and peace, until the armistice with Anglo-Americans') published in 1947. His name has been habitually misspelt as Fanetza. I am grateful to Enrico Cernuschi for the timely correction

71. 'Perhaps owing to mediocre ...'. Sutherland, p.116

72. 'sailing straight into the port'. Mortimer, *SBS* p.82

73. 'as calm as a mill pond'. Mortimer, *SBS* p.84

74. 'undiplomatic tumble'. Mortimer, *SBS* p.84

75. 'It was an Italian admiral...'. Holmes, p.187

76. 'looked physically and mentally...'. Sutherland, p.117

77. 'the Dodecanese could have ...'. Jellicoe, correspondence with Ian A. Powys, 21 Jan 2000

78. 'We certainly did not realize...'. Mortimer, *SBS* p.85

79. 'I believe we made...'. Parish, p.275

80. '24 MLs and 24 Dakotas (or the equivalent)'. Sutherland, *Appendix to Personal War Diary*, 7-14 September 1943, p.4

81. Sutherland made no mention of Jellicoe's first attempt to go to Simi and his return with Fanizza: 'Turnbull left for Simi to strengthen the Italians there, while Jellicoe and I headed north for Cos on ML 249'. (*He Who Dares*, p.118)

82. 'Their enthusiasm was almost...'. Jellicoe, *Rhodes Drop Operational Report*, p.13

83. 'The enthusiasm and joy of the inhabitants...'. Sutherland, p.118

84. 'A young man with [a] classical nose...'. Lassen, p.137
85. Sutherland, p.118
86. Capell, p.28
87. 'long enough... to verify the peaceful...' Lodwick, p. 80 (Lodwick, p.81, incorrectly spells Mascherpa as Mascheroa, as indeed Jellicoe himself referred to Colonel Fanetza as Campioni's Chief of Staff. He was Campioni's deputy and his name was Rugerro Fanizza)
88. Mascherpa's name is misspelt as Marscheroa in the *Rhodes Drop Operational Report*
89. Lt. Colonel David Pawson of MO4 led a mission to Samos on Friday, 10 September and then briefly visited Leros
90. 'difficult and odious character'. Lodwick, p.81
91. 'guide down a company of...'. Sutherland, p.119
92. 'lack of reliable information...'. Mortimer. *Men Who Made*, p.181
93. 'It was a cold, wet ride and...'. Mortimer, *Men Who Made*, p.182
94. 'the aircraft's Italian...'. Sadler, p.165
95. 'parading resplendent as though...'. Sadler, p.165
96. 'There was no depth in the defence...'. Sadler, p.166 quoting Lloyd Owen
97. Those billeted at the Navy House included Frank Ramseyer, Stewart Macbeth, Dick Harden, Charlie Clynes, Max Bally (the Davis Cup player, now an Intelligence officer) and Hugh Stowell (Captain Baker's Operations Officer)
98. 'a little gang consisting of ...'. Seligman, p.71
99. 'I am a cook, Signore, not fighting...'. Seligman, p.71
100. 'they were inhabitants of the thre *"palazzini"*...'. Seligman, p.57
101. 'embodied almost every deficiency...'. Hastings, *Finest Years*, p.414
102. 'stood on the highest point ...'. Thompson, p.266
103. Tony Rogers (*Folly*, p.108) stated that Tilney was 'acting on the instructions of his superior, Major General H. R. Hall'
104. 'to plan a defensive action...'. Bevan, p.17
105. See Tidy. The German air fleet now listed ninety Ju.88s and He.111s (Heinkel), fifty Me.109s (Messerschmitt) and sixty-five Ju.87s (Junkers)
106. 'proceed to naval docks, Haifa...'. (NA, *SBS War Diary*, 8 September 1943)

Chapter 8
1. 'make an ideal base for all raiding ...'. Sutherland, p.121
2. Silhouette Navigation relies on identifying key recognizable silhouette details of a piece of geography and then using its alignment as a navigational aid (See Langley, pp. 157–8)
3. Tidy
4. The airborne troops had been training with eight Dakotas of 216 Squadron, Palestine
5. Tidy
6. 'The operating room grew steamy ...'. Seligman, p.104
7. 'On the morning of 3rd October I awoke ...'. Tidy
8. 'upon which they focused ...'. Sutherland p.125
9. 'one of the most brainless and ...'. Sadler, p.168 quoting Lloyd Owen
10. 'I was ordered to go by night to Bodrum...'. Searle, p.149
11. 'She was a German-controlled Greek vessel with a German armed guard on board...'. Seligman, p.105
12. 'sixteen British officers and ...'. Sutherland, p.127
13. Hastings, *Finest Years*, p.409
14. Hastings, *Finest Years*, p.409
15. 'the most authoritative and highly respected...'. Lassen p.108
16. The senior Italian officer was Naval Lieutenant Andrea Occipinti. Under his command were 140 men manning nine 8mm and two 20mm machine guns
17. 'Three big strong Irishmen...'. Lassen, p.81. Suzanne said that Sean 'in particular was very devoted' to Andy

18. On 29 August 1943, the Danes scuttled their navy to prevent it falling into German hands. Thirty-two ships were sunk but a few – mainly minesweepers – managed to get away to join the Royal Navy. Lassen was elated as he had expressed severe doubts about his countrymen's abilty to resist
19. 'a bundle of nerves'. Lassen, p.81
20. Abbot Chrysanthos's sentiments were well known to his enemies. On 7 February 1944 he was killed by Fascist soldiers, along with his radio operator
21. 'Breakfast on Piscopi, dinner...'. Lassen, p.86 quoting Pomford
22. 'For the benefit of the RAF'. Tidy
23. 'FS Schofield is short-sighted...'.Tidy
24. 'labyrinthine'. Lewis. *Churchill's Warriors*, p.243
25. 'Lassen held his men back...'. Lewis. *Churchill's Warriors*, p.244
26. 'no idea there were Germans...' Lassen, p.90 quoting Sean O'Reilly
27. Lewis, *Secret Warriors*, p.162
28. 'withdrawn his men to the spot...'. Lewis, *Secret Warriors*, p.245
29. 'targeting them entire length...'. Lewis, *Secret Warriors*, p.246
30. 'counted 30 Germans wounded...'. Tidy
31. Lodwick, p.88
32. 'largely indiscriminate and...'. Lewis, *Churchill's Warriors*, p.247
33. 'worked for 27 hours, without rest...'. Jellicoe, correspondence re Porter Jarrell's war record
34. 'A fantastic bloke, with his Red Cross...'. Lewis, *Secret Warriors*, p.250
35. 'one of the most admired figures...'. Correspondence dated 23 Feb 2001. Jellicoe to Porter Jarrell's second wife, Edwina Moquin, with whom he had two sons
36. 'The Fascists on Simi...'. Langley, p.174
37. 'Between the Greeks and Italians...'. Lassen, p.85
38. 'a German major with 18 ...'. Morgan, p.159

Chapter 9
1. 'a large cowpat trodden...'. Sutherland, p.128
2. 'a series of formidable coastal batteries'. Mortimer, p.190
3. 'hardly featured in the battle'. Schenck
4. 'No Italian aircraft batteries ...'. Seligman, p.59
5. 'consignments of jeeps...'. Seligman, p.66
6. 'I am slowly becoming convinced...'. Alan Brooke Diary, 8 Oct 1943
7. 'Many congratulations on extricating...'. Note from Jellicoe to Ronald Watler, 11 November 1943
8. 'We know the Germans are going...'. Sutherland, p.130
9. Harder points out that Jellicoe later confused the orders he had given Sutherland. He was ordered to leave for Turkey, not (as appeared in Almonds, *British Achilles*, p.86) that Sutherland should 'join Lassen and the others on Samos'. Lassen had, indeed, gone to Samos with Wright, Holmes, Nicholson and Porter Jarrell
10. 'He had a guile which was almost uncanny in his ability to foresee how the enemy would react'. Sadler, p.170 quoting Lloyd Owen
11. 'He knew that disaster lay ahead'. Mortimer, *Men Who Made* p.192
12. 'an inexcusable failure', Peakman, p.116
13. 'Hallo! What ship?'. Schenk
14. 'Take no notice of that fool...'. Seligman, p.70
15. 'although 'this disruption meant...'. Peakman, p.113 (From RAF publication *Operations in the Dodecanese Islands September–November 1943*). They had been spotted at 0120 hrs
16. 'at least eight men'. Rogers, *Kos and Leros*, p.57
17. 'Is anybody doing...'. Peakman, p.117
18. 'who spoke in a quiet...'. (Peakman, p.112 quoting from Gander, *The Road to Leros*)
19. 'a pre-arranged signal...'. Schenk

20. 'A fleet of barges and other craft...'. Quotes by Olivey and Broderick, Mortimer, *LRDG*, p.174
21. Mortimer, *Men Who Made*, p.193
22. 'should not protect himself...'. Mortimer, *LRDG*, p.174
23. 'out sight and virtually...', Rogers, *Folly*, p.118
24. 'had achieved their immediate...'. Guard, p.139
25. 'shot cleanly through...'. Rogers, *Folly*, p.123
26. 'never took place due to...', Peakman, p.141
27. 'low dark cloud close to the sea'. Mortimer, *Men Who Made*, p.193
28. 'A warning had already been sent...'. Peakman, p.128
29. 'a matter of around 5 seconds'. Spencer, Battle for Crete, p.128
30. 'automatically assuming an X position'. Rogers, *Folly*, p.129
31. Beevor, *Crete*, pp.104–5
32. 'some 500 to 700 yards away...'.Blyth, *Leros Operational Report*
33. Manetas, *Ieros Lochos*, p.98
34. 'I was third out of the plane...'. Rogers, *Folly*, p.129
35. 'As the first man jumped...'. Mortimer, *Men Who Made*, p.194
36. 'the more reliable thirty-round ones'. Bevan, p.29
37. '...fired less at the paratroops in the air...'. Guard, p.140
38. 'I could see the frenzied attempts...'. Peakman, p.127
39. 'I have a nightmarish picture...'. Seligman, p.72
40. 'We went to Rachi searching for food...'. Peakman, p.129. Interview with Peter George Koulianus
41. '...could have shot a paratrooper...'. Bevan, p.24
42. 'Personal arms...were an automatic...'. Spencer, *Battle for Crete*, p.146 talking of the 1941 Crete drop. A section normally had 'one light machine gun (*Solothurn*), eight tommy gunners (*Schmeisser*) and two champion sharp shooters with special long-barrelled Mausers with telescopic sights ...'. (Clark, *Fall of Crete*, p.52). In the Crete drop (Clark p.55), officers's 'chutes were violet or pink, ORs black, medical supplies yellow and munitions white
43. 'The paras did not stop to dig in...'. Lucas
44. 'concentrated food, the safety...'. Lodwick, p.92
45. 'hasty re-deployment'. Rogers, *Kos and Leros*, p.59
46. 'failed to observe that...'. Lodwick, p.91
47. 'Of the 470 paratroopers who...'. Mortimer, *LRDG*, p.175
48. Recollections from Pauline Bevan, *Leros* Addendum Notes, add support
49. 'a British officer ordered his men...'. Mortimer, *LRDG*, p.175
50. 'almost a third of the total...'. Guard, p.141
51. 'strongly held'. Blyth, *Leros Operational Report*
52. 'If you were sensible...'. Peakman, p.138 quoting Lt. Jimmy James
53. 'in the teeth of a fierce gale'. Holmes, p.193
54. Guard, p.138
55. '...soon the vessel was a roaring...'. Peakman, p.147
56. 'There was a good deal of wind'. Peakman, p.134. Jellicoe's comment possibly references the second day's drop
57. 'the 200 who actually left ...'. Lodwick, p.92
58. '...one of the slow troop carriers...'. Rogers, *Folly*, p.143
59. 'white silk parachutes, like...'. Lassen, p.106. She is paraphrasing Marsland Gander's report
60. Les Nichols IWM Interview, quoted from O'Carroll, p.220
61. 'having reached that far unobserved...'. Rogers, *Folly*, p.149 quoting Lt. Pavlides
62. '...the Stukas seemed to be lined up...'. Rogers, *Folly*, p.157
63. 'intensified dramatically'. Rogers, *Folly*, p.159
64. 'skillful use of the new MG42...'. Lucas
65. 'firing from the shoulder...'. Rogers, *Folly*, p.152. The *Küstenjäger* commander was also wounded, command passing to his medical officer, Dr Martin Schrägle (Schenck)

66. 'his apparently aimless wanderings…'. Peakman, p.132
67. 'seemed to be constantly itching…'. Bevan, p.132
68. 'leaving them at a disadvantage…'. Peakman, p.170
69. 'it appeared impossible…'. Peakman, p.159
70. 'All radio messages destroyed…'. Rogers, *Folly*, p.149. Evidently this was Phipps's signal
71. 'Rapidly, methodically, wooden…' Peakman, p.173
72. 'As we continued to zig-zag…'. Rogers, *Folly*, pp.166–7
73. '…instructed the people there…'. Rogers, *Folly*, p.167
74. 'they were exhausted, had…'. Peakman, p.160
75. 'due to the somewhat confused situation…'. Rogers, *Folly*, p.169
76. 'The Stukas understood this…'. Rogers, *Folly*, p.170
77. 'Only twelve men had managed…'. Bevan, *Appendices* Day 4
78. 'An enemy mortar barrage…'. Rogers, *Folly*, p.174
79. 'bloody hand-to-hand combat…'. Lucas
80. 'The fighting is confused…'. Mortimer, *Men Who Made*, p.195
81. 'LRDG reckon that the island …'. Milner-Barry, Diary 16 Nov 1943
82. 'within grenade throwing range'. Rogers, *Folly*, p.178
83. 'If you reinforce Leros…'. Peakman, pp.184-5
84. 'just130 yards south-east of the battery CP'. Rogers, *Kos and Leros*, p.82
85. 'very fine rifle shot and personally…'. Letter, Jeremy Phipps, 27 Oct 2019
86. 'a twisted piece of metal…'. Rogers, *Folly*, p.190
87. 'Richie could not see what actually…'. Letter, Jeremy Phipps, 27 Oct 2019
88. '…saw a large number of Germans…'. Mortimer, *LRDG*, p.177
89. 'It is very probable that…'. GPRJ, Letters to Barrie Pitt, 21 July, 24 November 1983
90. 'as far as the Navy House…'. Peakman, p.189
91. 'Anyway, at the end…'. Peakman, p.189. Interview with Ewart Tassell
92. "George, I do apologize'. Interview with GPRJ, Tony Rogers 13 March 2001
93. 'I was assisting this officer…'. E. B. Horton, Rogers, *Folly*, p.250
94. 'exceedingly rare'. Maclean, Veronica. *Past Forgetting*, p.157
95. 'non vi crediamo…'. Cernuschi
96. 'My own company was decimated…'. Peakman, p.187
97. 'Anyway, the rest came out. One…'. Rogers, Folly, p.141
98. Figures differ: Searle (p.172) – '30 SBS and LRDG troops'; Ranfurly (p.201, 24 November, Cairo) – Jellicoe 'managed to escape with 60 men'; Milner-Barry (Diary, 19 Nov 1943) – 'George and David and 20 ORs are out of Leros'. O'Carroll (p.220) quoted Captain Saxton's operational report ('approx 70 men left Parteni Bay'). Including Greenwood's 10, 45 were LRDG
99. Some reports have it that it was an Italian MAS boat
100. 'local inhabitants insisted on…'. Blyth, *Leros Operational Report*
101. 'cattle-trucks pulled by a dilapidated…'. Holmes, p.203
102. 'both dressed in Turkish civilian clothes'. Ranfurly, p.201
103. 'about 36 other LRDG…'. Mortimer, *LRDG*, p.178
104. 'How long I had to hold the fort'. Thompson, p.270
105. 'A couple of miles from shore…'". Mortimer, *Men Who Made*, p.197
106. Thompson, p.274
107. Schenk, *War in the Aegean*
108. At the start, that meant around four raids by forty-one bombers a day but by the end, in the pre-assault period, eight raids by thirty-seven bombers a day
109. 'fired more than 150,000 rounds…'. Cernuschi
110. Source Enrico Cernuschi quoting from Gerhard Schreiber, *Die Italienischen Militarinternierten in Deutschen Machtbereich 1943–1945*
111. Ernrico Cernuschi and estimates Gavin Mortimer (*Men Who Made*, p.197) use the figure higher at 1,109 casualties (41 per cent of the invasion force)
112. Mortimer, *Men Who Made*, p.197

113. 'One could still make out…'. Bevan, p.57
114. 'at the last minute [it] pulled away without strafing or bombing…'. Rogers, p.168
115. 'The American Staff had enforced…'. Churchill, *Memoirs*, abridged, p.736
116. 'middle aged and deaf…'. Capell, p.13
117. Another source, Vlachostthopoulos (p.118), reported higher casualties: the first drop suffered 125 casualties, the second 7 per cent
118. 'If I am to break my legs…'. Lassen, p.101
119. 'Sutherland, is that enemy fire…' Sutherland, p.191
120. 'The fall of Leros ensured…'. Lodwick, p.94
121. 'In Vathy, a fifth of the houses…'. Harder, p.213
122. Harder (p.212) cites an official British report showing the total up to 23 November was 222 British, 358 members of the Greek Sacred Squadron, 400 Greek guerrillas and 2,978 Italians
123. 'politically too unstable to…', Lassen, p.112
124. 'thirty-seven heavily laden…', Lassen, p.113
125. 'A kind English lady who…'. Lassen, p117
126. Thassos Kanaris, interview on Leros, September 2017
127. Tidy has a slightly different total – 115 lost out of 260 aircraft
128. 'If I don't like you, you'll go'. Lodwick, p.100
129. 'The Regiment doesn't need…'. Holmes, p.230
130. 'modest and unassuming…'. Lodwick, p.218
131. Lodwick, p.216
132. 'took himself off to the *Tewfik…*'. Holmes, p.247

Chapter 10

1. 'to make the German occupation…'. Mortimer, *SBS*, p.124
2. 'separated the Aegean into two sectors…''.Kotzampopoulos, p.55
3. 'it participated, organized and executed…'. Raiding Forces and Sacred Squadron Club programme, Athens 1992
4. 'powerfully-built and dark …'. Kirk, p.93
5. 'over forty anchorages…'Kotzampopoulos, p.54
6. 'had temperamental engines…'. Lassen, p.119
7. 'mess room, ops room…'. Seligman, p.27
8. 'They were the scruffiest…'. Lewis, *Secret Warriors*, p.262
9. 'slinging rolls of loo…'. Seligman, pp.28-29
10. 'He owned an enormous metal tea pot…'. House, p.10
11. 'one officer in charge…'. Lassen, p.120
12. 'Andy had a quality which…'. Lassen, p.129
13. 'I took the Italians prisoner…'. Lodwick, p.110
14. 'they will give me a wound stripe…'. Lewis, *Secret Warriors*, p.273
15. 'not conspicuous for those qualities…'. Lodwick, p.111
16. 'bit annoyed'. House, p.13
17. …came in on a Monday morning…'. House, p.12
18. Photograph in Leslie, *A Story Half Told*
19. 'with a trunkful…'. Penny Perrick, p.70.The story was first presented in Leslie (p.55): 'she'd managed to bring three trunks of gorgeous clothes out of China'
20. 'under point blank fire …'. Seligman, p.64
21. 'even appealing vainly to Churchill…'. Sinclair, p.131
22. 'very inelegantly man-handled'. House, p.13
23. 'the operation would not…'. WW2 Talk
24. WW2 Talk, Alimnia patrol
25. 'wearing a tie throughout'. Read, p.18
26. '…unfortunately they made…'. Read, p.19
27. 'about 500 Greeks invaded the house…'. Read, p.17
28. 'Jellicoe's plan of attack…'. Lewis, *Secret Warriors*, p.287

29. 'Thirty-eight Italians and ten Germans had been reported'. Lassen, p.138
30. 'one of the reasons I'm trying…'. Mortimer, *SBS*, p.160
31. 'of the original sixty-eight…'. Warner, p.81
32. 'A huge bearded Greek came…'. Holmes, p.270
33. 'magazine full of Schmeisser…'. Kirk, p.118
34. Figures differ: Lassen (p142) and Lewis (*Secret Warriors*, p.301) both cite ten
35. 'Captain Lassen drank two…', Lassen, p.145
36. 'three additional companies…'. Read. p.25
37. 'ill-aimed machine gun fire'. Read, p.28
38. 'they left pandemonium…'. Read, p.30 quoting QMS Alexander Fraser
39. 'heavily weighted in …'. Read, p.30
40. 'because the enemy was now "standing to"…'. Read, p.30
41. 'was the signal for simultaneous…'. Read p.31
42. 'They came down the rocks…'. Read, p.31 quoting QMS Alexander Fraser
43. 'I radioed them five hours ago … '. Mortimer, *SBS*, p.175. Read p.31 states that it was six German planes, not three
44. Read (p.31) puts the total enemy killed or wounded at 185
45. 'The great raid on Simi marked…'. Kotzampopoulos, p.63, paraphrasing Mortimer (*SBS*, p.175) called it 'the last act of the SBS in the Aegean')
46. 'So effective were the SBS efforts…'. Warner, p.44
47. 'Is it true, Mr. Prime Minister…'. *Daily Mirror.* 'How modest Dick and his band of SBS "pirates" wreaked havoc on the enemy', 19 Oct 2013

Chapter 11
1. 'reached over and marked…'. Lowe, p.295. Stalin had literally written down the percentages on notepaper, a copy of which survived. Churchill had asked whether it should be destroyed. Stalin replied. "No, you keep it." (BBC, *Cold War*, 1/24)
2. 'throughout executed (and circumscribed) …'. Jellicoe, *Towanbucket Report*, p.1
3. 'crush ELAS'. Quoted in Lowe, p.298
4. 'was preparing to take control…', Harder, unpublished MSS
5. 'British military authorities…'.Woodhouse, p.248
6. '…received strict orders before leaving…'. Jellicoe, *Towanbucket Report*, p.4
7. 'Our so-called allies, the partisans…'. Memories, Alf Page, LRDG
8. ' did not discover…'.Smith, *Victory*, p.150
9. 'the brutality he suffered…'. Lowe, *Savage Continent*, p.304. He chose his nom de guerre, *Aris,* after the God of War (Henderson, *Xenia*, p.61, although spelt *Ares*. (Capell, p.42)
10. '…despite his considerable personal…detected an air of…'. Smith, *Victory*, p.150
11. 'established'. Woodhouse, p.251
12. Warner (p.93) states 24 (not 23) September
13. '…comprehensively looted…'. Jellicoe, *Towanbucket Report*, p.3
14. 'summary trials end executions…'. Jellicoe, *Towanbucket Report*, p.4
15. 'into a seaplane base within…'. Jellicoe, *Towanbucket Report*, p.4
16. '…the danger to which we were exposed…'. Jellicoe, Speech St Sophia
17. '…so much for this being a "Top Secret mission"'. Memories, Alf Page, LRDG
18. 'lying outside the harbour'. Jellicoe, *Towanbucket Report*, p.8
19. Al Page (LRDG Memories) remembers them as 2pdrs. The 2pdr was standard till 1942
20. '…we'd drive up the hills at night…'. Memories, Alf Page, LRDG
21. 'activities were camouflaged…'. Warner, p.94
22. 'fully cognisant of our numerical…'. Jellicoe, *Towanbucket Report*, p.6
23. 'consequent danger of a general…'. Jellicoe, *Towanbucket Report*, p.7
24. 'accept no responsibility for…'. Jellicoe, *Towanbucket Report*, p.7
25. 'Patras became a bitter battle'. Smith, *Victory*, p.151
26. Seymour, p.220

27. '…remember the Earl, George Jellicoe…'. Memories, Alf Page, LRDG
28. '…the centre of military gravity…'. Jellicoe, *Towanbucket Report*, p.9
29. 'with not a mark on him…'. Memories, Alf Page, LRDG
30. '[Jellicoe's] task was to pursue…'. Woodhouse, *Autobiography*, p.93
31. 'rumours of lootings …'. Jellicoe, *Towanbucket Report*, p.10
32. 'It was tricky…'. Holland interview, 2002, p.11
33. 'A piper from the Highland…'. Speech, Anglo-Hellenic, House of Lords, 14 Feb 2008, Kedros
34. 'Everything became very matey'. Smith, *Victory*, p.151
35. 'between 1,500 and 2,000…'. Almonds, *British Achilles*, p.99
36. 'only one execution took place…'. Jellicoe, *Towanbucket Report*, p.10
37. 'a rather splendid title…'. Jellicoe, Speech, University Dining Club, Athens, June 1981
38. 'on a sunken liner that was…'. House, p.26
39. 'a novel and exhilarating pursuit'. Jellicoe, *Towanbucket Report*, p.10
40. 'noticeably absent from…'. Warner, p.96
41. 'The Germans had as far as…'. Jellicoe, *Towanbucket Report*, p.15
42. 'With German forces in the…'. Jellicoe, *Towanbucket Report*, p.15
43. 'held up by a strong German…'. Jellicoe, Speech St Sophia
44. 'Their bearing, discipline and…'. Jellicoe, *Towanbucket Report*, p.15
45. 'I think it was the correct decision…'. Holland interview, 2002, p.12
46. 'as the men landed…'. Gander, *Capturing Athens. Air Troopers' Part*
47. 'The 4th Para Battalion was…'. Memories, Alf Page, LRDG
48. 'lined up on a path and during…'. House, p.27
49. 'If he drove himself over a mine…'. Waldegrave, p.23
50. 'many of them fell into the sea…'. Woodhouse, *Autobiography*, p.92
51. 'not know that Stalin, in a ruthless…'. Waldegrave, p.23
52. 'with prominent Greek collaborators…'. Mazower, p.357
53. 'needed some additions …'. House, p.27
54. 'the liberation of the center…'. Warner, p.97
55. 'the volcanic outbursts of joy…'. Gander, *Capturing Athens. Air Troopers' Part*
56. 'They threw flowers and kisses…'. Memories, Alf Page, LRDG
57. 'You must take the flowers…'. Smith, *Victory*, p.152
58. 'a comic element to Jellicoe's …'. Speech, Anglo-Hellenic, House of Lords, Kedros
59. Sedgwick was Marina Sulzberger's uncle. She was married to Cy Sulzberger of the *New York Times* and became my sister Zara's godmother. Mary Cawadias and Marina were close friends
60. 'The Englishman!' Tsatsos, p.125
61. 'The people are mad with joy'. Tsatsos, p.124
62. '…in handfuls rather…'. Woodhouse, *Autobiography*, p.93
63. '…this was deemed insufficiently senior…'. Harder, p.268
64. 'regarded by ELAS…'. Lowe, *Savage Continent*, p.298. EAM ministers resigned en masse from George Papandreou's government in December 1944
65. 'For the rest of the day, Jellicoe, Milner-Barry…'. Harder, p.268
66. 'parties and politics'. Jellicoe, *Towanbucket Report*, p.12
67. Waldegrave, Royal Society, Biographical Memoirs, p.172
68. 'the Primate of Greece sprinkled…'. Jellicoe, Speech St Sophia
69. 'tins of bully beef, which…'. Henderson, *Xenia*, p.106
70. 'clap whenever they see him…'. Ranfurly, p.296
71. '"serve" the commander of the SS camp'. Henderson, *Xenia*, p.83

Chapter 12
1. 'in 15 jeeps and four trucks'. House, p.28
2. 'his small detatchment was…'. Sarafis, p.415
3. 'the plain of Thessaly westwards…'. Woodhouse, *Autobiography*, p.94
4. 'bad marksmanship of the enemy'. Ladd, p.91

5. 'who spent less ammunition attacking...'. Ladd, p.91
6. 'The British did not fire a single shot...'. Smith, *Victory*, p.154 quoting Thanasis Hajis
7. 'because of bad weather'. Sarafis, p.417
8. 'devastating results'. Ladd, p.91
9. 'instructing us not to go...'. Mortimer, *LRDG*, p.205
10. 'It is indeed my hope that...'. Jellicoe, speech, St Sophia
11. At Skiathos, Lassen's group was reinforced by the LRDG. The SBS was now 6 officers and 55 ORs, the LRDG 2 officers and 13 ORs, a total of 8 officers and 68 ORs
12. '...a man who would play a key... Lewis, *Secret Warriors*, p.324
13. 'a particularly close friend'. Langley, p.239
14. Letter, W. K. Croxton, 1991. Before the war, Solomon had been the personal agent for John Mills, Hermione Gingold and Michael Wilding
15. 'more or less permanently'. Lewis, *Secret Warriors*, p.326
16. 'had sailed up when...'. Langley, p.240
17. 'were concerned only with their...'. Langley, p.240
18. 'shamed by his words and...'. Lewis, *Secret Warriors*, p.329
19. 'A very large allied convoy...'.Lewis, *Secret Warriors*, p.329
20. 'blocked their advance'. Lewis, *Secret Warriors*, p.334
21. 'Bren gun in one hand and...'. Lewis, *Secret Warriors*, p.336
22. 'England's prestige has been saved...'. Lewis, *Secret Warriors*, p.340
23. 'I shall never again have...'. Langley, p.245
24. 'I have the honour to report...'. Lewis, *Secret Warriors*, p.340
25. 'turned a reconnaissance of islands...'. Langley, p.245
26. '...his otherwise accommodating...'. Harder, p.278
27. 'cursing the little stitches...'. House, p.28
28. 'it only needs a match...'. Lowe, p.299
29. 'to act as if you were in a conquered city...'. Lowe, p.300

Chapter 13
1. 'lead the unit to the Far East...'.Harder, p.293
2. WW2 Talk
3. 'brought to the task breadth...'. Seymour, p.224
4. Milner-Barry, March 5 1943 (referred to as the 'Jellicoe Intruder'. He 'tested out collapsible rubber boat with George Jellicoe', 3 March)
5. Comment made by George Jellicoe when First Lord of the Admiralty
6. 'had lost his attention...'. Holland interview, 2002, p.10
7. '*Glanzpunkt*'. Henderson, *Old Friends*, p.108
8. Ranfurly, p.356, 2 May 1945
9. 'three of the closest friends...'. Holland interview, 2002, p.2
10. 'for courage, perserverance ...'. Lassen, p.102
11. 'with impressive foresight...'. Taylor, *Exorcising Hitler. The Occupation and Denazification of Germany*, p.166
12. 'opportunities for counselling, ...'. Lowe, *Savage Continent*, p.106
13. '4.8 million *internal* refugees'. Lowe, p.27
14. 'Germany in 1945 was one huge ant's...'. Lowe, p.31
15. Lowe, p.36
16. 'half the amount received by...'. Lowe, p.37
17. Woodhouse, speech, King's College, p.4
18. 'Central Europe was reverting...'. BBC, *Cold War*, Episode 2/24
19. 'a great and sullen suspicion...'. Lowe, p.105
20. 'fell afoul of the British authorities...'. Sinclair, p.158
21. 'It is clear from the official reports...'. Lowe, p.102
22. 'Liberation complex'. Lowe, p.105
23. 'entered into a criminal...'. Mather, *Aftermath*, p.104
24. 'To refuse is to...'. Mather, *Aftermath*, p.106 quoting Macmillan
25. 'more than a third died in captivity'. Lowe, p.117

Chapter 14

1. 'furious'. Bullock, p.199
2. 'at a loss how to deal'. Bullock, p.382
3. 'Thank you for your kind offer…'.Almonds, *British Achilles*, p.114
4. 'Britain and America chose to ignore…'. BBC, *Cold War*, Episode 1/24
5. 'bad tempered conference'.BBC, *Cold War*, Episode 1/24
6. Thomas, p.9
7. 'in the State Department …'. Talbot, p.148
8. 'sit together reading…'. Bethell, p.97
9. Bethell, p.96
10. 'convivial soul'. Philby, p.155
11. 'He was far from being a mere …'. Milne, p.174
12. Walter, *Guardian*
13. 'Philby was impressed both by…'. Macintyre, *Spy*, p.132
14. 'had arrived at Philby…'. Thomas, pp.68-69
15. 'I have a shock for you…'.Macintyre, *Spy*, p.142
16. 'I thought of the cigarette ends…'. Lownie, p.198
17. 'an outrageous figure…'. Bethell, p.171
18. 'dark, nicotine stained fingers'. Lownie, p.199
19. 'awful show-off…'. Lownie, p.216
20. 'the son of a former Cabinet minister…'. Macintyre, *Spy*, p.141
21. 'refused to have anything to do…'. Lownie, p.200
22. 'expressed at once a total disinterest…'. Lownie, p.200
23. 'not anything startling'. Lownie, p.201
24. Almonds, *British Achilles*, p.115
25. 'extraordinarily nice'.Almonds, *British Achilles*, p.115
26. Natasha Walter, *Guardian*, 10 May 2003
27. 'it was essential to rescue Maclean…'. Milne, p.217
28. '…the general view in SIS itself…'. Bethell, p.173
29. 'Incredibly, Wisner continued to…'. Thomas, p.70
30. Letter from Prof. Hugh Trevor-Roper to Kim Philby, 21 September 1968. Quoted in *One hundred letters from Hugh Trevor-Roper* (eds. Davenport-Hines, Richard and Sisman, Adam. Oxford, 2014, p.174)
31. 'He said he didn't really know…'. Masty, 28 November 2012
32. Reynolds, David. *The Origins of the Cold War in Europe: International Perspectives*. Yale University Press, 1994
33. 'it's important to make…'. Speech, Anglo-Hellenic, House of Lords, 14 Feb 2008, Viscount Norwich
34. 'I was outraged. It struck me…'. Bethell, p.173
35. On 24 March it was reported that the 180-ton *Dodeconesus* had sunk close to the Turkish coast between Simi and Kos. Only six out of thirty crew and passengers survived
36. J. R. Shaw to Jellicoe, 15 February 1958
37. 'I know that, at 39, an ex-diplomat…'. Sinclair, p.159
38. 'There are many among the management…'.Sinclair, p.159
39. Penny Perrick (p.142) quotes an undated reference in Anita Leslie's diary saying that Margot Fonteyn's 'amusing, witty Panamanian husband' had said that Patsy 'was given a black eye by George' after squabbling about the need for a divorce to be settled. I strongly doubt the validity of Roberto 'Tito' Arias's recollections: my father would never have raised his hand to any woman, let alone Patsy
40. 'he never had an easier…'. Henderson, *Old Friends*, p.112

Chapter 15

1. 'the lovely way in which he…'. Buckley, private correspondence
2. 'He liked to nurture talent when…'. Lord Howe, Interview 2017

3. 'was much more widely read...'. Waldegrave, Royal Society, Biographical Memoirs, p.174
4. 'not very bright'. Holland interview, p.2, 2002
5. 'not by nature a political animal...'. Henderson, *Old Friends*, p.112
6. 'This was the period of "Butskellism"...'. Waldegrave, Royal Society, Biographical Memoirs, p.173
7. 'as good a leader...'. *Hansard*, HL Debate 5 June 1973, and *The Times*, 6 June 1973
8. 'regret his departure...'. *Hansard*, HL Debate 05 June 1973 vol. 343 cc1-6
9. 'in our union we...'. William Kendall, *The Times*, 25 May 1973
10. 'among the bravest, ablest...'.Crossman, *The Times*, 30 May, 1973
11. 'protégés', Shawcross, p.209
12. 'a near legendary reputation...'. 1976 CIA Report quoted in Shawcross, p.189
13. 'The best golden caviar'. Almonds, *British Achilles*, p.222
14. 'George Jellicoe had bonded...'. Speech, Anglo-Hellenic, House of Lords, Kedros
15. 'the bravest man he'd ever met'. Leigh Fermor, *Spectator*, 'Remembering Lord Jellicoe'
16. 'George did a tremendous...'. Davenport-Hines and Sisman, p.268
17. Wikipedia
18. 'hugely admired on the democratic right...'. Waldegrave, p.24
19. 'I doubt whether the British Council...'. Jellicoe, George. Obituary, The Hon. Sir Steven Runciman CH FBA 1903–2000. *The Anglo-Hellenic Review*, No. 23, Spring 2001
20. 'George, like most real heroes...'. Waldegrave. p.23
21. 'had no right to this exalted rank...'. Jellicoe to Georges Bergé, 13 February 1991
22. 'We Greeks will be...'. George Papoulios, diplomat. Letter, 3 March 2007

Chapter 16

1. 'public service was both ...'. Lord Carrington, Memorial Service, Guards Chapel
2. 'the perhaps inappropriately jolly...'. *Daily Telegraph*, Obituary, 26 February 2007
3. 'frenzy of anxiety'. Philippa Jellicoe, conversational records 03.10.2016
4. Ziegler (Kindle p.409, LOC 7022) Jellicoe to Heath 2.6.73 NA PREM 15.1904. conversations with Lords Armstrong and Jellicoe
5. 'I am really not selling...'. Waldegrave, p.96
6. 'a man who had the ability...'. *Sunday Times*, Robert Lacey
7. Rita Gardner, Interview
8. *Independent*, 24 February 2007
9. 'It was all pretend'. Duke of Kent, Interview
10. 'anything about his war record...'. Duke of Kent, Interview
11. 'Leading a high-level British...'. Henderson, *Old Friends*, p.115
12. 'had the smallest increase of Aids...'. Almonds, *British Achilles*, p.232
13. Collette Jackson. Interview, 4 November 2016

Bibliography

* Publications to which George Jellicoe made written contributions

Almonds-Windmill, Lorna
—— *A British Achilles. The Life of George, 2nd Earl Jellicoe.* Pen & Sword, 2005
—— *Gentleman Jim. The Wartime Story of a Founder of the SAS and Special Forces.** Constable, 2001
Asher, Michael. *The Regiment: The Real Story of the SAS. The First Fifty Years.* Viking Books, 2007
Bagnold, Brig. R.A. *Early Days of the Long Range Desert Group.* Royal Society Presentation, 15 January 1945
Bally, Max. *A Player's War. Davis Cup to Guns of Navarone.* Unpublished draft text (French version *Le Joueur à la Guerre. De la Coupe Davis aux canons de Navarone.* Editions France-Empire 1984)
Beevor, Anthony. *Crete. The Battle and the Resistance.* Penguin, 1991
Bethell, Nicholas. *The Great Betrayal. The untold story of Kim Philby's biggest coup.* Hodder & Stoughton, 1984
Bevan M.A., Pauline
—— *Travels with a Leros Veteran.* MPG Books, 2000
—— *Travels with a Leros Veteran.* Addendum Notes, 75th Anniversary
Boyle, Andrew. *The Climate of Treason. Five who spied for Russia.* Hutchinson, 1979
Bullock, Alan. *Ernest Bevin: Foreign Secretary 1945–1951.* Heinemann
Capell, Richard. *Simiomata. A Greek Notebook 1944–1945.* MacDonald
Churchill, Sir Winston S. *Memoirs of the Second World War* (An abridgement by Denis Kelly). Bonanza Books, New York, 1978
Clark, Alan. *The Fall of Crete.* Cassell, 1962
Cooper, Johnny. *One of the Originals. The Story of a Founder Member of the SAS.* Pan Books, 1991
Courtney, G.B. *SBS in World War Two. The Story of the Original Special Boat Section of the Army Commandos.* Robert Hale, 1983
Cowles, Virginia. *The Phantom Major. The Story of David Stirling and the SAS Regiment.* Collins, 1958 (pagination in the Companion Book Club edition differs significantly)
Dillon, Martin and Bradford, Roy. *Rogue Warrior of the SAS: The Blair Mayne Legend. Lt. Col. Paddy Blair Mayne DSO, 3 Bars.* John Murray, 1987
Dinshaw, Minoo. *Byzantine Knight. The Byzantine Life of Steven Runciman.* Allen Lane, 2016
Eshel, David. *Daring to Win. Special Forces at War.* Cassell, 1998
Feebery, David. *Guardsman and Commando: The War Memoirs of RSM Cyril Feebery DCM.* Pen & Sword, 2009
Forgeat, Raymond
—— *Ils ont choisi de vivre la France libre.* Atlante editions, 1999
—— *REMEMBER. Les Parachutistes de La France Libre – 40 à 43* Service Historique de l'Armée de Terre. Vincennes, 1990
Gander, Leonard Marsland. *The Long Road to Leros.* McDonald & Co.
Guard, J.S. *Improvise and Dare. War on the Aegean 1943–1945.* The Book Guild, 1997

Harder, Thomas. *Special Forces Hero. Anders Lassen VC, MC.* Pen and Sword, 2021. An earlier, unpublished MSS is also quoted even if amended in his final book

Hargreaves, Andrew. *Special Operations in World War II: British and American Irregular Warfare*

Hastings, Sir Stephen

—— *The Drums of Memory. The Autobiography of Sir Stephen Hastings, MC.* Leo Cooper, 1994

—— *The SAS Raid on Benghazi.* Guards Magazine, Summer 2003

—— *The SAS in North Africa on 1942.* Guards Magazine, Spring 2003

Henderson, Lady Mary. *Xenia – A Memoir. Greece 1919–1949.* Weidenfeld & Nicholson, 1988

Henderson, Sir Nicholas. *Old Friends and Modern Instances.* Profile Books, 2001

Hoe, Alan. *David Stirling. The authorised biography of the founder of the SAS.* Little, Brown & Company, 1992

Holland, Jeffrey.* *The Aegean Mission. Allied Operations in the Dodecanese, 1943.* Greenwood Press, New York. 1988

Holmes, Richard. *Mediterranean Odyssey. A Squaddy's Tale. The Remarkable War Memoir of an Original WW2/SAS/SBS Special Forces Operator.* 2016

House, Angels. *Housie. The wartime memories of John House, his travels and adventures 1939–1945.* Unpublished pamphlet, 2001

Hunter, Robin. *True Stories of the SAS.* Weidenfeld & Nicholson, 1958

James, Malcolm. *Born of the Desert. With the SAS in North Africa.* Frontline Books, 2015 (actually the desert war memoirs of Malcolm Pleydell)

Johnson MC, Edward B. W. *Island Prize: Leros 1943.* The Kemble Press, 1992

Kay, R. L. *Long Range Desert Group in the Mediterranean.* Merriam Press, 2005

Kemp, Anthony. *The SAS at War. The Special Air Service Regiment 1941–1945.* John Murray, 1991

Kirk, Geoffrey. *Towards the Aegean Sea. A Wartime Memoir.* Square One, 1997

Koburger, Charles A. *Wine-Dark, Blood Red Sea: Naval Warfare in the Aegean, 1941–1946.* Praeger, 1999

Kofod-Hanse, Mogens. *Andy. A Portrait of the Dane Major Anders Lassen.** Friehdsmuseets Venners Forlag, 1991

Ladd, James. *Commandos and Rangers of World War II.* St Martin's Press, New York. 1978

Langley, Mike. *Anders Lassen VC, MC of the SAS.* Grafton Books, 1990

Lassen, Suzanne. *Anders Lassen VC.* Frederick Muller, 1963

Leslie, Anita. *A Story Half Told. A Wartime Biography.* Hutchinson, 1983

Lewes, John. *Jock Lewes. Co-Founder of the SAS.** Pen & Sword 2016 (originally published 2000)

Lewis, Damien

—— *Churchill's Secret Warriors: The Explosive True Story of the Special Forces.* Quercus, 2015

—— *SAS Ghost Patrol. The ultra-secret unit that posed as Nazi stormtroopers.* Quercus, 2018

—— *SAS Italian Job. The secret mission to storm a forbidden Nazi fortress.* Quercus, 2019

Lodwick, John. *The Filibusters. The Story of the Special Boat Service.** Methuen, 1947. Republished as *Raiders from the Sea*

Lowe, Keith. *Savage Continent. Europe in the Aftermath of World War II.* Penguin, 2013 (first published Viking, 2012)

Lownie, Andrew. *Stalin's Englishman: The Lives of Guy Burgess.* Hodder & Stoughton, 2015

MacDonaugh, Giles. *After the Reich. From the Liberation of Vienna to the Berlin Airlift.* John Murray, 2007

Macintyre, Ben

—— *A Spy among Friends. Philby and the Great Betrayal.* Bloomsbury, 2014

—— *SAS Rogue Heroes. The Authorized Wartime History.* Penguin Random House, 2016

---

* Holland, from the Holland & Holland family, had been a platoon Sergeant in the SBS and was MiD for gallantry on Racchi Ridge, Leros.

Maclean, Fitzroy. *Eastern Approaches.* Jonathan Cape, 1951

Maclean, Gavin. *The Governors. New Zealand's Governors and Governors-General.* Otago University Press, 2006

Maclean, Veronica. *Past Forgetting. A Memoir of Heroes, Adventure and Love.* Review, 2002

McCrery, Nigel. *The Complete History of the SAS.* André Deutsch, 2011

McLynn, Frank. *Fitzroy Maclean.* John Murray, 1992

Mamalakis, Constantinos E. *Sibard.* McFarland & Company, 2016

Manetas, Ioannis. Ιερός Λόχος *1942–1945 (The Greek Sacred Squadron).* Logothetis Publications, Athens 1996

Marrinan, Patrick. *Colonel Paddy. The Man Who Dared.* Pretani Press, 2013

Mather, Sir Carol

—— *Aftermath of War. Everyone must go.* Brasseys, 1992

—— *When the Grass Stops Growing. A war memoir.** Leo Cooper, 1997

Mazower, Mark. *Inside Hitler's Greece. The Experience of Occupation, 1941–1944.* Yale University Press, 1993

Milne, Tim, GMG, OBE. *Kim Philby. A Story of Friendship and Betrayal.* Biteback Publishing, 2014

Milton, Giles. *Churchill's Ministry of Ungentlemanly Warfare. The mavericks who plotted Hitler's defeat.* John Murray, 2017

Morgan, Mike. *Daggers Drawn: Second World War Heroes of the SAS & SBS.* Sutton, 2000

Mortimer, Gavin

—— *Stirling's Desert Triumph – The SAS Egyptian Airfield Raids 1942 (G)*

—— *The SAS in World War II. An Illustrated History.* Osprey, 2011

—— *Stirling's Men. The Inside History of the SAS in World War II.* Cassell, 2004

—— *The Men Who Made the SAS: The History of the Long-Range Desert Group.* Constable, 2015

—— *The SBS in World War II. An Illustrated History.* Osprey, 2013

—— *Churchill's Secret Warriors. The Explosive True Story of the Special Forces Desperadoes of WWII.* Quercus, 2015

—— *The Long-Range Desert Group in World War Two.* Osprey, 2017

Norén, Karl-Gunnar & Gyllenhal, Lars. *The Long-Range Desert Group. History and Legacy.* Helion, 2019

O'Carroll, Brendan. The Long Range Desert Group in the Aegean. Pen & Sword, 2020

Owen, James. *Commando: Winning the War behind Enemy Lines.* Little, Brown Book Group, New York, 2012

Paget, Julian (ed.) *Second to None: The History of the Coldstream Guards 1650–2000,* Leo Cooper for Pen & Sword, 2000

Parish, Michael Woodbine. *Aegean Adventures 1940–1943 and the End of Churchill's Dream.* The Book Guild, 1993

Parker, John. *SBS. The Inside Story of the Special Boat Service.* Headline Books, 1997

Peakman, Julie. *Hitler's Island War.The men who fought for Leros,* I B Taurus, 2018

Perrick, Penny. *Telling Tales. The Fabulous Lives of Anita Leslie.* Bloomsbury, 2017

Philby, Kim. *My Silent War. The Autobiography of a Spy.* Arrow Books, 2003

Pitt, Barrie. *Special Boat Squadron. The story of the SBS in the Mediterranean.* Century, 1983

Portier, David. *Les Parachutistes SAS de la France libre 1940–1945*

Ranfurly, Countess. *To War with Whitaker. The Wartime Diaries of the Countess of Ranfurly 1939–1945.* Arrow, 1998

Rogers, Anthony

—— *Churchill's Folly: Leros and the Aegean, 1943,** The History Press, 2017

—— *Swastika over the Aegean.* Toro, 2013

—— *Kos and Leros 1943. The German Conquest of the Dodecanese.* Osprey, 2019

Ross, Hamish. *Paddy Mayne, Lt. Col. Blair Paddy Mayne, 1st SAS Regiment.* The History Press, 2003

Sadler, John. *Ghost Patrol: A History of the Long Range Desert Group, 1940–1945.* Casemate, 2015

Sarafis, MajorGeneral Stefanos. *ELAS. Greek Resistance Army.* Merlin Press, 1980

Schenk, Dr Peter. *Kampf um die Agais. Die Kriegsmarine in den Griechischen Gewässern 1941–1945.* Hamburg, Mittler, 2000 (translated by John Guard, 2001).The pages of the pdf are, unfortunately, not numbered

Searle, Geoffrey. *At Sea Level.** Reprinted by the Book Guild, 1994

Seligman, Adrian. *War in the Islands. Undercover Operations in the Aegean 1942–1944.** Sutton Publishing, 1997

Seymour, William. *British Special Forces. The Story of Britain's Undercover Soldiers.* Reprinted Pen & Sword, 2006

Shawcross, William.*The Shah's Last Ride. The Fate of an Ally.* Touchstone, 1988

Sibard, Jack L.
—— *Mission en Crète.* Société des Études Historiques Crétoise, Heraklion, 2006
—— *Mission en Crète,* Juin 1942. (Memoires, Tome 2. Personal Notes and photo materials)

Sinclair, David. *Uncharted Waters. The Cayzer Family Firm, 1916–1987.* Cayzer Trust Company Publishing, 2010

Smith, E. D. *Victory of a Sort. The British in Greece 1941-1946.* Robert Hale, 1988

Smith, Peter C. and Walker, Edwin. *War in the Aegean.* William Kimber, 1974. (Reprinted 2008 by Stackpole Books. References are to the 2008 edition unless stated 1974, which contained materials dropped from the later editions.)

Spencer, John Hall. *Battle for Crete.* White Lion Publishers, 1962

Spigai, Prof. Vittorio. *Lero. La Battaglia per il Dodecaneso.* In Edibus, 2017

Stevens, Gordon. *The Originals. The secret history of the birth of the SAS in their own words.* Ebury, 2005

Sutherland, David
—— *He Who Dares.** Leo Cooper, 1998
—— *Appendix to Personal War Diary, 7–14 September 1943* (courtesy of Thomas Harder)

Taylor, Frederick. *Exorcising Hitler. The Occupation and Denazification of Germany.* Bloomsbury, 2011 (paperback edition, 2012)

Thomas, Evan. *The Very Best Men. The Daring Early Years of the CIA.* Simon and Schuster, New York, 2006 (first printed 1995)

Thompson, Julian. *War behind Enemy Lines.* Sidgwick & Jackson for the Imperial War Museum, 1998

Tsatsos, Jeanne (Tsatsou, Iōanna). *The Sword's Fierce Edge. A Journal of the Occupation of Greece, 1941–1944.* Vanderbilt University Press, 1969

Vlachostathopoulos, Anastasios G. *Ieros Lochos.* Eléftheri Sképsis

Waldegrave, William (Lord Waldegrave of North Hill PC)
—— *A Different Kind of Weather. A Memoir.* Constable, 2015
—— *George Patrick John Rushworth Jellicoe.* Biographical Memoirs. Royal Society, 2008

Warner, Philip. *The SBS, Special Boat Squadron.* Sphere, 1983

Waugh, Evelyn, *Memorandum on Layforce* (Diaries)

Wise, Michael T (ed.). *Joy Street. A Wartime Romance in Letters 1940–1942. Mirren Barford and Lieutenant John Lewes.* Little Brown & Co., 1995

Woodhouse, C. M.
—— *Modern Greece. A short history.* Faber & Faber, 1968
—— *The Autobiography of C. M. Woodhouse. Something Ventured.* Granada, 1982

Wynter Brigadier H.W., DSO
—— *Special Forces in the Desert War 1940–1943.* Public Records Office, 2001
—— *The History of the Long Range Desert Group. June 1940 to March 1943.* The National Archives, 2008

Archives

National Archives, Kew Gardens, London
—— CAB 106/603 Brig. Tilney's report on the Battle for Leros
—— WO 218/98
—— WO 218/97

—— WO 218/102 Signals
—— WO 218/106
—— WO 218/107
—— WO 218/170 (B Battalion, *LAYFORCE War Diary*)
—— WO 218/174 (Sardinia, Operation Hawthorn)
—— WO 201/2836 Read, Captain G W (Editor). *Raiding Forces. The Story of an Independent Command in the Aegean 1943–1945. Compiled from Official Sources and reports by Observer Offices of No.1 Pubilc relations Service, MEF*
—— SBS War Diaries. *Brief History of L Detachment, SAS Brigade & 1st SAS Regiment*
King's Own Royal Regiment Museum (KORRM), Lancaster. Regimental History, compiled October 1944

Private Papers, Speeches, Reports
Blyth, Captain. *Operational Report, Leros.* Part of Sutherland Scrap Book materials. Signed and Dated, Azzib, 7 December 1943
Carrington, Lord Peter. *Memorial Address*, Earl Jellicoe. Guards Chapel
Imbert-Terry, Edward. *An account of the 1943 Sardinia raid*
Irvine, James. *A Good Deal to do in Cairo*, Contribution to the Dobrski papers at the Liddell Hart Centre, Leeds, 2003. Dated 4 Nov 2003
Jellicoe, Lt. Col. Earl Jellicoe and Articles
—— *Report on Operation Towanbucket*, 1944
—— *Rhodes Drop Operational report*, September 1943 (Kindly sourced from David Sutherland's Scrap Book by Tony Rogers)
—— *Speech, University Dining Club*, Athens 6 June 1981
—— *Speech St.Sophia, Athens.* Undated
—— *SBS Reunion Dinner*, Poole, 13 September 1996
—— *The Origins of the Special Air Service*, Speech, Bryanston School, 7 May 1983
—— *Reflections on the Special Air Serice.* Undated manuscript with notes and corrections
Kedros, Tryphon (ex-SBS), Anglo-Hellenic League Commemoration, House of Lords, 14 February 2008
Malcolm, Kirsty. *SAS Project Film Proposal*, July 1995
Mavrikis, Jason. *The Big Bluff.* January 2000
Norwich, Viscount, CVO, FRSL, FRGS, FSA, Anglo-Hellenic League Commemoration, House of Lords, 14 February 2008
Soames, Lady. *Memorial Address*, Fitzroy Maclean of Dunconnel
Sutherland, David. *Appendix to Personal War Diary*, 7–14 September 1943
Woodhouse, Monty, DSO, OBE, MA, CM. *Speech, King's College*, 29 Nov 1990

Academic Texts
Gartzonikas, Panagiotis. *Amphibious and Special Operations in the Aegean Sea, 1943-1945. Operational Effectiveness and Strategic Implications.* MA Thesis submitted to the Naval Postgraduate School, Monterey, CA, USA. Dec 2003
Kotzampopoulos, Theofanis-Marios. *British-Greek Special Forces in the Aegean 1943-1945: A Case Study of 'Hybrid' war in German-occupied Maritime Greece.* Lancaster University, 2018
Nikoloudis, Nikos. *The Sacred Squadron.The struggles of an elite military unit from the deserts of Africa to the islands of the Aegean during WW2.* PhD Modern Greek Studies, King's College, London (undated)

Personal Interviews
Bernstorff-Gyldensteen, Bente. Copenhagen, 2017
Carrington, the Rt. Hon. Lord Peter
Canaris, Thassos, Leros September 2017
Gardner, Dr. Rita, CBE. Director of the Royal Geographical Society. 20 January 2017
Harder, Thomas, Author, Copenhagen

Holland, James. Interview with Earl Jellicoe, 31 October2002. Transcript kindly given to the author
Howe, The Rt. Hon, Earl, Minister of Defence. 21 January 2017
Jackson, Mrs. Collette
Jellicoe, Lady Philippa
Kent, HRH the Duke of. 23 January 2017
Lloyd, David, 26 June 2017
Rogers, Tony. Interview with Earl Jellicoe, 13 March 2001. Transcript kindly given to the author
Stewart, Lady Damaris, 20 January 2017
Tsigante, Eleni, Athens, Sept. 2018
Waldegrave, Lord William, Provost of Eton College, 21 January 2017

Private Correspondence Quoted – From George Jellicoe
Almonds, (Mrs Almonds)
Bergé, Georges, 13 February 1991
Lamb, R., 9 December 1992
Powys, Ian A. (*Comments on Battlefield Tour proposals*) 21 January 2000
Rodigan, Andrew. Reply 7 August 1991 (written to 7 July 1990)
Sandi, Fabio. 3 June 2005

Private Correspondence Quoted – To George Jellicoe
Croxton, William K. (re Martin Solomon). 11 July 1991
Jarrell, 'Joe' Porter. 4 November 1998
Mather, Sir Carol, MC. 12 March 1991
Powys, Ian (including proposal *'An Idea for a Dodecanese Battle Tour'*) 31 October 1999

Private Correspondence Quoted – Other
de la Billière, Sir Peter to Philippa Jellicoe, 9 March 2007
Buckley, Mary. 2 March 2007
Phipps, Major General Jeremy (to the author), 27 October 2019
Sutherland, David. Response to Dick Holmes' article, *Anders Lassen: The Man and the Myth*

Newspaper, magazine and newsletter articles
Arthur, Max. *Obituary: Major Pat Riley*. 31 March 1999 (*Independent*)
Bergé, Gen. Georges. *Commando Francais en Crète (Histoire)*
Caïtucoli, Georges (ex-National President of French SAS) *L'Épopée des SAS*
Cernuschi, Enrico. *Storia e retroscena della vicenda del MAS 522 nel settembre 1943 (Storia Miltaria)*
Faith, Nicholas. Peter *Wilson, Obituary (Auctioneer who lifted art to new heights)*. 20 June 1993 (*Independent*)
Gander, Marsland. *Capturing Athens. Air Troopers' Part* (*British Ministry of Information*)
Grant, Donald, journalist reporting on SBS operations in the Aegean (*Look* magazine, New York)
Hare, Alan. *George Jellicoe, Obituary* (*Independent*)
Kavanagh, Dennis. *Earl Jellicoe. Minister under Heath who made a successful return to public life after his involvement in a sex scandal*. 24 February, 2007 (*Independent*)
Lacey, Robert. *'A Touch of Evil'*. 22 February 1998 (*Sunday Times*)
Leigh Fermor, Patrick. *Remembering Lord Jellicoe. A tribute to the war hero, diplomat and politician*. 28 February 2007 (*Spectator*)
Lucas, James. *Strike on Leros* (*The Elite*, vol.3, issue 36, Orbis, 1985)
Malcolm, Kirsty. *SAS Project. Research Report*. July 1995. GPRJ papers
Maltoni, Luciano Alberhini. *Rodi 1943. L'anno decisive per le sorti del Dodecaneso* (June 2002) Summary notes for GPRJ prepared by Fabio Sandi 3 June 2005 *(Storia Miltaria) La Battaglia di Lero. Il ruiscito attacco Tedesco del novembre 1943 all picoola isola del Dodecanesco defisa da italiani e britannici.* Pt.1 October 2002 *(Storia Miltaria)*

Mortimer, Gavin. *The SAS and David Stirling's Leap of Faith.* 30 July 2012 (*The History Reader)*

Rhodesian Services Association Incorporated newsletter Jan 2010. Memories of Alf Page, LRDG (*Contact, Contact)*

Roth, Andrew. *Obituary,* 27 February 2007 (corrected 1 March 2007) (*Guardian)*

Selbourne, Lord. Obituary, Earl Jellicoe. Vol. 173, No. 2, June 2007, pp. 186–7 (*Geographical Journal)*

Sharman, Jon. *'I was just a kid': SAS Veteran speaks out, eight decades on from Second World War service.* 9 November 2018 (*Independent)*

Snelling, Steve. *Fens SAS Man's medals fetch £98,400 at Auction.* 22 November 2015 (*Eastern Daily Press)*

Stevens, Gordon. *The Special Air Service Originals.* 21 November 2012 (*Defence Media Network). How the SAS began: The Secret History.* 15 August 2016 (*Forces Network)*

Stone, Andrew. *Remembering the Ghost Patrol,* June 2020 (*Classic Military Vehicles*)

Stormonth Darling, Peter. November 2014. *The Trusty Servant*

Sutherland, Col. David, Speech, Athens, 11 November 1996 *Mars and Minerva (*SAS Regimental Magazine*)*

Walter, Natasha. *Spies and Lovers,* 10 May 2003 (*Guardian)*

Wilson, Peter, Obituary (Peter C Wilson, 71, is dead. Headed Sotheby's London), Rita Reif, 5 June 1984 (*New York Times)*

Eleni Tsigante, Athens, -----

Useful web sites

Cernuschi, Enrico, Post 24 January 2003 (*Feldgrau.net*)

Commando Veterans Association

Leigh Fermor, Patrick: *He drank from a different fountain.* Blog site set up after Paddy's death *(https://patrickleighfermor.org/*)

Noon, Ron. *The death of Saxon Tate & one of the last of the Tates to serve an apprenticeship in Love Lane.*2 October 2012 (*Love Lane refinery blog*)

Tidy, Squadron Leader D. P. *Dodecanese Disaster and the Batte of Simi 1943* in *Military History Journal* (*South African Military History Society*)

SBS in the Aegean – Late 1943. Posted 26 December 2016, *SBS in the Aegean – September 1943.* Posted 9 February 2017 (*Weapons and Warfare*)

World War Two Talk

Recorded and online materials

BBC. *The Cold War,* 24-part series, 2014

BBC. *The Last Word*

Ieros Lochos. Documentary. WhiteFox Films, Athens

The Secret War (Episode11: The Special Interrogation Group). Interview with Maurice Tiefenbrunner (https://www.youtube.com/watch?v=Kgu2SW_MCfk&t=579s)

Grenall, Mike. People's Stories. Liverpool Lives, 2011 (http://www.peoples-stories.com)

Haneuse, Pierre (Réalisateur) & Coty, Henri Rolland (Producteur) Interview (on camera) with George Jellicoe, Institut national del'audiovisuel)(www.ina.fr/video/CPD04002949)

Harder, Thomas. Lecture *Anders Lassen War in Greece.* Benaki Museum, Athens, (https://www.youtube.com/watch?v=2TL_Agjjz0c)

Imperial War Museum Sound Archives. Interview (audio) with George Jellicoe (www.Iwm.org.uk/collections/item/object). Catalogue No.13039

Kampouras, Nicholas. *The Battle of Leros and the Italian coastal batteries (Postazione Lero PL)*

Masty, Stephen (Senior Contributor) *Shanghaied by Yuletide Materialism?* An essay on Patricia, Countess Jellicoe (*The Imaginative Conservative)*

German action in the Kos and Leros campaigns, 1943. (www.ina.fr/video/AFE86002277/debarquement-allemand-dans-l-ile-dc-kos-video.html)

German capture of Leros 1943 (www.ina.fr/video/AFE86002357/prise-de-l-ile-de-leros-par-les-allemands-video.html)

Index